PRENTICE-HALL, INC. *Englewood Cliffs, New Jersey 07632*

MARKETING
RESEARCH
AND KNOWLEDGE
DEVELOPMENT

An Assessment
for
Marketing Management

John G. Myers
University of California at Berkeley

William F. Massy
Stanford University

Stephen A. Greyser
Harvard University

Library of Congress Cataloging in Publication Data

Myers, John G
   Marketing research and knowledge development.

   Includes bibliographical references.
   1.-Marketing research—United States. I.-Massy,
William F., joint author. II.-Greyser, Stephen A.,
joint author. III.-Title.
HF5415.2.M945   658.8'3'0973   80-13929
ISBN 0-13-557686-5

Editorial/Production Supervision and Interior Design by Natalie Krivanek
Manufacturing Buyer—Gordon Osbourne

Printed in the United States of America

10 9 8 7 6 5 4 3 2 1

Prentice-Hall International, Inc., *London*
Prentice-Hall of Australia Pty. Limited, *Sydney*
Prentice-Hall of Canada, Ltd., *Toronto*
Prentice-Hall of India Private Limited, *New Delhi*
Prentice-Hall of Japan, Inc., *Tokyo*
Prentice-Hall of Southeast Asia Pte. Ltd., *Singapore*
Whitehall Books Limited, *Wellington, New Zealand*

About the Book

This book deals with the nature of marketing research and marketing knowledge development in the United States over the past quarter century. Beyond its descriptive content, a major goal is to assess the relative impact of research and knowledge development activities on marketing management practices over the period. Much of the assessment material and many of the empirical findings and other data presented are based on studies done in connection with a project known as the Commission on the Effectiveness of Research and Development for Marketing Management. The objectives, membership, and other details concerning the Commission are described in the early chapters. The effort was initiated by the American Marketing Association and subsequently co-sponsored by the Marketing Science Institute.

Contents

3 CHANGES IN MARKETING RESEARCH AND KNOWLEDGE DEVELOPMENT 52

4 MARKETING'S RESEARCH AND DEVELOPMENT SYSTEM 101

5 THE KNOWLEDGE CREATION AND UTILIZATION PROCESS 167

6 ASSESSMENTS OF THE KNOWLEDGE CREATION AND UTILIZATION PROCESS 202

Preface

Marketing research and the development of new knowledge in the field of marketing has been a subject of considerable controversy in recent years. Although in the industrial sector a large and complex industry involved in the business of generating marketing research information for use in marketing management and decision-making now exists, there is wide variation in the degree to which managers either accept and/or utilize such information in their day-to-day operations. Even more controversial are managerial attitudes toward the stream of new marketing research knowledge being generated by marketing academics in the nation's leading business and management schools.

Concerning this latter type of research—what is often referred to as "basic" research in marketing—two fundamentally opposite positions with respect to its value and contributions to marketing management appear to be evolving. The first and most critical view is that most of this type of new knowledge, particularly that which has been generated over the past few decades, is basically irrelevant to marketing management practice, and is of little present or potential use to practicing marketing professionals. This negative position about the research base for the entire field of marketing, is quite widespread and is shared by some marketing academics and professional researchers as well as by many managers. It is manifest in criticisms of marketing journals and the work of leading marketing academics, in various forms of anti-intellectualism, and in numerous other attitudes and beliefs that are generally skeptical of the current nature of marketing scholarship and the directions it appears to be taking. It has been said, for example, that marketing scholars exist as a kind of island unto themselves, whose research work contributes little or nothing to improvements in marketing management practice or to advancements of knowledge in the basic social science disciplines.

This critical position appears to receive its greatest support from marketing academics whose approach to teaching and research in marketing is very different from those academics who currently generate much of the scholarly work in the field. This difference can be traced to a major shift in philosophy with respect to teaching and research in business education that occurred in the early 1950s. The shift was advocated by two commissions sponsored by the Ford and Carnegie Foundations. Each essentially argued that business education should be upgraded and should return to economics as the core of business training. This subsequently evolved into a social science core of economics, behavioral science, and quantitative methods which characterizes the foundation training of many of today's MBA programs. Business schools which adopted this philosophy became, during the intervening twenty-five years, the most productive generators of new knowledge in all business fields, including marketing. However, it is the nature of this productivity which is at the core of the controversy. There is little question that the ensuing scholarly work contributed significantly to the volume of available knowledge. There is a question, however, of what contributions it has made to advancing the state of marketing practice and the marketing management profession. The critic is most likely to answer the question with "none" or "not much!"

The second position views this kind of scholarly productivity as the essential ingredient to advancing marketing practice. It is, from this viewpoint, the source of the basic fuel which powers the marketing profession in all its diverse forms and applied aspects. Without a core of basic researchers, often working on seemingly obscure and esoteric things, the likelihood of "progress" in the field is vastly reduced. It is from this source that all new useful marketing management ideas flow—or so the argument goes.

Criticisms of basic research and scholarly efforts in marketing are part of a more broadly based skepticism concerning the value of basic research of all kinds, which has permeated many aspects of society in recent years. A hard-headed demand for demonstrations of relevance has, to a considerable degree, replaced a post World War II faith that knowledge is useful "in its own right." In marketing, the demand for such relevance has been extended from a focus on industrial marketing research, and the degree to which it contributes to corporate sales and profits, to considerations of academic marketing research and the extent to which it makes any contributions to the advancement of the profession.

This broadened viewpoint that postulates that academic marketing research is an integral part of a total system of marketing research and knowledge development activities in society has not been explicitly mapped out or evaluated in any careful and systematic way. This book represents a first attempt to do so. A basic departure point is that assessment needs to rest on a common understanding of the nature and scope of the whole system, how the parts interrelate, who plays what roles, and so on. Basically, we need a "macro" viewpoint on marketing research which identifies how new knowledge is created and developed, how it is diffused among various people and organizations in the system, and what the sources of the breakthroughs which impact significantly on improving marketing practice are.

With such a viewpoint, assessments concerning various aspects of the overall system should become more informed. Barriers and blocks to knowledge utilization, whether arising from the inherent irrelevance of the scholarly work or from other factors (or both), should be more readily identifiable and debates about marketing research effectiveness carried to a higher and more meaningful plane. The desirable goal of improving the rate of knowledge utilization by marketing management and, in this sense, of making meaningful advances in the marketing profession, should be enhanced as well.

The need for such a broadened perspective on the subject of marketing research derives from the types of controversy expressed in the two positions reviewed earlier. It was a major factor leading to the formation of the Commission on the Effectiveness of Research and Development for Marketing Management. The Commission, a group of eighteen distinguished academic and professional people in marketing (see Appendix 1-1 for the prospectus and membership), met three times in 1976–77 and initiated and served as the supervisory body for a number of studies reported in this book. About two-thirds of the content of this book comes directly from materials generated by the Commission's activities and the studies which it undertook. These are reviewed in Chapter 1, and data from them presented in all subsequent chapters. Other materials for the book were drawn from extant literature, as well as from our own insights and experiences as marketing educators. The scope is very broad and, being a new perspective, is by no means complete. The book nevertheless contains much that should be of interest to students, teachers, professionals, and anyone concerned with progress in the field of marketing. Much of its evaluative and prescriptive content is attributable to the Commission as well as to ourselves and, in general, represents the judgments, opinions, and advice of the full Commission. The viewpoint is much broader, less technical, and generally very different from that of most modern marketing research books. It essentially spans the marketing research-marketing management interface. Although we do not see the book as a substitute for either a marketing research or a marketing management text, it should be an interesting supplement to course materials concerning either type of subject.

Each of the authors was involved in the work of the Commission and in the subsequent development of this volume. Bill Massy conceived of the idea for the Commission at the beginning of his tenure as vice-president of the Education Division of the American Marketing Association in 1976–77. Bill wrote the prospectus shown in Appendix 1-1, served as its initial chairman, and in general shepherded the work through its many stages and phases. Steve Greyser agreed early on to join Bill as cochairman. An important consequence was that it became a jointly sponsored activity of both the American Marketing Association and the Marketing Science Institute. Steve sought out and appointed the staff members, and jointly chaired meetings. John Myers, who followed Bill as vice-president of the AMA's Education Division in 1977–78, served as a member of the Commission. John subsequently was heavily involved in organizing and drafting the final manuscript.

There are five major themes or topics treated in this volume:

1. A review of the previous published assessments of industrial marketing research effectiveness.
2. Identification of changes and the major forces of change in marketing management and marketing research over the past quarter century.
3. A presentation and discussion of the nature, scope, and current state of marketing's research and development system.
4. Presentations of various models and conceptual frameworks dealing with the knowledge creation and utilization process.
5. Assessments of the impacts and effectiveness of various components of marketing's research and development system from the management utilization viewpoint, and a series of recommendations which flow from these assessments.

The book is organized around seven topics and chapters. A reference bibliography is also provided. Chapter 1 presents a review of previous assessments of marketing research from literature which focuses on the impact and effectiveness of industrial marketing research. This chapter introduces the broader perspectives and viewpoints adopted by the Commission and presents an overview of the various methods used and the studies that were done. The prospectus and membership of the Commission are given in Appendix 1–1.

Chapter 2 presents commissioner views on the types of changes that took place in marketing management over the twenty-five-year period and the factors, other than marketing's research and development, that affected those changes. Much of the material for the chapter comes from a poll of commissioners taken in late 1976 and their replies to the question: "What major changes in the practice of marketing do you believe have occurred in the last twenty-five years?" We have attempted to organize and paraphrase the important themes in this chapter, but have also included the verbatim comments of all commissioner replies to this question in Appendix 2–1.

Chapter 3 is a parallel treatment of the changes that took place in marketing research and development over the assessment period. It begins with an analysis of the major changes in the marketing research industry and the changes in knowledge development which took place over the period. The results of content analysis studies of marketing journals and textbooks undertaken by the Commission are presented in this chapter.

Chapter 4 addresses the broad question of "marketing's research and development system." What is the size, nature, and scope of this system? What are the objectives of knowledge development? What kinds of knowledge development are there? What kinds of research appear to characterize the field of marketing? The chapter addresses these kinds of questions.

Chapter 5 elaborates on several aspects of marketing's R & D system with particular emphasis on the knowledge creation and utilization process. Several models and viewpoints are presented. The creation, diffusion, and utilization of conjoint analysis is presented as an illustrative example of how the process can work. The chapter also introduces the concept of an "innovator research group" within marketing, and the role this group appears to play in the overall system. The results of an iterative, delphi-like procedure used by the Commission to develop models of the process are also presented in this chapter.

Chapter 6 presents commissioner assessments of the roles and effectiveness of various components of the knowledge creation and utilization process. It also contains the results of an empirical study undertaken by the Commission on the extent to which thirteen different types of new knowledge are currently being used, and compares these results with another study on the subject. The combination of commissioner judgments and empirical research is used to develop various types of assessments of the effectiveness of marketing's research and development system, and to identify barriers and blocks within the system.

Chapter 7 presents overall conclusions, focusing particularly on research and development effectiveness, the forces that shaped marketing's R & D system, and assessments of its "creation" and "utilization" aspects. Factors that appear to inhibit knowledge utilization are presented. A section that addresses the role of the marketing academic community and the nature of research that appears to us to be most appropriate for them is included. The chapter ends with some reflections on whether the "fuel" of creative effort in our field is self-generating or whether it requires conscious efforts to maintain it, and some overall assessments of the investment in marketing's R & D.

Appendix A presents twenty recommendations spanning the entire work of the Commission and this book. Recommendations are arranged in sets, each directed to a specific constituency: "the academic community," "the business community," "government," and "associations, institutes and foundations." Several pertain to specific project reommendations applicable to any or all of these constituencies. Appendix B provides technical information on one of the major studies undertaken by the Commission.

This book could not have been written without the cooperation, contributions, and efforts of members of the Commission on the Effectiveness of Research and Development for Marketing Management. We want to thank members of the Commission both personally and on behalf of the American Marketing Association, Management Science Institute, and the marketing profession in general. It has been a joy to know them and to work with them. The financial support and encouragement of the officers and directors of the American Marketing Association and Management Science Institute are gratefully acknowledged. In particular, AMA past presidents, John G. Keane and W. Arthur Cullman, were very supportive and helpful. Numerous other people contributed to the work of the Commission and the writing of this book. In particular, we would like to thank Professor Christopher Lovelock, who headed up the staff and was crucial to the content analysis and survey research studies reported here. Chris also contributed major sections to earlier drafts, and we are greatly indebted for his insights and hard work. Also, we would like to acknowledge John Bateson for much of the analytical work in these studies and the project as a whole. Secretarial assistance was provided by June Wong, Berkeley, Roberta Callaway, Stanford, and Shannon Grady Vento, Harvard, and we want to thank them for the many contributions they have made throughout the long process of developing this book. Katherine Triest, at Berkeley, did an admirable job of typing the final manuscript, and we are indebted to our friends at Prentice-Hall for the excellent production work. Finally, our sincere thanks to three wives and a set of understanding children, who have patiently supported their husbands and fathers in connection with this project over the past four years.

John G. Myers
William F. Massy
Stephen A. Greyser

1

Introduction

The controversy surrounding the effectiveness of marketing research and knowledge development over the past twenty-five years goes beyond mere differences of opinion about the value of scholarly or basic research done by marketing academics. Opinions differ on the worth of *all* kinds of marketing research. Industrial marketing research is that which is done by the marketing research department of a corporation or by advertising agencies, media, or commercial research suppliers. The value of this kind of research in accomplishing corporate objectives, whether these objectives are measured by profits, sales, market share, or some other criterion, has received a great deal of attention over the years. A small but significant literature—speeches, editorials, and a few formal studies—has attempted to assess this aspect of the overall system of marketing research and knowledge development.

The chapter begins with a review of these assessment studies. Most of them refer to industrial marketing research. The broad question addressed is, "What is the worth or effectiveness of industrial marketing research?" The studies have been organized into sections covering assessment perspectives, methods of assessing effectiveness, and other assessments and issues. The final section of the chapter introduces the broader perspectives on marketing research and development adopted by the Commission and reviews the major methods of inquiry it followed.

It is useful to set the stage by reviewing some fundamental causes of the controversy that surrounds the entire subject. Much disagreement is rooted in basic differences in occupational position, values, and interests of the three primary groups that make up marketing's research and development system: educators, professional researchers, and managers. Educators, for example, differ in terms of educational philosophy; teaching and research pedagogy; interpretations of the meaning of ''effective'' knowledge; what students need to know to pursue a successful career in marketing; whether short- or long-run-based training is of most value; and so on. Professional marketing researchers differ strongly on which kind of research is of most value in solving a particular marketing problem; what kinds of information managers should have; and the relative value of behavioral versus economics methodologies. Managers and management often approach the whole question of marketing research effectiveness from the perspective of its return on their investment. An investment of X dollars on research in connection with a particular advertising campaign, or over an entire year of operations, should return Y dollars in sales or profits. Marketing-related R & D is treated as part of, or parallel to, the firm's overall R & D efforts and is evaluated from this viewpoint.

Managers, as a group, also disagree over the value and contributions of marketing research. Some believe that marketing management is inherently an intuitive activity. Research data and formal modeling are not as important as ''insight,'' ''adaptability,'' ''experience,'' and ''intuition.'' Marketing management, from this viewpoint, is more art than science. Others depend heavily on research for problem identification and problem solving. Marketing, in this sense, is more science than art. These viewpoints are expressed not only in different styles of operation and management, but also in relative differences in research expenditures among corporations in the same industry and between corporations in different industries. Some data on this phenomenon are presented in Chapter 4. Thus many built-in factors explain some of the controversy surrounding marketing research and marketing knowledge development.

The view that marketing research, funded by an individual corporation to serve its marketing objectives, is an investment for which a certain return (ROI) should be expected has motivated most of the assessment studies to date. This micro view does not, however, take into account the larger system of marketing research and knowledge development—a system that includes academic and other kinds of marketing research as well. This book represents a first attempt to describe and assess the nature, scope, and effectiveness of this larger system. It is a macro system made up of components whose interdependencies and workings have not been well explicated.

Objectivity in assessing the effectiveness of such a system requires some agreement on the nature of the system itself. What is lacking is an adequate model or theory on which objective assessment might be based. What criterion variables should be used? What really are the sources of new knowledge in the field? How do new ideas arise and reach, or fail to reach, operating line management? What is the degree of use of knowledge and research from this broadened perspective? These are some of the fundamental questions addressed in this book. The book does not attempt to present one grand overall design or theory about how the system works, but rather a series of models, perspectives, and ideas, many of which flow from the work of the Commission on the Effectiveness of Research and Development for Marketing Management.

ASSESSMENTS OF INDUSTRIAL MARKETING RESEARCH

This section presents some previous assessment perspectives, alternative methods for assessing industrial marketing research effectiveness, and additional issues and viewpoints concerning marketing research in the United States over the past twenty-five years. The first section attempts to capture the major perspectives and some of the controversial nature of the subject over this period.

Assessment Perspectives

As early as 1950, proposals were being made for conducting audits of commercial marketing research activities and expenditures. Sessions[1] laid out the basic approach for conducting such an audit. Although the idea of a "marketing audit" of the entire marketing operation seems to be gaining in popularity, it is doubtful that the formal procedures for auditing marketing research departments outlined by Sessions are in widespread use today. Jeuck[2] began the long history of controversy over the effectiveness of industrial marketing research by declaring that few if any of the notable successes in business were aided by marketing research. Roberts[3] published what is still considered a classic paper, "The Role of Research in Marketing Management," and this was followed by several published articles along the same lines (for example, see Adler, "Phasing Research into the Marketing Plan,"[4] and Newman, "Put Research into Marketing Decisions"[5]).

Two changes in perspective on both the meaning of "marketing research" and the ways it should be assessed were introduced in the early 1960s. Each called for an "interdisciplinary" approach to the study of markets and consumers. The first derived from the field of management science and stressed the idea of model building as the necessary first step in research and the key to linking research to a marketing management problem. The philosophy was elaborated by Massy and Webster in the lead article of the first issue of the *Journal of Marketing Research* in 1964.[6] The authors argued in the following way:

The relationship between behavioral and optimization models has often been obscured. While these two manifestations of the scientific method in business are different by virtue of their subject matter and skill requirements, they share a common orientation and neither can fully succeed without the other. The application of optimization techniques to marketing problems has sometimes been less than fruitful because of a failure to understand the importance of the underlying behavioral model that specifies the relationships among the variables of the problem. Formal optimization methods can succeed only if they are built upon sound behavioral foundations.[7]

This philosophy had far-reaching implications for marketing management and research and, among other things, led to the formation of the TIMS College on Marketing.[8] It has resulted in a long chain of model-building efforts, focused on each of the major marketing management decision areas (product, price, promotion, and distribution) and attempts to model the relative contributions of each of these marketing mix components as a whole. It also significantly changed the conception of the role of marketing research by highlighting the use of the computer for model building and testing as well as for data analysis and, in general, argued for the notion of a "marketing information system" (MIS). Amstutz's classic work[9] and the more managerially oriented work of Montgomery and Urban[10] did much to introduce MIS thinking to marketing. To the notion of DATA collection were added those of a MODEL bank, a STATISTICAL bank, and a computer DISPLAY UNIT.[11] Some marketing research textbooks subsequently evolved that were heavily based on the computer-marketing information systems perspective.[12]

From the assessment viewpoint, work subsequently focused on the validity and degree of use of the systems or the models themselves.[13] Criteria such as usefulness, adaptability, completeness, and robustness became the departure points for assessing the value of this type of "marketing research."

The second change in perspective introduced in the early 1960s was also interdisciplinary in nature but had its roots in the behavioral sciences. Marketing research became, in effect, "consumer research," and the emphasis was placed on developing theories of consumer motivation and behavior or consumer decision processes. Motivation research of the 1950s[14] and the work of researchers in psychology and sociology[15] were significant precursors of this stream of thought. The behavioral science emphasis on "theory and method" and "validity and reliability" was widely adopted as the basis for both doing marketing research and assessing its worth. Dozens of books on consumer or buyer behavior[16] subsequently evolved and, among other things, led to the formation of ACR (the Association for Consumer Research) in 1970 and the founding of a new journal, the *Journal of Consumer Research,* first issued in June 1974.

Most marketing research textbooks are heavily infused with behavioral science perspectives, primarily psychological or sociological. The books by Schreier and Zaltman-Burger, for example, are heavily sociological in orientation.[17] There is little question that the bulk of commercial marketing research services, particularly in the advertising-effectiveness and copy-testing areas, are based on methods flowing out of psychology or sociology. The existence of the industry itself has been cited as evidence that this kind of research has been "effective" in advancing marketing management practices. Consumer behavior research of all kinds tended to dominate scholarly work in the 1960s—much of it what is currently referred to as "basic" research in marketing. The nature of this work is reflected in the following list of article topics published in the *Journal of Marketing Research* between 1964 and 1969:[18]

Topic	Number of Articles
Consumer and market area research	141
Brand loyalty and preference studies	86
Attitude and opinion measurement	66
Media and advertising research	52
Regression and other multivariate methods	44
Experimental design	36
Data collection methods	35
Projective and other psychological methods	34

Several other perspectives evolved relating to research utilization and the role of marketing research departments. Boyd and Britt[19] were among the first to point out that research utilization could be increased by adopting general management principles or what they called the "administrative process": setting objectives, developing plans to achieve objectives, organizing to put plans into action, and controlling and reappraising the program that had been carried out. Their advice that "researchers and decision makers must strive to interact in such a way as to make explicit the use to which research information will be put"[20] is a theme that occurs repeatedly in later articles.

Krum[21] conducted two empirical studies on the role of marketing research departments within an organization. The broad issue that motivated these studies was whether any kind of objective, scientific research could be conducted in a bureaucratic organization, particularly where research generators and research users were in close contact and research could be used for many purposes other than the supplying of objective information. Howard[22] had noted earlier that one of the most complicated marketing problems has been the relationship between the executive and the marketing researcher. Krum's conclusions were that marketing research directors, their immediate supervisors, and their clients had very similar expectations about the role of the marketing research department and that standard criticisms (lack of objectivity and clarity, timing of research reports, ivory-towerism) were not substantiated. The major area of conflict revealed in the second study arose from marketing research directors' desires to take a more active part in management decisions and the resistance to such efforts by line and staff managers who were served by them.

Hardin,[23] in a *Journal of Marketing Research* editorial, provided some reasons for inherent conflict at the manager-researcher interface. Marketing research often appears to be critical and otherwise threatening to marketing management. Marketing management often uses research *after* decisions have been made, and research can become a sales promotion tool used by top management to justify marketing decisions and to encourage members of the marketing team to be "properly optimistic." Hardin's views in 1969 are interesting in comparison with some of those expressed by commission members in 1977 given in later chapters:

Marketing research now has the tools for making truly substantive contributions to marketing decisions and corporate profits. Refined information collection techniques, experimental designs, and Bayesian procedures provide valid decision contributions. The problem centers around management's general lack of awareness of the kinds of technical progress that have been achieved in this decade.[24]

The use of marketing research to satisfy manager needs other than those related to decision making has been called "pseudo-research" by Smith.[25] Marketing research can be used as a way for the manager to gain visibility and power; to justify decisions already made (if research results contradict the decision, the manager can declare the research invalid or ignore it); as a scapegoat for marketing decisions that do not accomplish objectives; as a promotion tool by advertising agencies or media to attract new business; as a means to soothe an anxious manager that "something is being done"; or simply as the "faddish thing to do."

Some of the barriers to effective use of marketing research by managers were identified in the Newman article cited earlier.[26] Some managers view research as a threat to their personal status as decision makers. They fear that marketing research information may conflict with or invalidate the "knowledge" gained from experience and judgment. In other instances, the lack of systematic planning and of common organizational objectives leads to a substitution of a manager's own objectives. Research may be used to support a manager's predetermined position in his struggle for power. Generally, managers who believe marketing research will enhance their position will favor it, and those who do not will oppose it. Newman goes on to point out that some managers are unable to work effectively with, understand, and use the knowledge and skills of research specialists, the interdisciplinary training of the specialists making this particularly difficult. Marketing research departments may be handicapped by low organizational status and lack of close contact with managers. In such situations the manager must take the initiative. Managers may be unfamiliar with the nature and role of research and unable to identify problems well enough to ask for help when they need it.

More recently, McCall[27] provided a review, from the advertising agency perspective, of what agency managers want from research, and Holbert[28] reported the results of a poll of brand managers (from forty corporations) on how managers see marketing research. Fourteen types of research were identified in the Holbert study, the most important from the viewpoint of amount of use being: continuing audits, advertising tests, product testing, consumer tracking studies, and concept testing. Respondents reported that product testing was the most indispensable. The two most important things researchers could do to be of greatest help were reported to be to show a greater interest and involvement in the actionability of projects and to understand marketing problems better. Holbert's conclusions on the subject are interesting:

It is simple (though not simple-minded) research projects that are best received by market-ers: projects that are written in the marketer's language, that seek an answer to a real marketing question, and an answer that can be implemented . . . neither undue elation nor undue distress is appropriate for marketing researchers. Indeed, as always, research effec-tiveness is not a destination but a journey. And if some clues may be deduced from this probe, then maybe there will be less *terra* as researchers seek a *firma* base for their existence in the marketing community.[29]

Methods of Assessing Effectiveness

How effective is marketing research in terms of return on investment or a cost-benefit perspective? Corporate management sees marketing research in terms of a budget. How much should be spent on this type of activity? Most current marketing research textbooks[30] suggest an attempt to determine the value of information associated with a particular decision problem. This approach is essentially an application of decision theory and Bayesian analysis. Alternative actions, states of nature, payoffs, and the decision maker's prior probabilities of the occurrence of each state of nature are specified. By estimating the validity and reliability of the proposed research, and developing so-called posterior prob-abilities, one can derive the value of marketing research information for any specific set of marketing decision alternatives. Schlaifer's book[31] was very im-portant in introducing the subject to marketers. Bass[32] published one of the first articles on its specific application to determining the value of marketing research.

Various other approaches have been developed. In 1964, Massy and Sarvas[33] introduced logical flow models as a way to model marketing manage-ment decision making and to control expenditures such as those for marketing research. Twedt[34] presented a simplified return-on-investment approach from the perspectives of his position as Director of Marketing Research at Oscar Mayer. He pointed out that a few projects have zero value, whereas others are highly valued for "negative" reasons—they result in decisions *not* to go ahead with product development. In a later study of 265 marketing research directors,[35]

Twedt found relatively little reliance on systematic methods of internal communication, control, and information retrieval. The majority of directors had no formal system for evaluating the worth of marketing research projects.

Myers and Samli[36] suggested yet other ways to (1) determine the value of marketing research (simple savings, present-value method, and Bayesian analysis), (2) control research projects (such as checklists, logical flow analysis, Gantt charts, and PERT networks), and (3) control and guide the total research program (advisory committees, audits, and budget controls). Mayer[37] introduced formal procedures for estimating nonsampling errors in research projects and did much to focus attention on this important problem.[38] Samli and Bellas[39] introduced GERT (graphical evaluation and review technique) for planning and control of marketing research, and Gandz and Whipple, [40] in an article titled, "Making Marketing Research Accountable," demonstrated the role of computer simulation in conjunction with field data in the assessment process.

Thus, over the twenty-five years much attention has been given to the "effectiveness" of commercial marketing research, how much to spend on it, and how to manage and control research expenditures. Also, several books have been written on marketing research management.[41] Again, most of the R & D in question concerns applied research done by marketing research personnel in the industrial sector, and generally does not encompass a macro view of all forms of marketing research. When considered on a project-by-project basis, some of the ideas—particularly those given in the Myers and Samli review[42]—are applicable to management and control of other forms of research. The reader should, however, appreciate the difficulties of attempting to use them to evaluate the effectiveness of all forms of marketing research and knowledge development efforts over a twenty-five-year period!

Other Assessments and Issues

Ferber, in an early *Journal of Marketing Research* editorial, recognized trends in marketing research and noted the underlying issues and controversies involved. In his words:

Market behavior is a multivariate, multidisciplinary problem. . . . This is not to deny statistical laws of aggregate market behavior, such as the negative binomial for consumer purchases. These regularities can be useful for certain marketing problems, but they cannot provide an explanation of the factors underlying market behavior. . . . Largely spurious is the long-standing distinction, or controversy, between the quantitative and qualitative approaches to marketing research. . . . One may specialize in either approach, but to be most effective one must be able to use each method as the situation demands . . . . Marketing researchers are becoming aware that they face the same problems that econometricians did about twenty years ago . . . the systems analyst appears to be to the 1960s what the motivation researcher was to the 1950s (and let's hope that he comes to a more glorious end). . . . Paradoxically, marketing research is becoming more intricate and specialized at the same time that awareness for a more simple comprehension of marketing problems is increasing.[43]

Some of the anticipated and unanticipated consequences of research specialization were discussed by Green the following year and a specific proposal put forward—the idea of the "research generalist." Green sets the tone in an opening paragraph:

The manager-versus-advisor conflict, the two cultures' schism, the clinician-versus-methodologist syndrome (all variations on a single theme) are favorite issues of current writers . . . the communications gap in marketing is turning into a chasm.

Today a single individual cannot encompass the breadth of material being ground out in the quantitative and behavior sciences. About all most of us can do is to obtain and retain a good foundation in general methodology (philosophy, mathematics, and statistics) and hope to be able to separate the few really innovative ideas from the welter of highly precise (and often highly mathematical) accounts of inconsequential notions. . . . For those already trained in methodology, I argue for more dilettantism rather than more concentration in the area of specialization.[44]

The research generalist role would serve to fill the gap between managers and researchers.[45]

Articles in the *Journal of Marketing* commemorating forty years of that journal's existence provided some useful insights on how marketing research and knowledge have changed over time. (See in particular the articles by Grether and Keane.[46]) In an earlier paper, Keane[47] looked at the marketing research assessment question from the perspectives of top management. He provided an estimate of marketing research investment in 1969 ($600,000,000), described the flow of marketing research information to top management, assessed the role of marketing research in top management decision making, summarized the obstacles to effective use of research in decision making, and offered suggestions for improving the research/top management interface.

Much has been written about communications within organizations, and many suggestions have been offered for improving it. Hulbert and others[48] described a method to produce descriptions of an organization's information processing and decision making system. Kover[49] explained the communications-gap problem between academics and professional marketers in terms of differences in career motivations and patterns. See also the article by Souder, "Effectiveness of Nominal and Interacting Group Decision Processes for Integrating R & D and Marketing."[50] Souder's results are interesting in terms of some of the later chapters. What is called a "combined group decision-making process" (including elements of "nominal" and "interacting") was found most effective in achieving statistical consensus and group integration.

A recent issue that has generated controversy among marketing researchers is the threat of new types of government regulation of marketing research practices, particularly in the area of personal interviewing. An excellent discussion of the underlying ethical issues involved was provided in an article by Tybout and Zaltman.[51] Day,[52] writing from the viewpoint of a practicing professional researcher, disagrees with some of the article's basic premises. Another useful paper on the subject of the controllable and uncontrollable environmental threats to marketing research was published in 1975.[53] More recently, one of the authors has set down specific examples of the types of academic marketing research that marketing managers should find useful.[54] To facilitate or accelerate the development of useful managerial research, we need to identify and define topics considered significant in the business community, have a mechanism for helping to develop and shape the research ideas to be employed in addressing those topics, and develop a base of funding to support the time and efforts of the researchers involved. The article spells out how this can be done and provides examples of priority topics in the advertising area.

The foregoing methods for assessing research effectiveness and the several types of controversy alluded to are, with a few exceptions, heavily focused on industrial marketing research. In these cases, research has been treated like any other business investment for which a reasonable ROI should be expected. In the next section, the perspectives of the Commission on the Effectiveness of Research and Development for Marketing Management and the methods used by the Commission are presented (to conserve space, we will refer to it as the ERDMM Commission, or simply, the Commission). As will be seen, the Commission's objectives were much broader than those of earlier assessment studies. The attempt was to understand and assess the effectiveness of all kinds of marketing research, including academic marketing research.

THE ERDMM COMMISSION

The Prospectus for the ERDMM Commission, which is a statement of objectives, rationale, and the mission with which the Commission was charged, is reproduced in its original form in Appendix 1-1. Also included is a list of the membership of the Commission. Eighteen distinguished people in marketing agreed to serve on it. Members represented a diverse group of academics and professionals and their respective interests. Eight were from universities, four from independent research, consulting, and advertising firms, and six from operating companies. The four from independent firms were professional researchers, and the six from operating companies were evenly split between the management and research functions.

The Commission's task was to assess the contributions of marketing research and development to the advancement of marketing management practice over the 1952–1977 assessment period. Early on, the Commission adopted the position that the objective of research should be to improve marketing management practice. A very broad view of what constitutes marketing research and development and what constitutes marketing management practice was also adopted. The Commission reasoned that there exists a system of "R & D" for marketing much as there exists a system of "R & D" for production. The latter, more usual meaning of "research and development" refers to activities such as basic and applied research in the physical (physics, chemistry, and so on) and biological sciences. This kind of research leads to new physical inventions and commercially viable products and services that make for material progress in a society. Marketing R & D, in contrast, is based largely on the social sciences of economics, psychology, and sociology and on engineering and statistics. It is the latter type of research and development on which the Commission focused. The system that underlies this type of R & D extends much beyond the industrial sector of the economy and includes work in the academic, governmental, and nonprofit organization sectors as well. The nature, scope, and effectiveness of this larger macro system of research and development, what became known as "marketing's research and development system," was the basic departure point of the ERDMM Commission.

The meaning of "marketing management" and "marketing management practice" adopted by the Commission was equally broad. All forms of marketing management were considered, including middle line operating managers, staff managers, and senior marketing executives in private corporations, or managers of any organization (private, government, or nonprofit) in which marketing management functions were being performed.

The Commission was charged with three basic tasks. The first was *descriptive*—to identify, describe, and explain various aspects of marketing's R & D system and the changes that took place in it over a twenty-five-year period. A great deal of effort was devoted to attempts to reach agreement on the basic creative and utilization aspects of the overall system. What were the sources of new marketing research knowledge? How was it diffused from one component to the next? Who played what roles?—and so on. The second task was *evaluative*—to assess the effectiveness of the system over this period. To what degree had marketing R & D led to improvements in marketing management practice? What was the rate of use of new knowledge and research? What barriers and blocks interfered with the utilization process? The final task was *prescriptive*. The Commission was charged with formulating a set of recommendations directed to various constituencies in the field of marketing based on the results of its deliberations and studies. (This charge is not alluded to in the Appendix 1-1 Prospectus, but was agreed upon in one of the early meetings of the Commission.)

To accomplish these three broad objectives, the Commission initiated and supervised several kinds of studies and held formal meetings of commissioners at which issues and perspectives were debated and discussed. Three all-day meetings took place in November 1976, June 1977, and November 1977, and exchanges of correspondence and various kinds of empirical studies were accomplished in and around this period. The staff of the Commission, headed by Professor Christopher Lovelock and John Bateson of Harvard University, conducted content-analysis studies of marketing journals and textbooks and did much of the legwork for a survey research study of marketing academics and professionals. The following section provides an overview of the work of the Commission and the various methods it used to carry out its mission.

An Overview of the Commission's Work

The work of the Commission involved five different operating methods and data generation procedures. First, commissioners and selected "friends" of the Commission[55] were polled for their opinions on four challenging questions: What were the major changes in the practice of marketing over the past twenty-five years? What major, new, useful approaches and techniques had been introduced over the period? What major problem areas remained? What major research approaches and techniques (in the respondent's judgment) had failed to fulfill their promise?

Second, several face-to-face meetings of the commissioners were held during 1976-1977. Much attention, particularly in the later meetings, was given to the discussion of viewpoints on the idea generation and diffusion process in marketing.

Third, a study was undertaken of changes in marketing journals and textbooks over the twenty-five-year period. The journal study involved content analyses over time of the *Journal of Marketing, Journal of Marketing Research, Harvard Business Review,* and *Journal of Consumer Research.* Examined were "hot topics" at the beginning and end of the period, topics that appeared to be a continuing source of interest as well as those that seemed to fade and those that were introduced, and the business/academic affiliation of authors. The textbook study involved content analysis of fifteen multiple-edition marketing textbooks ranging from Maynard and Beckman to Kotler, Enis, and Heskett.

A fourth type of effort involved a survey of American Marketing Association members on various aspects of idea generation and diffusion. The focus was on determining the amount of awareness and use of thirteen different types of analytical techniques, models, or research approaches.

Finally, attempts were made to elaborate on specific aspects of marketing's research and development system. Special interviews were conducted by the Commission staff to "track" the intellectual and applications evolution of new developments—in particular what many considered to be a highly successful example: that of conjoint analysis. Also, the Commission staff developed alternative skeletal views of the idea generation and diffusion process for use in Commission discussions of this process, and the cochairmen developed several "think pieces" on the types, nature, and functions of marketing research and the role of the marketing academic community.

Several important constraints were imposed on the Commission in carrying out its work. First, apart from secretarial costs and staff assistance, the effort was entirely voluntary. The commissioners were all senior academic and business people very busy with their normal activities. Second, the objectives of the Commission were, of necessity, very broad, and the measurement of concepts such as R & D and management practice very difficult. Finally, evaluative research, even if it is confined to evaluating the effectiveness of a specific program of activities, is very difficult to do. The Commission nevertheless provided a great many insightful and useful new ways to think about marketing research. Its work has extended our knowledge of this important topic and provided a base for future work.

In the next chapter we present our own and the view of many of the commissioners on the major changes and forces of change in marketing management over the twenty-five-year assessment period.

Appendix 1-1

PROSPECTUS

Commission on the Effectiveness of Research and Development for Marketing Management

Few would doubt that enormous changes have occurred in the profession of marketing, including marketing management, during the past twenty-five years. Indicators of change include: the adoption of the marketing concept itself; new approaches to planning, marketing, and advertising research methods, and much broader use of the same; mathematical models and applications of econometrics; information systems; concepts and analytical methods for market segmentation; and new approaches to consumer research. Progress has been made both in terms of conceptualization of marketing problems—learning about how to think about them, so to speak—and in terms of particular approaches and techniques. The work has been qualitative as well as quantitative, and has involved a variety of underlying disciplines such as behavioral science, operations research, and economics.

What is the origin of these changes? Where does the creative impetus lie? Where and with whom do the ideas incubate and concepts become articulated? Where are the new methods tested and the techniques refined? Where are the theories synthesized that, in their turn, give rise to a new generation of concepts? In short, what is the process of knowledge-creation in marketing?

The year 1976 is a good time to take stock of where we are in marketing and how we have gotten here. This is so not because of the bicentennial, though absent any other reason that is a good enough impetus for stock-taking. Rather, the length of the road already traveled is sufficiently long now for a review to be meaningful. There should be enough evidence for analysis; at the same time it is possible to set a beginning benchmark date that is not so far removed as to be inaccessible to memory.

Twenty-five years ago the computer emerged onto the business scene. Operations research and later the broader field of management science were born of the marriage of the computer and the thrust of analytical and scientific thinking that was a legacy of World War II. It was approximately twenty years ago that the Gordon and Howell and Pierson reports revolutionized and revitalized business education, and it was during this period that "new look" business schools such as M.I.T., Carnegie Institute of Technology (now Carnegie-Mellon University), Chicago, and later Stanford began to assume significant stature, and the more established schools such as Harvard, Wharton, and Berkeley began to introduce significant changes into their curricula. It is not unreasonable to assume that an acceleration of change in the practice of marketing management and research began during this same period.

More than curiosity defines the need for a better understanding of knowledge-creation in marketing. The great wave of support for science, basic research, and the financing of the intellectual community generally, that grew out of the experience of World War II, now has subsided. A "hard-headed" demand for demonstrations of relevance to clear and present problems has replaced, in the American culture, a faith that contributions to knowledge are good in their own right and worthy of support, and that they will in time yield handsome returns in ways not yet known or even knowable.

The field of marketing has not been immune to this trend. Serious debate has been joined. A better understanding of the process of knowledge-creation in marketing will lift this debate to a higher level and increase the probability that wise answers and actions will emerge.

We take as given the goal of long-run relevance to practice in marketing, including the determination of government policies that affect our field and the commercial research and consulting industries that support it. The question is, what has been the source of the intellectual fuel that runs the engine of practice and education for action? Can we take the supply of this energy for granted? Will the fuel renew and enhance itself solely by the process of its application, as in a breeder reactor, or does continued progress demand the explicit investment of talent and money in knowledge-creation? If investment is required, how should the process be managed and the necessary resources made available?

It is obvious that a knowledge-creating sector does exist in marketing. It runs from basic research—mostly done in universities—through applied work in the universities, in non-profit organizations, and in research and consulting firms. A growing number of journals related to marketing questions attest to the quantity, if not the quality, of what is intended at least to be knowledge-creation. However, the fundamental question is whether all or most of these segments do really create useful knowledge, even when ''useful'' is defined as being relevant in the long run rather than the short run. The creation of knowledge that is inadequate, either in terms of quality or because of the choice of topics, will not be viewed as an important investment. Those whose work is inadequate do not have a valid claim on resources.

By taking stock of where we are and how we got here, it should be possible to assess the adequacy of the output of the various knowledge-creating sectors in marketing. This can be done through a determination of the contribution of each sector to the major shifts in practice that have occurred during the last twenty-five years. If the investments in knowledge-creation have made a difference, some effects should be traceable. Linkages among people and institutions can be analyzed through hindsight, as can the evolution of important successful ideas. The fact that many research lines and concepts end up in blind alleys, and unexpected favorable insights and applications also occur frequently, makes it difficult or impossible for a researcher or a research sector to demonstrate, or even promise, relevance a priori. However, an ex post analysis should make it possible to uncover and document successful investments to the extent they are significant. Alternatively, if the process is more like the breeder reactor, that fact, too, can be uncovered.

This, then, is the objective of the Commission on the Effectiveness of Research and Development for Marketing Management. The Commission will consist of fifteen distinguished marketing people, drawn from marketing management, marketing research, and academia. The task of the Commission will be to assist in the design of the review and assessment effort, to contribute expertise, insight, and personal contacts to the information-gathering phase of the project, and to review and determine approval of the draft report. The Commission will be co-chaired by Dr. William F. Massy, Professor at the Stanford Business School and Vice President-Marketing Education of the American Marketing Association, and Dr. Stephen A. Greyser, Professor at the Harvard Business School and Director of the Marketing Science Institute.

(*Author's Note:* The original copy of the Prospectus reproduced above was written by Bill Massy in August, 1976. The Commission membership was later expanded to include eighteen members whose names, titles, and affliations appear on the following list.)

Commission Membership

Co-chairmen

WILLIAM F. MASSY
   Professor, Graduate School of Business and
   Vice President for Business and Finance
   Stanford University
   Vice President for Marketing Education (1976–1977)
   American Marketing Association

STEPHEN A. GREYSER
   Professor, Graduate School of Business Administration
   Harvard University
   Executive Director
   Marketing Science Institute

Commissioners

SEYMOUR BANKS
   Vice President, Media Research
   Leo Burnett Company

FRANK M. BASS
   Professor, Krannert Graduate School of Management
   Purdue University

ROBERT BURNETT
   President
   Meredith Corporation

ROBERT D. BUZZELL
   Professor of Business Administration
   Harvard Business School
   Harvard University

HENRY J. CLAYCAMP
   Vice President, Corporate Planning
   International Harvester

ROBERT FERBER
   Professor
   University of Illinois

RONALD E. FRANK
  Professor
  The Wharton School (University of Pennsylvania)

JOHN G. KEANE
  President
  Managing Change, Inc.
  (President, 1976–1977), American Marketing Association

PHILIP KOTLER
  Professor, Graduate School of Management
  Northwestern University

LARRY LIGHT
  Batten, Barton, Durstine & Osborn, Inc.
  Research Department

ELMER LOTSHAW
  Director Corporate Marketing & Economic Research
  Owens-Illinois

WILLIAM T. MORAN
  President
  Ad Mar Research

JOHN G. MYERS
  Professor, School of Business, University of California, Berkeley
  Vice President for Marketing Education (1977–1978)
  American Marketing Association

BART R. PANNETTIERE
  Director, Research, Development & Technology
  General Foods Corporation

W. R. REISS
  Marketing Director, Research
  American Telephone & Telegraph

DUDLEY M. RUCH
  Marketing Information Department
  The Quaker Oats Company

Staff

CHRISTOPHER H. LOVELOCK
  Associate Professor, Graduate School of Business Administration
  Harvard University

JOHN BATESON
Doctoral student in Marketing, Graduate School of Business Administration
Harvard University

NOTES

[1] Richard E. Sessions, "A Management Audit of Marketing Research," *Journal of Marketing,* 14 (January 1950), 111–19.

[2] John E. Jeuck, "Marketing Research: Milestone or Millstone?" *Journal of Marketing,* 17 (April 1953), 381–87.

[3] Harry V. Roberts, "The Role of Research in Marketing Management," *Journal of Marketing,* 22 (July 1957), 21–32.

[4] Lee Adler, "Phasing Research into the Marketing Plan," *Harvard Business Review,* May–June, p. 113.

[5] Joseph W. Newman, "Put Research into Marketing Decisions," *Harvard Business Review,* 40 (March–April 1962), 105–12.

[6] William F. Massy and Frederick E. Webster, Jr., "Model-Building in Marketing Research," *Journal of Marketing Research,* 1 (May 1964), 9–13, published by the American Marketing Association.

[7] Massy and Webster, "Model-Building in Marketing Research," published by the American Marketing Association, p. 13.

[8] William F. Massy, "The TIMS College of Marketing," *Journal of Marketing Research,* 5 (May 1968), 230.

[9] Arnold. E. Amstutz, *Computer Simulation of Competitive Market Response* (Cambridge, Mass.: M.I.T. Press, 1967).

[10] David B. Montgomery and Glen L. Urban, *Management Science in Marketing* (Englewood Cliffs, N.J.: Prentice-Hall, 1969).

[11] Another consequence was the beginning of the "Computer Abstracts" section of the *Journal of Marketing Research.* See David B. Montgomery, "Computer Uses in Marketing Research: A Proposal," *Journal of Marketing Research,* 4 (May 1967), 195–98.

[12] See, for example, Robert D. Buzzell, Donald F. Cox, and Rex V. Brown, *Marketing Research and Information Systems: Text and Cases* (New York: McGraw-Hill, 1969), and Kenneth P. Uhl and Bertram Schoner, *Marketing Research: Information Systems and Decision Making* (New York: Wiley, 1969).

[13] Jean-Claude Larreche and David B. Montgomery, "A Framework for the Comparison of Marketing Models: A Delphi Study," *Journal of Marketing Research,* 14 (November 1977), 487–98.

[14] See, for example, B. B. Gardner and S. J. Levy, "The Product and the Brand," *Harvard Business Review,* March–April 1955, pp. 33–39, and P. Martineau, "Social Classes and Spending Behavior," *Journal of Marketing,* 23 (1958), 121–30. For an early book on the subject, see R. Ferber and H. G. Wales, *Motivation and Market Behavior* (Homewood, Ill.: Richard D. Irwin, 1958).

[15] One of the first interdisciplinary books on the subject of consumer behavior was the collection of readings edited by Nelson Foote. See N. N. Foote, ed., *Household Decision-Making, Consumer Behavior IV* (New York: New York University Press, 1961). Examples of influential works of psychologists and sociologists published in the 1950s and early 1960s are G. Katona, *The Powerful Consumer* (New York: McGraw-Hill,

1951); P. F. Lazarsfeld, "Sociological Reflections on Business: Consumers and Managers," in R. A. Dahl, M. Haire, and P. F. Lazarsfeld, *Social Science Research on Business: Product and Potential* (New York: Columbia University Press, 1959); D. T. Campbell and D. W. Fiske, "Convergent and Discriminant Validation by the Multitrait-MultiMethod Matrix," *Psychological Bulletin,* 56 (March 1959), 81-105; L. Festinger, *A Theory of Cognitive Dissonance* (Stanford: Stanford University Press, 1957); W. S. Torgerson, *Theory and Methods of Scaling* (New York: Wiley, 1958); D. Krech and others, *Individual in Society* (New York: McGraw-Hill, 1962); M. J. Rosenberg, "Cognitive Structure and Attitudinal Affect," *Journal of Abnormal and Social Psychology,* 53 (1956), 367-72; E. M. Rogers, *Diffusion of Innovations* (New York: The Free Press, 1962); M. Fishbein, ed., *Readings in Attitude Theory and Measurement* (New York: Wiley, 1967); R. D. Luce and J. W. Tukey, "Simultaneous Conjoint Measurement: A New Type of Fundamental Measurement," *Journal of Mathematical Psychology,* 1 (February 1964), 1-27, and many books on attitude change published in the 1950s and 1960s.

[16]Examples published during the last half of the 1960s are F. M. Nicosia, *Consumer Decision Processes: Marketing and Advertising Implications* (Englewood Cliffs, N.J.: Prentice-Hall, 1966); D. F. Cox, ed., *Risk Taking and Information Handling in Consumer Behavior* (Boston: Graduate School of Business Administration, Harvard University, 1967); J. F. Engel and others, *Consumer Behavior* (New York: Holt, Rinehart and Winston, 1968); J. G. Myers, *Consumer Image and Attitude* (Berkeley, Calif.: Institute of Business and Economic Research, 1968); and J. A. Howard and J. N. Sheth, *The Theory of Buyer Behavior* (New York: Wiley, 1969).

[17]F. T. Schreier, *Modern Marketing Research: A Behavioral Science Approach* (Belmont, Calif.: Wadsworth, 1963); G. Zaltman and P. C. Burger, *Marketing Research: Fundamentals and Dynamics* (Hinsdale, Ill.: Dryden Press, 1975).

[18]The same articles are included in different categories, so the total should not be interpreted as the total number of articles published in the *Journal of Marketing Research* during this period.

[19]Harper W. Boyd, Jr., and Steuart H. Britt, "Making Marketing Research More Effective by Using the Administrative Process," *Journal of Marketing Research,* 2 (February 1965), 13-19.

[20]Boyd and Britt, "Making Marketing Research More Effective by Using the Administrative Process," p. 13.

[21]James R. Krum, "Survey of Marketing Research Directors of Fortune 500 Firms," *Journal of Marketing Research,* 3 (August 1966), 313-17, and "Perceptions and Evaluation of the Role of the Corporate Marketing Research Department," *Journal of Marketing Research,* 6 (November 1969), 459-64.

[22]J. A. Howard, *Marketing: Executive and Buyer Behavior* (New York: Columbia University Press, 1963).

[23]David K. Hardin, "Marketing Research—Is It Used or Abused?" *Journal of Marketing Research,* 6 (May 1969), 239, published by the American Marketing Association.

[24]David K. Hardin, "Marketing Research—Is It Used or Abused?" p. 239.

[25]Stewart A. Smith, "Research and Pseudo-Research in Marketing," *Harvard Business Review,* March—April 1974, pp. 73-76.

[26]Newman, "Put Research into Marketing Decisions."

[27]David B. McCall, "What Agency Managers Want from Research," *Journal of Advertising Research,* 14 (August 1974), 7-10.

[28]Neil Holbert, "How Managers See Marketing Research," *Journal of Advertising Research,* 14 No. 6 (December 1974), 41–46. Reprinted from the Journal of Advertising Research © Copyright (1974), by the Advertising Research Foundation.

[29]Holbert, "How Managers See Marketing Research," p. 46. See also V. P. Buell, "60 Years of Progress in Marketing Research, But Will It Meet New Opportunities, Problems?" *Marketing News,* March 14, 1975, p. 1.

[30]See, for example, Donald S. Tull and Del I. Hawkins, *Marketing Research: Meaning, Measurement, and Method* (New York: Macmillan, 1976); Gilbert A. Churchill, Jr., *Marketing Research: Methodological Foundations* (Hinsdale, Ill.: Dryden Press, 1976); Paul E. Green and Donald S. Tull, *Research for Marketing Decisions* (Englewood Cliffs, N.J.: Prentice-Hall, 1978).

[31]Robert Schlaifer, *Probability and Statistics for Business Decisions* (New York: McGraw-Hill, 1959).

[32]Frank M. Bass, "Marketing Research Expenditures: A Decision Model," *Journal of Business,* 36 (1963), 77–90.

[33]W. F. Massy and J. D. Sarvas, "Logical Flow Models for Marketing Analysis," *Journal of Marketing,* 28 (1964), 32–37.

[34]Dik W. Twedt, "What is the 'Return on Investment' in Marketing Research?" *Journal of Marketing,* January 1966, pp. 62–63.

[35]D. W. Twedt, *1973 Survey of Marketing Research* (Chicago: American Marketing Association, 1973).

[36]James H. Myers and A. C. Samli, "Management Control of Marketing Research," *Journal of Marketing Research,* 6 (August 1969), 267–77.

[37]Charles S. Mayer, "Assessing the Accuracy of Marketing Research," *Journal of Marketing Research,* 7 (August 1970), 285–91.

[38]For a recent discussion, see Churchill, *Marketing Research: Methodological Foundations,* pp. 317–44.

[39]A. Samli and Carl Bellas, "The Use of GERT in the Planning and Control of Marketing Research," *Journal of Marketing Research,* 8 (August 1971), 335–39.

[40]Jeffrey Gandz and Thomas W. Whipple, "Making Marketing Research Accountable," *Journal of Marketing Research,* 14 (May 1977), 202–8.

[41]See James H. Myers and Richard R. Mead, *The Management of Marketing Research* (Scranton, Pa.: International Textbook, 1969), and Lee Adler and Charles S. Mayer, *Managing the Marketing Research Function* (Chicago: American Marketing Association, 1977).

[42]Myers and Samli, "Management Control of Marketing Research."

[43]Robert Ferber, "Looking Back to 1967," *Journal of Marketing Research,* 4 (May 1967), 210–11, published by the American Marketing Association.

[44]Paul E. Green, "Where Is the Research Generalist?" *Journal of Marketing Research,* 5 (November 1968), 442, published by the American Marketing Association.

[45]The term "research generalist" had been introduced earlier by Newman, "Put Research into Marketing Decisions," and by Massy and Webster, "Model-Building in Marketing Research." Massy and Webster, for example, stated in their 1964 article (p. 13), "Progress in the application of scientific methods to marketing can be expedited if we continuously keep in mind the relationship between the marketing researcher (who studies behavioral phenomena), the operations analyst (who prescribes problem solutions), and the research generalist who can help bridge the gaps between the scientific approaches and between them and marketing management." A dissenting view on the idea of a research

generalist is provided in a paper by Lawrence H. Wortzel, "Finding the Research Generalist: Solution May Not Be Black or White But It Isn't Green Either," *Journal of Marketing Research,* 6 (November 1969), 498–99. Wortzel essentially argued that every marketing manager must be a research generalist and every researcher must have the orientations of a marketing manager, and that up-to-date MBA programs would produce these kinds of people. Little formal work in terms of marketing department organization implications appears to have been done on this issue since then. For an interesting discussion of the problems of communications among basic scientists, see Lewis Thomas, "Hubris in Science?" *Science,* 200 (June 1978), 1459–62.

[46]Ewald T. Grether, "The First Forty Years," *Journal of Marketing,* 40 (July 1976), 63–69, and John G. Keane, "A Business View: Forty Years and the Future," *Journal of Marketing,* 40 (July 1976), 70–73.

[47]John G. Keane, "Some Observations on Marketing Research in Top Management Decision Making," *Journal of Marketing,* 33 (October 1969), 10–15.

[48]J. Hulbert, J. U. Farley, and J. A. Howard, "Information Processing and Decision Making in Marketing Organizations," *Journal of Marketing Research,* 9 (February 1972), 75–77.

[49]Arthur J. Kover, "Careers and Noncommunication: The Case of Academic and Applied Marketing Research," *Journal of Marketing Research,* 13 (November 1976), 339–44. For a reply, see Charles M. Lillis, "Careers and Noncommunication: The Case of Academic and Applied Marketing Research—A Comment," *Journal of Marketing Research,* 14 (November 1977), 580.

[50]William E. Souder, "Effectiveness of Nominal and Interacting Group Decision Processes for Integrating R & D and Marketing," *Management Science,* 23 (February 1977), 595–605.

[51]Alice M. Tybout and Gerald Zaltman, "Ethics in Marketing Research: Their Practical Relevance," *Journal of Marketing Research,* 11 (November 1974), 357–68.

[52]R. L. Day, "Comment on 'Ethics in Marketing Research,'" *Journal of Marketing Research,* 12 (May 1975), 232–33.

[53]George S. Day, "The Threats to Marketing Research," *Journal of Marketing Research,* 12 (November 1975), 562–67.

[54]Stephen A. Greyser, "Academic Research Marketing Managers Can Use," *Journal of Advertising Research,* 18 (April 1978), 9–14.

[55]Particularly useful communications were obtained from Charles R. Adler of the Eastman Kodak Company, Paul N. Reis of the Procter and Gamble Company, C. R. Smith of Nabisco, Inc., and William D. Wells of Needham, Harper & Steers Advertising, Inc.

2

The Evolution of Marketing Management

The assessment period, 1952–1977, was a time of unparalleled growth in marketing research. Many commercial research supplier firms, for example, came into being and grew into sizeable and significant operations. Consumer packaged goods manufacturers and many other industrial and service corporations initiated or considerably expanded their marketing research departments. In the academic sector, a great deal of new theoretical and methodological knowledge was developed.

The assessment objective of the Commission was in part focused on evaluating the impact of this considerable amount of research and development effort on changes or improvements in marketing management practice. An initial point of departure was thus to determine what changes had taken place in marketing practice and what factors and forces brought them about. Obviously, many factors besides marketing research affected the evolution of marketing management practice. This chapter focuses both on the nature of these changes and on the nature of the forces other than marketing's R & D that appeared to contribute to them.

The review presented in this chapter of the evolution of marketing management from 1952 to 1977 is noncomprehensive in at least two senses.

First, it focuses on the evolution of marketing practices in large corporations, particularly in the consumer packaged goods area. Second, it highlights the types of changes in organizations that did indeed change their practices. The changes and the forces of change identified do not apply equally well to all types of organizations and marketing operations. Some corporations, for example, obviously changed a great deal, while others changed little or not at all.

The material in this chapter comes from a poll of Commission members conducted in 1976–1977 and from selected published writings on the subject. The first section deals with the types of changes that took place and is organized into subsections dealing with changes in such things as the marketing concept, planning, organization-implementation, and control. This is followed by a section on the factors influencing those changes. Specific attention is given to technological, social, governmental, and economic factors. The changes that took place in marketing research and details about the types of new knowledge that were developed over the period are discussed in Chapter 3. Subsequent chapters assess the materials from several different viewpoints. Here, we focus on changes in marketing management practice and those factors other than marketing research that appear to have strongly influenced the evolution of marketing management over the period.

The Commission poll asked the question: "What major changes in the practice of marketing do you believe have occurred in the last twenty-five years?" Thirteen commissioners provided insightful and lengthy replies. Much of the material in the chapter is based on this rich source of judgmental data. The flavor of the individual responses can be captured only by reading the verbatim reactions of each commissioner. To this end, Appendix 2-1, containing the important comments of each commissioner, has been included at the end of the chapter. Comments are organized by the individual's affiliation (academic, independent research-consulting-agency firms, and operating companies) and disguised so as to maintain the anonymity of each respondent.

An interesting aspect of these responses is their surprisingly high degree of consistency. Although language differs from one commissioner to the next, different individuals and interest groups have identified many of the same changes and forces of change. There is some obvious nonindependence of commissioners as "sampling units," given the fact that most of them knew each other, but each was independently solicited by private letter and asked for his judgments and opinions on the question. The responses of these thirteen can be characterized much more by their similarities than by their differences.

TYPES OF CHANGES IN MARKETING PRACTICE

Consider the nature of the marketing and selling efforts of a typical large corporation in 1952. How might these operations be expected to change in the subsequent twenty-five years? In retrospect, we know that the major change in most such organizations was one of scale of operations—that is, their sales or number of employees simply increased. There was little change in the basic functions or activities of marketing, such as the development, pricing, promotion, and distribution of new products. Each of these activities is, in some sense, a prerequisite to business operations, and any firm that continued to operate throughout the period would perform these functions in one way or another.

In what way, then, did marketing management practice change over the period? The next sections answer this question. Most important was a change in management philosophy that led to new or expanded kinds of marketing activities (such as marketing research) and new ways to plan, organize, implement, and control marketing operations. The manifest consequences of these changes can be seen largely as additions to, rather than subtractions from, the basic elements of marketing as it was being practiced in 1952. The change in managerial philosophy that had the greatest impact was, of course, the emergence of the marketing concept. The next section briefly reviews this fundamental idea and some of the changes in marketing operations that evolved from it.

The Marketing Concept

A "product concept" approach to organizing and running a business implies that little or no marketing or selling effort is needed—the product will "sell itself." Companies that adopted this approach concentrated strongly on such functions as production, finance, and accounting, and devoted few resources to marketing. A virtually opposite managerial philosophy is the "selling concept." In this case, selling, particularly "hard selling," is assumed to be vital to success. Organizations that take this approach tend to put exceptionally heavy emphasis on selling, promoting, and related activities. In neither case, however, is there a real need for consumer or marketing research. Each is essentially an internally oriented way of thinking, which emphasizes production or selling and ignores the needs, wants, and motivations of prospective customers.

Drucker[1] is generally credited with introducing the basis perspectives of the marketing concept in 1954.[2] The marketing concept is distinguishable from the product and selling concepts by (1) a customer orientation, (2) the argument that all marketing-related activities should be integrated and brought under one organizational planning/management unit, and (3) the resultant need to engage in consumer and marketing research. The basic argument was that an organization's goals (for example, the goal of maximum profits) could best be accomplished through integrated marketing and an increased understanding of which products and services satisfy consumers.

The *focus* of marketing management changed from internal (costs and products) to external (customer needs and competition). The *means* changed from an independent perspective of "selling," "pricing," "promoting," and so on to a coordinated perspective of "integrated marketing." And the *ends* changed from "profits through sales volume" to "profits through customer satisfaction." This externally focused attitude on how to run a business and the idea that various components of marketing such as product, pricing, promotion, and distribution should be integrated into an overall comprehensive marketing plan had far-reaching consequences for the evolution of marketing practice.

An external focus, for example, leads logically to a heightened awareness of and stronger motivation for marketing research. This undoubtedly helped increase academic and professional interest in understanding and predicting consumer behavior and was a major impetus to the emergence of consumer behavior as a field of study, the creation of the Association for Consumer Research, and the publication of numerous new textbooks and journals on the subject. The new focus gave increased stature and significance to marketing as a vital business function. The scientific and explicit use of information in decision making, the educational and university role in training managerial talent for marketing positions, and the development of numerous other trappings of a "profession" are traceable to this change in overall managerial focus. Even the modern-day concept of "marketing information systems" and the change of marketing research in some corporations from a purely data-gathering function to one that includes complex decision models and multivariate analysis are natural extensions of the fundamental idea.

Many of the commissioner replies to the previously cited poll (see Appendix 2-1) acknowledge the importance of the marketing concept and the relatively widespread adoption of this managerial philosophy during the period. As stated by one commissioner: "Probably the greatest change influence on methods of marketing decisions making has been the development of the Marketing Concept. This simple idea has had a revolutionary effect upon methods of marketing decision making. Almost every facet of change in marketing practice is related in one way or another to this concept." Some specific types of changes resulting from the new perspective were identified in the Commission poll as follows:

More systematic, sophisticated, and information-based planning, forecasting, implementation, and control functions.

The integration and coordination of key marketing activities based upon overall goals of consumer satisfaction and profitability. A change of emphasis from "product and selling" to "consumer and marketing."

A sharp increase in the amount of marketing research, in the quality and quantity of secondary sources of information, in syndicated services such as SAMI, Nielsen, and MCRA, and in the volume of corporate-initiated primary research studies, particularly in consumer research relating to concept testing, packaging, new product development, and advertising.

Introduction of many kinds of systems viewpoints into marketing management, such as "marketing information systems."

Numerous accompanying organizational changes including larger marketing research and planning staffs, adoption by many firms of a brand or product management approach, and general shifts in assigning responsibility and authority for marketing-related functions in the organization.

The marketing concept and the changes in marketing practice that flowed from it also did much to change the way marketing was taught in universities. There was, at the beginning of the period, a marked decline in commodity, institutional, and macro approaches to the subject and, at the end of the period, a virtual dominance of decision-making, management, and micro approaches across marketing curricula.[3]

The following sections elaborate on the changes in marketing practice associated with each of the major management tasks of planning, organization, implementation, and control. The material in these sections draws heavily on the Commission poll results and contains excerpts from the commissioner replies to that poll reproduced in full in Appendix 2-1. All quotations in these sections are excerpts from commissioner replies.

Planning

One change that took place over the period was the development of formal, written, and well thought out short- and long-run marketing plans, particularly in larger consumer packaged goods corporations. As stated by one commissioner:

Progress has been made in methods for planning marketing activities, of integrating marketing plans with those of other functional areas such as manufacturing and R & D, and in relating those to overall business objectives. One manifestation of this is the growing emphasis in marketing on profitability.... The time horizon for planning with respect to marketing actions has increased during the last twenty-five years.... [a]nnual and long-range plans [are now being made] for separate products, markets, and market segments.

Other comments such as "Major advances in marketing planning and its integration into business planning," "The time frame for marketing planning increased dramatically," "Systems evaluation of the marketing process," and "Increased financial evaluation of the results of marketing expenditures" all attest to the recognition of more formal and systematic planning as a major change.

Time-tested marketing strategies such as the product life cycle were refined, and numerous new views on strategic thinking with respect to demand and competition were introduced. Ideas such as market penetration and penetration rates, market segmentation (differentiation, concentration, and undifferentiation), demand states (negative demand, irregular demand, overfull demand, and so on), hierarchy models, and several other ways of viewing markets from a strategic perspective came into being. The classical economic view was extended to viewing competition in terms of consumer perceptions and preferences. A widespread interest in product positioning and perceptual mapping and a much broader view of the concept of "market structure" evolved. Many new models relating to the creative, screening, economic analysis, pretesting, and market monitoring stages of new product development were introduced, tested, and refined. Product portfolio analysis became yet another way to consider alternative marketing strategies and develop formal marketing plans.

As noted earlier, a customer orientation was the underpinning of many of these changes. Commissioners expressed this in various ways:

Caveat emptor is no longer a viable way of doing business.

There has been a growing emphasis on the consumer from a behavioral point of view, including recognition of the increasing complementarity and substitutability of different types of products on the one hand, and attention to the consumer's ever-increasing wants and vocalism on the other.

Many commissioners reported a general increase in the overall intensity of competition:

Markets, and the practice of marketing, have become more competitive. Whether this is being caused by the incidence of new decision-making tools, by government action and consumerism, or by basic economic changes is not clear. As competition increases, so also does the risk of wrong decisions.

The use of marketing research in planning was also recognized:

The span of issues that marketing research is perceived as capable of being addressed to has also broadened considerably. More marketing research is now being done on broader strategic development than used to be the case.

Finally, commission members recognized an increased consideration of government regulations, consumerism, and environmental-ecological issues in the development of plans and strategies. One referred to "vastly increased government involvement, including as indirect effects private antitrust as a competitive weapon," and another noted the "increasing need for legal appraisal of marketing decisions stemming from more complex regulations and increasing litigiousness generally. . . . [L]egal appraisal introduces a largely unfamiliar dimension into the marketing management process."

Organization and Implementation

Significant changes in practice took place at the organization and implementation stages of marketing management. Several Commissioners noted an increase in the overall scale of business and marketing operations over the period. It is highly likely that the amount invested in marketing-related activities within corporations increased relative to that invested in other functions such as accounting and finance. This implies larger departments, more people, and in some departments, such as marketing research or consumer affairs, new organizational structures.

The most significant organizational changes are traceable to the "integrated marketing activities" recommendation associated with the marketing concept. Previously separated activities such as "sales," "advertising," and "pricing" were brought together under one senior executive officer, often called the vice-president of marketing. Many companies that produced a variety of products adopted product management organization as an addition to functional organization, manifest in the "brand manager" or "product manager" approach to organization. Comments such as the following attest to these changes:

Organizing marketing activities to more effectively plan and implement marketing programs.

Systems invention of new products.

Widespread adoption of product division form of organization.

Various experiments with "market manager" and related forms of organization.

More educated marketing managers.

Implementation-related changes were particularly noteworthy at the levels of advertising/promotion and distribution/channel programs. In the former case implementation involved much heavier use of mass communications, particularly television (at least toward the end of the period). A brand manager, as a consequence, was forced to become expert in judging the effectiveness of this type of communications and to interact with numerous specialists associated with the use of television. The increased use of television and all forms of mass media was itself a major change in practice. As noted by one commissioner, the period was characterized by "greater communications to consumers directly from the producers rather than through complete dependence upon the mediating influence of distributors (wholesale and retail)."

Distribution and related channel decisions changed in both nature and scope. For mass market producers, improvements in physical transportation allowed for greater and faster distribution. New forms of wholesaling and retailing outlets and proliferation and improvements in media vehicles and transportation modes allowed products to be more precisely targeted and better matched with consumer needs. The evolution of retail institutions such as "shopping centers," "automated vending machines," and specialized distributors such as "rack jobbers" had a significant effect on the implementation of marketing plans. In the words of a commissioner, "Trade decisions on ordering increasingly became based upon shelf movement—first, their own shelf movement and later, thanks to syndicated retail and wholesale movement services, their competitors' shelf movement.''

Control

Major changes in marketing management practice took place at the control stage. Here, marketing research, both internal (done within the firm) and external (such as advertising agency and independent marketing research firm research), had its greatest impact. All phases of the company's operations became increasingly dependent on research information. A wide variety of complex, disparate, and often confusing sources of data became available for planning and control, significantly changing these practices. Among other things, marketing managers or their staff had to learn to analyze and interpret such data. ''Marketing audits'' and ''control by market monitoring'' became widely accepted ways of doing business.

Commissioners recognized these changes in several ways. Some pointed out the greater emphasis on financial evaluation of the results of marketing expenditures, the rise in the use of ''models'' to guide marketing research, and, in general, the development of various kinds of ''marketing information systems.'' Although, as stated by one commissioner,

a great variety of statistical methods, mostly developed by other disciplines for purposes other than marketing management, have been adapted, refined, and employed in the analysis of marketing data,

another pointed out that

the techniques utilized by most firms in research and information processing are primitive compared to those discussed in contemporary academic journals—yet the change in marketing practice has been dramatic compared to that of several years ago.

The following commissioner comment provides an interesting summary of the nature of the evolutionary process, particularly as it pertains to the acceptance of ''soft data'' in the control of marketing operations:

Producers have accepted ''soft data'' on market performance to permit comparison with competitive performance:

a. Share-of-market replaced factory shipment as the indicator of future profitability.

b. Later, share-of-mind and the whole current spectrum of intermediate criteria, including functional behavioral relationships such as repeat rates, came to be used for marketing control and planning.

c. Then came a growing awareness of the need to make explicit the implicit models behind the intermediate criteria which were being used.

d. Intermediate indices such as behavioral, perceptual, attitudinal data and demographic trends permitted forecasting from data obtained not only from outside the producer's internal information but (even more radically) from outside—and prior to—the distribution system.

e. The availability of such forecasts led to marketing resource allocation decisions based upon the market effects of prior decisions.

The overall increase in the size and scope of marketing research as an industry was noted in comments such as "increased size and sophistication of market research activities," "increased range of applications for market research," "systematic use of consumer surveys," "maintenance of regular time series data," "shift from trade to consumer research emphasis and from secondary to original data," "test marketing and test market simulation," "advertising testing," and "marketing information systems."

Other Types of Changes

Commissioners noted several changes that do not fit easily into the foregoing categories. First, it was generally agreed that marketing practice became more "professional" and its stature within the organization increased. In the words of two commissioners, there was:

An increase in the "professionalism" of marketing management manifest in better and higher-quality decision making, more systematic and sustained data gathering, such as panels and repetitive consumer surveys, and more well-educated managers.

A significant increase in the stature of marketing within the organization and greater recognition of and investment in marketing management as an essential business function.

One commissioner noted changes in the labor force involved in marketing practice—there was a "greater diversity in kinds of people available for and aspiring to marketing jobs—women, blacks, etc." Another pointed out the "continuing pressures to mechanize and/or simplify both management and marketing research due to rising labor costs." Several noted that marketing management practices began to be applied in the public and nonprofit organization sectors.

In summary, marketing management evolved in important new ways, most of which were reflections of the basic shift in top-management attitudes manifest in the marketing concept. Most changes were incremental to the basic marketing tasks of product development, pricing, promotion, and distribution and concerned new approaches to planning, organization, implementation, and control of marketing operations.

In the next section we will identify and discuss some major external forces that were operating in the economy over the twenty-five-year period. (Developments in marketing research and knowledge will be treated in the next chapter.) Once again, an attempt has been made to introduce specific commissioner comments relating to these types of externalities. All such comments are drawn from the verbatim replies to the Commission poll given in Appendix 2-1. Also, we leave to the reader the task of relating specific types of externalities to specific changes in marketing management practice. In most cases these should be obvious. The focus, instead, is on documenting some of the major factors that were operating on marketing management over the period—factors that in one way or another influenced its evolution.

FACTORS AFFECTING CHANGES IN MARKETING MANAGEMENT PRACTICE

No attempt is made to document all the conceivable "externalities" that affected marketing management over this period. Factors such as wars, politics, weather, population shifts, and inflation all exerted some influence but will not be treated in this review.[4] Rather, attention is focused on those that appeared to have the most direct impact on changes in marketing practice. They were the "facilitators" of specific changes during the period, both contributing to and influenced by marketing management. Three primary factors are emphasized, referred to below as (1) technological, (2) sociopolitical, and (3) economic.

Technological Factors

The period from 1952 to 1977 was characterized by an explosive growth of technological inventions and developments, many of which had significant effects on the evolution of marketing management practice. Two such innovations—computers and television—were of particular importance. Each became commercially viable and went through its period of greatest growth and development during the past quarter century.

Computers.   Although the logic of computing goes back to early work by mathematicians such as Alan Turing in 1937, and World War II did much to foster military interest in the subject, much of the commercial development took place in the 1950s and 1960s.[5] In 1958, for example, the transistor was incorporated into an integrated circuit (IC) at Texas Instruments, leading to a vast increase in computing power and applications of microprocessing over the subsequent decade. Peripherals of all kinds were developed during the period, the first CRT appearing in 1955 and the first stand-alone CRT in 1968. Minicomputers came into production during 1964 and 1965, and in 1969, Intel and Texas Instruments developed the first logic device on a single silicon chip, the essential ingredient for the development of microprocessors. The microprocessor, which characterizes modern-day computing, radically reduced the costs of a computer and increased the efficiency of computer production. Recent developments such as, home computers, the automation of cash registers in food retailing, and numerous others will undoubtedly have significant effects on marketing management practice over the coming quarter century.

Specific commissioner comments concerning the impact of computers on marketing practice were as follows:

It provided the *means* whereby many of the current practices of marketing managers and researchers are carried out—processing large amounts of data, using powerful statistical techniques, and implementing marketing information systems.

Its applications over the period have moved from essentially a cost-control-accounting tool to a tool used in marketing planning, decision making, data analysis, and data collection.

It is the pillar on which much of the new knowledge generated in marketing over the past quarter century rests.

Computers made possible the management of very large amounts of data in terms of both accessibility and analysis. This, in turn, stimulated the need for models, theories, and perspectives to guide the data collection and analysis process. Highly complex multivariate methods became feasible analysis alternatives, and a whole generation of model builders, statisticians, and computer specialists began to look at marketing as an applications area for pursuing their interests. Progress in adapting the computer to studies in the basic disciplines from which marketing researchers continued to draw their inspiration and insight—economics, psychology, sociology, and others—further emphasized and expanded the important role of the computer. The computer was a facilitating device for the making of marketing decisions rather than a contributor to the conduct of marketing per se. But that did not make it any less important. The computer's role in changing marketing was crucial precisely because it affected the research and decision-making process and, therefore, affected the knowledge-creating and knowledge-using activities in the field.

Television.   Television also saw its greatest growth and development during the assessment period. Although by 1950 there were ninety-six television stations operating in approximately fifty different markets, at the beginning of the period television was still a selective medium from a geographical coverage point of view.[6] By 1964, the number of stations had climbed to 569, and 98% of American homes were within range of at least one station. In 1950 the number of homes with TV sets was 3.4 million. By 1964 it was 52.6 million, and average home use ranged from five to seven hours per day. Developments such as pay TV, CATV, and Public Broadcasting TV expanded further the scope and reach of this significant communication medium.[7] By 1978 television made up 59.6%

of major media national advertising revenue.[8] In 1977 the nation's largest advertiser, Procter & Gamble Company, spent an estimated $460 million on advertising, about 76% ($350 million) of which was for Spot and Network television.[9]

The development of television and, indeed, developments in all media (radio, magazines, newspapers, and so on) over the period had significant effects on marketing management. To be used effectively, mass communications required the investment of significant amounts of funds, and marketing expenditures grew as a direct result. From the manager's viewpoint, such expenditures had numerous ROI and other implications. For example, a large and sophisticated industry of research suppliers and corporate and advertising agency research focusing on the question of advertising effectiveness developed. Marketing managers had to deal with a new class of specialists associated with an audiovisual medium—production experts, creative experts, media experts, and so on—and make decisions in this environment. Television offered marketers for the first time a truly national medium in which they could reach millions of families with an audiovisual message and reach them more efficiently in terms of reasonable costs-per-thousand. Commissioners noted the part television played in

Increasing the efficiency of marketing and opening a wide band of communication alternatives that were not previously available.

Allowing the targeting of persuasive messages to a truly mass audience at relatively low costs per thousand people reached.

Creating a new industry of specialists in the creative, media, and research aspects of marketing.

Opening up numerous new creative possibilities arising from the existence of a dynamic audio, and visual, medium of mass communications.

Television also resulted in the introduction of many new kinds of research into marketing. Methodologies that were developed in basic social science ranging from econometrics to pupilometrics and psychometrics were quickly adopted, refined, and in some cases rejected by marketing academics and commercial research firms doing television and advertising research. When a marketing manager's budget has been multiplied, the requirements and opportunities for use of marketing research data expand accordingly. The existence of the combination of dynamic audio and video stimuli opened up rich possibilities for advertising creativity and the behavioral sophistication of ad content.

Many other technological developments were, or could be, identified as facilitators of changes in marketing practice over the period. References were made to transportation, particularly the development of jet aircraft, space-associated technologies such as satellites, microprocessors, and specific kinds of new products that flow from them—digital watches, microwave ovens, hand-held calculators, and so on.

Sociopolitical Factors

Changes in the wants, needs, values, and aspirations of consumers, changes in government regulations and laws affecting marketing practices, and changes in public attitudes toward the environment also affected marketing management over the period. A brief review together with commissioner comments on some of the more important trends is given below.

Consumerism. The consumerism movement in the 1960s was parallel in scope and impact to that of the 1930s. With some considerable degree of irony, marketers who had adopted the "consumer satisfaction" criterion of the marketing concept as a way of doing business were faced with a great sea of consumer dissatisfaction in the mid- and late 1960s. Much has been written about this phenomenon,[10] and it is beyond our purposes to explain it here. Suffice it to say that these factors reflect a growing view that the quality of life is measured as much by the characteristics of goods and services and process of producing them as by the quantity of output and consumption. These are factors that may well be very important, but for which the marketplace does not provide adequate incentives or disincentives. Companies, particularly during the latter part of the period, were increasingly being asked to include social welfare matters in their portfolio of objectives and to weigh them more and more heavily in their decisions. Currently, the "asking" process is being buttressed with legislation and court action.

One specific indicator of the impact of consumerism over the period was the rise of the Department of Consumer Affairs as a corporate entity within large companies. Few companies had a formal consumer affairs unit before 1960, whereas by the mid-1970s, few major corporations were without one. SOCAP (Society of Consumer Affairs Professionals in Business) was established in 1973, and well over 500 firms are now represented in that organization[11]

Consumerism and the attendant call for increased "social responsibility" on the part of business firms added immeasurably to the complexities of marketing decision making and affected it at all levels—product decisions, pricing decisions, promotion decisions, and distribution decisions. Important consequences were the increased role and visibility of consumer protest groups as a force to be taken seriously and a spectacular rise in proposed government regulation concerning marketing activities.

Government. It has been reported that at one point in the late 1960s over 200 pieces of consumer and marketing-related legislation were before the U.S. Congress. There is little doubt that the period was characterized by heavy government involvement in marketing-related business activities, and that legal departments within corporations became important and necessary adjuncts to the marketing management team. Commissioners recognized this in comments such as:

Marketing decisions are increasingly constrained by the law—there are fewer degrees of freedom now than there were before with respect to the formulation of marketing policies.

Vastly increased government involvement, including—as an indirect effect—private anti-trust and class-action suits as a competitive or social-policy weapon . . . reflects an increasing tendency in the United States to rely on government and/or the legal adversary system for problem resolution.

Increasing need for legal appraisal of marketing decisions. This stems from more complex regulations and increasing litigiousness generally. Legal appraisal introduces a largely unfamiliar dimension into the marketing management process, and doubtless it affects decisions in countless subtle ways.

Environment. Ecological issues arising from public concern to protect the environment from secondary or "unanticipated consequences" of business activities also characterized the period. These issues were raised both at the production stage (for example, the pollution of rivers and streams from effluents) and at the marketing stage (such as pollution arising from nonbiodegradable packages). People became more aware of shortages of raw materials, of the nation's dependency on foreign sources of energy supply, and of "limits to growth" in many industries. Marketing practice was affected to the degree that any of these environmental factors affected decision making. One can only speculate, for example, on how many, and in what form, marketing plans were revised as a result of the Arab oil boycott. Commissioners pointed out the following:

The need to take into consideration potential raw material and energy shortages and potential environmental impact in developing and implementing marketing plans.

The growing demand for "social responsibility" by corporations in carrying out various types of marketing activities.

We have become aware of the impact of industrial growth on the environment and concerned about the depletion of natural resources. We have also seen the emergence of the postindustrial society and its emphasis on the quality of life, the rise of "consumerism" and decline of caveat emptor, and changes in the product/services mix.

Economic Factors

The final factors that significantly affected practice over the period were economic. The expanding population and gross national product of the nation as a whole and a corresponding growth in the size of corporations are examples. As noted earlier, many commissioners recognized an overall increase in the "scale" of marketing operations. This extends, of course, to multinational marketing, and many firms became much more involved in foreign operations, adding further to the general notion of increasing size and decision-making complexity. More weight or risk became associated with marketing decisions—a greater opportunity for gain and more risk of loss in each case. This, in turn, led to a greater need to bring information to bear to reduce uncertainties in decision making and a subsequent emphasis on marketing information systems and marketing research. More weight per decision implied several things:

1. There was more at stake each time the dice were rolled. Each decision carried with it a larger opportunity and more risk of loss.
2. The decisions were likely to be more complex, and it was likely to be harder to understand all their facets. In addition, greater corporate size was likely to mean that the marketing manager had less firsthand knowledge and had to implement his decisions through a longer chain of intermediaries.
3. More resources were used to help improve decisions. It was not unreasonable to spend hundreds of thousands of dollars researching and pretesting a multimillion dollar advertising campaign, whereas this would be absurd for a company with a small ad budget. Also the need to provide decision aids increased as complexity and risk increased.

SUMMARY

Marketing management evolved in important ways over the past quarter century. Many of the external factors that were operating on this process appeared to be the technological, sociopolitical, and economic forces that affected the economy as a whole. Internally, the greatest changes resulted from the overall shift in top-management philosophy with respect to the importance of marketing, which led to greater emphasis on planning, new organizational forms and ways of organizing marketing operations, new means to implement marketing plans and programs, and a vastly increased attention to consumer and marketing research.

All "externalities" contributed to making the practice of marketing more complex. For example, the need for legal review with respect to what the layman might consider arcane questions certainly reduces freedom of action. But even beyond the legal constraints, complexity was introduced by the need to consider multiple points of view when evaluating decision alternatives. The more significant factors there were, the more convolutions and surprises were likely to occur.

Most commissioners also believed that markets—and the practice of marketing—became more competitive. Whether this was caused by the incidence of new decision-making tools, by government action and consumerism, or by basic economic changes is not clear. Nevertheless, to the extent competition increased, so also did the risk of wrong decisions. Improvements in methods of marketing planning and decision making appeared in many instances to be motivated by needs to meet increased competition.

One commissioner believed that because of its increased scale, risk, complexity, and competitiveness, marketing needed to become more scientific. We doubt that marketing can ever be reduced to a science, but there surely is plenty of room and need for additional science.

Finally, the increasing availability of data from secondary sources and improvements in the technology for collecting primary data interacted with the other forces to effect a basic change in the practice of marketing. This was due in part to the computer, though advances in the social sciences and in statistical methodology were also important. When a vital decision had to be made, the tendency to guess (or even to ignore) was in many cases replaced by the tendency to measure.

Chapter 3 focuses on changes that took place in research and knowledge development during the assessment period. It begins by reviewing changes in industrial marketing research. The next section treats knowledge development during the period, and subsequent sections report on the results of content analyses of marketing journals and textbooks.

We should not conclude this chapter without urging readers to study the verbatim comments of the thirteen commissioners on the subject of the evolution of marketing management, as given in Appendix 2-1. We hope to have captured the major thrusts and insights, but many others were offered relating to what went on during this period, and our best advice is to read the commissioner comments in their original form.

Appendix 2-1

RESULTS FROM THE COMMISSION'S POLL

In late 1976 each commissioner was sent a personal letter from the cochairmen asking for his reactions to four questions: (1) What major changes in the practice of marketing do you believe have occurred in the last twenty-five years? (2) What have been the major new useful approaches and techniques to research in marketing over the same period? (3) What major problem areas in the practice of marketing remain, in your opinion, despite research efforts to address them? (4) What promising research approaches and techniques have, in your opinion, failed to fulfill their promise in terms of application?

This appendix provides the verbatim replies of thirteen commissioners to the first of these questions. Reactions to the other three questions are presented in later chapters. As noted earlier, three types of people participated in the

Commission, representing (1) academics, (2) independent research, consulting, or agency firms, and (3) operating companies. Eight members were university-affiliated, four were affiliated with independent research, consulting, or advertising agency firms, and six were from operating companies. To maintain anonymity, each member was assigned a letter (A, B, C, and so on) within each of the three groups (Academic, IRCA, and OPERC, respectively) on a random (scrambled) basis, and the responses are identified as such.

Only portions of the letters in question are reproduced, and these have been subject to a certain amount of editorial change to improve continuity. Also, it should be emphasized that commissioners were appointed at somewhat different times and tended to be active at different stages of the project. Hence these early letters are not necessarily indicative of overall participation.

Although members were not explicitly instructed to "speak for their constituencies" in any way, some did so as a natural consequence of the position they occupied. The first group of comments come from six academic representatives.

Academic Representatives

ACADEMIC C

In discussing the major changes in the practice of marketing it is, I think, useful to distinguish between *methods* of marketing decision making and *results* of marketing decision making. The results are visible and measurable while the influences which bear upon decision making are more subtle and less easily measured. The results include changes in marketing institutions and structures as well as changes in methods of communication. Examples of institutional changes include suburbanization and specialization of the distribution system. An example of changes in methods of communication is the development and maturation of television as an advertising medium with the concomitant effect of the development of television upon competing media. These examples of the results of marketing decision making reflect to a considerable extent the response to changes in technology and economics. Other examples of changes in results, such as a greater flow of new products, are in substantial part a reflection of changes in management philosophy.

Marketing practice responds to, but also influences, the environment. In studying the causes of change it may be enlightening to compare change in one society at different periods and to compare change in different societies during the same period. To what extent has research and development in marketing management practice influenced only the style of decision making and to what extent has it influenced the substance of decision making? In what ways would the decisions have been different if there had only been the natural response to economics and not the ideas and learning that stem from research and development? It is probably impossible to answer these questions definitively, but some insight into the answers may be gained by examining changes in the methods of marketing decision making.

In a global sense probably the greatest change influence on methods of marketing decision making has been the development of the Marketing Concept. The idea that products, in both a physical and psychological sense, are fixed and predetermined and that the function of marketing management is only to sell existing products has been replaced by the notion that it is profitable for the firm to adapt its resources in a fashion which will respond to the needs of consumers. This simple idea has had a revolutionary effect upon methods of marketing decision making. Almost every facet of change in marketing practice is related in one way or another to this concept. The concept implies that effective marketing decision making must be based upon information about the needs and desires of consumers. Perhaps every change in methods of marketing decision making has been the result of the development of formal *marketing information systems*. The details of information systems vary so that it is only possible here to sketch in broad and incomplete outline some major and minor examples.

Twenty-five years ago consumer surveys were a part of marketing practice, but few firms utilized surveys in a systematic way. Today most well-managed firms will maintain periodic survey data on their products and will measure consumer beliefs and attitudes toward their products and their competitors' products. Advertising-awareness, brand-preference, and brand-switching data are collected and analyzed on a regular basis. Sample design, interviewing methodology, and methods of measuring attitudes and awareness have been developed, adapted, and refined and extended by the research and development area of marketing.

The maintenance of regular time-series data on consumer purchase as measured by store audit, warehouse withdrawal, consumer panels, and surveys has become a much more widespread practice over the past twenty-five years. To the extent that these data may be matched with data which measure the effects of decisions such as advertising, promotions, product changes, and pricing policies, it is possible to make inferences about the influence and impact of decision variables upon consumer choice.

As methods of data collection have become more widely employed, more systematic, and more extensive, so too have methods of data analysis. A great variety of statistical methods, mostly developed by other disciplines for purposes other than marketing management, have been adapted, refined, and employed in the analysis of marketing data. Because of the emergence of the computer it is now possible to maintain, retrieve, and analyze vast quantities of data at a relatively low cost. In most cases the cost of data analysis is trivial compared with the cost of data collection. The marketing research and development sector has been responsible for the adaptation and extension of methods of data analysis for marketing purposes.

Emerging marketing management concepts such as "market segmentation," developed by marketing academics and practitioners, have been given operational meaning and precision by the data analysis methods as applied to marketing. Econometric analysis of marketing time series date, factor analysis and discriminant analysis, multidimensional scaling, and numerous forecasting methodologies have become almost routine among corporate staff groups dealing with the analysis of marketing data.

Marketing decision models for advertising media selection, advertising expenditure levels, and product development and selection, among others, have been developed and are being used in varying degrees and with mixed acceptance. Only rarely are marketing decision models used explicitly and uncritically without taking into account other factors including, among others, corporate politics.

The influence of formal marketing information systems and related methods of data analysis and decision making upon marketing management is difficult to assess. Marketing decisions are made by generalists who have only limited understanding of the methods employed in the development and the analysis of data. Because marketing information systems appear to grow in scope and influence, however, it does appear that these systems have been accepted by management and that they are contributing to corporate learning.

ACADEMIC H

Numerous changes in the nature of problems confronting marketing executives. Most of these changes reflect exogenous forces, such as shifts in the economy and materials shortages. Marketing practice always has been responsive to these kinds of changes. Basically the methods employed to *be* responsive are the same now as in 1950, with the possible exception of more sophisticated forecasting techniques and "what-if" types of simulations (see below).

Some important changes in the *organizational setting* of marketing management are as follows.

1. Increased average size of corporations.
2. Increased diversity.
3. Widespread adoption of product division form of organization.
4. Increased use of strategic planning and formal planning systems.
5. In many companies, "upgrading" of marketing planning to a broader business planning function.
6. Various experiments with "market manager" and related forms of organization.
7. Much more extensive use of marketing research.

Finally, a number of very important changes have occurred outside the walls of the company itself.

1. Numerous changes induced by use of, and increasing competence with, computers.
2. More educated marketing managers—especially because of immense increase in number of MBA's since 1950. Has led to generally more "sophisticated" outlook, greater willingness to use abstract concepts, adopt "theoretical" approaches.
3. Greater diversity in kinds of people available for and aspiring to marketing jobs—women, blacks, and others.
4. Vastly increased government involvement, including—as an indirect effect—private antitrust as a competitive weapon.
5. Continuing pressures to mechanize and/or simplify both management and marketing research, owing to rising labor costs.

ACADEMIC A

Among major changes in the practice of marketing in the past twenty-five years I would include the following:

1. The numerous effects due to the computer, including its use for record keeping, inventory control, billing and service operations, and data analysis.
2. The growing emphasis on the consumer from a behavioral point of view, including recognition of the increasing complementarity and substitutability of different types of products on the one hand, and attention to the consumer's ever-increasing wants on the other hand. I would also include under this heading reactions to the increasing voc-

alism of the consumer and recognition of the need to provide better service if consumer wants are to be satisfied.

3. The application of marketing concepts to areas other than the traditional ones of selling goods and services.

4. More sophisticated attempts to divide markets into meaningful segments and develop products and strategies for meeting the needs of each of these segments.

ACADEMIC E

Here are the major changes that I think have occurred in the past twenty-five years or so—I'm singling out those things with which I am most familiar.

1. The time horizon for planning with respect to marketing actions (as well as with respect to most decisions) has increased during the last twenty-five years. This is hard to pin down but I am virtually certain that it's true.

2. The substantive content of corporate planning has changed in that the marketing concept has been accepted by a much higher percentage of firms. Stemming from that concept, consumer-oriented issues pervade the planning process from beginning to end for a much higher percentage of corporations now than twenty-five years ago. In some ways this may be the most important change—it's not a change in the procedures that are related to practice but instead a change in the way of thinking about marketing practice.

3. There is a markedly increased need for the legal appraisal of marketing decisions. This has accelerated during the last several years, but if one looks at the twenty-five year time period I am pretty sure that there has been a consistent trend of increase in the role of legal issues in making marketing decisions. One might argue that closely related to this is yet another change in that marketing decisions are increasingly constrained by the law—there are fewer degrees of freedom now than there were before with respect to the formulation of marketing policies.

4. There is a marked increase in the recognition of marketing research as an important contributor to the formulation of marketing strategies in the execution of marketing tactics. One piece of evidence for this might be gained by going through the American Marketing Association's surveys that have been conducted for five-year intervals for at least the past fifteen and maybe the past twenty years.

5. Not only the overall importance of marketing research increased but the span of issues to which marketing research is perceived as capable of being addressed has also broadened considerably. In general, problems at the top corporate levels are now considered amenable and appropriate for marketing research, whereas in the past marketing research would have been principally buried within a division or even within a small span of a single product or products. More marketing research is now being done on broader strategic issues that relate to corporate objectives and long-term development than used to be the case.

ACADEMIC B

In my view these are the major changes that have occurred in the practice of marketing in the last twenty-five years:

1. Greater planning from the point of view of the customer rather than the firm (customer orientation).

2. Greater use of marketing research to establish customer needs, wants, perceptions, motivations, preferences, and behavior.
3. The preparation of annual and long-range plans for separate products, markets, and market segments.
4. The coordination of formerly separate customer-impinging functions (advertising, sales promotion, sales force, product design, marketing research, etc.) under the rubric of marketing.
5. Increased financial evaluation of the results of marketing expenditures.

ACADEMIC G

As a writer of marketing cases in the mid-fifties and a user of such cases in the mid-seventies, I have a strong impression that much about the *practice* of marketing and the problems faced by marketing managers across this 20-year time span has not changed appreciably. Nevertheless, much that has happened in those years undoubtedly has affected how managers relate and deal with decision making in marketing. In sum, the major ingredients that managers deal with—such as product, price, distribution, and promotion decisions and the attendant consumer, competition, and government forces that affect such decision areas—have been largely constant through time, but the nature of the people, organizations, tools, and techniques used to deal with them have changed a great deal.

Some of these changes as I see them are discussed below:

1. *From "art" toward "science."* This means that as corporations become larger, as risks of mistakes become more costly, and as "customer orientation" and the marketing concept are adopted, and even as the intensity of competition within an industry increases, management has become more concerned with (and willing to invest in) *information* and marketing research of all kinds. This has increased the size and sophistication of marketing research activities, created the subfield of marketing information systems, and, I think, made the present-day marketing manager much more prone to use "hard data" than he was 25 years ago. In model terms, managers may not have reached the mathematical model stage, but do try to make decisions with a much greater variety of data and information than they did 25 years ago.

2. *Technology.* The practice of marketing also has been changed by major technological developments over the period. The two things with probably greatest impact on marketing management are *computers* and *television*—computers because they have created a whole new generation of marketing specialists to which modern managers must relate, and television for much the same reason. Each did not exist in any usable form 25 years ago. Computers have allowed the introduction of multivariate techniques into the applied world of marketing, are now being introduced to management as interactive tools for decision making, and will probably be important in the data-generation function in the future. Television has created vast numbers of subsidiary industries, many of which affect marketing decision making, particularly the television research industry. There are those who argue that television alone has so expanded man's horizons of communications, needs, attitudes, and values that all aspects of private- and public-sector decision making are affected in many ways by this one technological accomplishment. This theme could be pursued for at least the following types of technological developments and their impact on management:

a. Air travel and transportation developments.

b. Telephone and telecommunications developments.

c. New retailing institutions—shopping centers, discount operations, cash register control, etc.

d. Space, NASA, and the whole gamut of scientific discoveries during the period.

3. *Demand analysis and consumer behavior.* The most visible changes in theories and techniques of marketing management pertain to the area of demand analysis and consumer behavior. Thirty-plus textbooks have been written on the subject in the past fifteen years; a new association (ACR) and a new journal (*JCR*) have been formed. Forecasting models based on panel data and perceptual mapping procedures rather than sales projections per se have been introduced. Many new ways to think about markets, including the concept of *market segmentation,* also characterize the period. Market segmentation affects management both as a framework for strategy and planning and as a set of techniques for measuring markets. *Market structure* is another way to capture these developments, using notions of industrial organization theory, brand share, utility, and decision theory as well as psychometric notions of brand positioning, perceptual mapping, and multidimensional scaling.

4. *Other significant changes*

a. Consumerism, environmental issues, social responsibility:

(1) Management has had to give much more attention to these types of externalities manifest in consumer protection agencies and individuals of various kinds.

(2) Two empirical indicators of impact are the number of large corporations that now have a Department of Consumer Affairs and the formation and rapid growth of SOCAP, the Society of Consumer Affairs Professionals.

b. Marketing management in nonprofit organizations:

(1) The period spans the existence of the Advertising Council founded in 1945 and its activities in the nonprofit sector.

(2) Marketing managers and professors are increasingly becoming involved as consultants to such organizations, witnesses in legal cases, and so on.

c. New research techniques and approaches: It is likely that there is a commercial application for every methodological technique or perspective yet developed in the social sciences (economics, psychology, sociology, etc.). Stochastic models, semantic differentials, Skinnerian procedures, econometric methods, clinical psychology (motivation research), psychometrics (multidimensional scaling), advances in survey research and so on, all have been quickly introduced and adapted in marketing.

Independent Research, Consulting, Agency Representatives

IRCA D

The following are five major areas of change which I believe have occurred in marketing during the past twenty-five years and which, unfortunately, I believe have flowed causally one from the other.

1. Consumer-goods companies, first, began to recognize that not only utility to the consumer but utility to the producer could more effectively be meshed through greater

communications to consumers directly from the producers rather than through complete dependence upon the mediating influence of distributors (wholesale and retail). This change came to be known as "consumer pull" vs. "dealer push." This conceptual change produced a number of results.

a. More use of communications directly to consumers.

b. The use of consumer criteria rather than the opinions of the trade on advertising copy choices in consumer media.

c. Reduced allocation of media (and even promotion) budgets to regional sales managers and to dealers.

d. The creation of the marketing function to integrate sales activities, consumer information, and even production scheduling and the priorities and criteria of R & D.

   (1) The creation of the marketing function led to demand-responsive marketing resource allocation.

   (2) The resultant increase in the breadth of functional responsibilities encompassed by the marketing function created a need to subdivide the enlarged task some other way. Thus, the product manager system was born.

2. Changes began to occur in retailing practices that dovetailed with the "consumer pull" concept.

a. Self-service retailing became possible and efficient for the retailer as well as the producer.

b. Aside from the decision on initial stocking and inventory levels for a new product (or line extension), trade decisions on ordering increasingly became based upon shelf movement—first, their own shelf movement and later, thanks to syndicated retail and wholesale movement services, their competitors' shelf movement.

3. The next major conceptual change was producers' acceptance of "soft data" on market performance to permit comparison with competitive performance.

a. First, share-of-market replaced factory shipments as the indicator of future profitability.

b. Later, share-of-mind and the whole current spectrum of intermediate criteria, including functional behavioral relationships such as repeat rates, came to be used for marketing control and planning.

c. Then came a growing awareness of the need to make explicit the implicit models behind the intermediate criteria that were being used.

d. All these indices of marketing performance originally were used for "marketing controllership." Later, however, such data were employed for forecasting as the then radical idea arose that intermediate criteria (the notion of models) permitted forecasting. These intermediate indices such as behavioral, perceptual, and attitudinal data and demographic trends permitted forecasting from data obtained not only from outside the producers' internal information but (even more radical) from outside—and prior to—the distribution system.

e. The availability of such forecasts led to marketing resource allocation decisions based upon the market effects of prior allocations.

4. The success experienced in marketing controllership and marketing resource allocation decisions based upon past allocations led to increasing demand by marketers for means of forecasting prior to marketwide allocation decisions to reduce risk. This desire led to the extensive use of market experimental designs such as test markets, checkerboard designs, and limited-exposure advertising copy tests.

5. Most recently, the desire to use intermediate indices and market experiments to reduce type 1 error risks has been joined by a desire to shorten feedback time in order to reduce type 2 error risks. As a result, there is a substantial increase in the analytic treatment of allocation: performance ratios from ongoing market activities. These analyses are to reveal demand response elasticities by geographic area, demographic group, product category, brand, and marketing function—i.e., advertising, promotion, price, etc. Such information permits rapid reaction to changing competitive market situations, with appropriate resource reallocations being based on current information about market behavior rather than on historical examples.

IRCA A

Here is a list of major changes in the practice of marketing during the past twenty-five years.

1. Overall practice of and reliance upon marketing research.
2. Use of test marketing and development of test-market simulation.
3. Development of and dependence upon marketing information systems.
4. Extension of marketing principles and practices to nonprofit organization management.
5. Multichannel distribution.
6. Integration of marketing planning (the process) and marketing plans (the output) into the marketing function.
7. Advertising research, particularly its creative development and pretesting aspects.
8. Shift of emphasis from trade to consumer research and from secondary to original data in the process.
9. Much more scientific approach to sales forcasting.
10. Market segmentation.
11. Steady shift upward in the attention, time, and resources companies devote to marketing relative to other business functions (i.e., the marketing orientation).

Operating Company Representatives

OPERC B

In putting together a list of major changes in marketing during the past quarter-century, it is important to keep in mind the conditions of the time. Marketing practice contributed to changes that occurred during this period; and many changes in marketing practice themselves either were facilitated by external developments or were responses to them.

The years since World War II were at first ones of reconstruction and then of development that resulted in a rise in affluence, principally in North America, Europe, and Japan. Toward the end of this period we became aware of the impact of industrial growth on the environment and concerned about the depletion of natural resources. We also saw the emergence of the postindustrial society and its emphasis on the quality of life, the rise of "consumerism" and decline of caveat emptor, and changes in the product/services mix.

Among technological advances, three that stand out as being of great importance in marketing are developments in transportation, communications, and computers. All three enlarged and changed our markets. Computers, in particular, have had a great impact on marketing practice. The impact of the auto and airplane reached maturity and produced major changes after World War II; TV and computers are products of the past twenty-five years.

One problem in identifying major changes in marketing is distinguishing between such things as changes in channels of distribution, new types of retailing (discounting and shopping centers), new advertising media, etc. on the one hand, and changes in marketing practices (planning, organizing, forecasting, etc.) on the other. I'm assuming we are going to focus on the latter.

So far as marketing R & D is concerned, Jacque Barzun's statement to the effect that "through the middle of the nineteenth century, science learned more from the steam engine than the steam engine learned from science" could also be applied to marketing through the third quarter of the twentieth century. I don't think this is too surprising, because in most areas marketing science has had neither the tools nor the resources to get ahead of practice until recently. In the future, it could be different.

My thoughts on some major changes in marketing practice are discussed below. They obviously reflect personal experience in research and planning, primarily in industrial marketing.

1. *Broad acceptance of the marketing concept.* There is, of course, continuing debate as to what the marketing concept is and what its relevance is to practice—just as there is about "Keynesian economics"—but there is general acceptance of the idea that marketing must be consciously concerned about the satisfaction of customer needs (and wants) if a business is going to compete successfully. In earlier times, this was less of a problem—goods were not as abundant, and businesses and markets were smaller, making it easier to understand customer needs. Now, however, because of the size and complexity of businesses and markets and the impact of technological changes that offer new ways of serving customer needs, marketing management has had to learn to think in terms of abstractions like customer needs rather than tangibles—i.e., railroads, steel, and telephone service.

2. *The rise of consumerism and the decline of caveat emptor as a viable way of doing business.* We are still a long way from the millennium, but there is growing recognition of a much broader responsibility to both the customer and the community-at-large than was true before. This does not mean the marketer has become an altruist but, rather, that he is recognizing the necessity of factoring in a much broader range of considerations in making marketing decisions than ever before.

3. *The use of segmentation as the basis for development of marketing plans and action programs.* This has come from the more intimate knowledge of customer needs—whether individual consumers, businesses or institutions—and what motivates action.

4. *Organizing marketing activities so as to more effectively plan and implement marketing programs.* The use of brand, product, and market managers to develop and execute marketing programs has grown extensively in the past twenty-five years. Sales organizations and distribution channels are more carefully tailored to specific market situations. Special organizational arrangements are provided for new-product planning and development.

5. *Major advances in marketing planning and its integration into business planning.* Planning itself is obviously not new, but it has been surprisingly fragmentary and ad

hoc. In the past decade in particular, much progress has been made in methods for planning marketing activities, for integrating marketing plans with those of other functional areas such as manufacturing and R & D, and for relating those to overall business objectives. One manifestation of this is the growing emphasis in marketing on profitability. The development of modelling and simulation capabilities has played an important role here.

6. *Extensive and intensive use of market and marketing research.* The number of companies with research departments has grown enormously since World War II, as has the scope of research activities. This has been chronicled in recent years by the periodic survey conducted by the AMA. Even companies without research departments invariably use the results of research conducted by government and trade associations, or make use of consultants and independent research firms.

7. *Application of quantitative methods to research and planning.* The advent of computers and, specifically, time-sharing made this technically and economically feasible. Economic theory and behavioral science that formerly found little application in marketing are now widely used; and, of course, the body of management and marketing science has grown enormously as well. The important thing is that this is now finding its way into practice.

OPERC A

The major change in the practice of marketing is the application of the systems approach to all of its aspects.

1. Systems applied to planning.
2. Models simulating the effect of changes in marketing forces on profit and share.
3. Systems in "invention" of new products. The individual entrepreneur in new-products marketing has pretty much disappeared. The concept of the commercial laboratory, first introduced by Thomas Edison in Menlo Park, has reached its fruition.
4. Systems in evaluating the marketing process. As in the control of the manufacturing of products, systems have been introduced to control the effectiveness of the marketing process. The technology employed here is incomplete, but it is adequate for systems control of the process.
5. Radical changes in systems of distribution. The emergence of giant retailers has led to a situation in which competitive "conflict" between retailer and manufacturer becomes an issue. The roles of wholesaler, jobber, etc., have been diminished.

OPERC E

In my view the major changes that have occurred in the practice of marketing during the past twenty-five years are as follows:

1. The direction of marketing efforts to specific segments of customers.
2. The study of consumer motivations underlying purchase behavior.
3. The use of panel data to trend customer demographics, media usage, and purchase behavior.
4. The expansion and wider implementation of the product management concept.
5. The development and implementation of the market management concept.

6. The availability to market managers of expanded demographic, psychographic, and attitudinal descriptions of consumers.

7. The development of marketing departments in corporations that did not have these specific responsibilities.

8. The recognition by corporate heads that the future growth of their business lies in the expanded role of marketing.

9. The development and expanded role of marketing information organizations.

10. The use of TV as the principal method of advertising.

11. The development of point-of-sale promotions as a major motivator of customer purchase.

12. The interdisciplinary approach to consumer research.

13. The institutionalization of the methods and procedures for new-product development.

OPERC F

Rather than address myself to the four substantive questions raised in your memorandum, may I suggest that the Commission consider the future role of R & D in marketing management rather than historical perspective.

Without question, we have had major innovations in marketing during the past twenty-five years and, although the cost-efficiency results may not have been what we would hope for, the effectiveness of the system has been greatly improved. But that is a matter of the past; whether it was good or bad, how it came about, who was responsible for bringing it about, are now in the hands of historians.

Looking ahead, on the other hand, may serve a very useful purpose in determining what we must do as individuals and as groups of individuals to identify problems and develop programs for coping with them. How serious, for example, are the problems of escalating costs in marketing distribution and communication? What adverse effects can be expected from government regulations? How do we cope with the rising tide of consumerism reflected currently in product-liability litigations? What effect will all these future implications have on the cost and efficiency of our marketing system?

It appears to me that it would be more useful and productive to look ahead rather than to the past . . . which is becoming less and less a prologue of the future.

OPERC D

While it is undoubtedly impossible to support the position with objective data, I have the strong belief that a material change has taken place in the general quality of marketing decision making during the past twenty-five years. That is, if one were to place a typical contemporary firm using current marketing practice in the competitive environment of twenty-five years ago, it would be highly successful, whereas the reverse would not be true.

Given the validity of this assumption, I believe it is possible to identify three major changes that have been instrumental in bringing this situation about:

1. *Increased recognition of "marketing" as a management function requiring integration of formerly separate functions.* Before the 1950s and '60s there was little recogni-

tion of the need to coordinate and systematize the activities of the firm impinging on middlemen and consumers. For example, sales, advertising, physical distribution, and pricing tended to be separate and equal functions, product development tended to be an engineering and research function, and so on.

During the past twenty-five years, increasing numbers of managers have subscribed to the belief that benefits were to be had from integrating these activities and have altered their organizations in an attempt to realize these benefits.

To a large extent this change was probably brought about by the popularization of the catch phrase "the marketing concept." Undoubtedly, the business community had never before seen so much made of such a simple idea. In fact, so much that was written and spoken about this subject was so ambiguous that an enterprising manager seeking change could use "the marketing concept" as the basis for almost any change in organization and management style he might want to make.

Regardless of the causes, pronounced changes have taken place in organizations, individual tasks, and the way decisions are made about elements of the marketing mix.

2. *Maturation of planning in marketing.* Recognition of marketing as an area of management concern consisting of a number of interrelated functions brought with it a new problem—how to coordinate the activities of a large number of people that are designed to influence independent middlemen and consumers to behave in a desired way at some point in the future. In essence, it intensified the need for planning.

Concomitant with this development was the emergence of planning as a discipline in virtually every organized activity.

Within marketing the most marked change in practice is in the number of companies that at least go through the ritual of identifying target markets, setting market-penetration objectives, and establishing budgets for individual elements of the market mix.

In the more sophisticated companies, planning also includes a formalized procedure for researching potential marketing opportunities, planning and developing a desired product portfolio, pretesting strategy and tactics, ex post evaluation of effectiveness, monitoring postsale customer satisfaction, and so on.

3. *Quality and quantity of information.* Perhaps the most dramatic change in the past twenty-five years is the quality and quantity of information used in marketing decision making.

While the growth of planning provided the framework needed to make much of the information currently used meaningful, it was the development of the computer that made it practical.

Much of the impact has been a result of the firm's ability to use internally generated data that before the maturation of the computer and EDP systems were simply too voluminous to process and use in a meaningful way—e.g., customer files, sales contact records, prospecting systems.

In terms of state-of-the-art technology most of the systems currently in use are very elementary and mundane—yet they have had a dramatic impact on the amount of information available for decision making.

Similarly, significant changes have taken place in the availability of externally generated data. The most dramatic examples are found in the consumer-goods industries—e.g., SAMI, Nielsen, MRCA. The value of proprietary-research-generated data banks has also been recognized in industrial marketing firms; e.g., our own Truck Tracking Studies generate estimates of annual sales by model type, by competitor, and by market segments for the entire U.S. and Canadian truck industry.

Again, the techniques used by most firms in research and information processing are primitive compared to those discussed in contemporary academic journals—yet the change in marketing practice has been dramatic. For example, the availability of the data described above and a simple planning framework has altered nearly every aspect of the way we market trucks.

I used the example of my own company in order to dramatize the point that it was not until there was a management recognition of the need to integrate marketing functions that real acceptance of planning was achieved and resources were allocated to create a data bank to provide the information needed for intelligent decision making.

There is considerable evidence that the above changes have strengthened our market position and that if the approach to marketing practice described above had been used earlier, many decisions would have been made differently.

Yet, interestingly enough, all of the techniques employed have been within the state-of-the-art in marketing for years.

NOTES

[1]Peter F. Drucker, *The Practice of Management* (New York: Harper & Row, 1954).

[2]For early articles specifically addressed to marketing implications, see Fred J. Borch, "The Marketing Philosophy as a Way of Business Life," *The Marketing Concept: Its Meaning to Management,* Marketing Series No. 99 (New York: American Management Association, 1957), pp. 3–5; John B. McKitterick, "What Is the Marketing Management Concept?" *The Frontiers of Marketing Thought and Action* (Chicago: American Marketing Association, 1957), pp. 71–82; Arthur P. Felton, "Making the Marketing Concept Work," *Harvard Business Review,* March–April 1959, pp. 117–27; and Theodore Levitt, "Marketing Myopia," *Harvard Business Review,* July–August 1960, pp. 45–56.

[3]For a discussion of a fourth type of managerial philosophy referred to as the "societal marketing concept," see P. Kotler, *Marketing Management: Analysis, Planning, and Control,* 3rd ed. (Englewood Cliffs, N.J.: Prentice-Hall, 1976), p. 18. Kotler defines the societal marketing concept as "a management orientation aimed at generating customer satisfaction and long-run consumer and public welfare as the key to satisfying organizational goals and responsibilities."

[4]Although there was no world war during the assessment period, major conflagrations such as the Korean and Viet Nam wars had significant effects on the United States and undoubtedly on the evolution of marketing management practice. Numerous other such factors could be cited. Shifts in the nation's eating habits, dress styles, population movements, and so on all had obvious effects on practice.

[5]The first operational electronic computer, ENIAC, was developed at the University of Pennsylvania during 1944–1946. Von Neuman at Princeton University did much to develop a stored-program-binary-use machine in the period 1946–1952. It was adapted at the University of Illinois in the development of ILLIAC and by IBM in the IBM-701. Transistors were invented at Bell Laboratories in 1948, and Sperry Rand manufactured a vacuum-tube machine, UNIVAC I, in 1951. UNIVAC I was used at the Census Bureau for twelve years and was a major source in the development of early programming languages. IBM is credited with the first operational FORTRAN in 1954. For useful references on the development of the computer, see Harold Sackman, *Computers, System Science, and Evolving Society* (New York: Wiley, 1967); William F.

Sharpe, *The Economics of Computers* (New York: Columbia University Press, 1970); and Edwin Schlossberg, John Broackman, and Lyn Horton, *The Home Computer Handbook* (New York: Bantam Books, 1978). Good articles on the uses of computers in various branches of science can be found in the September 1966 issue, Vol. 215, of *Scientific American*.

[6]John S. Wright and Daniel S. Warner, *Advertising* (New York: McGraw-Hill, 1966), 220 ff.

[7]Transmission of color signals—that is, color television—was authorized by the Federal Communications Commission in 1953, but color television developed slowly. By 1965, however, there were 2,860,000 color TV sets in the United States (Wright and Warner, *Advertising,* p. 222).

[8]*Advertising Age,* September 25, 1978, p. 30.

[9]*Advertising Age,* August 28, 1978, p. 182.

[10]David A. Aaker and George S. Day, *Consumerism: Search for the Consumer Interest,* 3rd ed. (New York: The Free Press, 1978).

[11]Claes Fornell, *Consumer Input for Marketing Decisions: A Study of Corporate Departments for Consumer Affairs* (New York: Praeger, 1976).

3

Changes
In Marketing Research
and
Knowledge
Development

Chapter 3 parallels in scope and perspective the analysis over time of Chapter 2. Here, attention is directed not to changes in marketing management, but to changes in marketing research over the twenty-five-year assessment period. Some of the important aspects of the evolution of the marketing research industry are identified and discussed. New knowledge developments are presented from several different perspectives.

The chapter is organized into four major sections. The first deals with the comments of commissioners and other leaders in the field concerning the major changes that took place in the marketing research industry. Additional information on the current state of the industry is given in Chapter 4. In the present chapter, the focus is on broad-scale patterns of change and development in the industry between 1952 and 1977.

The second section considers new knowledge developed over the period. It reviews the evolution of marketing research textbooks and gives examples of new types of knowledge introduced. It also gives commissioner replies to the question: "What have been the major new useful approaches and techniques to research in marketing over the same period?"

The third section presents the results of a content analysis of four marketing journals, focusing on the nature of the changes in their content between 1952 and 1977. It is one of two content analysis studies performed by the Commission's staff to extend and supplement commissioner impressions of the development of new knowledge over the period.

The fourth section presents the results of the second content study, which focused on the evolution of marketing textbooks over the period. Data are presented on changing patterns of topical emphasis and on other aspects of the changing nature of marketing literature as reflected in marketing textbooks over the period. Much of the assessment of the impact of the marketing research industry and new knowledge developments on improving marketing management practice is reserved for later chapters. Here, attention is directed to factual reporting on how the industry changed and what types of new knowledge were developed.

CHANGES IN THE MARKETING RESEARCH INDUSTRY

The marketing research industry, made up of "internal" marketing research conducted by corporations and "external" marketing research done by advertising agencies, media, and marketing research supplier firms, grew in size, diversity, and scope between 1952 and 1977. Several of the largest marketing research supplier firms of today, such as Selling Areas-Marketing, Inc. (SAMI), Burke Marketing Research, Audits & Surveys, and Daniel Yankelovich, Inc., were founded and grew to their present multimillion dollar size in this period. Commissioners alluded to this industry growth in various ways:

Increasing size and sophistication of market research activities—increased range of applications for market research—systematic use of consumer surveys—maintenance of regular time-series data—marketing information systems—test marketing and test-market simulation—advertising testing.

Greater use of marketing research to establish customer needs, wants, perceptions, motivations, preferences, and behavior.

Use of test marketing and development of test-market simulation; development of and dependence upon marketing information systems; shifts from trade to consumer research emphasis and from secondary to original data in the process.

Hardin[1] reported that in 1974 the industry was growing at a rate of about 10% to 11% per year. If inflation was taken into account, however, this rate was not particularly impressive. The industry, like many industries, has been affected by business cycles in a predictable way. Twedt,[2] in a 1973 survey of marketing research departments done under the auspices of the American Marketing Association, reported that marketing research budgets were growing faster in non-consumer-goods companies, even though in an absolute sense consumer goods companies still tended to dominate marketing research spending. Between 1968 and 1973 the mean percent rise in outside research budgets among manufacturers of consumer goods was 5%; for industrial-goods manufacturers it was 28%; for retailers, 28%; and for publishers and broadcast (media), 88%. The overall size of the industry has been estimated at from $500 million to $1 billion or more, depending on what is included.

Although the leading market research supplier firms are large multimillion-dollar companies,[3] the industry per se is still not very large compared to other industries in the private sector. Also, many of the firms are privately held, making overall size and growth patterns difficult to estimate. Lehmann, after discussing the nature and size of the top ten research suppliers, for example, observes:

These are all substantial firms. Yet in a relative sense, they are small. Procter and Gamble's annual advertising budget would more than pay for all of the services of all of these firms for a year. Similarly R & D budgets typically dwarf marketing research spending. This fact more than anything else typifies the position of research—an important activity with a limited budget.[4]

In comparison to what we have referred to as production R & D, marketing R & D comprises a small fraction of a corporation's overall research and development efforts.

Changes in the nature of the industry have been discussed from a historical perspective.[5] Zaltman and Burger, for example, identify six phases of marketing research, beginning in the 1880s and ending in the 1970s: (1) the industrial statistics phase, 1880–1920; (2) the random sampling, questionnaire, and behavioral measurement development era, 1920–1940; (3) the management awareness phase, 1940–1950; (4) the experimentation phase, 1950–1960; (5) the computer analysis and quantitative methods phase, 1960–1970; (6) the consumer theory development phase, 1970 to date.[6] The authors emphasize that the phases are not mutually exclusive. The computer analysis and quantitative methods phase, for example, did not start suddenly in 1960 and end in 1970. A diagrammatic representation of the chronology of marketing research is given in Figure 3-1.

Figure 3-1 also shows the approximate publication date of three marketing research textbooks, the dates of the founding of the *Journal of Advertising Research,* the *Journal of Marketing Research,* and the *Journal of Consumer Research,* and the period in which the Hollerith card was invented. From the Commission's perspective, the relevant period begins at "D" and extends over the next twenty-five years.[7] The authors note that the significant change in perspective from "market research" to "marketing research," in which marketing changed its emphasis from economics to management, occurred in the 1940s.

FIGURE 3-1

A CHRONOLOGY OF MARKETING RESEARCH

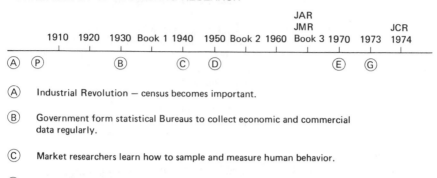

Ⓐ   Industrial Revolution — census becomes important.

Ⓑ   Government form statistical Bureaus to collect economic and commercial data regularly.

Ⓒ   Market researchers learn how to sample and measure human behavior.

Ⓓ   Market research becomes marketing research, i.e., the emphasis changes from economics to management as the central role of marketing.

Ⓔ   The computer becomes a major part of marketing research.

Ⓖ   Consumer theories become organized.

Ⓟ   Mr. Hollerith of the Census Bureau invents the paper card with holes punched, leading to mechanical tabulation of data.

Book 1 = Brown, Book 2 = Boyd and Westfall, Book 3 = Green and Tull.

JAR   = *Journal of Advertising Research*

JMR   = *Journal of Marketing Research*

JCR   = *Journal of Consumer Research*

Source: Gerald Zaltman and Philip C. Burger, *Marketing Research: Fundamentals and Dynamics* (Hinsdale, Ill.: The Dryden Press, 1975), p. 5.

They further argue that the important characteristic of the 1970s was "the adoption of an integrated, *scientific* approach to marketing research blending quantitative and qualitative analysis. . . . [M]arketing research has over time emerged as a science."[8]

Much marketing research is, in effect, advertising research, and advertising research has also been studied from a historical, over-time, developmental perspective. Maneloveg,[9] for example, traces the media research and audience measurement industry back to 1914, when ABC (Audit Bureau of Circulations) came into existence. About 1931, Gallup conducted the first national survey of weekly magazines. Crossley had made comparable surveys for radio about 1929. Many of the audience measurement firms of today such as A. C. Nielsen, W. R. Simmons and Associates, ARBITRON (American Research Bureau), Starch INRA Hooper, Inc., Burke Marketing Research, and A.S.I. (Audience Studies, Inc.), have evolved from these early beginnings.[10]

Gerhold provides an interesting summary of the advertising research industry and why its impact has not been more significant:

The promise of scientific gain through advertising research has been mostly unfilled. The reason is not hard to find; it hinges on our continuinmg inability to quantify the returns from brand advertising and learn from such quantification. Management engineering could demonstrate the tangible benefits of science in increased production and reduced cost of manufacture. National brand advertising and the research related to it were never able to achieve the authority that might have come from similar measures of accomplishment. . . . Much of what we did was bright, and technical, and impressive, but in the end, it never said which advertising was making money for which brands.[11]

Dunn gives some useful reflections on the advertising agency research department. As of 1974, Dunn argued, even though many agency people were indifferent to or disliked research, it was becoming more acceptable in advertising agencies.

The staffs of agency research departments today are better trained in the social sciences. Their training better enables them to measure and understand consumer needs and reactions. But more important than their training, they are better integrated into the process of developing advertising than was true just five years ago. . . . How research is used in an agency is the key to attitudes toward it. Those who use it well, "like it," and those who don't, dislike it or are indifferent to it. Let's hope that the "dislikers" and "indifferents" change their attitudes because, as we believe, "It's not creative unless it sells," and it's getting harder and harder to sell something about which you know little to people about whom you know less.[12]

What are some of the factors that have shaped the industry over the twenty-five years? The demand for marketing research was to a considerable extent created by the shift in managerial philosophy discussed in the last chapter. That is, a change from a product or a selling concept to a marketing concept creates the need for consumer research as well as for someone in the corporation to take charge of it. Each of the managerial tasks discussed earlier—planning, organization, implementation, and control—requires research, as do all aspects of marketing operations.

Research, like management practice, was affected by the "externalities" reviewed in Chapter 2. The computer allowed significant advances in the analysis and interpretation of data. Subsequently, it became important in decision-model development, simulation, and marketing information system/interactive modes that went beyond so-called batch-processing of marketing research information. Toward the end of the period, the computer began to be used not only for data analysis, but for some aspects of the data-collection phase of marketing research. Computers, for example, are currently being used to automate the cash register checkout function in supermarkets,[13] to assist in telephone interviewing, and, as does the INTERQUEST System developed by Market Facts of Chicago, to fully automate the personal interview procedure.

Marketing research has also been affected by the fact that it has historically served the grocery and drug product manufacturers. Budgeting by these types of companies has been a major factor in controlling the growth of the industry. Hardin, for example, observed that:

Historically, the market research industry has been concentrated among the major consumer non-durables-grocery and drug product manufacturers. Some of these companies commit as many dollar resources for marketing research as entire industry groups, such as the appliance, housing, clothing and furniture industries. Accordingly, budgeting by major food and drug companies has largely controlled the growth of the industry, and budgeting by companies in this area has become somewhat bearish compared to the rapid growth experienced during the decade of the 60's.[14]

Hardin goes on to state that the concentration of the marketing research industry in the grocery and drug area is coming to an end, and industrial-goods manufacturers, retailers, publishers, and broadcasters, in terms of research budget commitments, are growing much faster. He also noted four major trends in marketing research: (1) more shared-cost studies, (2) greater use of low-cost interviewing techniques, (3) increased use of basic strategy studies, involving relatively sophisticated statistical techniques, and (4) a more balanced research commitment between industries. In sum, the types of corporations doing research and the types of firms supplying it have become more diverse. The bulk of all marketing research, however, is still initiated by the consumer-goods manufacturers and by those who make large investments in consumer advertising.

Toward the end of the period the industry was affected by the tendency for many marketing research firms to be taken over by outside parent organizations. Honomichl,[15] for example, in a study of 154 research "influentials" reported that the majority viewed the "take-over" of marketing research firms by outsiders as a "bad" thing that was likely to continue. The majority also believed that having *one* trade association would be preferable to the current pattern of having as many as six.

NEW KNOWLEDGE DEVELOPMENTS

In this and the final sections we attempt to document some of the more important new knowledge developed over the period. The Commission was primarily interested in identifying new approaches or techniques that had significantly improved marketing management practice. This chapter provides some examples. Other more specific cases will be illustrated in subsequent chapters, where we discuss the nature of marketing knowledge and the process whereby new knowledge in the field is created and diffused.

Readers should be aware that truly "new" knowledge in marketing, particularly that which has significantly changed marketing management practice, is very difficult to document. In medicine, the discovery of penicillin, X-rays, and drugs for the control of diseases such as polio, tuberculosis, and syphilis, are clearly definable events. In marketing, no "drug" has yet been invented that will "cure" the problem of new-product failures. Also, much that is new in marketing (for example, new research techniques or data-analysis procedures) is an adaptation of something that was developed at an earlier date in the basic social sciences. This is not to deny the importance of the "adaptation" function but rather to demonstrate the difficulty of thoroughly tracing the roots of each new development.

The first section provides a brief overview of new knowledge, focusing on changes in the nature of marketing research textbooks and specific examples of new types of "useful" knowledge reported in the Commission's poll. In that poll, commissioners were also asked, "What have been the major new useful approaches and techniques to research in marketing over the same period?" Their responses are reported on here. The latter two sections present results of content analyses of selected marketing journals and marketing principles textbooks over the twenty-five years. Details of each study are given in the introductory portions of each of these final sections.

Analyzing the nature and content of marketing research textbooks is one way of finding how marketing research knowledge changed over the period. The earliest books by Brown[16] and Ferber[17] tended to have a strong economics and classical statistics orientation and to reflect the corresponding statistical methodologies. Boyd and Westfall[18] introduced a more managerial orientation by, among other things, introducing actual case examples of management problems involving marketing research. Their book also broadened the perspective to include behavioral science topics such as motivation and survey research and attendant issues such as questionnaire construction and interviewing techniques.[19] Data-analysis procedures in these early texts were still rather "univariate" in orientation and tended to draw upon classical statistics and the traditional topics of inference and hypothesis-testing.

Green and Tull[20] did much to position marketing research as a marketing-management-related activity in a formal decision-theory sense and to formalize the relationship between managerial decision making and research information. Decision-theory principles were drawn upon to make the link. Subjective probability and Bayesian statistics were introduced to marketing research as extensions to, rather than replacements for, classical "relative-frequency" views of probability. Several subsequent marketing research texts introduced the Bayesian view of marketing research information.[21] This view appears to be deemphasized, however, in the most recent texts. As stated in the closing paragraphs of Kinnear and Taylor, "For the present, the decision theory approach remains a powerful theoretical tool that has obtained some usage in sophisticated organizations. It is for the future to judge its long-term practical value."[22]

Marketing research texts published over the period also underwent other kinds of specialization and orientation. The model-building perspective was set down in an early book by Montgomery and Urban,[23] and numerous kinds of marketing management model-oriented books were subsequently published. Some marketing research books evolved that treated the subject primarily as a "marketing information system,"[24] and others were heavily based on sociological perspectives and methodologies.[25] As several commissioners observed, the summary impression of these developments was of an overall increase in quantitative and behavioral science sophistication, particularly with respect to formal model development and the use of sophisticated statistical multivariate methods of data analysis. Every recent book, for example, has some treatment of topics such as "measurement," "multidimensional scaling," and the "dependence" (for example, multiple regression, multiple discriminant analysis) and "interdependence" (for example, factor analysis) methods of multivariate statistical analysis.

The Commission poll generated a wide-ranging list of "new useful approaches and techniques." Commissioners tended either to mention specific theories, approaches, models, and techniques or to describe types of research or activities that had been introduced to the field over the period. Table 3-1 organizes in this way a sampling of commissioner responses to the question. These might be thought of as "top-of-the-head" recollections about the knowledge developed over the period and the kinds of things that made important contributions to the field.

In Chapter 4 we will discuss the development of knowledge in greater depth. Here we will try to classify the commissioner comments about "new knowledge" and provide other examples of knowledge that was introduced to the field in the 1952–1977 period. Four kinds of knowledge were developed. The first type, known as *discipline-based theories* or theory development, includes general theories such as those of the 1960s that attempted to describe consumer behavior, as well as numerous kinds of "middle-range" theorizing—theories of attitude change, innovation diffusion, and so on.

Managerial frameworks and approaches are another type of knowledge. Although often cast as paradigms or conceptual classification schemes (for example, the classification of products as Cash Cows, Stars, Dogs, and Problem Children in the Boston Consulting Group view of product portfolio analysis, or the product life cycle, DAGMAR, and so on), they are not fully developed theories or models but frameworks for management planning and strategy.

Models and measurement is distinguishable from these more conceptual efforts. This category includes work that is both mathematically based and often decision and/or optimization oriented. Response functions and underlying relationships are formally specified, and the goal is often to find an optimum solution. Work on measurement is closely related because of its axiomatic and formal/quantitative perspectives. Where human subjects are involved, modeling

TABLE 3-1

MAJOR NEW USEFUL APPROACHES AND TECHNIQUES INTRODUCED, 1952-1977[1]

Theories, Approaches, Models, Techniques Mentioned

Market segmentation	Standard multivariate techniques
Product positioning	Psychometric methods
Numerous minitheories	Multidimensional scaling, conjoint
Product/SBU portfolio	analysis
analysis (BCG, PIMS, etc.)	Taxonomic analysis, cluster analysis
Stochastic models of buyer behavior	Motivation research
Decision models (MEDIAC, CALLPAN,	Pretest market technology
etc.)	Focus groups
Computer simulation	Experimental design—ANOVA
General planning simulation models	Eye camera devices
Computer modeling and sensitivity	Information load research
analysis	

Other Descriptive Ideas Mentioned

Beginnings of a theory of consumer behavior.

Efforts to develop general theories (Howard-Sheth, etc.)

A-I-O studies (not really theoretical, but apparently more useful than general personality theories)

Image and attitude research (new theories and approaches to multiattribute models, weighted belief models, utility and decision theory)

Measurement of the character of the population (beyond demography, with attempts to characterize the direction of shifts in behavior)

Specific measurement of behavior changes

Systems concepts (e.g., the work on agribusiness systems)

Early operations research approaches (mostly standard models such as linear programming)

More specific models of market process and marketing decision structure

Regression, time-series, discriminant, and factor analysis

New focus on advertising research

Refinement of consumer product-acceptance technology

Attempts to partition the effects of media technology

The development of probability sampling methods or, more broadly, general improvements in sample survey methods

Greater emphasis on panel technique and on studying change by this technique

---

[1]Source: Commissioner poll. Based on replies to the question: "What major new useful approaches and techniques had been introduced over the period?"

entails a more complicated form of measurement, but the attendant issues and perspectives have much in common with marketing models per se. Thus, new forms of multidimensional scaling and attitude measurement introduced over the period generally fit into this category.

The fourth type of knowledge is in the category of *research methods and statistical techniques.* An impressive characteristic about the marketing research industry is that virtually every kind of economic or behavioral science methodology yet invented has its counterpart in some commercial firm offering a research service relating to it. Hundreds of examples, ranging from econometrics through pupilometrics and clinical, experimental, and other techniques, could be cited in support of this generalization.

Rather than providing an exhaustive list of the knowledge developed over the period, we have selected examples of each type. Some are drawn from the reactions of commissioners and others are from our own impressions. Table 3-2 lists sixty-four examples of new marketing knowledge developed during the period from 1952 to 1977, organized into the four categories: (1) discipline-based theories, (2) managerial frameworks and approaches, (3) models and measurement, and (4) research methods and statistical techniques. The list is illustrative only and is intended to provide a sampling of the waterfront of identifiable new theories, concepts, methods, and techniques.

Much new knowledge in marketing is an application and refinement of basic theories and methods from the social sciences. An interesting characteristic is also the comparative speed with which marketing academics and professional researchers have adopted or "tried out" those new ideas. In general, marketing knowledge generated over the period 1952–1977 increased in quantitative and behavioral science sophistication. The introduction of a management science/ engineering perspective to the field moved it closer to an applied science and allowed it to be viewed as a kind of "social engineering."

Readers should note in these examples the effect of externalities, particularly the computer and television, on the nature of the "new knowledge" generated. *Marketing and the Computer,* edited by Alderson and Shapiro in 1963,[26] contained papers by a new generation of eager young students such as Al Kuehn, Ralph Day, Paul Green, Hans Thorelli, Purnell Benson, Bill Massy, and Arnie Amstutz and was, in retrospect, a major precursor of things to come. The largest commercial marketing research service, A. C. Nielsen, Inc., is currently one of the largest users of computers in the world. Television required the development of new theories of consumer behavior and communication, new methods to study its effects (for example, dozens of new commercial services such as Burke's DAR, AD-TEL, and ASI In-Theater Testing), and significant new models of advertising decision making such as MEDIAC, ADBUDG, POMSIS, and ADMESIM. (For a current review of the relative value of and references to these and other such models, see Larreche and Montgomery.)[27]

The foregoing examples of changes in marketing research textbook materials, together with the new theories, managerial frameworks, models, and statistical techniques introduced over the period, reflect the nature of the new knowledge developed in marketing. A more systematic and rigorous approach is content analysis of representative publications. A publication is classified into content categories and examined for changes in these content categories at pre-specified time intervals, such as five years. Graphs of trends in content categories are subsequently developed. The staff of the Commission undertook two such studies, the first focusing on marketing journals and the second on marketing

TABLE 3-2
EXAMPLES OF KNOWLEDGE DEVELOPMENT IN MARKETING, 1952-1977

Discipline-Based Theories	Managerial Frameworks and Approaches	Models and Measurement	Research Methods and Statistical Techniques
Demand and utility theory	Marketing concept	Stochastic models of brand choice	Motivation research and projective techniques
Market segmentation	Marketing mix—4 P's	Market-share models	Survey research
General and middle-range theories of consumer behavior	Development of marketing cases	Marginal analysis and linear programming	Focus groups and depth interviewing
Image and attitude theory	DAGMAR	Bayesian analysis	Experimental and panel designs—ANOVA
Theories of motivation, social personality, social class, life style, and culture	Product life cycle	Advertising models, e.g., Mediac, Pomsis, Admesim, Brandaid, Adbudg	Advances in probability sampling
	Marketing plan	Causal models	
	State approaches to strategy development	Sensitivity analysis and validity tests	Hypothesis formulation, inference, significance tests
Expectancy-value theory	New-product development process	Response functions	Multivariate dependence methods—multiple regression and multiple discriminant analysis, canonical correlation
Theories of advertising processes and effects	Physical-distribution management	Weighted belief models, determinant attributes	
Information-processing theory	Marketing information systems	Simulation and marketing games	
Attitude-change theories (consistency and complexity theories)	Product positioning and perceptual mapping	Multidimensional scaling and attitude measurement	Multivariate interdependence methods—cluster and factor analysis, latent structure analysis
Attribution theory	Segmentation strategies	Sales management models, e.g., Detailer, Callplan	
Perceptual processes	New marketing organization concepts, e.g., brand management	New-product models, e.g., Demon, Sprinter, Steam, Hendry	Advances in forecasting, econometrics, and time-series analysis.
Advertising repetition	Territory design and salesman compensation		
Distribution theory	Marketing audit	Bid pricing models	Trade-off analysis and conjoint analysis
Refutation and distraction hypotheses	Demand-state strategies	Computer-assisted marketing cases	Psychographics and A-I-O studies
Theories of diffusion, new-product adoption and personal influence	Creative approaches and styles	Product planning models: Perceptor, Accessor	Physiological techniques—eye camera, GSR, CONPAAD
Prospect theory	New search and screening approaches		Unobtrusive measures, response latency, nonverbal behavior
	Refinements in test-marketing approaches		

62

textbooks. In the next section the results of the journal study are presented and compared with other studies of journal content over the period. The final section presents results from the textbook study.

Readers should appreciate that the task of documenting *all* new knowledge in marketing over a period of twenty-five years is virtually impossible—for at least two reasons. First, the number of potential records on which one could draw is enormous. Marketing knowledge is documented in journal articles, textbooks, corporate records, computer records, government statistics and reports, working papers, reports of nonprofit organizations (for example, Marketing Science Institute), pamphlets and other materials from research supplier firms, and so on. The second reason is perhaps even more significant. Marketing scholars often write ''state-of-the-art'' papers with the objective of summarizing and discussing all or most of what is known about a certain topic up to a particular point in time. Regardless of how valuable such works might be for fostering additional scholarship, they are always incomplete because they invariably rely on published information. Many commissioners pointed out that much knowledge in marketing is not published or written down. It exists in the minds of practicing professionals as ''experience,'' ''intuition,'' and executive ''judgment.'' The lack of time or motivation to record such knowledge (although, of course, many professionals in marketing have done such writing), as well as the competitive nature of the industry and the question of confidentiality, are further reasons for the incompleteness of recorded marketing knowledge. The following content analysis studies, which report on changes in the knowledge base of marketing between 1952 and 1977, should be viewed with these qualifications in mind.

MARKETING JOURNALS: 1952–1977

Four journals, the *Journal of Marketing (JM)*, the *Harvard Business Review (HBR)*, the *Journal of Marketing Research (JMR)*, and the *Journal of Consumer Research (JCR)*, were content analyzed at selected intervals over the twenty-five years. Both *JM* and *HBR* were in continuous publication throughout the period and were studied at five-year intervals (1952, 1957, 1962, 1967, 1972, and 1977). *JMR*, which began publication in 1964, was examined at three-year intervals, and *JCR*, which began in 1974, at one-year intervals. The trends and patterns presented concerning these four journals thus represent a sampling of their content over time. Although they are among the more important journals in which marketing-related materials are published, they are but a sampling of all such journals. A recent study by Browne and Becker,[28] for example, evaluated the status ranking of fifty-three journals in which marketing articles were published. Journal article writers in marketing now have at least this number of possible journal outlets for their work. Many journals such as the

Journal of Advertising, the *Journal of Communications,* and the *Journal of Applied Psychology* as well as many others in the basic disciplines and important trade magazines such as *Business Week,* the *Wall Street Journal,* and *Fortune,* were not included in the study and could be added to the list. Out of this large number of journals, we have chosen to analyze only four, but they are among the most prestigious, widely read, and important journals in marketing and were ranked among the top six of the fifty-three journals studied by Browne and Becker.

The Journal of Marketing

The first issue of *JM* was published in July 1936, and thus it was about forty years old at the end of the period. It was founded by the then newly formed American Marketing Association with Paul H. Nystrom as its first editor. In 1976 its circulation had reached about 25,000. An excellent review on the first forty years of the journal is given in Grether.[29] He and his associates conducted a content analysis of all forty years of its existence. It is interesting to compare their study with the Commission's work covering the past twenty-five years. Subject matter in the Grether study was divided into twelve content categories and further classified into three "interest" groups as follows:

Low Relative Interest	*Medium and Stable Interest*	*High Continuing Interest*
1. Historical	4. Societal role	10. Marketing management
2. Industry studies	5. International marketing	11. Marketing mix variables
3. Marketing education	6. Marketing theory	12. Marketing research
	7. Marketing institutions	
	8. Role of government	
	9. Consumer role & behavior	

Figure 3-2 shows the pattern of content change in high- and low-interest topics at three-year intervals beginning in 1936 and ending in 1975. During the Commission's assessment period, 1952–1977, the low-interest topics of historical, industry studies, and marketing education continued to be a low proportion of *JM* content and showed a generally declining trend. In the high-interest group, research articles showed a sharp decline from the peak of nearly 50% in the 1950s to about 11% in 1975. The establishment of the *Journal of Marketing Research* in February 1964 is a significant cause of this pattern. In contrast, marketing management and marketing mix articles showed a slight positive (but erratic) trend, and together these topics made up about 43% of *JM*'s content in the 1952–1977 period.

Some interesting patterns also appear in the medium-interest group

FIGURE 3-2

PATTERNS OF CHANGE IN LOW-INTEREST AND HIGH-INTEREST TOPICS, *JM,*
1936–1975

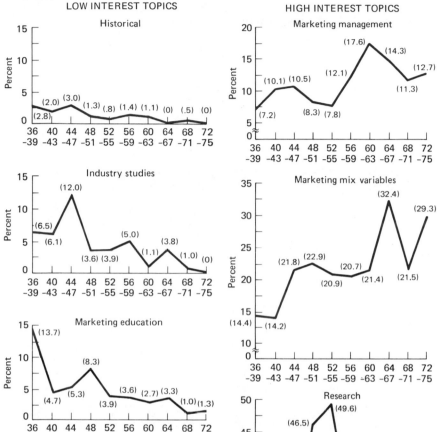

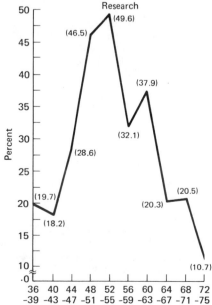

Source: Ewald T. Grether, "The First Forty Years," *Journal of Marketing,* 40 (July 1976), p. 65 and 67;
published by the American Marketing Association.

FIGURE 3-3
PATTERNS OF CHANGE IN MEDIUM-INTEREST TOPICS, *JM*, 1936–1975

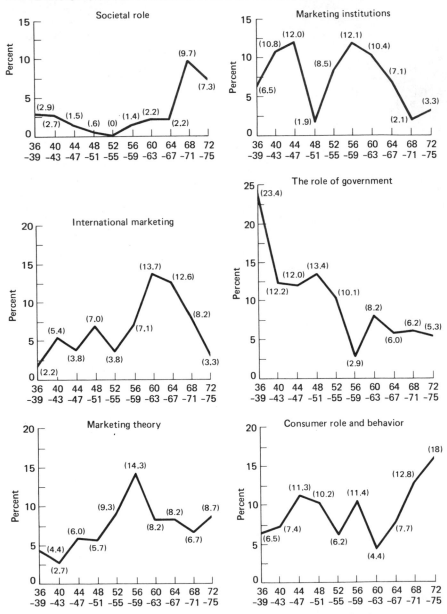

Source: Ewald T. Grether, "The First Forty Years," *Journal of Marketing,* 40 (July 1976), p. 66, published by the American Marketing Association.

(Figure 3-3). Space devoted to marketing institutions peaked at 12.1% in the period 1956–1959 and declined thereafter to 3.3% in 1972–1975. Surprisingly, international marketing also declined after its peak of 13.7% in 1960–1963, whereas, beginning in the early 1960s, consumer role and behavior displayed a sharp upward trend. In sum, concerning *JM* content over the entire forty years, Grether stated:

> Inevitably, and appropriately, the articles published in the *Journal of Marketing* mirrored the economic, political, scientific, and technological changes in the movement from the Great Depression, through World War II, and into the postwar aftermath. But even more significantly, the evolving discipline of marketing participated in and contributed to the enormous strides taken in scientific discourses and tools, especially in the behavioral sciences and in quantitative, statistical, and econometric methodologies. The marketing literature of recent years is a far cry from the nascent first two decades of this century.[30]

The Commission staff's analysis of content considered a whole year of *JM* issues, rather than any individual issue from that year. In 1977 an exception was made—only the first two issues were available, so both were used. In each

FIGURE 3-4

PATTERNS OF CHANGE IN *JM* CONTENT, 1952–1977, BASED ON COMMISSION STUDY

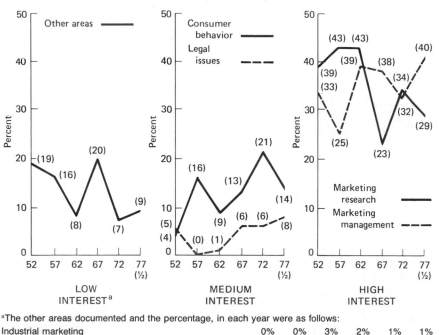

aThe other areas documented and the percentage, in each year were as follows:

Industrial marketing	0%	0%	3%	2%	1%	1%
International marketing	2%	1%	5%	5%	2%	1%
Marketing education	2%	5%	3%	2%	1%	0%
Biographical sketches	0%	4%	4%	4%	4%	0%

journal the analysis was confined to articles and did not include such things as legal notes, editorials, or other content.

The method involved subjectively assigning each article into one *or more* subject categories. Thus the level of interest in a topic should be determined by the amount of emphasis per topic, not the number of articles per se. During this process no account was taken of either the length of the article or the number of authors per article. It is thus difficult to make direct comparisons to the Grether study. Figure 3-4, however, does show that general patterns of content change were at least similar. There was, for example, a general decline in the low-interest categories lumped together in Figure 3-4 as "other areas." An identical pattern of consumer behavior content appears as a general growing trend through the period 1952–1972, with a drop-off in 1977, probably owing to the introduction of *JCR* in 1974. Legal issues shows a pattern generally similar to

TABLE 3-3

PATTERNS OF CHANGE IN SPECIFIC CONTENT AREAS, *JM*, 1952–1977
BASED ON COMMISSION STUDY

	1952	1957	1962	1967	1972	1977 (½)
Marketing Management						
General management and strategy	16%	8%	36%	28%	15%	46%
Marketing institutions	37	23	24	28	27	0
Marketing functions	47	69	40	44	58	54
Control	1	3	1	1	0	1
Pricing	3	2	2	2	2	0
Product	0	1	3	1	5	2
Advertising and promotion	4	2	4	8	7	2
Sales management	0	1	2	1	2	2
Channels of distribution	1	1	2	1	2	0
Market research	0	0	1	0	0	1
Consumer Behavior						
Theory	1	4	2	4	1	1
Phenomenon description	0	1	0	0	6	1
Concepts testing and validation	1	1	5	4	7	3
Research and Quantitative Methods						
Empirical research	41	40	48	73	80	91
Concepts and methods	59	60	52	27	20	9
Research design	0	0	1	1	0	0
Sampling	1	0	0	0	0	0
Survey techniques and measurement	4	4	5	3	1	0
Data analysis	0	0	2	0	0	0
Research concepts and approaches	8	6	7	2	0	1
Management science	0	3	3	0	4	0

TABLE 3-4

COMPARISON OF SPECIFIC ARTICLE TITLES IN *JM*, 1951-1952 AND 1976

1951-1952	1976
a. "Customer Patronage of a Parent and New Branch Store" D. F. Blankertz, October 1951, Vol. XVI, No. 2, pp. 152-157.	"Risk and Personality-Related Dimensions of Store Choice" J. F. Dash, L. G. Schiffman, and C. Berenson, January 1976, Vol. 40, No. 1, pp. 32-40.
b. "Sherman Act Enforcement" K. J. Cunan, April 1952, Vol. XVI, No. 4, pp. 449-452.	"Consumer Protection: More Information or More Regulation?" W. H. Cunningham and J. C. M. Cunningham, March 1976, Vol. 40, No. 2, pp. 63-68.
c. "What Economists Should Know about Marketing" G. H. Brown, July 1951, Vol. XVI, No. 1, pp. 60-66. "Marketing as a Science: an Appraisal" K. D. Hutchinson, January 1952, Vol. XVI, No. 3, pp. 286-293.	"Nature and Scope of Marketing" S. D. Hunt, July 1976, Vol. 40, No. 3, pp. 17-28. "Contributions to the Marketing Discipline" W. Lazer, July 1976, Vol. 40, No. 3, pp. 74-78.
d. "Mail Questionnaires and the Personalized Letter of Transmittal" W. M. Weilbacher and H. R. Walsh, January 1952, Vol. XVI, No. 3, pp. 331-336.	"Mail Questionnaire Response Rates: Updating Outmoded Thinking" D. R. Berdie and J. F. Anderson, January 1976, Vol. 40, No. 1, pp. 71-73.
e. "The Group Interview as a Tool of Research" E. P. Shapiro, April 1952, Vol. XVI, No. 4, pp. 451-452.	"The Application of Focus Group Interviews in Marketing" K. R. Cox, J. B. Higginbotham, and J. Burton, January 1976, Vol. 40, No. 1, pp. 77-80.
f. "Studying Consumer Behavior in Retail Stores" W. Applebaum, October 1951, Vol. XVI, No. 2, pp. 172-178.	"Bank Selection Decisions and Market Segmentation" W. T. Anderson, E. P. Cox III, and D. G. Fulcher, January 1976, Vol. 40, No. 1, pp. 40-46.

that of what Grether refers to as societal role (rising in interest through the period), and the general pattern of rising share of content on marketing management and falling share on marketing research in the highest-interest categories is quite similar. Again, the introduction of *JMR* in 1964 appears to have reduced the proportionate share of marketing research content in *JM*.

Table 3-3 shows percentages of content change over the period within specific categories such as marketing management and research and quantitative methods.[31] Within marketing management, for example, articles devoted to general management and strategy increased from a low of 8% in 1957 to 46% in

1977. The functions or "mix" category shows a fluctuating trend similar to the Grether results, whereas marketing institutions show a general decline, with 0% in the first six months of 1977. In the category of research and quantitative methods, concepts and methods articles dominated at the beginning of the period but empirical research articles dominated at the end. Because of duplication in assigning articles to categories, neither the marketing functions breakdown nor the concepts and methods breakdown sums to the appropriate percentage.

One observation about *JM* content was the comparatively large number of articles with similar titles at the beginning and end of the period. Table 3-4 compares titles of specific articles appearing in 1951–1952 and in 1976. Although many of the articles had similar titles, there were major variations across the set. Some were very similar in scope (for example, pair *e*), whereas others in the consumer behavior area (pair *f*) showed some differences of focus. Unlike the pure empiricism of the 1951 paper, the 1977 paper had a theoretical base for its empirical study. Generally, for all pairs, there was a major increase in rigor witnessed by, for example, statistical significance testing. All pairs show how far marketing articles in *JM* have moved away from economics (pair *c* in particular). Yet despite the differences, many of the issues and debates remained the same.

The Harvard Business Review

The *Harvard Business Review* is more widely read by practicing executives and managers than is *JM* and has the potential for directly influencing their decision making. The attempt to conduct a parallel analysis revealed that the number of marketing articles in any one issue of *HBR* was comparatively small.

Table 3-5 shows the number and proportion of marketing articles relative to the total number of articles in the journal at five-year intervals over the period. As can be seen, the proportion has fluctuated between 11% and 18% and reached a low point in the 1967–1971 period. In 1971 only two articles out of sixty were devoted to marketing topics. As would be expected from the editorial stance of *HBR*, general management and organizational articles predominate.

Figure 3-5 shows graphs of the topical patterns organized into categories similar to those used in the Grether study of *JM*. As can be seen, by far the largest proportion of content concerns marketing management articles. Consumer behavior and legal issues make up a minor proportion, and all other

TABLE 3-5
NUMBER AND PROPORTION OF MARKETING ARTICLES IN *HBR*, 1952–1976

	1952–1956	*1957–1961*	*1962–1966*	*1967–1971*	*1972–1976*
Marketing	37	55	48	33	48
Total	287	306	301	306	375
Proportion	13%	18%	16%	11%	13%

FIGURE 3-5

PATTERNS OF CHANGE IN *HBR* CONTENT, 1952-1977[a]

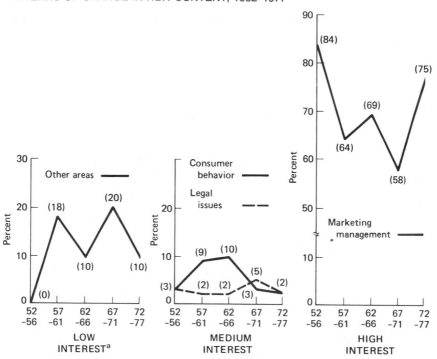

[a]The other areas included industrial marketing, international marketing, marketing education, and biographical studies.

marketing-related topics (industrial marketing, international marketing, marketing education, and biographical studies) are also relatively minor compared with marketing management.

Table 3-6 breaks down the marketing management category into general management and strategy topics and marketing functions or mix topics. The relative proportion of general management and strategy articles generally increased even though attention to specific marketing functions dominated at both the beginning and end (77% and 65%) of the period. Pricing was relatively popular at the beginning of the period but declined in importance toward the end. Sales management, advertising and promotion, and product-related articles were consistently popular.

The Journal of Marketing Research

Analysis of *JMR* content was done at three-year rather than five-year intervals because the journal had only been in existence for thirteen years by

TABLE 3-6

PATTERNS OF CHANGE IN SPECIFIC MARKETING MANAGEMENT AREAS, *HBR,* 1952-1976

	1952		*1957-1961*		*1962-1966*		*1967-1971*		*1972-1976*	
General management and strategy	7	23%	8	22%	8	23%	11	50%	14	35%
Marketing functions	24	77%	28	78%	27	77%	11	50%	24	65%
Total	31	100%	36	100%	35	100%	22	100%	38	100%
Marketing functions:										
Control	0		1		0		0		0	
Pricing	6		6		6		0		1	
Product	4		3		5		1		5	
Advertising and promotion	6		6		7		1		5	
Sales management	4		4		3		5		6	
Channels	3		4		4		3		4	
Market research	1		4		2		1		3	

mid-1977. Also, given that the entire journal is devoted to marketing research, a different system of classifying content was used. First, all content was assigned to one of two broad categories: research concepts and methods, and other marketing topics. The former refers to articles on topics such as research design, sampling, measurement, and data analysis methods. The latter includes the marketing function or "mix" variables—advertising, pricing, and so on.

Figure 3-6 shows the pattern of change of relative content between these two categories at three-year intervals between 1964 and 1977. The first half of the period shows a progressive decline in the proportion devoted to research concepts and methods and a corresponding increase in the other marketing topics category. This pattern is reversed in the 1972-1977 period and it would appear that there was a resurgence of interest in methodological issues toward the end of the period.[32] The proportion devoted to specific marketing management decision areas such as advertising, pricing, and so on dominated content throughout the thirteen years. It is important to note that these marketing management topics were in general *not* being treated from an overall "general marketing management planning, strategy, and conceptual-verbal frameworks development" approach but rather as specific decision areas to which multivariate statistical methods, computer simulation, and so on could make a contribution. From another perspective, much of the content of *JMR* up to the present can be said to deal with demand analysis either as various developments in forecasting, market structure and segmentation, or studies of the determinants of consumer and buyer behavior (group influences, diffusion, family decision making, attitudinal components—beliefs, affects, and so on).

Table 3-7 shows the patterns for each of the two broad categories and

FIGURE 3-6

PATTERNS OF CHANGE IN *JMR* CONTENT, 1964–1977

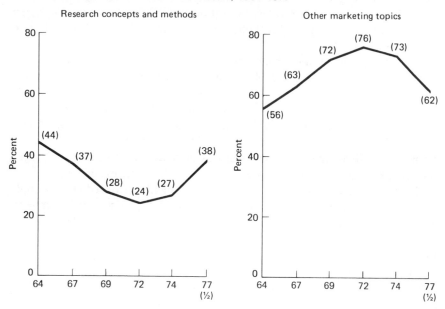

TABLE 3-7

PATTERNS OF CHANGE IN SPECIFIC CONTENT AREAS, *JMR*, 1964–1977

	1964	1967	1969	1972	1974	1977 (½)
Research Concepts and Methods						
Research design	1%	2%	1%	0%	1%	1%
Sampling	4	0	0	1	0	0
Survey and measurement	6	7	4	6	4	4
Data analysis (methods)	3	4	6	5	4	1
Research concepts and approaches	5	6	5	7	7	3
Management science and models	2	3	3	2	1	3
Total	21	22	19	21	17	12
Other Marketing Topics						
Advertising and communication	6	4	7	10	6	4
Pricing issues	1	1	3	5	2	0
Product issues	4	1	4	1	1	0
Sales management issues	0	2	0	0	4	3
Distribution issues	0	0	2	3	1	1
Retailing and wholesaling	1	3	2	2	4	1
Consumer behavior	8	21	25	42	23	8
Others	7	5	6	5	5	3
Total	27	37	49	68	46	20

the dominance of consumer behavior and advertising-related articles throughout the history of this journal. In 1972, for example, over 50% of *JMR* was devoted to articles in these two categories, even though decision areas such as pricing, product, sales management, distribution, retailing and wholesaling have been of continuing but lesser interest.

   JMR content was characterized by a move from univariate, single-criterion studies of marketing phenomena or "two-way cross'classification, survey research" analysis to "multivariate, multiple-predictor, and single-criterion variable" modeling. These new studies dealt either with pure demand-type variables or with a model linking demand to a marketing decision variable such as advertising or pricing. Studies tended to be based on data that were either "objective," involving no direct measures of human judgment (for example, sales, market share, advertising expenditures—econometric in outlook), or "subjective," in which consumer responses were directly measured (for example, beliefs, attitudes, opinions—psychometric in outlook). The former approach analyzes demand from the perspective of microeconomics, and the latter does so from the perspective of psychology, sociology, and the behavioral sciences. The founding of the *Journal of Consumer Research* in 1974 was probably based in part on the recognition of the need to have a separate outlet for predominantly behavioral science materials. If marketing research is best described as "applied social science," then it may be that *JMR* is becoming the dominant outlet for "applied economics" approaches to marketing management and *JCR* the dominant outlet for "applied behavioral science" approaches.

The Journal of Consumer Research

   JCR was launched in 1974 as an interdisciplinary journal for the study of consumer behavior with financial support from the American Marketing Association and other support from eight additional associations. During its short history it has become dominated by publications of marketing professors with a social psychological or sociological orientation. Wind, in a comment published in the journal in mid-1977, noted that "Articles on consumer behavior from the perspective of the other disciplines are missing, and even more noticeable by their absence are truly interdisciplinary papers."[33]

   This pattern is evident in Figure 3-7, which traces three of the most popular topics in *JCR* over the period from 1974 to 1977. Articles on attitude/choice models were essentially social psychological in focus, those on social issues tended to embody the viewpoint of marketing professors trained in either social psychology or sociology, and those on group influence were dominated by marketing professors trained in sociology. Except during 1976, attitude/choice models, particularly the expectancy-value formulations of Fishbein, continued to be the dominant content of *JCR* and to be authored by marketing professors trained in social psychology.

FIGURE 3-7

PATTERNS OF CHANGE IN *JCR* CONTENT, 1974–1977

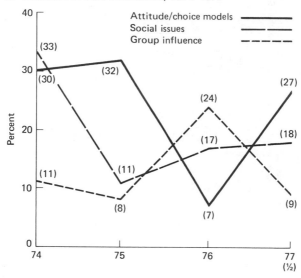

Table 3-8 provides a breakdown of the 116 articles published in *JCR* between 1974 and 1977 in terms of the three categories given in Figure 3-7 and four additional ones. Another popular topic, highly related to attitude/choice models in terms of social psychological focus, was information processing. It made up 19% and 18% of 1974 and 1977 content, respectively. The years 1975 and 1976 saw a marked rise in empirical studies dealing with specific constructs such as social class, learning, time, confidence, personality traits, situational variables, source credibility, and so on.

TABLE 3-8

PATTERNS OF CHANGE IN SPECIFIC BEHAVIORAL SCIENCE AREAS, *JCR*, 1974-1977

	1974	1975	1976	1977 (½)
Attitude/choice models	30 %	32 %	7 %	27 %
Social issues (consumer socialization, government, advertising to children)	33	11	17	18
Information acquisition and processing	19	8	7	18
Group influence, family decision making, diffusion, adoption processes	11	8	24	9
Specific constructs (social class, learning, time, confidence, traits, situations, credibility)	0	18	21	5
Specific methods (content analysis, segment congruence, latent class analysis)	0	0	3	9
Other (macro theories, validity, pricing, retail, research notes)	7	23	21	14

TABLE 3-9

FAMILIARITY AND OVERALL QUALITY RATINGS OF 53 MARKETING JOURNALS

Familiarity Rank	Journal Name	All Respondents (Total of 151)				Business Schools with 60 or more faculty		Business Schools with less than 60 faculty	
		Number Aware	Familiarity Index	Weighted Average	Weighted Average Rank	Familiarity Index (Rank)	Weighted Average (Rank)	Familiarity Index (Rank)	Weighted Average (Rank)
1	Harvard Business Review	151	1.000	1.719	5	1.000 (2)	1.732 (6)	1.000 (2)	1.71 (4)
2	Journal of Marketing	150	.993	1.520	2	.972 (7)	1.563 (2)	1.000 (2)	1.48 (1)
3	Journal of Marketing Research	150	.993	1.406	1	.972 (7)	1.332 (1)	1.000 (2)	1.51 (2)
4	Advertising Age	146	.966	3.172	41	.986 (4)	3.284 (39)	.950 (4.5)	3.07 (40.5)
5	Journal of Advertising Research	146	.966	1.905	9	1.000 (2)	1.915 (10)	.938 (6)	1.89 (9)
6	AMA Conference Proceedings	145	.960	2.218	14	.972 (7)	2.302 (15)	.950 (4.5)	2.14 (13)
7	Business Horizons	144	.953	2.287	17	.972 (7)	2.244 (13)	.937 (7)	2.32 (16)
8	Journal of Business	143	.947	1.771	7	1.000 (2)	1.662 (5)	.900 (11)	1.88 (3)
9	Journal of Retailing	142	.940	2.260	15	.972 (7)	2.244 (14)	.912 (10)	2.27 (15)
10	Marketing News	140	.927	3.417	49	.930 (11.5)	3.515 (48)	.925 (8.5)	3.32 (46)
11	Sales Management	140	.927	3.022	35	.930 (11.5)	3.195 (37)	.925 (8.5)	2.86 (34)
12	California Management Review	139	.920	1.970	10	.958 (10)	1.929 (11)	.887 (12)	2.01 (11)
13	Collegiate News	134	.887	3.722	53	.901 (14)	3.825 (53)	.875 (13)	3.63 (52)
14	Journal of Consumer Research	133	.880	1.742	6	.901 (14)	1.765 (7)	.853 (14)	1.72 (5)
15	Business Topics	132	.874	2.525	22	.901 (14)	2.436 (20)	.850 (15)	2.60 (25)
16	Progressive Grocer	127	.841	3.538	51	.887 (16)	3.602 (51)	.800 (16.5)	3.47 (50)
17	Public Opinion Quarterly	123	.814	1.881	8	.845 (18.5)	1.983 (12)	.788 (18)	1.78 (5)
18	Industrial Marketing	122	.807	3.039	38	.845 (18.5)	3.217 (38)	.775 (19)	2.39 (12.5)
19	Michigan Business Review	122	.807	2.272	16	.817 (20)	2.827 (39)	.800 (16.5)	2.73 (32)
20	Management Science	122	.807	1.614	3	.859 (17)	1.605 (4)	.763 (20)	1.62 (3)
21	Journal of Academy Marketing Sci.	108	.715	2.817	32	.732 (21)	2.923 (32)	.700 (21)	2.71 (29.5)
22	Journal of Business Research	104	.688	2.501	20	.690 (23.5)	2.408 (18)	.688 (22)	2.58 (23.5)
23	Decision Sciences	102	.675	2.184	12	.690 (23.5)	1.915 (9)	.653 (23)	2.17 (14)
24	Marquette Business Review	98	.649	3.151	40	.704 (22)	3.360 (42)	.600 (26.5)	2.94 (39)

25	Southern Journal of Business	97	.642	2.679	28	.634 (25)	2.709 (26)	.650 (24)	2.65 (28)
26	Journal of Consumers Affairs	93	.615	2.592	26	.592 (28)	2.645 (23)	.637 (25)	2.63 (27)
27	Operations Research	88	.582	1.705	4	.620 (26)	1.691 (3)	.550 (28)	1.32 (7)
28	J. of Marketing Research So.	86	.569	2.184	13	.535 (30.5)	2.396 (17)	.600 (25.5)	2.02 (12)
29	Miss. Valley J. of Business Econ.	85	.562	3.285	44	.629 (26.5)	3.409 (44)	.512 (31.5)	3.15 (43.5)
30	Akron Business Review	79	.523	3.408	48	.577 (29)	3.512 (47)	.475 (34)	3.29 (47)
31	Industrial Adv. and Marketing	79	.523	3.102	39	.507 (35.5)	3.305 (40)	.538 (29)	2.93 (37.5)
32	Bell Journal of MS	78	.516	1.935	11	.521 (33)	1.890 (8)	.513 (30)	1.98 (10)
33	Industrial Marketing Management	75	.496	2.971	34	.521 (33)	3.051 (34)	.475 (34)	2.89 (35.5)
34	Direct Marketing	72	.476	3.558	52	.437 (39.5)	3.584 (50)	.512 (31.5)	3.54 (51)
35	Journal of Contemporary Business	71	.470	2.803	31	.507 (35.5)	2.806 (28)	.438 (36)	2.80 (33)
36	Pittsburgh Business Review	68	.450	3.221	42	.535 (30.5)	3.345 (41)	.375 (30)	3.07 (40.5)
37	Business Management	68	.450	2.897	33	.423 (41)	2.898 (30)	.475 (34)	2.89 (35.5)
38	European Journal of Marketing	68	.450	2.517	21	.521 (33)	2.457 (21)	.388 (37)	2.58 (23.5)
39	Baylor Business Studies	60	.397	3.483	50	.465 (37)	3.606 (52)	.337 (41.5)	3.33 (49)
40	Advanced Management Journal	60	.397	2.464	19	.451 (38)	2.469 (22)	.350 (40)	2.46 (20)
41	Marketing Times	58	.389	3.327	45	.437 (39.5)	3.484 (46)	.337 (41.5)	3.15 (43.5)
42	Trans. and Dist. Management	55	.364	3.037	37	.366 (44)	3.154 (35)	.363 (39)	2.93 (37.5)
43	Journal of Int. Business Studies	52	.344	2.616	27	.380 (42)	2.778 (27)	.313 (43)	3.64 (53)
44	N. C. Review of Business & Econ.	49	.324	3.368	47	.366 (44)	3.539 (49)	.288 (45)	3.17 (45)
45	The Logistics & Trans. Review	47	.311	2.554	24	.366 (44)	2.423 (19)	.263 (46.5)	2.71 (29.5)
46	Transportation Journal	46	.304	2.457	18	.352 (46)	2.320 (16)	.263 (46.5)	2.62 (25)
47	Canadian Marketeer	44	.291	3.250	43	.282 (50)	3.400 (43)	.300 (44)	3.13 (42)
48	Journal of Industrial Economics	42	.278	2.548	23	.310 (47.5)	2.592 (25)	.250 (48)	2.50 (21)
49	International J. of Physical Dist.	40	.264	2.575	25	.310 (47.5)	2.591 (24)	.225 (49.5)	2.55 (22)
50	International Marketing Mgmt.	39	.258	2.718	30	.296 (40)	3.000 (32)	.225 (49.5)	2.39 (12.5)
51	Marketing in Europe	29	.192	3.032	36	.169 (52)	3.168 (36)	.213 (51)	2.72 (31)
52	J. of Med. & Phar. Marketing	27	.178	3.333	46	.155 (53)	3.459 (45)	.200 (52)	3.25 (46)
53	Omega-International J. of MS	26	.172	2.692	29	.197 (51)	3.001 (38)	.150 (58)	2.33 (17)

Source: Boris W. Becker and William G. Browne, "Perceived Quality of Marketing Journals," Journal of Marketing Education, Nov. 1979, pp. 6–15.

Cross-Journal Comparisons

This section presents a few comparisons of each of the four journals. It is useful to begin with a brief overview of journals that publish articles in the areas of marketing management and research. The Browne and Becker[34] study cited earlier solicited reactions from 151 marketing department chairpersons concerning their awareness of and familiarity with fifty-three journals and trade papers that publish marketing-related articles. Table 3-9 shows awareness, familiarity, and weighted-average-rank data for the fifty-three journals broken down by large and small business-school faculty size.

Concerning the four journals studied by the Commission, the *HBR* received the highest familiarity or awareness rating, followed closely by *JM* and *JMR*. *JCR* placed fourteenth on this basis. Department chairman were also asked to rate each journal as to relative "quality." The top six marketing journals from this perspective were:

Rank	Journal
1	*Journal of Marketing Research*
2	*Journal of Marketing*
3	*Management Science*
4	*Operations Research*
5	*Harvard Business Review*
6	*Journal of Consumer Research*

There were some interesting rating differences between chairmen of large and small business schools, however, as shown below.

Rank Order Given by Large-School Chairmen	Rank Order Given by Small-School Chairmen
1. *Journal of Marketing Research*	1. *Journal of Marketing*
2. *Journal of Marketing*	2. *Journal of Marketing Research*
3. *Operations Research*	3. *Management Science*
4. *Management Science*	4. *Harvard Business Review*
5. *Journal of Business*	5. *Journal of Consumer Research*
6. *Harvard Business Review*	6. *Public Opinion Quarterly*
7. *Journal of Consumer Research*	7. *Operations Research*

JMR and *JM* remained near the top of the list in each case. The sponsorship of these journals is interesting also. Of eight journals listed above, six are sponsored by associations (AMA-3, ORSA-1, TIMS-1, AAPOR-1) and two by universities (Harvard and Chicago).[35]

An analysis was made of journal editorships over the period (Table 3-10) and of the proportion of academic versus nonacademic authorships (Table 3-11). Journal content is to some degree determined by the editor-in-chief, and

TABLE 3-10

EDITORS OF THREE MARKETING JOURNALS, 1936-1978

Journal of Marketing

Paul Nystrom	1936-37	D. M. Phelps	1945-49
N. H. Engle	1936-39	Ralph Cassidy, Jr.	1947-51
R. S. Vaile	1937-41	E. R. Hawkins	1949-53
E. T. Grether	1939-43	A. W. Frey	1951-55
Reavis Cox	1941-45	Lincoln H. Clark	1953-57
C. F. Phillips	1943-47	G. L. Mehren	1955-58
Steuart H. Britt	1958-67		
Eugene J. Kelley	1968-73		
Edward W. Cundiff	1973-76		
Edward C. Bursk	1976-78		
Yoram Wind	1978-		

Journal of Marketing Research

Robert Ferber	1964-69
Ralph L. Day	1969-72
Frank M. Bass	1973-75
Harper W. Boyd, Jr.	1976-78
Gilbert A. Churchill, Jr.	1978-

Journal of Consumer Research

Ronald E. Frank	1974-76
Robert Ferber	1977-

the particular orientations and academic backgrounds of these persons had much to do with changes in content. Table 3-11 shows that throughout their history *JM, JMR,* and *JCR* have been dominated by university-affiliated authorships, which generally increased as a percent of the total in all three journals over the period studied. In contrast, *HBR* has a more balanced ratio of authorship, even though the proportion of university-affiliated authors also increased over the twenty-five years. A recent study[36] provides a somewhat finer-grained break-down of sources of author affiliation for *JMR* and *JM* from 1970 to 1974.

Author Affiliation	*JMR*	*JM*
Marketing academics	78.4%	80.1%
Public administration, management	8.1	6.9
Practitioners	7.3	9.3
Journalism	.5	1.2
Government	.3	.4
Other	5.4	2.0

A final way to look at content changes in the four journals is to examine specific "hot" topics around which much writing and controversy took place. Table 3-12 lists such topics over the time period.

TABLE 3-11

PROPORTIONS OF UNIVERSITY-AFFILIATED AND NON-UNIVERSITY-AFFILIATED AUTHORSHIP OF FOUR JOURNALS, 1952–1977

	1952	1957	1962	1967	1972	1977
Journal of Marketing						
All articles:						
University-affiliated	62%	60%	55%	70%	97%	70%
Other affiliations	38	40	45	30	3	30
Research-oriented articles:						
University-affiliated	56	64	59	70	96	67
Other affiliations	44	36	41	30	4	33
Journal of Marketing Research	1964	1967	1969	1972	1974	1977
University-affiliated	63%	78%	80%	92%	95%	96%
Other affiliations	37	22	20	8	5	4
Journal of Consumer Research						1977
University-affiliated						100%
Other affiliations						

Harvard Business Review	1952–56	1957–61	1962–66	1967–71	1971–76
University-affiliated	35%	49%	44%	47%	58%
Other affiliation	65	51	56	53	42

What can be said about the changes in development of marketing knowledge over the period from the viewpoint of changes in journals? First, an expanding volume of new knowledge is indicated by the publication of new marketing journals, such as *JMR* and *JCR*. The fifty-three journals listed in the Browne-Becker study suggest the scope and nature of marketing-related journal material. As will be discussed in later chapters, the most important journals for the development of new knowledge in marketing are those in the basic social science disciplines, such as economics, psychology, sociology, and statistics, and it is quite evident that a surge in the number and nature of journals in these disciplines also took place over the period.

Concerning changes in content, the two management-oriented journals, *JM* and *HBR,* displayed significant shifts in topical interest over the period.[37] Research topics associated with developments in multivariate methods of data analysis, which were beginning to find their way into *JM* in the mid-1960s, were picked up and given full-focused attention in *JMR*. Similarly, the behavioral science materials beginning to fight for space in *JMR* in the early 1970s were picked up in the new *JCR*. This proliferation of specialized topics is a healthy characteristic of a natural evolutionary process in the development of any basic or applied science.

As noted, the authorship affiliation of *JM, JMR,* and *JCR* was heavily dominated by academics over the period, and none of these journals approaches the fifty-fifty industry/university proportions of *HBR* authorships. This issue is examined further in later chapters.

The next section reports on a parallel analysis of marketing textbooks over the twenty-five-year period.

MARKETING TEXTBOOKS: 1952–1977

What changes in marketing knowledge are reflected by changes in textbook content? First, the Commission noted that hundreds, if not thousands, of textbooks on marketing or marketing-related topics (e.g., advertising) had been published over the twenty-five years.[38] The subject-matter scope of this stream of books is suggested by the typical recipe of courses in a fully developed marketing program of a major university (particularly one with an undergraduate as well as an MBA program). Course offerings could include

Marketing	Consumer Behavior
Marketing Management	Advertising
Marketing Research	Retailing (and/or related topics such as Channels, Wholesaling, Physical Distribution Management)
Marketing Models	Sales Management
	Product Management
	Pricing

as well as other specialized topics:

Social Marketing (including Marketing for Nonprofit Organizations)

Government and Marketing Regulation (and/or Industrial Organization Theory and Methods)

Methodological Specialty Courses (Econometrics, Psychometrics, Measurement, and so on)

International Marketing

Each of the fourteen topics listed above is itself a "field." There are hundreds of books, for example, on the subject of advertising, written from perspectives that range over economics, institutional views, behavioral science, sociology, political science, and professional know-how. There are now over fifty books titled *Consumer Behavior* or something close to it.

The Commission chose to focus on nonquantitatively oriented "principles" or "general" marketing management textbooks published over the period—those that were the most appropriate to courses on Marketing or Market-

TABLE 3-12

MAJOR TOPICS IN JOURNALS, 1947-1977

Year	Journal of Marketing	Harvard Business Review	Journal of Marketing Research	Journal of Consumer Research
1947	FTC retail price maintenance FTC false advertising Legal aspects of price discrimination Sampling issues (method, quality) Advertising effectiveness and response rate Marketing's role in getting back to sound prosperity			
1952	Implications of the Robinson-Patman Act Mail survey, questionnaire, group interview Role and value of market research Measuring advertising expenditures Consumer behavior in retail stores and responses to sales promotion	Qualitative research Pricing		
1957	Motivation research (conceptual) Attitude research (conceptual) Mail questionnaires Cost and efficiency of marketing Advertising	Pricing Market research		
1962	Personality image research (some empirical work) Surveys	Advertising World markets		

Year			
1964	Models in marketing Need for formal strategy Advertising still important, but more articles in other areas	Sales management	Advertising and media research Markov chains Sampling
1967	Government and regulations' impact on the market and marketing Consumer dissonance Marketing in a specific international market	No topic more than once	Attitude research Correlating socioeconomic and demographic variants with consumer behavior Data collection methods
1969		No topic more than once	Advertising effectiveness New products (demand forecasting) Attitude and preference measurement
1972	Advertising and promotion—attitudinal framework Cognitive dissonance Marketing theory (generic concept of marketing; marketing as a communication system) Unit pricing Consumerism		Attitude models Brand loyalty and switching Minority marketing Advertising
1974		Sales forces	Information load and processing Diffusion of innovation Salesmen issues Attitude theory research
1977	Services		Consumer information processing Family decision making Children and communication Attitude models Consumer information processing and attitude models Interpersonal influence on consumer behavior Household economics

ing Management and that were most often used in introductory courses at the MBA or undergraduate level.

Introductory marketing textbooks that are adopted by a professor for a first course in marketing differ from journals and other specialized books in at least two important respects.[39] First, their essential purpose is the effective *dissemination* of knowledge rather than its creation and development. Basic texts thus tend not to represent the latest developments in the field. Long lead times are required to develop and publish a text, and in order to be commercially successful it must be pitched to appeal to students in large introductory courses coming from a diversity of academic backgrounds. Second, the purpose of a text is to integrate and consolidate what is known about the field and often to put this material in a managerial framework. In contrast, except for review articles, most journal articles must be prepared to address new issues or present new approaches in their efforts to advance understanding of the field. Risk taking in basic textbooks tends to be confined to presentation, format, and emphasis. There is relatively little room for conjecture and theory development, since an introductory course must present a solid foundation of learning, serving the needs of those who are starting at "square one" (and who may not go on to take more advanced courses). Exploration of the frontiers must be left to elective courses and more advanced texts, as well as to assignments including recent articles, papers, and monographs.

An evaluation of basic marketing textbook content over time nevertheless reveals important dimensions of knowledge development in the field. Such textbooks embody the basic core of training received by marketing managers at the undergraduate or master's levels. They reflect not only changes in teaching orientation over the years but also developments in management practice and marketing applications.

Authors are naturally interested in selling their books, which means they have to fit the market's needs and interests. Instructors in required introductory courses are generally eager to keep students interested and involved in the subject—for, among other reasons, they hope that many of them will decide to major in marketing. This encourages the author of such a text to strive for an interesting presentation and to emphasize recent applications of marketing concepts and tools in real-world situations.

The Commission thus chose to focus on the most widely used and popular basic marketing management and principles textbooks. The study was done by members of the Commission staff at the Harvard Business School and involved the following five-step procedure:

1. Identify all marketing textbooks advertised in the *Journal of Marketing* during the periods 1951–1953 and 1975–1977.
2. Select those that appeared from their titles and the advertising copy to be general marketing texts.

3. Search the libraries at the Harvard Business School and at the MIT Sloan School of Management to identify which of these general marketing texts were included in the library collections.

4. Review all available editions of each general marketing book published during the period 1951–1977 and found in these two libraries' collections, *focusing on those texts that ran to two or more editions.*

5. Undertake a content analysis of each multiple-edition text (plus Heskett's 1976 text, *Marketing*[40]) and assess changes over time in topics covered, relative emphasis given to specific topics (as a percentage of total text content), developments in text structure, and general trends in presentation.

As a result of this procedure, fifteen books were selected for in-depth content analysis. (Several, of course, are no longer in print.) In addition, a very brief review was made of more specialized texts to determine trends in content and focus over time.

The procedure adopted may have biased the analysis in several ways, as noted below:

1. It excluded books (except Heskett) that had gone through only a single edition. The rationale was that single-edition books presumably are less successful, sell fewer copies, and have less influence in diffusing ideas about marketing tools, concepts, and strategies to students.

2. Casebooks and looseleaf cases distributed by the Intercollegiate Case Clearing House were excluded. In case teaching, the transmission of knowledge and concepts depends largely on *how* the cases are taught. A content analysis of instructors' teaching notes rather than cases would be needed.

3. The study was restricted to textbooks available in the collections of two leading graduate business schools. While these two schools represent very different philosophies of marketing education, their libraries are selective in purchasing textbooks, so that the resulting collections exclude several moderately successful texts designed primarily for use in undergraduate and junior college programs. It seems reasonable to assume that, overall, books excluded from this study are (a) less successful, (b) less comprehensive, and (c) pitched at a slightly lower level.

4. It was not possible to review all editions of every text, since library holdings were not complete. Fortunately, however, the two libraries complemented each other reasonably well in this respect.

Characteristics of Marketing Principles Textbooks

Table 3-13 provides a listing of the fifteen textbooks studied, showing the dates of publication of the first edition, the principal author or authors, and the title, publisher, and dates of subsequent editions. All the books have been revised in the 1970s except two (Clark's *Principles of Marketing* and Converse's *Elements of Marketing*), so there appears to be a continuing market for most of

TABLE 3-13

FIFTEEN MARKETING PRINCIPLES TEXTBOOKS, 1952–1977

Book No.	Date of First Publication	Author, Publisher, and Dates of Subsequent Editions
1	1922	CLARK, FRED. *Principles of Marketing.* New York: Macmillan Co., 1922; 2d ed., 1932; 3d ed., 1942 with CARRIE P. CLARK; rev. ed., 1962, by R. D. TOUSLEY, EUGENE CLARK, and F. E. CLARK.
2	1927	MAYNARD, H. H., T. N. BECKMAN, and W. C. WEIDLER, *Principles of Marketing.* New York: The Ronald Press Co., 1927; 2d ed., 1932; 3d ed., 1939; 4th ed., 1946; 5th ed., 1954; 6th ed., 1958, with W. R. DAVIDSON; 7th ed., 1962 by BECKMAN and DAVIDSON; 8th ed., 1967, with J. F. ENGEL; 9th ed., 1973, by BECKMAN, DAVIDSON, and W. WAYNE TALARZYK.
3	1930	CONVERSE, PAUL D. *Elements of Marketing.* New York: Prentice-Hall, Inc., 1930; rev. ed., 1935, with H. W. HUEGY; 2d ed., 1940; 3d ed., 1947; 5th ed., 1952, with ROBERT V. MITCHELL; 6th ed., 1958; 7th ed., 1965.
4	1938	PHILLIPS, C. F. *Marketing.* New York: Houghton Mifflin Co., 1938; rev. ed., with D. J. DUNCAN, as *Marketing, Principles and Methods.* Chicago: Richard D. Irwin, Inc., 1948; 2d ed., 1948; 3d ed., 1956; 4th ed., 1960; 5th ed., 1964; 6th ed., 1968; 7th ed., 1973, by J. M. CARMAN and K. P. UHL.
5	1956	HANSEN, HARRY L. *Marketing: Text Cases, Readings.* Homewood, Ill.: Richard D. Irwin, Inc., 1956; rev. ed., 1961; 3d ed., 1967; 4th ed., 1977.
6	1960	McCARTHY, E. J. *Basic Marketing: A Managerial Approach.* Homewood, Ill.: Richard D. Irwin, Inc., 1960; 2d ed., 1964; 3d ed., 1968; 4th ed., 1971; 5th ed., 1975.
7	1961	BUSKIRK, R. H. *Principles of Marketing.* New York: Holt, Rinehart, and Winston, 1961; rev. ed., 1966; 3d ed., 1970; 4th ed., 1975.
8	1964	BUZZELL, R. D., et al. *Marketing an Introductory Analysis.* New York: McGraw-Hill Book Co., Inc., 1964; 2d ed., as *Marketing: A Contemporary Analysis,* 1972.
9	1964	STANTON, W. J. *Fundamentals of Marketing.* New York: McGraw-Hill Book Co., Inc., 1964; 2d ed., 1967; 3d ed., 1971; 4th ed., 1975.
10	1973	CUNDIFF, E. W., R. R. STILL, and N. A. P. GOVONI. *Fundamentals of Modern Marketing.* Englewood Cliffs, N.J.: Prentice-Hall, Inc., 1973; 2d ed., 1976.
11	1957	HOWARD, J. R. *Marketing Management: Analysis and Decision.* Homewood, Ill.: Richard D. Irwin, Inc., 1957; rev. ed., 1963; 3d ed., 1973.
12	1961	DAVIS, K. R. *Marketing Management.* New York: The Ronald Press Co., 1961; 2d ed., 1966; 3d ed., 1972.
13	1967	KOTLER, PHILIP. *Marketing Management.* Englewood Cliffs, N.J.: Prentice-Hall, Inc., 1967; 2d ed., 1972; 3d ed., 1976.
14	1974	ENIS, BEN M. *Marketing Principles: The Management Process.* Santa Monica, Calif.: Goodyear Publishing Co., 1974; 2d ed., 1977.
15	1976	HESKETT, JAMES L. *Marketing.* Macmillan Co., 1976.

these books, even though the first editions of Maynard et al. and of Phillips were published in the 1920s and 1930s. Most of the major publishers of marketing books are involved, as shown below in terms of numbers of these books each published over the period:

Irwin	4	Ronald	2
Prentice-Hall	3	Holt, Rinehart, Winston	1
McGraw-Hill	2	Goodyear	1
Macmillan	2		

Figure 3-8 shows the publication dates of subsequent editions for each of the reference texts. It can reasonably be assumed that a book that has not appeared in a new edition since 1972–1973 is probably selling at present in very small quantities (if not already out of print). In short, if a text is not revised it will die.

Change and evolution can take place in two ways—by revision or by replacement. Some texts have remarkably long lives. Figure 3-8 shows that four texts selling in the early 1950s were carry-overs from prewar editions. A major new cycle was started in 1960 with the publication of McCarthy's *Basic Marketing: A Managerial Approach,* which, with its strongly managerial orientation, rapidly eclipsed all existing competitors.

During the 1950s and early 1960s most marketing textbooks appeared to be on a four- to six-year republication cycle. By the 1970s the cycle had shrunk to three to four years, reflecting greater competition in a larger market. Many new publishers had entered the marketing texts field, and some publishers had two or more entries in the market.

Revisions provide an opportunity to add to or delete from a text, as well as to restructure and update its contents and focus. However, many revisions seemed primarily to involve repackaging. Clearly, knowledge and new applications were not the only reasons for revision. Important motivations for frequent new editions were the growth of a secondhand market (which cannabalizes sales) and the need to revise exercises and assignments whose answers had found their way into fraternity files.

A key difference between 1952 and 1977 was that in 1952 books had much longer selling spans. New editions frequently added authors, who presumably undertook the labors of revision. Converse, Phillips and Clark, for example, each added authors. In 1977, authors appeared to labor alone more frequently and to revise more often to meet the constraints of a shorter selling span and a more competitive text market. However, as the long listings of names on the "acknowledgements" page often testify, a new edition reflects inputs from numerous sources—colleagues at both the author's own institution and elsewhere, graduate students and research assistants, and sometimes editorial assistance from the publishers. (Acknowledged inputs from practicing marketing

FIGURE 3-8

PUBLICATION DATES OF EDITIONS DURING ASSESSMENT PERIOD, 1952-1977

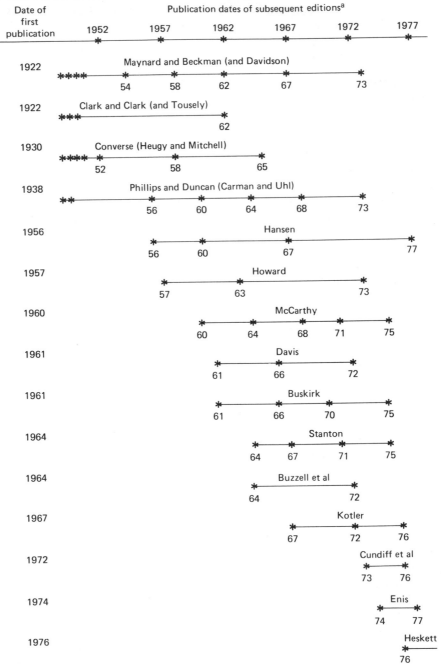

[a]Author names refer to the line immediately below. Asterisks signify dates of subsequent editions.

88

managers, however, are conspicuously absent from most texts.) The practice by publishers of employing faculty at other schools as reviewers formalizes this process, although the quality of such inputs varies widely.

Information about specific new marketing tools and concepts is more apparent in some books than in others. Some authors have deliberately adopted an "encyclopedic" approach, and the sources of their ideas are evident from extensive footnoting of journal articles, conference papers, specialist texts, news stories, and even competing texts.

In the case of Philip Kotler, who is a frequent author of journal articles, the reader can often recognize concepts developed earlier in articles or papers as they appear in his texts. Perhaps the most notable example occurs in his 1975 specialist volume, *Marketing for Nonprofit Organizations,* which draws heavily from his papers and articles as well as from the second edition of *Marketing Management: Analysis, Planning and Control* (1972). In turn, some of the material in the nonprofit book found its way into the third (1976) edition of *Marketing Management.*[41]

The books available in 1952 were characterized by their uniformity. In 1977 there was much greater diversity. Three market segments are discernible:

1. Basic texts (undergraduate or junior college); e.g., Stanton, Cundiff, Still, and Govoni
2. Comprehensive (undergraduate level) texts; e.g., McCarthy.
3. Advanced introductory (graduate level) texts; e.g., Kotler; Buzzell et al.

The content analysis included all three categories of books. However, the depth of treatment varies between segments (and, on a given topic) between texts.

Changes in Textbook Content: 1952-1977

Table 3-14 summarizes changes in the relative emphasis given to different topics between 1952 and 1977 in leading marketing principles textbooks. The seven topics shown on the left were of major interest in 1952. These evolved into those shown at the center of the figure and subsequently to those of dominant interest in 1977 (to the right). Certain topics (such as a discussion of agricultural commodities and of marketing institutions) virtually disappeared, while others (such as the environment of marketing, consumerism, and what the future may bring) have become significant in recent years. This figure also highlights (1) changes in emphasis on marketing applications (although this area received a similar proportion of total text space over the years, the topics have changed); (2) the evolution of discussions of the consumer from a primarily descriptive treatment to one emphasizing insights from the behavioral sciences; (3) a shift to a more strategic, managerial orientation; and (4) the rise of the marketing concept.

Table 3-15 shows examples of typical textbook organization and topics

TABLE 3-14
TWENTY POPULAR TOPICS IN MARKETING PRINCIPLES BOOKS, 1952–1977

1952	Mid-Period	1977
Nature and Significance of Marketing Consumer in marketplace	Hierarchy of needs	Marketing Concept Psychological, Sociological buyer behavior; modes of behavior Channels woven into text
Institutional marketing Functional marketing	Retailing and wholesaling Marketing mix and marketing program	Marketing management
Applications; commodities agriculture Cost and efficiency of marketing	Applications: more emphasis on manufacturing, services, foreign trade Planning; audit of marketing	Applications: more on international, services, nonprofit marketing Control and implementation of strategy; environmental changes and marketing
Marketing of commodities		Public policy; environment, consumerism, and future

TABLE 3-15

TYPICAL TEXTBOOK ORGANIZATION AND TOPICS IN 1952, 1967, AND 1977

1952	1967	1977
INTRO—NATURE AND SIGNIFICANCE OF MARKETING	ANALYZING MARKET OPPORTUNITIES Marketing concept, environment, segmentation, buyer behavior	MARKETING CONCEPT
CONSUMER IN MARKETPLACE Demographic—consumption income	ORGANIZING FOR MARKETING Goals, planning, decision making, marketing research, models, creativity	MARKETING AS A SYSTEM Planning overview
MARKET STRUCTURE Economic analysis	PLANNING THE MARKETING PROGRAM Product policy, new product, price, channel, distribution, advertising, sales management, law	CONSUMER BEHAVIOR Behavioral—motivational
WHOLESALING } INSTITUTIONAL Much detail	CONTROLLING THE MARKETING EFFORT Marketing control, sales and cost analysis audit	MARKETING MANAGEMENT Information collection, product analysis, distribution logistics, price system, promotional activity
RETAILING Much detail		SPECIAL FIELDS Service, international, social
FUNCTIONAL MARKETING Sales, advertising, pricing		MARKETING STRATEGY Planning, implementation program
APPLICATIONS Commodities, services, manufacturing		NEW ENVIRONMENT OF MARKETING AND FUTURE Law, government, consumerism, public policy
COST AND EFFICIENCY OF MARKETING PROGRAM		
MARKETING ARITHMETIC		
Descriptive *Institutional* *Static*	*Decision Orientation* *Analytical Approach*	*Behavioral* *Systemic* *Strategic*

in 1952, 1967, and 1977. The 1967 type is most closely exemplified by Kotler's first edition and that of 1977 by Heskett's recent book.

In 1950, marketing was "underdeveloped" and still had its roots in static market description and economics theory. Alderson and Cox clearly were groping for a theoretical framework. In the process, they offered a grab bag of concepts: (1) demography, (2) vector psychology, (3) survival theory, and (4) pluralistic competition. The turning point came about 1960, when functionalism developed into marketing-mix analysis, highlighted by the "four P's" conceptualization developed by McCarthy. In the mid-sixties, theories of consumer behavior blossomed and quantitative market research advanced rapidly. Concepts such as the life-cycle and segmentation permeated most of the textbooks. The publication of Kotler's book in 1967 can be seen as the beginning of a new wave of marketing texts that incorporated the behavioral sciences and quantitative methods explicitly as part of the general thrust of the book (and not just as an appendix or afterthought). It is interesting to note that Kotler's first edition included a complete chapter on the then trendy topic of motivation research, but this was downplayed in the otherwise comprehensive second edition (1972).

The 1952 textbooks were characterized by sections on the consumer expressed in terms of sociodemographic profile, income levels, and geographic spread—typically 10% to 12% of the content. This percentage remained the same in 1977, but the content dramatically changed, drawing much more heavily from behavioral science concepts applied to marketing.

One interesting verbal chain through the textbooks is:

MIDDLEMEN	WHOLESALING	DISTRIBUTION	PHYSICAL DISTRIBUTION SYSTEMS	CHANNELS LOGISTICS MANAGEMENT

Wholesaling generally took around 20% of a 1952 textbook; in 1977 it was included as part of channels. The institutional content (wholesaling and retailing) slipped from a joint content of around 40% and developed in two ways: it became assimilated into channels (around 3%) or it was incorporated into the topic of distribution (e.g., McCarthy).

Commodities virtually disappeared from the textbooks. This was a prime topic in 1952 texts and took around 15% to 17% of the content. Commodity markets and pricing also were discussed elsewhere in the 1952 texts. Only the revised Phillips and Duncan (1973) retains a section on agricultural products.

Another typical word chain is:

MERCHANDISING   PRODUCT DEVELOPMENT   PRODUCT PLANNING   PRODUCT MARKET STRATEGIES

It has grown in content from less than 3% to between 5% and 10%.

Heskett claims that many aspects of current marketing involve a complex system-type product. This is the extreme end of another line of development, reflecting changes in emphasis on areas of application.

1950s	1960s	1970s
agriculture	foreign trade	international
commodity	services	services
industrial	industrial	public/nonprofit
manufacturing		enterprises

Note that Heskett treats marketing in public/nonprofit organizations on an equal footing with traditional business marketing and not as some rarefied extension of it. He denigrates the notion that marketing is concerned only with selling soap powder, but he does not shrink from using a major (but unpopular) industry such as cigarettes to illustrate marketing of fast-moving, branded consumer products. Enis also weaves public/nonprofit marketing into the mainstream of his book.

Almost all 1952 books ended with a chapter on "Marketing Costs and Efficiency," comprising around 4% of the content. Occasionally the term *market program* emerged. This has developed into the concepts of marketing plans, goals analysis, planning, strategy, implementation, control, and evaluation. Planning currently takes 17% to 24% of modern textbooks, especially those targeted at more advanced students.

Perhaps the most noticeable change between editions of a specific textbook occurred in Buskirk, between the second and fourth editions. He decided to round off the third edition by calling Section VII "Potpourri," which included topics such as market intelligence, control and evaluation, ethical problems, legal constraints, international, and administration. There was then a major revision to a strategy-based conclusion for the fourth edition of the book.

A major philosophical change was the adoption of *systems* concepts (see Phillips & Duncan, 1973) and *planning and strategy* (Kotler's development). In this regard, the 1952 books typically included only a final chapter on "The Program." This treatment is still evident today in books such as the Cundiff, Still, and Govoni volume. In their 1973 edition this chapter was entitled "Overall Marketing Strategy" and included the interaction of marketing and society and overall strategy. By contrast, Heskett developed at the outset a flow diagram of "marketing strategy formulation," which provided the basic organizational structure for the rest of the text.

Another key development of the 1970s was consumerism. This generally merited a chapter or section representing 2% to 4% of the total. However, Duddy and Revzan had included a section on "the consumer movement" as early as 1952. Generally the position of the consumerism chapter has shifted toward the end of a book, into the "environment and future" section.

Functionalism evolved into marketing management, a concept devel oped by McCarthy in what became the largest-selling marketing textbook to date.

Discipline bases have changed *away from* (1) economics of markets and (2) pricing *toward* (1) psychology and motivation and (2) quantitative emphasis. Early books usually had an appendix on "marketing arithmetic," which persisted into the 1960s (Buskirk).

Although the Harvard Business School's *Problems in Marketing* casebook (originally prepared by Melvin T. Copeland) has been in almost continuous publication since 1920, Cannon and Weichert (1952) claim the first marketing text and cases book. Hansen followed in 1956. At first there was a reluctance to incorporate cases. McCarthy, Buskirk, and Stanton each began by presenting short ones (two-page caselets) at the end of the book, later bringing them into individual chapters. The trend seems to be toward more use of cases, and Enis has a number of short-to-medium-length cases in his second edition (1977), in contrast to the caseless first edition (1974). Certain authors, especially those associated with case-oriented schools, have incorporated case-type material into the text. Buzzell and others draw quite heavily from Harvard cases, while Heskett opens his book with a presentation of a real-world marketing situation, from which various marketing lessons can be drawn. Rather than illustrating a point with a follow-up case history, he *starts* with the case and uses it to highlight some basic marketing concepts and strategies. Meanwhile, *Problems in Marketing* has added progressively more text material, and the most recent (fifth post-war) edition in 1977 had twelve short textual notes comprising some 8% of the total content.

Style has changed dramatically, as evidenced by Heskett's bold introduction. Increased editorial assistance together with economic pressure to reduce overall length has resulted in clearer, more concise writing. Layout incorporates more design elements, better graphics, and in some books (e.g., Enis) even photographs and cartoons. Color has become fashionable as printing techniques have improved and print orders grown larger. This trend will undoubtedly continue, being supplemented by increasingly sophisticated instructors' manuals and teaching aids, such as overhead transparencies.

In summary, it is evident that until the mid-1960s many marketing textbooks were operationally prewar in approach. The changes that occurred (and that outmoded these earlier books) can be seen by comparing the 1952 and 1967 structures in Table 3-13. The movement was away from books "about market*ing*" to books "for market*ers*."

The movement from 1967 to date is more subtle. Although the 1967 books were cast in a decision-making mode and included marketing performance evaluations, they did not present a formal feedback process. What was *not* in these books was the sense of a marketing operation both under managerial control and also adaptive to changing conditions. The transformation since 1967 has been the addition of a feedback mechanism to give a true feeling of the "adaptive loop."

Specialist Texts

As compared to basic texts, specialist books in marketing may have several alternate foci:

1. Areas of application (e.g., international, nonprofit).
2. Specific functional areas (e.g., advertising, personal selling).
3. Marketing-related disciplines (e.g., consumer behavior).
4. Research methodologies (e.g., sampling, multivariate analysis).

Marketing theorists and researchers working at the cutting edge of the field often draw heavily from work, concepts, and tools in other fields.

To some extent, specialist texts can be seen as an intermediate form of dissemination via publication, lying between journal articles and basic texts. However, some of the functional texts are really quite similar to the basic texts except for their concentration on a specific function. Some of them go through numerous editions and have been used to train generations of students in such required or elective courses as "Principles of Advertising" or "Principles of Selling." Marketing research texts, reviewed earlier in the chapter, are another example of specialist texts.

Books in specific areas of application tend to have shorter life spans, reflecting the fact that the subject matter of elective courses in such applications may eventually be subsumed into basic or functional courses. International marketing appears to be following such a life cycle, and some predict the same for public/nonprofit marketing (although the growth of a management curriculum in schools of government, education, and public health may generate a lasting need for specialist marketing texts in these fields). However, the limited number of industrial marketing texts on the market have typically run to several editions over time.

In 1952, new specialist marketing texts were typically confined to such areas as sales, distribution, advertising, and purchasing. During the 1960s, logistics and industrial and international marketing came to the fore. In the 1970s, the subjects noted above remain and have been joined by a growing number of volumes emphasizing such topics as quantitative methods and modeling, applications of the behavioral sciences in marketing (e.g., psychographics), consumerism, marketing and society, and, most recently, marketing applications in public and nonprofit organizations.

SUMMARY

Over the past quarter-century major changes took place in the marketing research industry and in the storehouse of marketing knowledge available to the marketing practitioner. This chapter has attempted to document some of these changes while recognizing that much important practitioner-utilized information is inherently nondocumentable, existing in the minds and mores of practicing managers themselves. The marketing research industry increased in size, scope, and sophistication over the period, even though, in terms of expenditures on production-related research and development or other types of corporate investment, the industry itself is not very large. We will reexamine some aspects of the nature of the industry in Chapter 4.

The storehouse of knowledge represented in marketing journals and textbooks also grew explosively. At the end of the period there were at least fifty-three journals publishing marketing-related materials, as well as hundreds of trade papers, newsletters, and reports. The pattern of knowledge development in the major marketing journals can be seen as one of continuing specialization, the *Journal of Marketing* playing the initial role, followed by the *Journal of Marketing Research* as quantitative and multivariate methods of data analysis came to the fore, and subsequently by the *Journal of Consumer Research* as behavioral-science-oriented marketing professors sought yet another outlet for their research productivity. Journal content moved from descriptive, univariate, and classical representations at the beginning of the period to predictive, multivariate, and often Bayesian representations at the end. Economic, management science, and problem-oriented views are still clearly distinguishable from behavioral scientific, social psychological, and theory-oriented views, even though both perspectives are often brought to bear on the same marketing topic.

An explosive growth also took place in textbook writing in the field. In terms of the Commission's examination of basic principles texts, the predominant changes were from the "commodity," "functional," and "institutional" approaches to a "management" approach exemplified in the McCarthy and Kotler texts of the mid-1960s. The study of marketing as an interesting subject to think about and reflect on gave way to a much more action-oriented view of the training of potential marketing managers in the art and science of decision making and marketing management. Textbook content shifted toward less institutional, more conceptual materials, particularly as the latter encompassed ideas from economics and the behavioral sciences. However, none of the texts studied (representing most of the largest sellers even today), come close to the quantitative sophistication of other types of basic marketing management books, such as Montgomery and Urban's *Management Science in Marketing* or Simon and Freimer's *Analytical Marketing*. These more quantitatively oriented books on marketing management have served a much smaller segment of marketing faculty and students over the time period.

The next chapter presents a new perspective on marketing research and knowledge development referred to as "marketing's research and development system." In this context it addresses the question of the purpose of knowledge development in marketing. The chapter also reviews other ways to think about marketing knowledge and marketing research as a prelude to Chapter 5's explaining various aspects of how new knowledge is created, diffused, and used (or not used).

NOTES

[1] David K. Hardin, "Lower Profits Put Pinch on Researcher," *Advertising Age,* July 15, 1974, 26 ff. Reprinted with permission from the July 15, 1974 issue of Advertising Age. Copyright 1974 by Crain Communications, Inc.

[2] D. W. Twedt, *1973 Survey of Marketing Research* (Chicago: American Marketing Association, 1973).

[3] See Jack J. Honomichl, "Research Top Ten: Who Are They and What They Do," *Advertising Age,* July 15, 1974, p. 24, for data on the top ten research supplier firms. The largest company, A. C. Nielsen, for example, was estimated to have had $148,700,000 in gross revenues in 1974. By 1977, A. C. Nielsen had grown to $205,300,000 in gross research revenues, and the top twenty research supplier organizations had combined revenues of $494,300,000. The revenues of these companies as a group grew by 19% or had real growth of about 12.4% in 1977. See Jack J. Honomichl, "Research Top 20: Companies Posted 19% Gain Last Year," *Advertising Age,* April 24, 1978, 3 ff. Additional information on the marketing research industry is presented in Chapter 4.

[4] Donald R. Lehmann, *Market Research and Analysis* (Homewood, Ill.: Richard D. Irwin, 1979), p. 8.

[5] Lawrence C. Lockley, "History and Development of Marketing Research," in Robert Ferber, ed., *Handbook of Marketing Research* (New York: McGraw-Hill, 1974), pp. 1-3 to 1-15.

[6] Gerald Zaltman and Philip C. Burger, *Marketing Research: Fundamentals and Dynamics* (Hinsdale, Ill.: Dryden Press, 1975), p. 5.

[7] Other interpretations of the chronology of marketing research could be made. The first comprehensive theories of consumer behavior were developed in the early and mid-1960s. Although there was interest in consumer-theory development in the 1970s, more attention seems to have been given to decision-model development and theory testing.

[8] The authors define science as "the set of activities which concern studying a system which is measurable, performing studies which are reproducible, and being objective in terms of not influencing the results to fit one's own predilections." They note that marketing research is weakest on the "create reproducible experiments" criterion of scientific method.

[9] Herbert D. Maneloveg, "Media Research's Future: Is There Any?" *Advertising Age,* July 15, 1974, 23 ff.

[10] For an interesting review of "the founding fathers of advertising research," see the June 1977 issue of the *Journal of Advertising Research.* The life and contributions of eight leaders are reviewed: Ernest Dichter, George Gallup, Alfred Politz, Henry Brenner, A. C. Nielsen, Sr., Hans Ziesel, Frank Stanton, and Archibald Crossley.

[11]Paul E. J. Gerhold, "Sweeping Changes Seen in Brand Ad Research," *Advertising Age,* July 15, 1974, 23 ff. Reprinted with permission from the July 15, 1974 issue of Advertising Age. Copyright 1974 by Crain Communications, Inc.

[12]Theodore F. Dunn, "How Agencies Use Research," *Advertising Age,* July 15, 1974, p. 69. Reprinted with permission from the July 15, 1974 issue of Advertising Age. Copyright 1974 by Crain Communications, Inc.

[13]For a discussion of the implications of electronic cash registers and computerized checkout counters for marketing and advertising management, see Gerhold, "Sweeping Changes Seen in Brand Ad Research."

[14]Hardin, "Lower Profits Put Pinch on Researcher," p. 26. Copyright 1974 by Crain Communications, Inc.

[15]See Honomichl, "Research Top Ten: Who Are They and What They Do," p. 66.

[16]Lyndon O. Brown, *Market Research and Analysis* (New York: Ronald Press, 1937).

[17]Robert Ferber, *Statistical Techniques in Market Research.* Used by permission, © 1949 by McGraw-Hill, Inc., pp. 3–4.

[18]Harper W. Boyd, Jr. and Ralph Westfall, *Marketing Research: Text and Cases* (Homewood, Ill.: Richard D. Irwin, 1956). This definition was proposed by the Definitions Committee of the American Marketing Association and reported in the *Journal of Marketing,* 12 (October 1948), p. 210.

[19]Some of the earliest books that emphasized behavioral science methodologies were in advertising. See Walter D. Scott, *The Psychology of Advertising* (Boston: Small Maynard & Co., 1913); Darrel Lucas and C. E. Brown, *Psychology for Advertisers* (New York: Harper and Bros., 1930). Lucas and Britt published the first books specifically devoted to advertising research. See D. B. Lucas and S. M. Britt, *Advertising Psychology and Research* (New York: McGraw-Hill, 1950), and *Measuring Advertising Effectiveness* (New York: McGraw-Hill, 1963), by the same authors.

[20]Paul E. Green and Donald S. Tull, *Research for Marketing Decisions* (Englewood Cliffs, N.J.: Prentice-Hall, 1966).

[21]See, for example, Donald S. Tull and Del I. Hawkins, *Marketing Research: Meaning, Measurement, and Method.* Copyright © 1976 by Macmillan Publishing Co., Inc.; Gilbert A. Churchill, Jr., *Marketing Research: Methodological Foundations.* Copyright © 1976 by The Dryden Press, a division of Holt, Rinehart and Winston. Reprinted by permission of Holt, Rinehart and Winston.

[22]Thomas C. Kinnear and James R. Taylor, *Marketing Research: An Applied Approach* (New York: McGraw-Hill, 1979), p. 617.

[23]David B. Montgomery and Glen L. Urban, *Management Science in Marketing* (Englewood Cliffs, N.J.: Prentice-Hall, 1969).

[24]See, for example, Robert D. Buzzell, Donald F. Cox, and Rex V. Brown, *Marketing Research and Information Systems: Text and Cases* (New York: McGraw-Hill, 1969), and Kenneth P. Uhl and Bertram Schoner, *Marketing Research: Information Systems and Decision Making* (New York: Wiley, 1969).

[25]For example, F. T. Schreier, *Modern Marketing Research: A Behavioral Science Approach* (Belmont, Calif.: Wadsworth, 1963); G. Zaltman and P. C. Burger, *Marketing Research: Fundamentals and Dynamics* (Hinsdale, Ill.: Dryden Press, 1975).

[26]Wroe Alderson and Stanley J. Shapiro, eds., *Marketing and the Computer* (Englewood Cliffs, N.J.: Prentice-Hall, 1963).

[27]Jean-Claude Larreche and David B. Montgomery, "A Framework for the

Comparison of Marketing Models: A Delphi Study,'' *Journal of Marketing Research,* 14 (November 1977), 487–98.

[28]William G. Browne and Boris W. Becker, ''Journal Awareness and Quality: A Study of Academicians' Views of Journals,'' School of Business, Oregon State University, January 1977.

[29]Ewald T. Grether, ''The First Forty Years,'' *Journal of Marketing,* 40 (July 1976), 63–69, published by the American Marketing Association.

[30]Grether, ''The First Forty Years,'' p. 64.

[31]It is interesting to note that the number of multiple-authored articles increased rather dramatically over the period.

[32]As is true for all journals, some of this may reflect different editorial policies of the editors of the *Journal of Marketing Research.* See Table 3-10 for a list of the editors of *JMR* over the period.

[33]Jerry Wind, ''New Directions for JCR,'' *Journal of Consumer Research,* 4 (June 1977), 59–60. For a follow-up article on the same subject, see Robert Ferber, ''Can Consumer Research Be Interdisciplinary?'' *Journal of Consumer Research,* 4 (December 1977), 189–92.

[34]William G. Browne and Boris W. Becker, ''Journal Awareness and Quality: A Study of Academicians' Views of Journals,'' Working Paper, School of Business, Oregon State University, January 1977.

[35]Other university-sponsored marketing journals are included in the list, but none apparently have achieved the familiarity and quality rankings of the *Harvard Business Review* and Chicago's *Journal of Business.* Examples of other university-sponsored journals are *California Management Review* (Berkeley), *The Wharton Magazine* (Pennsylvania), *Journal of Retailing* (New York University), and *Business Horizons* (Indiana).

[36]J. T. Russell and C. H. Martin, ''Sources of Scholarly Publications in Marketing, Advertising, and Public Relations,'' *Journal of Advertising,* 5 (Summer 1976), 29–34. The other journals studied were the *Journal of Advertising, Journal of Advertising Research, Public Relations Journal,* and *Journalism Quarterly.* The article also provides some interesting statistics concerning which universities contributed the greatest number of articles to *JMR* and *JM.* Wharton, Columbia, Purdue, Texas, and Illinois lead the list for *JMR,* followed by Stanford, UCLA, Northwestern, Indiana, and Georgia. For *JM* the ranking was Northwestern, Wharton, Columbia, Texas, USC, Illinois, Georgia, and Washington. The study was based on articles appearing in respective issues of the journals between January 1970 and December 1974.

[37]It is perhaps presumptuous to classify *JM* as management-oriented, given the long history of controversy surrounding this journal. Grether, for example, noted that some respondents in a 1956 survey referred to it as ''a stodgy, long-hair booklet written by impractical scholars, in terminology not understood by laymen, containing boring articles arranged in a way which makes them hard to find,'' Grether, ''The First Forty Years,'' p. 68.

[38]If, for example, twenty publishers maintained a marketing list of only ten titles, each produced on a five-year cycle, then 1000 textbooks would have been published between 1952 and 1977.

[39]How to position and teach the basic marketing course has been a subject of ongoing interest and debate throughout the period. The course's importance stems from its role as the foundation on which all other aspects of a marketing course program and specific specialty course offerings are based. It also reflects the basic pedagogical teaching style that is adopted by a particular marketing faculty or department. The subject has been

consistently reviewed and discussed in the "teaching" tract of the AMA's marketing educator conferences down through the years.

[40]James L. Heskett, *Marketing*. Reprinted by permission of Macmillan Publishing Co. Although it was not a multiple-edition text, Heskett's book was included because it did appear to represent a departure in basic marketing books. For an example of another type of departure, which takes marketing plans as its basic perspective, see G. David Hughes, *Marketing Management: A Planning Approach* (Reading, Mass.: Addison-Wesley, 1978). Also, the Commission textbook study did not attempt to content-analyze numerous types of quantitatively oriented marketing management books published during the period.

[41]For a history of marketing textbook development, see Robert Bartels, *The History of Marketing Thought,* 2d ed., (Columbus, Ohio: Grid Press, 1976).

4

Marketing's Research and Development System

Chapters 2 and 3 reviewed some of the changes that have taken place in marketing management and marketing research over the twenty-five-year assessment period. The Commission essentially was charged with assessing the impact of the latter on the former and with addressing questions such as: Has the investment in marketing research and development been worthwhile? and, Does the research investment need conscious effort to maintain it, or is it essentially self-generating? A fundamental assumption was made that a knowledge-creating sector does exist in marketing, spanning both basic and applied forms of research. In other words, an essential departure point for the Commission was that marketing has a ''system'' of R & D analogous to such systems for other fields and professions.

The problem in attempting to assess the investment in marketing's research and development system is that no organization in the public or private sector has, to date, attempted to study the field of marketing and marketing research from this point of view. There have been no comprehensive studies made of marketing's R & D system and, indeed, no attempts to map out and rigorously define its components and boundaries. Assessment from this broadened point of view requires an assumption that marketing R & D is an important *national resource* and that the subject be studied and assessments made accordingly. The necessary viewpoint is one of national accounting, in which investments in various aspects of the system such as basic research, applied research, and development are monitored, preferably on an annual basis, and judgments about desirable levels of funding and resource allocation arrived at. This is not now done, and the necessary data base from which to work does not exist. The situation for marketing is in sharp contrast to that for other forms of R & D. There are few subjects about which we know more than research and development in the physical sciences. Hundreds of studies, books, reports, and materials have been generated about this form of national R & D investment.[1] The National Science Foundation, for example, has provided a detailed annual report on the state of the economy from this point of view since 1953. There is no parallel report on the state of the economy from the marketing R & D viewpoint to which one might turn.

There are many reasons for the lack of good data on marketing research and development as a national resource. The major one is that the system itself has not been specified nor described in terms that would make such accounting a feasible undertaking. We do not now have answers to such fundamental questions as what constitutes basic research, applied research, and "development" in marketing. All national accounting of R & D, at this point, explicitly *excludes* any investments associated with marketing or marketing research.

Another reason is that the disciplinary base for marketing R & D, at least from a national accounting perspective, has neither been formally recognized nor spelled out. We know, for example, a great deal about the role of basic sciences such as physics, chemistry, and biology in the overall system of developing new technological products and processes, but very little about the scientific underpinnings of the system that produces new knowledge in the marketing area. Many people feel that marketing does not have (or should not have) a scientific disciplinary base. Each of those who takes an opposite position and argues that the base is essentially "social science" is counterbalanced by hundreds, if not thousands, of social scientists who want nothing to do with marketing. Only a comparatively few social scientists make any attempt to align themselves with the field of marketing or see their work as in any way of potential use in a marketing application. Many appear to make great efforts to disassociate themselves from the field. Engineering is perhaps the most difficult field to relate to marketing from the R & D investment and utilization point of view. Management science, computer science, operations research, and engineering in general are obviously important to marketing R & D, but the distinction between "social" engineering and "physical" engineering, from a national resource accounting perspective, has not been made.

A third reason for the lack of good data by which to assess the investment in marketing R & D is merely the lack of incentive for investing in such studies at the national level. No vested interest group lobbies for marketing research at the federal level, nor does the federal government invest to any significant degree in basic or applied research in the field.[2] In contrast, multibillion dollar investments are made in science and technology R & D, particularly in connection with national defense, and there is a correspondingly high interest in accounting for these types of investments.

Marketing R & D is nevertheless an important national resource about which much more needs to be known. In this chapter we present a national accounting viewpoint that constitutes a new perspective on the entire field of marketing and marketing research. To study the system at anything like the level at which science and engineering (or what we will call "production R & D") is now studied would require significant funding. The chapter thus does not report precise investment and national accounting information because the data at this point do not appear to exist. Rather, it offers some perspectives on the system and provides some judgmental estimates of investments in its private-sector aspects only. We trade off elaborate specification for what appears to be needed—a new perspective on how to think about marketing and marketing research. From a national accounting viewpoint, we are quite confident that no one knows what the investment in marketing R & D really is. In this chapter we offer some useful concepts on which potential studies of the system could be based.

We begin by discussing the meaning of research and development and the origins of the term *marketing's research and development system*. Basically, we assume that at least *two* broad types of national research and development systems are operating in the United States, one serving production and one serving marketing. National accounting is currently done on the former but not on the latter. It is from the examination of national accounts of production's R & D, particularly from studies conducted by the National Science Foundation, that many of the ideas on marketing's R & D presented here evolved. Much of the discussion is comparative in the sense of looking at basic similarities and differences in these two types of systems. Three central propositions motivate the organization and structure of the chapter:

1. Analogous to a national system of research and development for production, there is a national system of research and development for marketing, which is not now formally recognized, monitored, or researched in any systematic way.
2. Marketing's R & D system in many ways parallels production's R & D system, but it differs in at least two important respects: (a) it is much smaller, and (b) it rests on a different set of scientific disciplines.
3. Marketing's R & D system is a national resource about which not much is known and that needs to be better understood by government, industry, and education.

Much of the chapter elaborates on these basic propositions. Later sections discuss some aspects of the overall system. This discussion is followed by sections on marketing research and development in the industrial and other sectors and on alternative ways to think about marketing knowledge and knowledge development activities within the context of the system. We discuss the objectives of knowledge development in marketing, the various types of knowledge, and the different kinds of research that appear to characterize the system.

The views expressed in this chapter evolved by extrapolation from the current federal model of R & D to the field of marketing. This approach has two advantages. First, the model provides a rigorous definitional base for specifying various components of marketing's R & D system. The goal is operational definitions—ones that could be used in studying the system from a national investment point of view. Second, the approach provides an opportunity to present precise figures on something that we know much about and compare them with gross estimates of something we know little about. The national system of production-related R & D is the comparison point for examining various aspects of the national system of marketing R & D. Each rests on a multisector view of resource allocation, and this provides the basic departure point for specifying the full complexity of the marketing system.

The chapter also serves to introduce Chapter 5, which focuses on the ways in which some aspects of the overall marketing system appear to work or not work. Chapter 5 attempts to explain the process of knowledge creation and utilization in marketing. In the present chapter we try to map out a national accounting perspective on the system itself.

PERSPECTIVES ON RESEARCH
AND DEVELOPMENT

The following two definitions are currently used to classify research and development expenditures from the perspectives of national accounting. The first was developed by the National Science Foundation in conjunction with its annual studies of R & D in the United States. The second is used by the Financial Accounting Review Standards Board (FASB).

Research and development—Basic and applied research in the sciences and engineering and the design and development of prototypes and processes. This definition excludes *quality control, routine product testing, market research, sales promotion, sales service, research in the social sciences or psychology* and other nontechnical activities or technical services.[3]

R & D expenses are those costs for all activities that lead to new technical knowledge as well as to the development of new products and processes. It *excludes:* (1) research performed under contract for others, such as the federal government, (2) *all market research,* (3) follow-on engineering cost and "normal" product improvement and quality control, *including product testing,* and (4) virtually all expenses associated with computer programming, whether the programming is by the manufacturer in support of its products, or by computer users.[4]

Notice that each definition explicitly *excludes* any expenditures connected with marketing activities or marketing research. At the federal level, no agency at this point appears to systematically record, monitor, or study investments in the excluded categories, and formal analysis of R & D trends, manpower resource allocation, sector investments, and so on, is done only on the *included* portions of the definition. We adopt throughout the chapter the concepts of "production R & D" and "marketing R & D," where the former refers to activity in the included portion and the latter to marketing-related activity in the excluded portion of these definitions.

Neither concept is particularly good, and the reader need only reflect briefly on the various meanings of "product" or "production" research to understand why. We want, however, to recognize at least two broad classes of national R & D, one associated with production activities and the other with marketing activities. The distinction is not without precedent in marketing literature. Ferber,[5] for example, in 1949 recognized something analogous to the two concepts in a classic book on the subject of market research. Actually, five ideas set down in the introduction to Ferber's book are germane to the contents of this chapter. First, a distinction is made between production research and market research. The basic arguments were as follows:

The efficient operation of the production processes is necessarily based on *production* research. The reason for this is that any particular product may be produced by a number of alternative methods and, usually, in a number of different shapes or forms. It is only through continual experimentation and through scientific and laboratory research that the most efficient production methods may be established. Production research is also responsible for the development of new and better products. Today (1949), the indispensability of production research is universally recognized, and few producers of any significant size are without such research.

Just as the efficiency of production is dependent upon production research, so the efficiency of marketing is dependent on *market research*. By market research is meant, broadly, the development of the most efficient means of marketing and, as in production research, the discovery of new and better methods of marketing—more economical means of distribution, new markets, better means of selling, and other marketing aids.[6]

Second, estimates of the relative investments in production research and market research were reported in the book as follows:

In 1936, American industry spent 200 million dollars on production research but only 3 million dollars on market research. . . . Eight years later, in 1944, the annual sum spent on market research had risen to about 12 million dollars.[7]

Third, the objectives or purposes of market research were alluded to in phrases such as "improving the efficiency of marketing," "the development of the most efficient means of marketing," and "the discovery of new and better methods of marketing . . . more economical means of distribution, new markets, better means of selling, and other marketing aids.''[8] We discuss this subject at greater length in the closing sections of the chapter.

Fourth, Ferber acknowledged the discrepancy in the amount of investment in market research relative to marketing costs as compared with the amount of investment in production research relative to production costs. He observed that ''over 50 cents of the consumer's dollar was (and is) estimated to have been spent on marketing costs,''[9] whereas the comparative research expenditures in each are far from equal.

A fifth and final point relevant here is his cautiously worded prediction (made in 1949): ''In due time it is entirely probable that market research will be conducted by American industry on a scale commensurate with production research.''[10] One interpretation of this assertion is that industrial investments in production research and market research would eventually approach the same level.

Today, thirty-odd years later, this has not happened. Although, as we have noted in earlier chapters, there has been an explosive growth in marketing research, particularly during the past two decades, the investment in production research as an industrial, academic, or governmental exterprise still far outweighs the investment in marketing research. What is equally important is that we know in great detail, and with great accuracy, the national investment in production research but know very little about the national investment in marketing research. Few subjects are better researched in this country than production-related R & D, and few subjects are worse researched than marketing-related R & D. For example, none of the thirty-odd textbooks on marketing research written since 1949 attempts to look at the whole system of marketing research and development from a national-level accounting viewpoint.[11] Most treat the subject as applied research, acknowledging in most cases that ''basic research'' is done in marketing but making no attempt to map out or analyze the larger system that this implies.

The excellent series of studies by the Census Bureau for the National Science Foundation on production R & D provide a very useful departure point for understanding marketing's R & D system. There is a significant parallelism of perspective, and the definitions and methods of data collection, data analysis, and data presentation provide a model to which marketing should aspire. For example, the annual *Research and Development in Industry* reports, published in the Surveys of Science Resources Series, are usually about one hundred pages long and contain numerous tables, charts, and graphs on funds expenditures, sources of support, manpower utilization, type of science, type of research (whether basic or applied), and numerous other analyses. The data are collected by the Bureau of the Census via a mail questionnaire sent to companies. The census is not complete, but all manufacturing companies with 1000 employees or more are included with certainty, and smaller companies by rates depending upon industry and employment size. Nonmanufacturing companies are also included on a selected basis. About 8000 manufacturing and nonmanufacturing companies, for example, were included in the 1971–1975 sample.[12]

The definitions of basic research, applied research, and development used in these NSF-sponsored R & D studies are germane to the field of marketing and marketing research:

Basic Research—Original investigations for the advancement of scientific knowledge not having specific commercial objectives, although such investigations may be in fields of present or potential interest to the reporting company.

Applied Research—Investigations directed to the discovery of new scientific knowledge having specific commercial objectives with respect to products or processes. This definition differs from that of basic research chiefly in terms of the objectives of the reporting company.

Development—Technical activities of a non-routine nature concerned with translating research findings or other scientific knowledge into products and processes. Does not include routine technical services to customers or other activities excluded from the above definition of research and development.[13]

One can conceive of parallel definitions for marketing, although we know of no agency that currently attempts to *assess* marketing from this point of view. The first two definitions probably would need no major changes. We do, however, provide some elaborations of each at the end of the chapter. The third—and the question of what exactly is *development* in marketing—has, to our knowledge, not been specified, and the concept has not found its way into marketing research textbooks. There is certainly no information available on how much of the nation's resources go into marketing research "development." By comparison, we know rather precisely what the nation invests in all categories of production R & D in any given year. In 1975, for example, $702 million went into basic research, $4.4 billion went into applied research, and the vast majority of dollars, $18.4 billion, went into development.[14]

To this point we have been using the concept of development as essentially referring to "knowledge development" activities. This is not the meaning inherent in the NSF definition, which emphasizes the *translating* function—translating research findings or other scientific knowledge into products and processes. It is not difficult to conceive of similar functions in marketing, and indeed much of the work of marketing academics might well be considered inherently "development" work in terms of its purpose and objectives.

A parallel definition of development in marketing might be: "technical activities of a non-routine nature concerned with translating research findings or other scientific knowledge into concepts, methods, and decision aids useful forr planning, control, and decision-making."[15] At this pont there is, to our knowledge, no use of such a definition for national accounting purposes, and there are no systematic studies that would allow estimates of how much of the nation's resources go into basic research, applied research, and development in marketing. What is known is that about 3%, 19% and 78% of all production-related R & D went into basic, applied, and development activities, respectively. About all we are confident of is that these figures are *not* very appropriate for marketing, particularly in the academic sector. If social scientists are considered to be doing "basic" research, and marketing professors either "applied" research or "development," there is little question that, in terms of either numbers of scientists or research funding, the former group by far dominates the latter.

Other problems would face the investigator interested in assessing the national investment in marketing's R & D. Suppose we modify the NSF definition to define marketing R & D as follows:

Marketing Research and Development—Basic and applied research in the sciences and engineering and the design and development of information systems, theories, models, and decision aids for marketing and corporatewide planning, decision-making, and control functions. The definition excludes basic, applied, and development activity pertaining to production-related research and development activities.

The obvious problem is to decide where investments in activities such as "product testing" and "product development" belong. In the case of the development of a new missile system, one might argue that such expenditures are not part of marketing research. For a new toothpaste, on the other hand, and for hundreds of other products[16] marketing textbooks now consider "product development" as part of marketing. The definition above avoids the issue by excluding references to product development. Many people would consider research expenditures now accounted for as production research to be marketing research. In the estimates presented later in the chapter concerning marketing R & D in the industrial sector, we adopt an operational definition: marketing R & D is what the marketing research department and related supporting institutions do, and production R & D is what the research and development department and its related supporting institutions do. Similarly, concerning the scientific base for each kind of system, we adopt the generalization that marketing R & D tends to rest on new knowledge development in the social and allied sciences, and production R & D on new knowledge development in the physical, biological, and allied sciences. Engineering can be considered applicable to both, but it should be distinguished in terms of different forms of engineering. "Social" engineering is an appropriate subject for marketing R & D, and "physical" engineering an appropriate subject for production R & D.

Marketing research textbook definitions of marketing research do not define the terms "marketing research and development" or "marketing's R & D system."[17] Definitionally, marketing research is considered to be *applied* research, whose general purpose is the identification and solution of marketing problems. Chart 4-1 lists twelve definitions drawn from books published over the last twenty-five years. Although there are differences of wording and emphasis,

CHART 4-1

Definitions of marketing research

The study of all problems relating to the transfer and sale of goods and services between producer and consumer, involving relationships and adjustments between production and consumption, preparation of commodities for sale, their physical distribution, wholesale and retail merchandising and financial problems concerned.[a]

Marketing and distribution research is the use of scientific method in the solution of marketing or distribution problems for the purpose of increasing sales, decreasing marketing and distribution costs, and maximizing profits.[b]

Marketing research is the gathering, recording, and analyzing of all facts about problems relating to the transfer and sale of goods and services from producer to consumer.[c]

Marketing research describes, explains, evaluates, and predicts what people do, think, feel, and want when they acquire or distribute goods and when they prepare for and follow up these activities; and it serves as a basis for making marketing decisions.[d]

Marketing research is a cost incurring activity whose output is information of potential value for management decisions. [and] Marketing research is the systematic and objective search for and analysis of information relevant to the identification and solution of any problem in the field of marketing.[e]

A distinction should be made between *research* and other sources of marketing information. The term "research," properly speaking, denotes formalized procedures, based on the principles of scientific method and especially on statistical techniques, for collecting and analyzing information. . . . Research should be viewed as *part* of a company's marketing information system, not the whole of it or as something distinct and separate from the other elements of the system.

Marketing research involves the diagnosis of information needs and the selection of relevant inter-related variables about which valid and reliable information is gathered, recorded, and analyzed.[g]

Marketing management is the process of making decisions with respect to marketing problems. . . . Marketing research is a formalized means of obtaining information to be used in making marketing decisions.[h]

Marketing research is used to assist the marketing manager to make better decisions within any (either the controllable or noncontrollable) domains of the manager's responsibility. . . . An alternative way of viewing the types of marketing intelligence provided by the research function is by the managerial use to which the information is put after it is gathered. Some marketing research is employed for planning, some for problem solving, and some for control.[i]

Research is the process of generating useful information. All the activities involved in planning the strategy to secure information, collecting data from various sources, processing and analyzing this data, and transmitting the resulting information to the appropriate decision makers are a part of research. . . . If the questions of interest are theoretical in nature the investigation may be called *basic research*. When the questions relate to a concrete managerial decision within some institution the investigation is called *applied research*. Applied research is of most concern to the marketing manager and is the topic of concern here.[j]

CHART 4-1 (continued)

Marketing research [is] the systematic and objective approach to the development and provision of information for the marketing management decision-making process. Marketing research studies can be classified as being basic or applied in nature. *Basic* (pure or fundamental) *research* seeks to extend the boundaries of knowledge regarding some aspect of the marketing system. There is little concern with how this knowledge can be used in the marketing management process. In contrast, *applied research* studies or investigations are concerned with assisting managers in making better decisions. . . . This textbook is primarily concerned with applied research.[k]

Marketing research is the collection, processing, and analysis of information on topics relevant to marketing. It begins with problem definition and ends with a report and action recommendations . . . Set in a business environment, marketing research is practically oriented . . . Yet in juxtaposition with this pragmatic framework is the connotation of research—scientific, scholarly, logical pursuit of truth . . . this juxtaposition leads to perpetual conflict between the demands of expediency and truth seeking . . . Marketing research and analysis is something of a hodgepodge of different approaches and heritages.[1]

---

[a] U.S. Department of Commerce, *Market Research Agencies* (Washington, D.C.: U.S. Government Printing Office, 1932).

[b] Lyndon O. Brown, *Marketing and Distribution Research,* 3rd ed. (New York: Ronald Press, 1955), p. 5. Copyright © (1955, John Wiley and Sons, Inc.). Reprinted by permission of John Wiley & Sons, Inc.

[c] Harper W. Boyd, Jr., and Ralph Westfall, *Marketing Research: Text and Cases* (Homewood, Ill.: Richard D. Irwin, 1956), p. 4. This definition was proposed by the Definitions Committee of the American Marketing Association and reported in the *Journal of Marketing,* 12 (October 1948), p. 210.

[d] Fred T. Schreier, *Modern Marketing Research: A Behavioral Science Approach* (Belmont, Calif.: Wadsworth, 1963), p. 8.

[e] Paul E. Green and Donald S. Tull, *Research for Marketing Decisions* (Englewood Cliffs, N.J.: Prentice-Hall, 1966), pp. 2, 32.

[f] Robert D. Buzzell, Donald F. Cox, and Rex V. Brown, *Marketing Research and Information Systems: Text and Cases* (New York: McGraw-Hill, 1969), pp. 15–16.

[g] Gerald Zaltman and Philip C. Burger, *Marketing Research: Fundamentals and Dynamics* (Hinsdale, Ill.: Dryden Press, 1975), p. 3.

[h] Donald S. Tull and Del I. Hawkins, *Marketing Research: Meaning, Measurement, and Method* (New York: Macmillan Publishing Co., Inc. © 1976), pp. 2–3.

[i] Gilbert A. Churchill, Jr., *Marketing Research: Methodological Foundations.* Copyright © 1976 by The Dryden Press, a division of Holt, Rinehart and Winston. Reprinted by permission of Holt, Rinehart and Winston.

[j] Danny N. Bellenger and Barnett A. Greenberg, *Marketing Research: A Management Information Approach* (Homewood, Ill.; Richard D. Irwin, 1978), p. 85. © 1978 by Richard D. Irwin, Inc.

[k] Thomas C. Kinnear and James R. Taylor, *Marketing Research: An Applied Approach* (New York: McGraw-Hill, 1979), pp. 20–21.

[l] Donald R. Lehmann, *Market Research and Analysis* (Homewood, Ill.: Richard D. Irwin, 1979), pp. 3–4.

predominantly the subject is treated as an applied science, applicable to problem identification and problem solving in industrial marketing contexts.[18] Most recent texts are built around some conception of the "research process"; the content of each, focusing on methods of data collection and data analysis, follows accordingly. None to date takes a macro national accounting view or provides a thorough and systematic analysis of what we are calling marketing R & D.[19]

AN OVERVIEW OF MARKETING'S R & D SYSTEM

The system of marketing research and development that serves marketing management and the profession of marketing in general is currently characterized by diversity, specialization, and change. All these factors make it difficult to capture the full scope of the system and to provide systematic analysis of its workings, the roles that organizations and people play, and its overall effectiveness. The system is diverse in terms of the different types of organizations that use and supply information. It is diverse also in terms of the people who engage in marketing research and in terms of their talents and training. There is, for example, currently no university degree program that awards a degree in "marketing research," nor is there any kind of university-based formal certification or licensing program analogous to the professions of accounting, law, or medicine. Marketing researcher training can vary from business MBA or Ph.D. degrees through all kinds of basic social science degrees or to degrees in the physical, engineering, computer, biological, and other sciences. In sum, many different kinds of people can be found whose career commitments and work activities are labeled "marketing research." A common characteristic is, however, that the majority in positions of responsibility have had graduate university training, and a significantly large number of them hold master's or doctoral degrees in business, economics, or one of the behavioral sciences.

There is diversity in the types of methodologies used in marketing research and in the organization of the marketing research function from one corporation to the next. All kinds of data-collection and data-analysis procedures can be found to be associated with marketing research and the "R & D" system involved. Organizations in every sector differ in terms of both the amount of resources invested and the way the activity is organized. In some, for example, marketing research is close to the top in the organization and plays a vital role in overall planning and decision making. In others it has a lower-level position servicing a particular department or group, and in many organizations there is no such thing as a formal marketing research department.

Specialization is another characterization of marketing's research and development system. As the riskiness of decision-making grows and more funds are invested in the research process, and as research projects grow in size and complexity, so do the needs and opportunities for specialization. There are specialists in sampling, forecasting, survey research, physiological methods, computers, and dozens of other areas. Such specialization sets up barriers to communication and information flows.

Finally, the system is characterized by change. It is dynamic in many important respects, particularly regarding the use of computing and mass-communication technologies. Advances in either of these tend to result in corresponding advances in marketing research and knowledge development. In sum, the system of marketing research and development is still young and changing, susceptible to methodological fads, and involves much that is difficult to specify in terms of hard facts and objective data.

What is the national scope of this system? Where does marketing research and development get done from the viewpoint of the nation as a whole? Who are the users and suppliers of marketing research and development? In answering these questions, we adopt the four-sector view of the economy used by the National Science Foundation and other government agencies in the analysis of production R & D. Marketing research and development is done in the industrial sector, the government sector, the nonprofit-organization sector, and the university-college or academic sector.[20] Figure 4-1 is a schematic diagram of the four sectors. The sectors are interconnected, and funds, knowledge, communications, and people flow among them.

At this level of abstraction, it is possible to see that organizations within each sector can be considered as either "users" or "suppliers" of research. If one adopts a broadened view of the marketing concept,[21] then the successful management of *any* organization requires investment in some form of marketing research. A university, for example, does marketing research in terms of alumni fund-raising activities or to forecast student enrollments. A government agency, such as the Department of Motor Vehicles at the state level, does marketing research to develop, for example, driver rehabilitation programs. It is not only corporations in the industrial sector that are users of marketing research, although the investment in the industrial sector probably far exceeds that in any other.

From the perspective of supplying research, it is also possible to argue that organizations in each sector are, in effect, suppliers of marketing research and development. This concept is most clearly defined and readily understandable in the industrial sector, where commercial marketing research firms specialize in supplying research to manufacturing, retailing, and other corporations in that sector. Much that we know about funds flows and marketing's R & D system is confined to this sector and to the idea of *manager users* and *research suppliers*. But, from the national perspective, research information is also "supplied" by government organizations in the form of national census data and other statistics, by nonprofit organizations such as the Marketing Science Institute, and by basic and applied research done in the academic sector. Even a

FIGURE 4-1

THE FOUR SECTORS INVOLVED IN MARKETING'S RESEARCH AND DEVELOPMENT SYSTEM

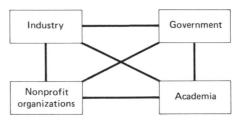

TABLE 4-1

PRODUCTION RESEARCH AND DEVELOPMENT EXPENDITURES IN THE
UNITED STATES, 1975

Sector		$ Billions	Percent
Industrial sector		$23.5	67%
Federal government supplied	$8.8 b.		
Company supplied	$14.8 b.		
University laboratories		3.4	10
Federally funded research and development centers		.7	2
Other noncommercial research		7.4	21
Total U.S. production R & D expenditures		$35.0	100%

Source: Adapted from *Research and Development in Industry, 1975,* Surveys of Science Resources Series, National Science Foundation, NSF 77-324 (Washington, D.C. 20402: Supt. of Documents, U.S. Government Printing Office).

supposedly "user" firm in the industrial sector such as General Foods Corporation can also be considered a supplier in the sense that researchers associated with the firm publish and make presentations at national conferences, and so on. It is in this sense of suppliers and users that all four sectors are connected and that the analysis of funds flows, communication, and research and development generally can proceed.

Little is known about the nature of marketing's R & D system or the investments associated with it. Research studies have not been done to supply the answers. The situation with respect to production research and development is quite different. On the production side, we not only have the answers but have them with a high level of precision and accuracy. For example, Table 4-1 shows the sector breakdown of production-related R & D for 1975 as given in one of the annual reports of the National Science Foundation. Of the $35 billion spent on this form of R & D in 1975, the largest share, $23.5 billion or 67%, was spent by corporations in the industrial sector (note that the federal government supplied $8.8 billion of this amount). The balance, $12.5 billion or 33%, represents the share of investments by other sectors. University laboratories absorbed $3.4 billion (10%), other organizations in the nonprofit sector $7.4 billion (21%), and federally funded research and development centers (FFRDC's) $700 million (2%).[22]

A great many other answers about the nature of production R & D in the United States can be derived from these reports. Below we provide a representative sampling of ten interesting questions and the appropriate answers in each case.[23]

1. How much was invested in basic research, applied research, and development in 1975?

Of the total of $23.5 billion invested by the industrial sector, $702 million went for basic research, $4.4 billion for applied research, and $18.4 billion for development.

2. What federal agencies supply most of the funds to the industrial sector for R & D investments?

Of the $8.8 billion contributed by the federal government, $5.9 billion came from the Department of Defense, $1.4 billion from NASA, and $1.5 billion from all other agencies, particularly the Energy Research and Development Administration, the Department of Health, Education, and Welfare, and the National Science Foundation.

3. Which industries invest most in production R & D?

The electrical equipment industry, the chemical industry, and the machinery industry were the leaders in 1975. Two industries, aircraft/missiles and electrical equipment, received the major share (about 80%) of federal support funding.

4. How is the basic research investment broken down by scientific field?

Of the $702 million spent by industry on basic research, chemistry and engineering received the bulk of the funds (53%), biology and life sciences were second (18%), other physical sciences received 15%, environmental sciences 2%, and all other sciences 10%.

5. How many scientists and engineers are employed in production-related R & D?

In 1975 approximately 1,562,000 scientists and engineers were employed in the United States, 1,031,000 of them in industry. Of these, 361,600 were identified by NSF as being employed in R & D.

6. Of the industrial investment, how much was contracted to outside organizations—universities and colleges, nonprofit institutions, and other companies?

Industry reported that $310 million (a relatively small amount of the total) was contracted to these types of outside organizations.

7. What is the ratio of R & D professionals to total employment for all industries?

In 1975 the answer was 27. There is great variability over industry, and data are available for each industry.

8. What percent of sales by manufacturing companies is spent on R & D?

The overall average was 3.1% of net sales, which, in 1975, represented a slight increase from the previous year (3.0%) but a decrease from the 1964 peak of 4.6%. The company portion of the investment amounted to an overall average of 1.9% in both 1974 and 1975.

9. What is the impact of company size on the amount of R & D investment?

Although an estimated 11,000 firms perform R & D in the United States, a relatively small number undertake the majority of the effort. The 116 R & D-performing companies with employment greater than 25,000 accounted for 73% of total investment. Forty companies reported R & D budgets in excess of $100 million in 1975. Four of the companies accounted for 6% of total net sales of manufacturing firms and 7% of the total employment.

10. Which state does the major share of overall R & D?
The answer in 1975 was California (21%). New York, Michigan, Pennsylvania, New Jersey, Ohio, Massachusetts, and Illinois followed with 10%, 8%, 7%, 7%, 5%, 4%, and 4%, respectively. All other states accounted for 34% of total spending.

Dozens of other similar questions could be answered. Since the surveys have been done annually since 1953, numerous kinds of trend analyses are possible. For example, total R & D spending by industry increased from about $4 billion in 1953 to $23.5 billion in 1975. The federal government share of this amount began to decline in about 1965, resulting in a flattening out of overall R & D investments in the 1965–1975 decade, when measured in constant dollars. The point is that virtually anything one would want to ask about the national investment in production R & D is now answerable from these types of NSF reports.

Similar questions concerning marketing R & D cannot be answered, because the necessary studies from which the answers would be derived have not been done. We have not even found conceptual articles that explicitly attempt to map out the nature and scope of marketing R & D from this national accounting perspective. The well-known Surveys of Marketing Research conducted periodically by the American Marketing Association under the direction of Professor Dik W Twedt,[24] for example, do not attempt to document the extent of government, academic, or nonprofit-sector participation, nor do they attempt to isolate the relative amounts of investment in basic research, applied research, and development in marketing.

What might the overall system look like from the perspective of a large industrial manufacturer in the private sector? We know, for example, that most such companies have both an "R & D" department and a "Marketing Research" department. On the production side, the nature and scope of the system can be understood within the confines of the previously cited NSF-sponsored studies. The nature and scope of the system on the marketing side is more diverse and less well defined, but there is little question that it does exist. One possible view is presented in Figure 4-2.

The figure suggests that the corporation invests in and draws upon many external agencies and institutions for each kind of R & D effort. These resources are referred to as "production's R & D system" and "marketing's R & D system," respectively. The importance of each system to the firm will vary greatly. For an aerospace manufacturer, the marketing R & D system may be insignificant. For large retailers, financial services and communications firms, there is no significant production R & D system, at least where products refer to physical products.

Each system is represented as resting upon different branches of science. For the production system the emphasis is on the physical, biological, engineering and related sciences, whereas for the marketing system the social sciences of economics, psychology, sociology, and allied disciplines seem most important. Although the figure suggests that these sciences reside in academia, which thus is the base for each kind of system, it should be obvious that scientists of each kind of persuasion work in virtually all sectors. The idea that basic research is confined solely to the academic sector is not true on the production side and, as we will argue in connection with the concept of an "innovator research group" in marketing, is not true on the marketing side.

FIGURE 4-2

MARKETING'S RESEARCH AND DEVELOPMENT SYSTEM FROM THE CORPORATION VIEWPOINT

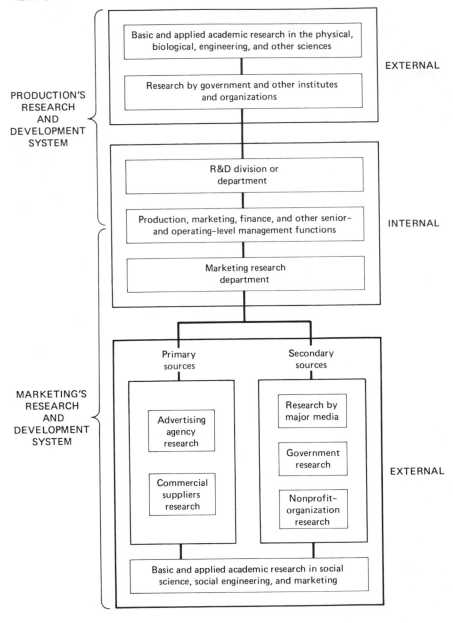

Figure 4-2 also suggests that there is an "internal" and "external" component to each system. R & D activities are conducted internally within the corporation by an R & D division or department and by a marketing research department. The diagram shows the basic external sectors on the production side as encompassing government and nonprofit organizations and the academic sector. This aspect, on the marketing side, captures some of the more important components of marketing's R & D system. In addition to the academic sector, five kinds or levels of external R & D activity can be recognized. The first two are essentially primary sources of research information from the corporation's viewpoint. By primary sources, we mean centers of research activity that conduct research specifically for a particular corporate problem or decision-making situation.[25]

As suggested in Figure 4-2, this type of research tends to be initiated at the level of the corporation's own marketing research department and to be done by that department, by outside organizations such as the advertising agencies it employs, or by commercial research suppliers it employs. It is important to recognize that both marketing and production R & D in some sense serve *all* types of managerial functions in the organization. Ferber, for example, in his book, *Market Research,* reported in 1949 on a study of 563 companies with marketing research departments and identified eleven normal functions of market research and where they were used with respect to problems and decisions in production, sales, advertising, finance, and general administration.[26]

Secondary sources are centers of research that provide data that may be germane to a problem or decision but that publish data collected for purposes other than the specific research needs at hand. In this category are research by major media (television, radio, magazines, newspapers, direct mail), by government, and nonprofit organizations. The notion of primary and secondary *data* applies to the internal aspects of corporation research as well. Sales records, for example, are often considered "secondary" data. Academic research can be considered either a primary source, in the sense of an academic consultant working with any of the three primary source levels, or secondary in the sense that much academic research is not done specifically for the research needs of a particular corporate problem.

In the sections that follow we will examine the size and nature of each of these centers of marketing research activity. At this point, Figure 4-2 is intended to convey the full scope of a corporation's marketing's research and development system. A corporation's "marketing information system" is really much broader and more complex than suggested by the usual treatment in marketing management or marketing research textbooks, and it encompasses research and development centers, external to the corporation, of many diverse types and forms. Much of the balance of the book concerns elaborations of the links among components of this system, particularly the academic sector–industry sector connections. Numerous other types of analysis could be done. For example, it should be recognized that advertising agencies and the major media, as well as corporations, have their *own* marketing research departments, and they also purchase research information from marketing research suppliers. Figure 4-3 shows the kinds of structural relationships involved in this type of subsystem, which is embedded in the overall system.

Managers (users) of research can be found at each of the institutional levels shown in Figure 4-3. For example, the brand or product manager is a user at the corporation level, the account executive is a user at the advertising agency level, and the media representative is a user at the media level. All make use of research supplier services, as well as having their own marketing research departments. The concept of "corporation" in Figure 4-3 is also completely general. The corporation could be a retailer, such as Sears, Roebuck, a consumer- or industrial-goods manufacturer, or, in the broadest sense, *any user* of mass media, such as a government or nonprofit organization. The reader should not have to dwell on these ideas very long to appreciate the numerous ways in which communications, funds, and other types of flows could be analyzed between any components in the system.

The next section addresses the question of the overall investment in industrial-sector aspects of the system. In this sector some hard data are available, and several types of studies have been done of various kinds of marketing R & D investment. The section following provides some impressions of the nature and scope of marketing R & D in other sectors.

MARKETING RESEARCH AND DEVELOPMENT IN THE INDUSTRIAL SECTOR

The Industrial-Sector Investment in Marketing R & D

This section focuses on the nature of the industrial marketing R & D subsystem shown in Figure 4-3. The general question is: How much did the industrial sector invest in marketing research and development in the year 1977? The "industrial sector" here refers to companies with marketing research departments and includes advertising agencies and media and research supplier firms. We generate an estimate of the investment using procedures explained below, and then we compare it with estimates derived from other studies of various aspects of this subsystem.

Although there have been studies of marketing research in the industrial sector, comparatively few researchers have ventured a guess as to the overall investment by this sector in marketing R & D. Ferber reported early estimates made by Coutant and LaClave[27] that in 1936 American industry had spent $3 million on market research and that by 1944 the annual investment was about $12 million. Dutka[28] reported that by 1969 the figure had reached $600 million. Our

FIGURE 4-3

AN INDUSTRIAL-SECTOR VIEW OF MARKETING'S RESEARCH AND DEVELOPMENT
SYSTEM

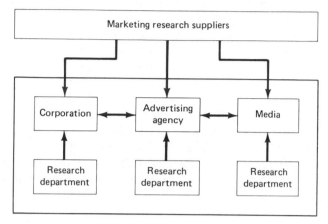

estimate is that in 1977 industry probably spent something over $1 billion on
marketing R & D. In that same year, a survey of production R & D expenditures
of industrial corporations reported an estimated $18 billion as the total.[29] The
definition of R & D used in the survey was similar to the NSF and FASB
definitions in *excluding* all marketing-related research. Based on this type of
accounting, it would appear that in 1977 marketing R & D expenditures were
about 5½% of production R & D expenditures by corporations in the private sector.

   In what follows, we present the logic behind the $1-billion-plus esti-
mate. First, it must be recognized that large firms and not small ones generally
invest in either production R & D or marketing R & D. Also, in general, it is only
manufacturers who invest heavily in production R & D. Manufacturers also
invest in marketing R & D, but so do many other industry groups such as
financial service firms, retailers, and communications firms (media), even
though nationally the investment by all such firms is much smaller. One characteristic of the marketing R & D investor/user group is that they are also heavy
"users" of mass media. Companies (manufacturers, financial service firms,
retailers, and the media) who have significant investments in marketing R & D also
make significant investments in commercial advertising. We use this fact in deriving
an estimate of the national investment in marketing R & D by the private sector.

   It is not true that all marketing research is advertising research, but there
appears to be a relatively strong association between the amount of mass-media
use and the amount of marketing R & D investment. In the United States about
17,000 companies advertise,[30] and all large firms, not just consumer-goods manufacturers, use mass media to some degree. General Motors, the nation's largest
Company in 1977, for example, was the second largest commercial advertiser.
Procter and Gamble, the largest commercial advertiser, was the nation's twentieth

119

largest company. The fourth largest advertiser was a retailer, the Sears, Roebuck Company.[31] Thus, although there is a tendency for consumer packaged-goods manufacturers to dominate the list of "top advertisers," many nondurable, industrial, service, and other types of corporations such as retailers are also heavy users of mass media.[32] The point is that we know something about the size of the advertising industry, we assume that research use tends to be associated with mass-media use, and the assumption provides a convenient base for generating estimates about marketing R & D investments.

A second assumption is that, as indicated in Figure 4-2, large corporations who invest in marketing R & D allocate some share of funding "internally" for primary and secondary research by their own research departments and allocate some share "externally." This leads to a third assumption that the principal external sources of primary research data are (1) marketing research supplier firms and (2) advertising agencies. In effect, most of the research done by these two groups is ultimately paid for by the client/user organizations. One must realize that most advertising agency research expenditures are made on behalf of their clients, and that agencies themselves are very large firms. Of the more than 4000 advertising agencies,[33] the top 583 had gross income of $2.86 billion on overall billings of $19.4 billion in 1977.[34] Three agencies in that year surpassed $1 billion in total world billings: J. Walter Thompson ($1.259), Young & Rubicam ($1.133), and McCann-Erickson ($1.084).[35]

Using these ideas and some gross assumptions about spending rates, we derived an estimate of $1.050 billion for private-sector marketing R & D investment in 1977. The size of the advertising industry in 1977, measured in terms of total media expenditures, was $38.120 billion.[36] We chose a base figure of $21.000 billion, representing the national advertising investment, as most closely associated with large advertisers. Table 4-2 shows the basic calculations involved. It was assumed that corporations, on average, invest about 5% of overall advertising expenses on marketing R & D. Compared with the 1.9% of sales spent by industrial manufacturing firms on production R & D, this works out to a much smaller rate—on average (for the top advertisers) something less than one-tenth of 1% of sales (.0008%) expended on marketing R & D.[37] This assumption generates the base figure of $1.050 billion in Table 4-2. Assuming that these expenditures are divided equally between internal and external research and that, of the external component, advertising agencies absorb about 5% and research suppliers about 95%, then $25 million and $500 million would have been spent on each source, respectively. Obviously, research represents only a small fraction of the agencies' revenues, whereas for most of the research suppliers it represents the bulk of their revenues.

In the sections to follow, we report on the results of selected industry studies and compare them with these estimates. For example, Honomichl[38] reported in a study of research supplier companies that the top twenty had 1977 revenues of $494.3 million from their research activities. Our purpose in this

TABLE 4-2

ESTIMATES OF PRIVATE-SECTOR MARKETING RESEARCH AND DEVELOPMENT
EXPENDITURES IN THE UNITED STATES, 1977

Account	$ Millions
Total investment in national media advertising [a]	$21,000
Estimate of marketing R & D expenditures [b]	1,050
Internal marketing R & D estimate [c]	525
External marketing R & D estimate [d]	525
Advertising agency research [e]	25
Commercial research suppliers [f]	500

[a] In 1977, $21,055 million was invested in national media advertising and $17,065 million in local advertising (*Advertising Age,* January 8, 1979, p. S-8).
[b] The assumption is that 5% of the advertising investment is equivalent to the total marketing R & D investment.
[c] Based on an assumption that about 50% of the marketing R & D investment is spent "internally" by the marketing research department.
[d] The external total is assumed to be accounted for by advertising agencies (5%) and commercial research suppliers (95%).
[e] Fifty-one advertising agencies accounted for $25.5 million in 1977 (see *1978 Survey of Marketing Research,* p. 28).
[f] The top twenty research suppliers accounted for $494.3 million in 1977 (see *Advertising Age,* April 24, 1978, p. 3).

exercise is to present some reasonable ballpark figure by which to think about the size of the industrial marketing R & D investment, as well as to suggest the need for a national-level accounting approach to the estimation problem. Obviously, studies of the thoroughness and scope of NSF's *Research and Development in Industry* would provide much better information.

The best currently available information on the industrial-sector investment on marketing R & D appears to be the series of studies done by the American Marketing Association under the direction of Twedt.[39] The studies focus on marketing research directors in corporations, media, and advertising agencies but not on supplier firms.[40]

Based on 1977 fiscal year spending, an estimate of $325 million is reported. We think this figure is too low to represent the "size of the industry" in 1977. It is difficult to reconcile with the Honomichl report that research revenues of the top twenty suppliers (and presumably representing only external R & D) were nearly $500 million in that year. Also, the estimate is based on only 687 (25%) of the total of 2780 marketing research directors sampled. The estimate derives from a sample rather than a census (or near census) of all possible private-sector organizations.

We nevertheless draw heavily upon these studies in elaborating various aspects of the industrial marketing R & D system in what follows. They represent the best data base at this point from which to work. Readers should be cautioned, however, that not only do these studies not represent a census, but they are based on a sampling frame drawn from the membership list of the American Marketing

Association, and this frame itself may be biased. Unlike the NSF-initiated studies referred to earlier, these do not carry the weight of the Census Bureau in eliciting investment estimates, nor are 8000 organizations sampled. Also, unlike the NSF studies, no sampling error statistics are provided and no attempt is made to estimate how much marketing R & D is either basic research, applied research, or development, or what other sector investments might be involved.

In what follows, we present some additional materials on the nature of expenditures and research activities associated with corporation marketing research departments, advertising agencies, commercial research supplier companies, and media. Subsequent sections deal with the nature of research in other levels and sectors of the overall system represented in Figure 4-2.

The Marketing Research Department

What do we know about this internal organization entity that lies within the corporation and is part of marketing's research and development system? Among all components, it is likely that most is known about this one. It has been, in many respects, the subject of two books[41] and of the aforementioned surveys sponsored by the American Marketing Association.

The AMA's 1978 survey[42] listed 545 companies (manufacturers of consumer products, publishing and broadcasting, manufacturers of industrial products, financial service firms, advertising agencies, and others) with marketing research departments, 250 of which had been formed in the preceding decade. The number of departments had grown steadily since 1922. The study also found that between 1973 and 1978 there had been a substantial increase in the proportion of marketing research budgets spent for outside services. For all but the top three job levels, compensation of research people had failed to keep up with inflation, and women in marketing research were still being paid substantially less than men.

The role of marketing research and of the research director was found to vary greatly among companies. In some, marketing research directors were senior members of the marketing or corporate management team, participating in all major policy and operating decisions, while in others they were much less influential in decision making. Also, the salary of directors of marketing research showed wide variability. The most impressive growth in formation of departments occurred in financial services companies. Of 102 such companies surveyed, 74% had formed departments within the preceding ten years.

Respondents were asked to estimate their total expenditures for marketing research for the fiscal years 1972–1973 and 1977. For the total sample, there was a 65% increase in the average marketing research budget over this four-year period. Advertising agencies' budgets increased least (29%), publishers' and broadcasters' most (84%). Consumer-goods companies outspent industrial-goods companies for every size classification. The ratio of research to sales tended to decline with increasing size; that is, larger companies spent a smaller proportion of sales on research. Also, the percent of sales or billings devoted to marketing research was usually greater for agencies and media than for manufacturers of comparable size, and agency research directors also tended to be paid more than manufacturers' research directors.

What kinds of research do corporations do? The 1973 AMA study provides a good base for considering this question. That study divided all corporate marketing research into two broad classes: (1) problem-identification research and (2) problem-solving research. Table 4-3 shows seven types of problem-identification research conducted by companies in the early 1970s. Heading the list are market-potential and market-share studies. The majority of companies, however, do all seven types of problem-identification research, and in 1973 the vast majority of each type was done by the marketing research department rather than by other departments or outside firms. Outside firms were doing a proportionately larger share as of 1978.

Problem-solving research is made up of four subtypes called product research, pricing research, advertising and sales research, and distribution research. These in turn are classifiable into fourteen additional kinds of research specific to each category. Table 4-4 shows the percentage of companies doing these kinds of research, and where it was done, as of 1973.

In 1977, thirty-two types of research were reported, organized into five categories: advertising, business economics and corporate, corporate responsibility, product, and sales and market. The basic distinctions between problem-identification and problem-solving research can still be seen in this new classification, and we will discuss them in later sections.

TABLE 4-3

PROBLEM-IDENTIFICATION RESEARCH CONDUCTED BY COMPANIES [a]

		Percentage of Studies Done by		
	Percentage of Companies Doing	Marketing Research Department	Other Departments	Outside Firms
Market potential	68	81	11	8
Market share	67	81	12	7
Market characteristics	68	84	8	8
Market analysis	65	65	32	3
Short-range forecasting	63	65	33	2
Long-range forecasting	61	64	33	3
Studies of business trends	61	71	25	4

[a] 1322 companies responded.

Source: Adapted from D. W. Twedt, *A Survey of Marketing Research* (Chicago: American Marketing Association, 1973), p. 41.

TABLE 4-4

PROBLEM-SOLVING RESEARCH CONDUCTED BY COMPANIES [a]

		Percentage of Studies Done by		
	Percentage of Companies Doing	Marketing Research Department	Other Departments	Outside Firms
Product research				
Competitive-product studies	63	75	13	12
New-product acceptance and potential	64	75	16	9
Testing existing products	57	57	32	11
Product-mix studies	44	47	35	18
Packaging research	51	67	30	3
Pricing research	56	55	42	3
Advertising and sales research				
Establishment of order quotas, territories	57	39	59	2
Studies of advertising effectiveness	49	48	13	39
Sales-compensation studies	45	24	72	4
Promotional studies of premiums, deals, etc.	39	56	30	14
Copy research	37	41	15	44
Media research	44	34	21	45
Distribution research				
Distribution-channel studies	48	57	37	6
Plant and warehouse location studies	47	37	57	6

[a]1322 companies responded.

Source: Adapted from D. W. Twedt, *A Survey of Marketing Research* (Chicago: American Marketing Association, 1973), p. 41.

The number and formation of marketing research departments is crucial to understanding the nature of marketing R & D in the industrial sector. Most departments were formed in the 1963–1973 period, but, as of 1973, less than half of consumer- and industrial-goods manufacturers with annual sales of under $50 million had research departments. Wilson[43] has described the evolution of the research department as a five-stage process: (1) the research department is new, small, and concentrates on generalized studies of market size and market structure; (2) as it grows, it tends to concern itself with more specific studies such as product development, product mix, distribution mix, or competitive response; (3) the next level sees the department involved in profitability studies, and studies attempting to evaluate the return on investment of advertising or the sales force; (4) then the department gets involved in studies of feasibility of new projects or alternative investments, and test marketing; and (5) the department attempts complex studies that span interrelated functions such as the development of an information system, long-range forcasts, and integrated inputs into planning. Many kinds of events can trigger within a company the recognition that it needs a formal research department. For example, Adler and Mayer[44] state: "Many a modest-sized firm is astonished to discover that they may be spending between $200,000 and $400,000 a year on research, without having previously even perceived that they were doing any research."

In a recent study, "B for Marketing Research Departments," Krum[45] updated his earlier studies of marketing research directors and departments. Although two-thirds of the eighty-nine departments studied had been established for at least ten years, Krum concludes that many are not yet well integrated into the marketing activities of the firm. The question is not lack of competency. Rather, criticism by users centers on the lack of creativity and initiative by marketing research people. Many research directors, on the other hand, were dissatisfied with the extent to which their departments' capabilities were being used. Problems are not always brought to the department early enough to allow for adequate research. Role conflict between researchers and their clients is cited as the root cause of this difficulty. Research directors and research users were found to have significantly different perceptions on eleven of fifty-four role-expectations items. Many users believe that researchers should remain somewhat aloof from ongoing activities. At the same time, users criticize the lack of creativity and initiative of marketing research departments and question the relevance of their work.

Let us look at an abbreviated case example of a highly centralized and successful marketing research department—that of the General Foods Corporation, headquartered in White Plains, New York. The company may not have solved all of the problems of the researcher-manager interface, but it addresses them in very imaginative ways in its marketing research organization, shown in Figure 4-4. First, we consider production R & D and marketing R & D investments by this company. In fiscal 1977–1978, the company had gross sales of $5.389 billion and marketing, general, and administrative expenses of $1.476 billion.[46] Included in these latter expenses were $293.8 million for advertising and $58.5 million for production-related R & D. The company maintains a large R & D complex called the General Foods Technical Center in Tarrytown, New York. It encompasses food sciences laboratories doing basic research on topics

FIGURE 4-4

ORGANIZATION OF THE MARKETING RESEARCH DEPARTMENT OF GENERAL FOODS

Source: *Careers in Marketing Research at General Foods,* a brochure published by General Foods Corporation, 250 North Street, White Plains, N.Y.

such as proteins, product safety, and food additives. Worldwide, about 1450 professional researchers were employed by the company in these kinds of research in 1977–1978.

Neither Security and Exchange 10-K reports nor the company's annual reports break down the marketing R & D investment. Lehmann[47] has noted that "just under 200 people" are employed by the company in connection with marketing research. One could generate estimates of the investment by using a production-R & D expense per employee figure of $40,360 on this 200-employee base to arrive at $8,072,000. Alternatively, using a 5% of advertising figure generates an estimate of $14,687,650. Using 5.5% of production R & D gives a third estimate of $3,220,000. Regardless of which figure is the more accurate, the company's annual investment in marketing R & D is considerable.

Unlike many multidivisional companies, General Foods has a centralized marketing research function; that is, marketing research is a separate corporate function rather than a part of marketing, and the emphasis is on supplying a total business service and access to top-level management. It is nevertheless structured so as to provide individualized services to the many, varied parts of GF's broad business. Figure 4-4 shows the overall organization of the department. Three different units report to the Department Director: Division Services, Functional Research, and Research Development & Technology.

In the Division Services unit, Marketing Research Managers provide the link to a specific Strategic Business Unit (SBU) and are, in effect, part of both the SBU and the MR Department. The MR Manager has primary responsibility for seeing that marketing research is brought into play whenever a program or problem of the operating unit calls for it. This unit plays the major interface role with marketing managers involved in the day-to-day operations of each SBU. The Functional Research unit conducts marketing research for all GF units and is the unit mainly responsible for hiring and overseeing the use of outside research suppliers, as well as conducting research on its own. The four areas of specialization managed by this unit are: Product Evaluation Research, Test Marketing Research, Communications Research, and Strategy Research.

The third unit, Research Development & Technology, encompasses central information services, development and application of advanced statistical and marketing models, GF's "in-house" survey operations, and quality control. Working with the Functional Research unit, it is dedicated to improving the state of the art and developing new techniques.

This example provides some insights into the organization of a well-run marketing research department, illustrates the nature of the difference in production R & D and marketing R & D, and reflects the corporation's commitment to marketing research activities. There are, of course, many other ways to organize the marketing R & D function. A good review of the alternatives is given in Adler and Mayer.[48]

Advertising Agency Research

There are about 4000 advertising agencies in the United States,[49] and the top agencies are now "billion-dollar" companies. It is naive to assume that every agency has a marketing research department, but the number that do is significant. Of 51 agencies responding to the 1978 AMA survey, for example, 35 reported having a marketing research department, and $25.5 million was invested in research. There is great variability in the commitment to research by agencies and in the make-buy decision of whether to have the research done by the agency itself or contracted out to a research supplier. Agencies do research ranging over all kinds of consumer survey studies, panels, focused groups, and many other aspects of marketing research in addition to specific copy, media, and "advertising" research. The Leo Burnett USA Company, headquartered in Chicago, has a large marketing research department and illustrates some of the scope of advertising agency research.

Leo Burnett USA with overall world billings of $795.1 million in 1977 has a staff of about 100 people working in marketing research.[50] The company is unique in having a relatively small number of clients compared with other large advertising agencies. The company does all its own creative and copy research and has been a leader in innovative new research procedures such as a program involving over-time sampling of 1000 households called CAPP (Continuous Advertising Planning Program), lifestyle analysis, and numerous others. The company owns a large research and testing center on the outskirts of Chicago, in which most of the advanced methods for measuring communication effectiveness are incorporated. A stream of leaders in the marketing research field—for example, John Maloney, Clark Leavitt, Seymour Banks, John Coulson, and Joseph Plummer—have, down through the years, been associated with Leo Burnett USA.

We will return to the theme of research leadership in Chapter 5. Our impression is that certain agencies have been particularly visible in this regard, and names such as Alvin Achenbaum, John Keane (J. Walter Thompson), Russell Haley, Shirley Young (Grey Advertising), Ted Dunn (Benton & Bowles), Lawrence Light (BBDO), Kenneth Longman (Young & Rubicam), Ruth Ziff (Doyle, Dane), and many others all attest to the significance of advertising agency research in marketing's research and development system.

Commercial Research Suppliers

Marketing research supplier companies numbered more than 500 as of 1977.[51] Studies by Honomichl provide useful insights into the nature of the leading firms in this industry. Honomichl defines a marketing research company as "a for-profit corporate identity which has as its main enterprise the development of proprietary measures in the field of marketing, public attitudes, media consumption or advertising stimuli that are basically related to the sales of goods and services."[52]

Table 4-5 gives a list of the top twenty companies as of 1977. They had combined revenues of $494,300,000 from their research activities alone in that year.

Like many other aspects of marketing's R & D system, this component has not been studied rigorously in some systematic over-time national-level accounting sense. Basic questions about the structure of the industry remain to be answered. Suppliers are probably classifiable in terms of whether they specialize in servicing particular components of the system (e.g., whether consumer or industrial corporations and whether broadcast or print media, and within media, whether specializing in television, radio, newspaper, or magazine research, etc.). Another feature is whether they offer a "syndicated" service in which reports are supplied on a regular and repetitive over-time basis, or whether they

TABLE 4-5

LARGEST U.S. RESEARCH COMPANIES [a]

Rank	Organization	1977 Research Revenue (in millions)	Percent Gain (loss) Over 1976	Percent of Revenue from Outside U.S.
1	A. C. Nielsen Co.	$205.3	18%	45
2	I.M.S. International	61.9	17	60
3	Selling Areas-Marketing	40.8	20	—
4	Arbitron Co.	29.0	16	—
5	Burke Int'l. Research	23.1	24	33
6	Booze, Allen & Hamilton	17.5	47	—
7	Market Facts	17.1	19	—
8	Audits & Surveys	12.2	20	—
9	ASI Marketing Research	10.2	(5)	29
10	Marketing & Research Counselors	10.0	33	—
11	Westat Inc.	8.4	29	—
12	National Family Opinion	7.9	27	—
13	Ehrhart-Babic Associates	7.9	13	2
14	Data Development Corp.	7.7	10	—
15	NPD Research	7.3	27	—
16	Yankelovich, Skelly & White	6.9	15	—
17	Louis Harris & Associates	5.8	18	28
18	Walker Research	5.2	26	—
19	Chilton Research Services	5.1	19	—
20	U.S. Testing Co.	5.0	14	—
		$494.3	19%	

[a]Based on 1977 marketing/advertising research volume only.

Source: Jack J. Honomichl, "Research Top 20: Companies Posted 19% Gain Last Year," *Advertising Age*, April 24, 1978, p. 3. Reprinted with permission from the April 24, 1978 issue of Advertising Age. Copyright 1978 by Crain Communications, Inc.

do only "contract" research. Methodology specialization offers another possible approach. Some concentrate on focused-group interviewing, others on survey research (whether by mail, telephone, personal interview, or so-called "intercept" procedures), others on panels with either the consumer or an institution (retail or wholesale) as the analysis unit, and still others on cable television, in-theater testing, physiological laboratory techniques (pupilometrics, CONPAAD, tachistoscopes, etc.), and motivation or social-class research. The industry encompasses companies that basically work with secondary data as well, many using government statistics and sophisticated econometric techniques as the focus of the services they offer.

What is important to recognize about the diversity in these companies is that they are the commercial equivalent of the "social sciences" in an academic disciplinary sense. Just about any social science discipline (e.g., economics, psychology, sociology), from a methodological point of view, is represented by a commercial research supplier company in this industry. For example, in psychology one can find marketing research supplier firms whose methodological orientations tend to be clinical, cognitive, stimulus-response learning (behaviorism), social psychological (attitude formation and change), personality trait (inventory), mathematical, psychometric, and so on. And this phenomenon holds true with respect to many of the methodological underpinnings of economics, sociology, anthropology, and political science. From a social science viewpoint, the nation has on the one hand a set of disciplines being taught and researched at a basic level in university settings, and on the other hand a commercial equivalent in the structure and makeup of this industry. Each, we think, should be considered from a national accounting viewpoint as a part of the overall system of marketing R & D.

Media Research

Thirty-four out of forty-seven publishers and broadcasters reported in the 1978 AMA surveys had a marketing research department. A total of $17.8 million was spent on marketing R & D. In broadcasting, the bulk of this effort goes for program testing and the generation of what, for the manufacturer, is "secondary" data on basic media statistics (the bulk of audience-measurement activity, however, is done by marketing research supplier companies—A. C. Nielsen, ARBITRON, Standard Rate and Data Corporation, etc.). It should be recognized that major networks such as ABC, CBS, and NBC are themselves "advertisers" and thus have need for research on their own account. In 1977, for example, CBS, NBC, and Time, Inc. were among the nation's top 100 advertisers, spending $96.4, $26.8, and $46.0 million, respectively.[53]

Print media are heavily engaged in marketing research, mainly because of the vast quantity of statistical and other information generated by commercial firms in this sector. In other words, publishers are included here as a class of "marketing researchers," and one need only think of the hundreds of directories, fact books, and other materials generated by companies such as Dun & Bradstreet, McGraw-Hill, Thomas Publishing, Simon and Schuster, Moody's, National Register, and others to appreciate the scope of the investment involved.

We have attempted in this section to provide some insights into the "investment" in marketing R & D by the industrial-sector component of the overall system. As with any such exercise in national accounting, and especially in a case such as this where "hard" data are not available, great variability can occur in the estimates. We have argued that the $325 million estimate given in the 1978 AMA Survey of Marketing Research may be too low. Our best guess is that the 1977 investment by the industrial sector in each of these two forms was about $18 billion and $1.05 billion, respectively. Marketing R & D, in this sense, was about 5½% of production R & D.

As noted in the NSF study cited earlier, other sectors are involved in production R & D, and we proposed the analogous situation for marketing R & D. The next section provides some impressions of the nature and scope of marketing R & D in other sectors.

MARKETING RESEARCH AND DEVELOPMENT IN OTHER SECTORS

Much of the material in this section is either speculative or highly impressionistic, but it should give the reader some additional ways to think about "marketing's R & D system." Three other sectors—government, nonprofit, and academic—are reviewed. Organizations in each sector can be considered both "suppliers" and "users" of marketing research: they supply the industrial sector with vast quantities of "secondary" data, and they use marketing research in varying degrees to manage their own affairs. Some thoughts from the supplier perspective and from the user prospective are presented for each sector.

Government

Although governments at all levels, federal, state, and local, both use and supply marketing research information, the focus here is on federal government activities. The first question addressed is: Does the federal government conduct "marketing research" for purposes of managing the programs, departments, and agencies it administers? We refer here to programs generally falling under the legislative and executive branches of government, and we will be focusing on those departments and agencies in which government invests research and development funds.

One approach to answering the question is to examine the index that lists all of the statistical publications printed by all federal departments, bureaus, and agencies for a given year. It is called the *American Statistics Index,* is published by the Congressional Information Service, and is reputedly a complete record of all unclassified publications. Titles are referenced by key subject words, and one can readily find everything published on a particular topic in a given year. In 1977, 7000 titles including 800 periodicals were listed in the index. One finds that "marketing research" is not a topic into which any of the 7000 titles is placed. Neither marketing research nor marketing R & D exists as a title in the index. One might argue that the marketing concept has made no formal inroads into the management of federal government agencies as of 1977,[54] at least in terms of its publications or their classification.

Kotler has argued that "the role of marketing in the (government) agency is to establish the needs of its various publics, develop the appropriate products and services, arrange for their efficient distribution and communication, and audit the degree of satisfaction. In this way it achieves its goals as an agency."[55] Although some federal government departments and agencies may have been adopting this perspective in 1977, it does not seem reflected in the publications they produce. We will show shortly that the term *is* used in the allocation of certain kinds of R & D funds.

Rathmell[56] took on the difficult task of attempting to estimate the amount of "market-related sales" of the federal government. He identified three classes of transactions: (1) government agency transactions, (2) mixed-venture transactions, and (3) withholding transactions. The first category, for example, included over 300 possibilities identified in the United States Budget of 1973 (representing actual 1971 transactions). Such things as sales of military hardware, agricultural products, postal services, and so on were included, and his estimate was that over $21.4 billion was market-related "sales" of this kind in 1971. Mixed-venture transactions were identified as those involving agencies having a special relationship with the federal government, such as the Federal Reserve Board and the Federal Home Loan Banks. The total here was $2.9 billion. Withholding transactions were items such as the Old Age and Survivors Insurance Trust Fund and the Unemployment Trust Fund. Rathmell argued that withholdings, rather than being considered as tax, should be considered a payment for an explicit intangible good sold by the federal government and purchased by the citizen. The total in this category was over $44.8 billion, leading to his conclusion that federal government market-related "sales" revenue for 1971 amounted to some $69 billion. Rathmell did not, however, discuss whether any of these types of sales involved marketing research.

Marketing research *is* used to classify some of the total federal government spending on research and development. Table 4-6 shows the pattern of all federal R & D obligations by function through fiscal years 1969–1978.

The report from which these data are drawn begins with a statement that "More than one-half of the national R & D effort is supported with federal funds, and thus the federal government plays the major part in determining the nature of the national R & D effort and the impact of that effort on national objectives."[57] It is also important to note that the figures in Table 4-6 do not represent the total expenditures of all federal agencies and functions, but only the R & D component associated with each.

There is no "function" called marketing research or marketing R & D on this list, but the term does appear in connection with reporting R & D obligations for specific functions. For example, those of the food, fiber, and other agricultural products function are divided into "production" R & D and

TABLE 4-6

FEDERAL R & D OBLIGATIONS BY FUNCTION:[a] FISCAL YEARS 1969-1978
[DOLLARS IN MILLIONS]

Function	1969	1970	1971	1972	1973	1974	1975	1976	1977[b]	1978[b]
Total	$15,641.1	$15,340.3	$15,545.0	$16,497.8	$16,800.1	$17,414.7	$19,013.3	$20,758.6	$24,465.3	$26,316.7
National defense	8,353.7	7,976.3	8,106.1	8,897.7	8,997.9	8,974.6	9,620.9	10,346.2	11,917.0	12,906.8
Space	3,731.7	3,509.9	2,893.0	2,714.3	2,601.3	2,477.6	2,511.3	2,863.2	2,972.4	3,140.0
Energy development and conversion[c]	327.9	317.3	323.6	382.7	441.6	605.1	1,109.7	1,387.6	2,390.4	2,797.7
Health	1,126.8	1,125.8	1,338.0	1,588.8	1,624.3	2,096.4	2,176.9	2,365.5	2,622.2	2,682.6
Environment	315.2	354.1	464.6	533.3	651.5	693.0	837.1	899.4	1,100.7	1,098.3
Science and technology base	513.4	524.6	523.8	601.2	604.7	694.6	781.6	839.2	952.6	1,059.9
Transportation and communications	458.1	590.2	778.7	614.6	630.1	702.9	640.5	635.7	768.8	804.8
Natural resources	201.0	237.5	326.0	354.0	341.0	340.8	444.6	488.8	546.9	609.8
Food, fiber, and other agricultural products	225.0	240.6	246.9	290.7	296.9	291.0	348.5	388.3	444.0	488.3
Education	154.8	146.6	186.1	190.7	214.2	173.5	149.1	142.4	283.8	269.2
Income security and social services	96.7	105.6	127.8	125.2	157.2	133.8	148.5	133.4	155.9	148.0
Area and community development, housing, and public services	49.4	91.1	88.7	87.4	96.7	96.4	101.8	104.2	110.5	99.2
Economic growth and productivity	55.8	80.0	98.9	62.8	75.1	71.9	67.1	83.9	98.1	96.8
International cooperation and development	26.8	32.2	32.3	29.5	32.9	26.7	29.8	44.5	53.3	70.8
Crime prevention and control	4.8	8.6	10.3	25.0	34.8	36.3	45.9	36.3	48.9	44.4

[a]R & D plant excluded.
[b]Estimates based on the President's 1978 budget to Congress.
[c]The inclusion of R & D plant obligations for energy would add $266.7 million in 1976, $508.9 million in 1977, and $522.4 million in 1978.
Source: National Science Foundation. *An Analysis of Federal R & D Funding by Function, Fiscal Years 1969-1978* (NSF 77-326). (Washington, D.C. 20402: Supt. of Documents, U.S. Government Printing Office).

"marketing and distribution" R & D. In 1977, for example, of the total of $444 million of R & D obligations for this function, 81.2% went for production R & D and 18.3% for marketing and distribution R & D. Two agencies, the Agricultural Research Service and the U.S. Department of Agriculture, received all of the marketing and distribution research funds. The categories of marketing obligations were marketing efficiency, expansion of agricultural exports, consumer services, economic research service, and farmer cooperative service. Marketing research associated with this function, to a considerable extent, means "distribution research," and over $81 million was obligated to it by the federal government in 1977.

The term "marketing research" appears once more in this extensive report of federal R & D obligations. For the function of "economic growth and productivity," which received $98.1 million in 1977, $4.1 million went to the Forest Service and the U.S. Department of Agriculture for "forest economic and marketing research." Other than these two mentions, however, the term marketing research is not used to classify any other kinds of R & D activity in which the federal government invested in these years.

If one were to pick one of the fifteen functions as most closely representing the federal government's marketing R & D, the best candidate would be the economic growth and productivity function. The bulk of the 1977 obligations of $98.1 million were earmarked for RANN and NSF for "industry and productivity research." The function includes many other department and bureau obligations that might also be broadly interpreted in this way. R & D obligations for the Bureau of the Census, Department of Commerce, Bureau of Standards, and others are included in the $98.1 million in addition to "forest economics and marketing research."

Other than these kinds of interpretations, however, we do not attempt to estimate federal government obligations for marketing research and development on its own behalf. It seems unreasonable, for example, to argue that the sum of the above agriculture and economic growth and productivity functions ($179 million—about three-fourths of 1% of the total of $23.5 billion R & D obligations in 1977) is a "good" estimate of the government's marketing R & D obligations. We thus revert to some broad impressions, as follows.

The federal government does invest in marketing R & D in several ways, among which are:

1. Distribution Research—probably the bulk of all problem-oriented or problem-solving research that could be called "marketing research," in the user sense of the term.

2. Organization Research—compilation of vast quantities of statistics on the nation's organizations in every sector of the economy. This might be called "marketing research" in the sense of government agencies as suppliers of statistical data for use in marketing management.

3. Consumer Research—in the same supplier sense with the focus on people/citizens as the research unit, e.g., population census. Also, the federal government has supplied

small amounts of funds through RANN for conducting primary research studies on consumer behavior.

4. Forecasting Research—dozens of federal agencies are involved in various kinds of forecasting, particularly in the area of economic forecasting, and increasingly in the area of social indicator-type forecasting.

5. Advertising Research—particularly in connection with military recruitment campaigns for the Department of Defense. The federal government was the nation's thirty-fourth largest advertiser in 1977, spending an estimated $116.2 million on media advertising. Also, about one-half of Advertising Council activity is done on behalf of federal government departments and agencies, but not very much advertising research is associated with these campaigns.

6. Basic Research—if basic research in the social sciences is considered the foundation of marketing knowledge, the federal government does invest in these kinds of research activity. We discuss this further in the section on education.

An interesting exercise is to estimate grossly, in categories such as Very Much, Some, and Very Little, the extent of federal research activity in each one of the types of industrial "problem-identification" and "problem-solving" research used to classify marketing research in the AMA surveys. In the problem-identification category, for example, the government obviously does a lot of short- and long-run forecasting research, but probably not very many "market-share" studies! There also seems to be a recent trend for government agencies to engage the services of commercial marketing research suppliers. Honomichl,[58] for example, reported that the 47% gain in gross revenues for the sixth largest supplier, Booz, Allen & Hamilton, from 1976 to 1977 was largely attributable to a survey for the U.S. Department of Agriculture estimated to have cost $3.8 million.

The federal government is a very significant "supplier" of secondary statistical information used in marketing research in the industrial and other sectors. One indicator of the scope of this contribution is the lists of government reference sources that can be found in any marketing research textbook. We thus consider all "governments" to be part of marketing's R & D system in the sense that marketing research is done to support their operations and manage departments and agencies, and they are suppliers of data used in marketing research activities by organizations in other sectors of the economy.

Nonprofit Organizations

Organizations in this sector can also be considered either users or suppliers of marketing research. As an example of a nonprofit organization that is to a considerable extent a supplier of "marketing research" information to the federal government, one could choose The Brookings Institution. It is an independent nonprofit organization devoted to nonpartisan research, education, and publication in economics, government, foreign policy, and the social sciences generally. Its principle purposes are to aid in the development of sound public policies and to promote public understanding of issues of national importance.[59] We cite this extreme example (few would classify this organization as a "marketing research" organization) to dramatize how far the concept of marketing can be broadened to include nonprofit organizations. Under many interpretations of the idea of marketing by nonprofit-sector organizations, The Brookings Institution would be defined as a marketing research organization supplying information to public policy decision makers. The econometric underpinnings for much of its research differ in no significant methodological respect from those for similar work done in the private sector to support policy formulation and decision making in private-sector organizations.

There is a strong interest among marketing scholars in extending the concept of marketing to the management of nonprofit organizations. Marketing is an appropriate subject for the management of such organizations if one adopts the view that "marketing is human activity directed at satisfying needs and wants through exchange processes."[60] That is, *exchange* is the fundamental characteristic of marketing. Business concerns exchange goods and services for money from customers. Service organizations, such as hospitals, exchange services for fees from patients, and so on. Every organization faces a number of "publics" whose wants and needs can be identified and for whom the managerial aspects of the organization can be adjusted accordingly.

The growing interest in this topic in marketing is reflected in the following list of books and articles published on the subject since 1969. This list represents only a sampling. As of 1977 there were about 150 nonbusiness cases, many of which focused on marketing issues, available through the Harvard Intercollegiate Case Clearing House.[61] An extensive bibliography of published articles and books is provided in the Lovelock and Weinberg volume given below.

Books

WILLIAM LAZER AND EUGENE J. KELLEY, eds., *Social Marketing* (Homewood: Ill.: Richard D. Irwin, 1973).

JAGDISH N. SHETH AND PETER L. WRIGHT, eds., *Broadening Marketing's Horizons* (Urbana, Ill.: University of Illinois, Bureau of Economic and Business Research, 1974).

PHILIP KOTLER, *Marketing for Nonprofit Organizations* (Englewood Cliffs, N.J.: Prentice-Hall, 1975).

RALPH M. GAEDEKE, ed., *Marketing in Private and Public Nonprofit Organizations* (Santa Monica, Calif.: Goodyear Publishing Company, 1977).

CHRISTOPHER H. LOVELOCK AND CHARLES B. WEINBERG, eds., *Readings in Public and Nonprofit Marketing* (Palo Alto, Calif.: The Scientific Press, 1978).

VIJAY MAHAJAN AND C. CARL PEGELS, *Systems Analysis in Health Care* (New York: Praeger, 1979).

Articles

PHILIP KOTLER AND SIDNEY J. LEVY, "Broadening the Concept of Marketing," *Journal of Marketing*, 33 (January 1969), 10–15.

JAMES M. CARMAN, "On the Universality of Marketing," Institute of Business and Economic Research, University of California, Berkeley, Calif., September 1973.

GLEN L. URBAN, "A Model for Managing a Family-Planning System," *Operations Research*, March–April 1974, 205–33.

WILLIAM L. WILKIE AND DAVID M. GARDNER, "The Role of Marketing Research in Public Policy Decision Making," *Journal of Marketing*, 38 (January 1974), 38–47.

JOHN G. MYERS, "On the Search for Management Science and Marketing in a Nonprofit Organization," a paper presented at the TIMS College on Marketing Annual Meetings, Portland, Oregon, August 1974.

MICHAEL L. ROTHSCHILD, "An Incomplete Bibliography of Works Relating to Marketing for Public Sector and Nonprofit Organizations," 2d Edition, #9-577-771 (Boston: Intercollegiate Clearing House, 1977).

CHARLES B. WEINBERG, "Building a Marketing Plan for the Performing Arts," *Association of College, University, and Community Arts Administrators Bulletin*, May 1977.

ADRIAN B. RYANS AND CHARLES B. WEINBERG, "Consumer Dynamics in Nonprofit Organizations," *Journal of Consumer Research*, 5, September 1978, 89–95.

RICHARD J. SEMENIK, "The Contribution of Marketing Research to the Arts," a paper presented to the Western Marketing Educators Conference, San Jose, Calif., April 1978.

We have not found any studies that attempt to document the degree to which nonprofit organizations (at least all those that are neither government nor educational institutions, which is our focus here[62]) have marketing research departments or some parallel organizational unit. Nor do we know much about the national investment in marketing R & D from this viewpoint. The first book on marketing research that has been explicitly positioned to encompass *both* public- and private-sector organizations is now in preparation,[63] and we anticipate that harder data will become available on the subject. For the present, we resort to some insights and impressions. First, some reflections from the "user" viewpoint.

Although the name "marketing research department" is probably not common in organizations in this sector, many nonprofit organizations, particularly large ones, probably do forecasting studies and other kinds of data-gathering and analysis activities that could be called marketing research. Religious organizations, unions, hospitals, museums, symphonies, and a large number of so-called "third-world" organizations undoubtedly do systematic work on analyzing their publics and constituencies. It is also useful to note that nonprofit organizations are heavy "users of mass media," even though the dominant pattern is to use nonpaid time and space made available by the FCC public service advertising rule in media licensing. This advertising occurs at the "national'' level through the facilities of The Advertising Council and at the ''local'' level through thousands of health, education, welfare, police, religious, and other organizations that make announcements of various kinds in local media. From a national point of view, associated with public service advertising there is a media-user system that differs from public media such as the Public Broadcasting Network and from the advertising in commercial media. Nonprofit organizations are heavy users of this system. From a research viewpoint, our impression is that very little advertising-effectiveness research gets done in connection with this system at either the national or local level.[64]

The concept that nonprofit organizations are part of marketing's R & D system in the sense of being ''suppliers'' of secondary information (see Figure 4-2) is readily understood if we examine trade and professional (nonprofit organizations) in the private sector. The following, for example, all produce ''marketing research'' information of one kind or another: American Marketing Association (AMA), American Management Association (AMA), Association of National Advertisers (ANA), American Association of Advertising Agencies (AAAA), American Advertising Federation (AAF), Advertising Research Foundation (ARF), National Association of Broadcasters (NAB), Radio Advertising Bureau (RAB), Station Representatives Association (STA), Television Bureau of Advertising (TvB), American Newspaper Publishers Association (ANPA), and Magazine Publishers Association (MPA). These are some of the largest and most important associations generating advertising and media-related information, and over one hundred such associations are involved in the communication aspects of the overall system alone. If one extends the idea to include associations connected with specific manufacturers (electronic, chemical, paper, etc.) and retailers (e.g., Supermarket Institute), the amount of marketing research data generated (and the accompanying investment) in this nonprofit aspect of the system must be considered sizeable and significant.

Two other categories in this general area are worth mentioning because of their importance to marketing R & D and the system as a whole. First are foundations such as the Ford Foundation, the Carnegie Foundation, the Markle Foundation, and the Russell Sage Foundation. Although we do not have figures that document their support for marketing R & D, some of their activity, at least, could be interpreted as such. The Ford Foundation in particular, in the early 1960s supported a significant amount of marketing research scholarship. The other category includes specialized institutes in the nonprofit sector that focus the majority of their efforts on advancing the state of marketing research and development. The best example is The Marketing Science Institute in Cambridge, Massachusetts. MSI is dedicated to advancing the science of marketing through marketing research, and it is one of the few explicit ''bridges'' with this orientation between the academic and industrial sectors. The Educational Foundation of the AAAA has, over the years, played a somewhat analogous role in funding academic and professional research in the marketing and advertising areas.

We leave to future analysts the task of putting an explicit dollar figure on the size of the national investment in the nonprofit sector of marketing's R & D system. Hopefully, our reflections will motivate some imaginative research in this direction, and the reader will at least take away the impression that the national investment in these kinds of R & D activities is sizeable and significant.

Universities and Colleges

The term "universities and colleges" is used by the National Science Foundation to document funds flows to this sector, and we adopt it here. We begin with the general proposition that organizations in this sector also are users and suppliers of marketing research. Given the Commission's focus on the interface between the academic and industrial sector, we will concentrate on the academic "supplier" concept. There is a burgeoning literature, however, on universities and colleges, and educational institutions in general, as "users" of marketing research information in the management process. As Kotler and Dubois[65] have noted, the education industry is one of the largest service industries in the United States, employing (in 1970) over three million people in over 120,000 establishments, and serving over sixty million students at an annual cost of about $74 billion (about 7% of the Gross National Product). We do not attempt to estimate the size of the national investment in marketing R & D done by universities, colleges, and other educational institutions. If one adopts the broadened view of marketing that encompasses educational institutions, then surely the vast majority of these institutions are doing some form of "marketing research" in connection with fund raising, predicting student enrollments, alumni relations, and numerous other "problem-identification" and "problem-solving" issues associated with managing the institution.[66] However, our focus is on this sector as supplier of marketing R & D to other sectors.

From this point of view, the first question addressed is: What kinds of academicians do marketing research in the academic sector? Many people would answer by identifying professors of marketing in business and management schools as the relevant group. Although these people have aligned their career commitments with the subject and are the nation's "marketing researchers" from an academic point of view, the academic system that supports marketing research involves many more people and a much larger commitment of national resources. A psychologist, for example, doing basic research on attitude change, may not view himself or herself as "doing marketing research," but from a national accounting systems viewpoint, that basic research can be the key to an important breakthrough in the marketing area. As suggested in Figure 4-2, the marketing R & D system rests to a considerable extent on the social sciences and social engineering. From a national accounting perspective, these sciences are part of marketing's R & D system. Some additional reflection may help to clarify this fundamental proposition.

As stated earlier, many scholars working in the social sciences are unenchanted with private-sector applications of their work, particularly if it has anything to do with commercial advertising. One is hard-pressed to find basic scholars in economics, psychology, or sociology who will, for example, attend and contribute to a "marketing" conference. Granted, there are a handful of such people, but they are only a tiny minority of the thousands of scientists working in these disciplines. The professional connection, if there is one, of most of these scientists is to organizations, agencies, and groups in the nonprofit sector, particularly the government sector. Advancing the knowledge base of economics, for example, often appears more motivated by the likelihood of some contribution to policy formulation or decision making in the public rather than the private sector. Explanations may lie in the fact that the public sector, particularly the federal government, is the primary source of funding for much of the basic research done in the social sciences, or perhaps the appeal is in the fundamental sociopolitical value differences involved.

We now adopt a "broadened" view of the marketing concept. If nonprofit organizations can be more effectively managed using marketing principles of sensitivity to consumer wants and needs, integrated marketing, and marketing research, then it is but a simple step to argue that the core of research (basic research) for managing the marketing aspects of such organizations rests in basic social science. Including *both* private and public organizations as potential "users" of such knowledge for more informed policies and decision making leads to a macro view of the system with these sciences as its base.

Figure 4-5 shows one possible way to view the academic sector from this broadened point of view. At the center of the diagram are typical content areas on which marketing scholarship in business and management schools tends to be focused. This activity, historically devoted solely to private-sector concerns, has now been broadened to public-sector concerns.

The system as shown encompasses basic social science disciplines and engineering sciences and applications to "social" rather than "physical" engineering problems. The facilitating sciences have been purposely arranged to highlight some typical patterns and orientations of the business/management school group. For example, marketing professors in many institutions tend to work *directly* with people in the basic supporting disciplines. This work is often very "basic" in character and can be at the "cutting edge" of that discipline in either a theoretical or methodological sense. On these grounds we later argue there is "basic research" *in* marketing, even though the vast amount of work that gets done can also be described as "applied research" or "development."

Shown in the diagram are several other kinds of sciences that are more "applied" in perspective and outlook than the basic sciences. Marketing scholars may be found whose main orientation is at this level and with one of these sciences. The American Association for Public Opinion Research (AAPOR), for example, provides the link between many marketing academics and social psychologists and sociologists working in Institutes of Mass Communications and

Survey Research centers across the nation. Ph.D. degrees are now granted in mass communications at places such as The Institute of Mass Communications at Stanford and Wisconsin, and Ph.D. degrees in advertising are now granted, for example, by the School of Advertising of the University of Illinois.

Much of the model-building and quantitative work that gets done in marketing research emanates from the engineering sciences, particularly from industrial engineering and electrical engineering. The analogous "more applied"

FIGURE 4-5

ELABORATION OF THE ACADEMIC-SECTOR COMPONENT OF MARKETING'S RESEARCH AND DEVELOPMENT SYSTEM

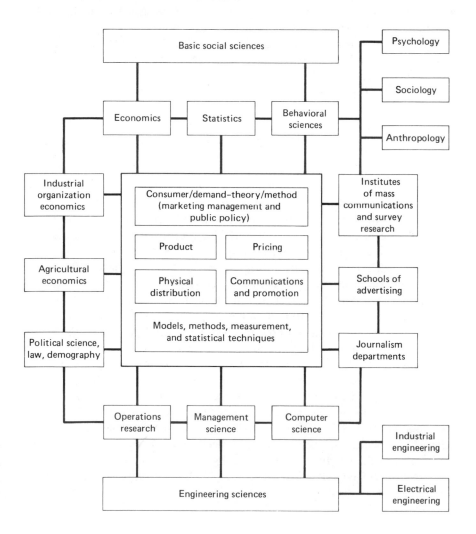

sciences here are operations research, management science, and computer science. It is interesting to note that few schools of engineering appear to departmentalize along the lines of "physical" and "social" engineering as two branches of the subject, and the physical orientation still seems to dominate the organizational structure of most engineering schools. A likely reaction from engineering schools is that "social engineering is done by people in the school of business!"

What is the national investment in this kind of system? We do not offer an overall estimate, but with some imaginative analysis of government and association statistics it could be derived. Employment of scientists in each area would probably be easier to estimate than the R & D investment. For example, we know there are about 30,000 members of the American Psychological Association, 18,000 members of the American Economic Association, and 8000 members of the American Sociological Association. In contrast, there are only about 2000 academic members of the American Marketing Association—a much smaller base of academic talent from a national accounting viewpoint. One might then attempt to estimate about how much of each pool is active in research and is contributing to the knowledge base at either the "basic," "applied," or "development" levels. In marketing, the group of active researchers is very small compared with the scope of social science or social engineering in general—probably some 500 to 800 people. The marketing professor memberships of associations such as the Association for Consumer Research and the TIMS College on Marketing would be indicators of the core of the most active academic people in marketing research. Neither is very large, and if allowance is made for joint memberships, probably only about 200 to 300 people are involved.[67]

If we assume that, say, 500 marketing professors are active in research (and thus are the major source of scholarly articles and textbooks in marketing), even this small number amounts to a significant national investment. Suppose the average annual salary plus research expenditure for an individual professor amounts to $50,000. The total annual investment would be $25 million, with perhaps as much as $5 to $10 million being accounted for by research.

Hard data do exist on how much of the federal government's R & D investment is devoted to basic research in the social sciences. Of the fifteen categories of federal R & D obligations (see Table 4-6), the appropriate statistics can be found in the "science and technology base" function. Table 4-7 shows federal obligations in various areas of basic research in the sciences in 1977. Two categories, "behavioral and neural sciences" and "social sciences," accounted for a total of about $48 million. Compared to investments in the basic physical sciences, particularly physics, these two account for a relatively small share (about 5%) of the nearly $1 billion of obligations to basic science research in 1977. All the behavioral and social science funds were funneled through NSF. Nearly half of all funds went to physics, largely in connection with national defense research.

TABLE 4-7

FEDERAL GOVERNMENT INVESTMENTS IN BASIC SCIENCE RESEARCH AND THE
SCIENCE AND TECHNOLOGY BASE ($ MILLIONS)

Type of Science	1977 Estimates	Percent
Physics (ERDA and NSF) [a]	$420.5	44%
Engineering (NSF)	41.7	4
Chemistry (NSF)	36.2	4
Mathematics (NSF)	21.2	2
Behavioral and neural science (NSF)	25.1	3
Social sciences (NSF)	22.9	2
All other sciences	385.0	40
Total science and technology base	$952.6	100%

[a]The agencies shown in parentheses are those disbursing the funds in each case.

Source: Adapted from *An Analysis of Federal R & D Funding by Function, 1969–1978,* Survey of Science Resources Series, National Science Foundation, NSF 77-326, p. 72. (Washington, D.C. 20402: Supt. of Documents, U.S. Government Printing Office).

National investment aspects of marketing's research and development system are summarized at the end of the chapter. We turn now to some fundamental ideas on what kind of knowledge is developed by this system, how, and why. Considering why knowledge is developed leads to a discussion of the objectives of knowledge development in marketing. Considering what kind of knowledge is developed leads us to discuss types of marketing knowledge and to present commissioners' views on this subject. Considering how knowledge is developed leads to an examination of the nature of "marketing research" and the various types of research associated with the system.

THE DEVELOPMENT OF MARKETING KNOWLEDGE

As we have noted, marketing knowledge is developed and used by organizations in all four sectors of the economy. The use of the term *knowledge development* throughout this section should not be confused with the formal definition of *development* in the R & D context. We focus here on basic ideas of what marketing knowledge is, on how and why it is developed, and on the research side of the R & D concept. Thus, by knowledge development we do not mean an activity separate from research; rather, we are referring to "knowledge" as the basic output of the system. The material presented is also focused largely on two sectors, industrial and academic, because these seem to be the major centers of knowledge-development activity in marketing.

A basic assumption adopted by the ERDMM Commission and reflected in its Prospectus was that the broad purpose of knowledge development in marketing should be to improve, or make more effective, marketing management. Marketing's R & D system, it can be argued, has this as its fundamental goal. Toward this goal, knowledge is used in many ways. It also exists in various states. Similarly, various kinds of research are done to bring about knowledge development. In effect, knowledge development is a "means-ends" chain; and this model was adopted as a basic departure point by the Commission. Figure 4-6 shows the three components involved.

The ends are broadly stated as *effective marketing management*. The major inputs to the accomplishment of these ends are *intervening states* or types of knowledge. The Commission recognized two broad types: context-specific and context-free; these are examined in a subsequent section. The means to the ends are various types of knowledge development: basic research, problem-oriented research, and problem-solving research. The third section examines this aspect. An important point, which guided much of the Commission's work, is that the second stage, types of knowledge, was *not* considered to be the objective of knowledge development in the field of marketing. The Commission's views on objectives are presented next.

Objectives of Knowledge Development in Marketing

From the perspectives of marketing's R & D system, the objectives of knowledge development *within* sectors can be stated in terms of the overall goals of a typical organization in each sector. Thus, for example, within the industrial sector, knowledge development should contribute to the overall goal of "con-

FIGURE 4-6

STAGES IN THE DEVELOPMENT OF MARKETING KNOWLEDGE

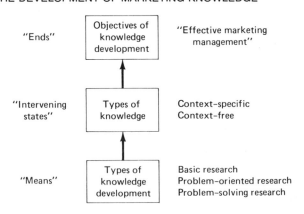

sumer satisfaction at a profit.'' For government, marketing knowledge has numerous purposes—from ''winning the next election'' to effective management of myriads of government-sponsored programs. Within the nonprofit sector a foundation, for example, needs marketing information to accomplish a goal of ''funding socially desirable research.'' In the academic sector knowledge development may help an organization achieve goals of ''creating and disseminating knowledge'' or, more simply, ''research and teaching.''

The implication is that ''marketing managers'' and, hence, users of marketing knowledge exist in some form in organizations in each of the four sectors. The main focus of the Commission, however, was on user-managers within the industrial sector. The principal objective of knowledge development in marketing, after all, should be to improve marketing management practice in this sector. Although much basic research in marketing is generated for ''its own sake,'' the Commission's view was that if marketing knowledge over the long run is to be considered ''effective,'' it should contribute something to improved decision making or other aspects of marketing management practice in the industrial sector. Earlier we cited Ferber's views on the purposes of marketing research, stated in 1949, which had an essentially parallel emphasis. He did, however, and we think rightly so, stress the potential contributions to *all* aspects of business management, and not just marketing. Marketing research can inform financial accounting, production, and numerous other aspects of business management.

The ''effective marketing manager'' criterion is nevertheless a useful point of focus. What is an effective marketing manager? More generally, what is an effective marketing organization? In answering either question, it is common to consider effectiveness in ''bottom-line'' terms of sales or profits. Successful managers are those whose work results in maximum profits or sales. These criteria, however, do not distinguish between *good judgment* and *good luck*. Marketing is a field where external factors play a key role in determining outcomes. For one thing, there is head-to-head competition, and even the best often lose. Managers should be accountable partly in terms of the *quality of decisions* as well as the sweetness or sourness of outcomes.

There was general agreement with the views of one Commissioner that a marketing manager must always make his or her decision within the constraints of a specific consumer psychological context. The context and the prevailing state of mind of the consumer determine the parameters within which the manager operates. The essence of an effective marketing manager is an ability to understand that context and to isolate the factors that will be critical *this time*.

The effective marketing manager will be able to explicate *why* he or she proposes to act in a certain way. While strong elements of uncertainty will always be present these should be identified and separated conceptually from more firmly held views based on data, coherent theory, and logical reasoning.

An inability to articulate the reasoning that led to a decision suggests muddy thinking. This in turn raises questions about the person's sensitivity to important issues, ability to learn from experience, and credibility in convincing others both up and down the management ladder who are important to a venture's success. Needless to say, articulation of one's thinking makes it easier for others to judge it; and favorable judgment provides some degree of personal insulation from the corrosive effects of unfavorable outcomes.

The first rung on the ladder of progress in a profession is a recognition that the "why" of things is important. Concern with the "what" to the exclusion of the "why" leads to the deification of assertion as a method of managerial decision making, as in extreme authoritarianism or a "cult of the personality." The "why" element represents the science in marketing. The "what" does, too, but always in juxtaposition with the "why." There is a great deal of art in marketing as well as science, but the contexts of marketing problems move too rapidly for anyone to be confident that the virtuoso of yesterday's concert will perform successfully today. An audition is required *before* each concert, and this means the examination of facts and the testing of concepts.

Progress in the practice of marketing has meant improving the ability of managers to understand why they want to take certain actions and avoid others. The *marshalling of facts* represents one kind of progress. The more that is known about a phenomenon, the better the situation for the one who must predict or attempt to influence it. The last twenty-five years have seen great improvements in the stock of "off-the-shelf" facts relevant to marketing and the resources available for seeking new facts when necessary. Facts are the raw materials for the making of decisions.

Additional progress is represented by improvements in *techniques of analysis* and the development of an array of decision rules. These techniques and rules extend the range of analysis and/or permit a faster or less expensive response to situations as they arise. They make up the kit of tools of the modern marketing practitioner.

Effective *theory* is the most important component of progress in any profession. For many workers in marketing and other applied fields the word suggests blue-sky speculation. More appropriate, however, is the vision of a hard-nosed, vigorous review of logic and evidence to determine just what can, or cannot, be said about a particular set of issues.

Good theory implies the ability to *conceptualize* problems in order to see the common factors and differences and to sort out cause and effect. Theories about attitudes and other aspects of consumer behavior are examples; so, too, are economic theories about consumer and industrial markets. The "theory" of market segmentation is another, in terms of both exploring market heterogeneity and determining effective segmentation strategies. A "theory of managerial modeling" in marketing is beginning to develop. This deals with alternative modeling approaches and the factors that enhance or inhibit their success in helping managers make decisions. Finally, the marketing concept itself exemplifies an operationally meaningful theory in marketing and the kind of influence a good theory can have. Theory tends to be context-free, hence it can provide greater leverage for managers than a long list of contingent decision rules applicable to specific situations. Effective concepts deal with "the problem"; thus they can be more powerful than decision-making techniques that deal with "how to analyze the problem." As a very experienced industry member of the commission put it, "There is nothing so practical as a good theory."

A review by another commissioner for his own firm pointed up the difficulties facing a line manager when an adequate conceptual structure is lacking:

The marketing plans being produced were not really plans but a snapshot of some data, and the setting of a few objectives, and quotas. There was little or no attempt at strategy development. Under strategy there was much talk of product "life cycle." However, further probing showed that there was no agreement on what "life cycle" really meant. A literature review to produce a workable strategy-development tool based on life cycles gave virtually no assistance. The articles simply were not operational and generalizable.

The "theory" of the product life cycle was found to be insufficient in this case, but this very finding emphasizes the importance of a sufficient theory. "Theory" has tended to be unpopular in marketing because it has gotten a reputation as something abstract and irrelevant. There *is* a lot of theory that is not well connected to the world of affairs or that simply is not very good or very important in and of itself. But the converse is true, too: a good theory or conceptual framework will help the decision maker organize his facts and direct his analysis and thus better understand "why this way this time."

Developing a set of overarching concepts about one's industry, one's customers or consumers, one's competitions, and one's resources—that is, a good set of theories—represents progress in one's job. The same holds true for a profession, including that of management: "You can't manage something you don't understand." Theory is more than the raw material or tools in a kit; it is the basic intellectual resource that guides their deployment for the solution of managerial problems.

Books have been written on the qualities of a good manager.[68] A marketing manager needs a whole bundle of qualities captured in the notion of "leader"—the capacities to motivate people, to manage efficiently substantial funds and expenditures, and to make difficult and risky decisions in an environment of great uncertainty. Increasingly, however, marketing managers must be capable of managing large amounts of complex data that can be used to reduce the uncertainty in decision making. To do so, they need to be able to recognize and conceptualize important problems and to distinguish the important from the trivial.

The modern manager, that is, must be a good planner. He or she must develop a good marketing plan in which realistic and worthwhile objectives are carefully specified, the resources marshalled to carry them out, and control mechanisms introduced to evaluate them. The manager must also be able to guide research efforts, to marshall facts and data relevant to stated objectives, and to analyze and interpret complex information. The ideal manager must be able to bridge the gaps between an original theory/model specification, the research design actually used to generate data, and the interpretation of the final data results themselves. Essentially, modern managers should display at least some of the characteristics of the scientist—a willingness to use theories, models, and concepts, a capacity to identify important problems, and a healthy respect for the value of objective information and research in seeking answers to problems. Managers need to know the "why" of their operations in the sense of a theory or model, the "what" in the sense of relevant facts and data that pertain to them, and the "how" in terms of the implications of implementation and control.

The difficulty of documenting that marketing managers were "better" at the end of the period than at the beginning should be obvious. The Commission did not attempt to test this proposition. We do know that more managers held the MBA degree, that much more marketing research information was available, that the demands for in-company information systems and information to support decisions were higher, and that there was a marked rise in the size and scale of the marketing research industry generally. The criterion of "better practice" was thus left implicit rather than explicit in the Commission's deliberations, and the focus directed to better understanding the nature of marketing knowledge and its creation and dissemination.

Types of Marketing Knowledge

Marketing knowledge essentially exists in one of three forms. First, there are written materials that extend over journal articles, books, monographs, reports, newsletters, corporate memoranda, association publications, and so forth. Second, much marketing knowledge exists in the form of computer data banks. Third, it exists as "executive experience"—the fund of wisdom extant in the minds of marketing managers.

Numerous other views have been put forward concerning the nature of marketing knowledge. For example, management science scholars often speak of four levels of model development: (1) nonverbal models—the unwritten set of hunches or decision rules that a manager uses in making many marketing decisions; (2) verbal models—the explicit spelling out of what a manager thinks will happen in a given situation (e.g., sales will increase 1% if we lower price by 5 cents); (3) logical flow models—the describing of a situation in terms of several constructs or abstractions linked together in some form of logical order or causal chain; and (4) mathematical models—the use of the power of mathematics to specify relationships, make deductions, and so on. Marketing knowledge exists in all of these forms.

Marketing knowledge may also be thought of in the context of a marketing information system. Here, knowledge is essentially reducible to three forms captured in the concepts of *model bank, statistical bank,* and *data bank.* A fourth component, a *computer terminal,* links these forms of "knowledge" and the manager-user. External information enters the system via the data bank and is subsequently processed into forms on which marketing management decisions are based.

Most marketing research textbooks speak of marketing "information" rather than marketing "knowledge." The implication is that information is what the manager seeks in problem identification or problem solving. Much attention is given to formal procedures to determine the value of information in the context of a particular marketing problem.

Marketing knowledge can be thought of as either secondary data or primary data. A formal definition of each is given below:

Secondary data are already published data collected for purposes other than the specific research needs at hand. Such data can be classified as internal or external. *Internal secondary data* are available within the organization (e.g., accounting records and sales reports), whereas *external secondary data* are provided by sources outside the organization (e.g., reports, periodicals, books). *Primary data* are collected specifically for purposes of the research needs at hand. For example, if a retailer collects data from shoppers regarding store image, the resulting data would be primary.[69]

A sociological view of marketing knowledge would emphasize the interchange among managers and staffs and the social relations and small-group behavior within and between organizations that affect and guide marketing practice and decision making. Advertising budgets, for example, are determined as much by intergroup bargaining in large corporations as they are by formal normative analysis of how much should be spent on this activity.

The Commission developed yet another view of marketing knowledge. Referring back to Figure 4-6, we can ask: What is the nature of the "intervening states" of marketing knowledge that exist between the means and ends? The Commission recognized two broad types of marketing knowledge and various subcategories of each as follows:

1. Context-specific
   a. Product/industry-specific
   b. Situation-specific
2. Context-free
   a. General facts or "laws"
   b. Theories or conceptual structures
   c. Techniques

Knowledge that is context-specific can be specific either to a particular product or industry (e.g., the automotive, industry, household detergent products), or to a particular situation (a sudden rise in energy prices, a consumer boycott, a competitor's reactions). Context-specific knowledge in marketing is usually proprietary, particularly if it is current. Probably also it is the most useful empirical evidence on which general facts and laws in marketing could eventually be based. That is, by looking for regularities across product-, industry-, or situation-specific cases, we might reach more useful and relevant generalizations in the field of marketing. There are examples of this type of work,[70] but they are comparatively rare.

Context-specific and context-free knowledge differ primarily in the degree to which the knowledge is linked to a specific marketing management problem or setting. The context-specific "fact" or "cause-effect relationship" deals with one's own industry, product, problem, or situation. If correct, it tends to fit nicely into the body of day-to-day experience. Context-specific knowledge is relevant almost by definition. In principle the importance of such knowledge can be gauged without difficulty, because it is couched in familiar context-oriented terms. It is the raw material of the managerial decision process. Many "experts" have earned the title because they know more about a particular market than most other people. While there may be questions about the quality of a particular expert, the value of expertise per se is seldom questioned.

At the other end of the spectrum is "context-free" knowledge. (Ignoring the semantic difficulty that little marketing knowledge is purely context-free, we use the term to emphasize a high degree of generalizability across companies, products, segments, and so on.) A classical type of context-free knowledge is scientific "laws." These are relationships between constructs that have been found to hold empirically true in a wide range of situations. Examples abound in the physical sciences, and there are some in the social sciences, too. An example of a general "fact" in marketing would be the advertising-to-sales ratios of Fortune 500 companies. What we know about the duration effects of advertising, and about patterns of brand loyalty and switching from stochastic brand-choice research, approaches the notion of general laws. Some other examples proposed in marketing are "Agostini's constant" in magazine audience research and Andrew Ehrenberg's general brand-switching relationships.

Unfortunately, discoveries of operationally meaningful general laws in marketing are few and far between. Most research results having a claim to such status are *so* general as to afford little leverage for the marketing manager. This is illustrated by the economic "law" that states that increases in relative price usually result in diminished demand. Finding that a particular situation is an exception to the "law" (e.g., that there is a strong price-quality relationship) can be very important, but other than that, the "law" does not help the operating manager or planner.

Theories or conceptual structures do not purport to provide "facts."

Instead they define a useful way of looking at a problem or organizing facts. Examples are the "experience curve" and "product portfolio" concepts developed by the Boston Consulting Group, and contrasting theories of advertising effects such as consistency theories, low-involvement theories, and conflict theories. The marketing concept itself, first articulated at General Electric, is another example.

Techniques or methods differ from theories in that they are specific processes for organizing and transforming facts (e.g., data), developing plans, and so forth. Where the theory gives an overall map of the terrain, the technique defines a flight plan for getting from one particular point to another. Examples of techniques are market experimentation, models for budgeting advertising, new-product predictions and sales forecasting models, zero-base budgeting, and attitude-measurement and copy-testing procedures. Obviously there is a grey area between techniques and concepts, since techniques may be defined only in general terms. Or one may adopt the "concept" upon which a technique is based and then invent one's own technique. However, there is an important operational difference.

There is considerable confusion in marketing about the definition of a technique. For instance, some might think of techniques as applying only to marketing research, and indeed that is where the bulk of R & D in marketing has been concentrated. This leads to a certain skepticism about R & D on the part of managers. As one of the friends of the Commission put it:

The title of the Commission's project is general. It talks of research and development for marketing management. The questions seem to imply concentrating this on development of new techniques and methodologies of market research. I think it should first be noted that the marketing line manager's main preoccupation is in developing the appropriate strategy and techniques to accomplish his operating plan. This occupies a great majority of his thought and effort. His first reaction to new techniques or concepts would tend to be directed to new approaches to sales campaigns, salesmen motivation, creative advertising and promotion, etc., rather than to new techniques in market research—although these could provide supporting information to accomplish his chief objectives. In fact, referring to your phrase, one of our managers said, "The line manager does not have a tool kit; he has a staff."

Our discussion of techniques is addressed to all kinds of techniques that are intended to aid managerial decision making, including but not limited to marketing research. At least three different kinds have been used to aid managerial decision making; examples were given in Chapter 3. First are *managerial frameworks and approaches*. Although often cast as paradigms or conceptual classification schemes (e.g., the classification of products as Cash Cows, Stars, Dogs, and Problem Children in the Boston Consulting Group view of product portfolio analysis, the identification of stages of development and decline in the product life cycle, DAGMAR), they are not fully developed theories or models.[71] (Although many would consider managerial frameworks to be "models," we treat them as a different class of techniques.) Second are *models and measurement*. Models and measurement represent work whose main focus is on formal, mathematical specification of the underlying relationships or functions involved. Work on measurement is included because, where human subjects are involved, modeling usually entails a more complicated form of "measurement" than where they are not involved. Much of marketing's "new knowledge" over the last half of the assessment period has been in this area. Finally, a recognizable class of developments in the technique category are *research methods and statistical techniques*. These encompass new ways to *collect* data as well as new ways to *analyze* them. The reader is referred to Table 3-2 of Chapter 3 for specific examples of new knowledge developments in each category.

Types of Knowledge Development

The development of new knowledge in any scientific field is above all a creative process, combining elements of insight, wisdom, and often pure luck. Inductive and deductive reasoning are involved, normative-positive approaches, denotative-connotative meaning, and many complicated concepts associated with the subject of the philosophy of science. Measurement, issues such as reliability and validity, formalization, and mathematics are pertinent subjects.[72] One basic proposition of knowledge development, for example, is that it is always the properties of objects that are measured rather than the objects themselves. We do not attempt here to expound on the types of possible knowledge development in marketing from this fundamental viewpoint. Rather, the focus is on identifying and elaborating different types of research that appear to characterize the field of marketing.

Marketing research textbooks generally classify *industry* research in marketing as either problem-identification research or problem-solving research. Problem-identification research usually is exploratory or descriptive and is done to identify problems the company is currently facing or may face in the future. Problem-solving research often is causal or "experimental" and is used to solve a specific company problem: Should a new brand be launched? Which version of advertising copy should be used? There are numerous varieties of each kind of research; some examples were given in Tables 4-3 and 4-4.

Problem-identification and problem-solving research together are often called *decisional research* to distinguish them from *basic research*. The purpose of basic research is to "advance the state of knowledge" in a field such as marketing. Decisional research, on the other hand, as described by Tull and Hawkins, is "concerned with helping to identify and solve problems."[73] The Commission recognized yet another important type of research, which as yet appears *not* to have been explicitly identified in marketing research textbooks:

problem-oriented research. Also, it was recognized that decisional research as currently used is largely focused on problem-solving rather than problem-identification research, and that "problem-solving" is a sufficient term to capture the nature of this class of research. In what follows, we discuss some of the similarities and differences among (1) problem-solving, (2) problem-oriented, and (3) basic research in marketing.

Problem-solving and basic research. Problem-solving research differs from basic research in several ways. First, consider the five points of difference from the perspective of differences in the stages or steps of a research process:[74]

	Basic Research	Problem-Solving Research
Step 1.	*Formulate a hypothesis* about the problem of interest.	*Develop alternative solutions* for the problem.
Step 2.	*Make a prediction* based on the hypothesis.	*Describe possible outcome* if each alternative is adopted.
Step 3.	*Devise a test* of the prediction.	*Devise means of predicting* actual outcomes.
Step 4.	*Conduct the test.*	*Make the measurements necessary* for the prediction.
Step 5.	*Analyze* to determine if test results are *statistically significant.*	*Analyze* the results to determine the *probability level* of each outcome.

Problem-solving research is done for the specific interests of an individual firm or organization, whereas basic research is done for the good of the field as a whole or, in general, "to advance knowledge." Numerous other differences in basic and problem-solving research are important for understanding marketing's R & D system and, in particular, for attempting to assess the "effectiveness" of the system.

Basic research is performed mostly in universities; its agenda is dictated by the internal logic of the discipline in question (e.g., marketing, management science, and so on). The drive to create arises from the intrinsic interest of the subject matter and the perceived opportunities for advancing the state of general knowledge. While practical applications may be envisioned at the outset (and perhaps articulated in the process of seeking financial support or data), they are not really the driving force. The conventional wisdom in universities tends to be that basic research is a necessary first step in the process of knowledge creation in marketing as in many other disciplines. Obviously, decisions need to be made about the level of support for basic research and who is to do it. Thereafter, however, it is important to leave the assessment of results to professional researchers. "Meddling" in the process of basic research or making premature demands for relevance will almost always guarantee a loss of productivity and a waste of some of the resources committed to basic knowledge creation.

The distinctions between problem-solving and basic research can be further elaborated by considering various "organizational" differences and various differences associated with "costs and value." Table 4-8, for example, presents ten criteria associated with organizational differences between these two ways of developing marketing knowledge. Differences occur in terms of purpose, orientation, client, sponsor, research, researcher-client relations, researcher-study relations, generalizability of results, focus on absolute or relative effects, and the time frame for research. Perhaps the most striking differences have to do with purpose, orientation, researcher-client relations, and the time frame. Each type of research serves a different purpose, although even basic research in marketing should make some contribution to "solving a specific business problem" or "improving the effectiveness of marketing management."

TABLE 4-8
TEN ORGANIZATIONAL DIFFERENCES IN BASIC AND PROBLEM-SOLVING RESEARCH

Criterion	Basic Research	Problem-Solving Research
Purpose	"Advancing knowledge"	"Solving a specific business problem"
Orientation	*Theories* and *hypotheses* developed from past research in the area	*Models* and *alternative solutions* from problem situations and decision-maker choice criteria
Client	"Scientific community"	"Managers/decision makers"
Sponsor	Often university, government or research foundation	Often corporation
Researcher	Often academic and individual	Often project team in marketing research department
Researcher-client relations	Impersonal; distant	Personal; close working relationship with client
Researcher-study relations	Objective; findings independent of the researcher	Greater use of subjective researcher judgment
Generalizability of results	Universal if done with appropriate design	Specific to firm; each research situation is unique
Absolute/relative effects	Focus often on *absolute* effects; e.g., how much change in *Y* is caused by *X*?	Focus often on *relative* effects; e.g., is alternative A more or less effective than alternative B?
Time frame for research	Often *long* with no immediate pressure for results	Often *short* and determined by the immediacy of problem to be solved

The orientation of the researcher also differs. In basic research the orientation is to theories and the test of hypotheses derived from extant literature and past research in the area. In problem-solving research the orientation is to the particular business problem that needs to be solved.

Differences in researcher-client relations have important implications for the way in which the research gets done. In basic research it is distant and impersonal. The researcher often does not know who will be reading his work or how it might eventually be used. In problem-solving research the relationship is (or should be) personal and close. The marketing research department or supplier exists primarily to serve the needs of marketing management. The client is explicitly known and in most cases is involved in a day-to-day or week-to-week basis as the research proceeds. Differences in the time frame for research are also important. Problem-solving researchers are invariably under pressure arising from deadlines set up in the scheduling of a project and the immediate needs to provide research inputs to the management problem.

Other dimensions of difference are more fundamental and are associated with basic differences in the costs and value of doing problem-solving and basic research. Table 4-9 shows ten criteria for distinguishing the two forms on this basis. Problem-solving research does not (and should not) be as "pure" as basic research in the classical scientific sense of research inquiry. The extra costs of random sampling, objective error measurement, and many things that a basic researcher takes for granted may not be justified in terms of the "value added" by the research information for improving (making more profitable) a marketing decision. The oft-cited criticism of problem-solving research—that it is "sloppy" or "useless" because many aspects of a formal design are ignored or left out—is at best naive and at worst ignorant of the basic functions of this kind of research. Problem-solving research, for example, is not often "replicated" (a basic criterion in the advancement of science) because each problem situation that faces a marketing manager differs in important respects, or because replication does not add significantly to the anticipated value of the research results.

The most important difference from the viewpoint of the Commission's inquiry has to do with determining the value of research. How should basic research be evaluated? This is a perennial problem in all fields, because the character of the work requires evaluation by peers and this can lead to an actual or perceived lack of accountability to those who provide the resources. But there is no way to avoid this, so there is always a built-in tension at the boundary between basic research and the world of affairs.

People with responsibility for basic research in universities tend to use the following two criteria in making judgments about programs, people, and projects.

1. Is the work of high quality? Does it contain deficiencies or omissions or is it internally consistent, rigorous, and highly linked to related findings? Is it shallow or deep? Is it

TABLE 4-9

TEN COST AND VALUE DIFFERENCES IN BASIC AND PROBLEM-SOLVING RESEARCH

Criterion	Basic Research	Problem-Solving Research
Costs of research	"Value-added" by random sampling, error measurement, etc. often worth the costs	"Value added" by these things often not worth the costs
Sampling	Often probability (random) sampling	Often nonprobability (judgmental) sampling
Measurement of error	Objective measurement of sampling and nonsampling errors	Subjective estimation of errors and even biased measures may be preferred
Validity and reliability	Construct validity (causation) and test-retest reliability very important	Focus often on predictive validity only
Statistical significance	Need to know *statistical significance* of results	Need to know *probability level* that an outcome will occur
Statistical focus	Often *classical statistics* and *relative-frequency probability*	Often *Bayesian statistics* and *personal subjective probability*
Replication	Study design must allow for replication by other researchers	Seldom any need for replication; each situation is unique
Confidentiality	Nonconfidential; all aspects open to public domain	Often confidential and proprietary research
Form of output	Often published as journal article	Often produced as internal company "research report"
Determining value of research	Based on contributions to *knowledge* and on peer-group assessments of quality of research	Based on contributions to *profits* and on Bayesian methods for determining value of research

new or is it a rehashing of old results? In other words, does it truly contribute to the stock of knowledge?

2. Is the subject of the work intrinsically important? Does the work address important questions or is it trivial? Is such a contribution to knowledge likely to lead to other answers or even other questions? In other words, is the work relevant to the future evolution of basic research?

Note that relevance is at issue, but it is relevance in terms of the internal logic of the field rather than in terms of external standards. Payoff is defined in terms of knowledge for its own sake rather than the facilitation of some external goal. It is hard to make judgments about even the "internal" relevance of specific basic research results, because tomorrow the conception of the field may be changed by some new finding. Therefore the most hard-nosed evaluations of basic research are based on the first criterion—quality—as judged by peers.

Problem-oriented research.

Problem-oriented research.   Problem-oriented research is a recognizable class of marketing research activity that, in many ways, lies *between* basic and problem-solving research. In other words, it *combines* many of the perspectives of basic and problem-solving research as presented in Tables 4-8 and 4-9. Although textbooks do not identify this as a particular type of marketing research, it is nonetheless the essential orientation of much of both the academic *and* professional work done in the field of marketing. The purpose of problem-oriented research can be broadly stated as "advancing knowledge with respect to a particular problem or decision area such as marketing."

Problem-oriented research may be fundamental or highly applied, but its driving force is the desire to make a contribution to the solution of an important practical problem. Such work is done in universities, in research institutes, and in business firms. Problem-oriented research may "look like" basic research. Communications among researchers may be highly arcane. However, the motivation of the researcher distinguishes it from basic work, affecting the choice of topics, the strategy of the research, and the standards by which it should be judged.

Problem-solving research differs from problem-oriented research in that it is undertaken in response to a specific, and typically an immediate, problem with the expectation that the work will in fact contribute materially to the solution of that problem. In other words, the work is specific and demonstrably relevant at the outset. Problem-solving research is performed mostly by and for business firms. Additions to the stock of general knowledge will occur as byproducts, but "breakthroughs" are not to be expected. Problem-solving research is done by company marketing research departments, by external marketing research firms, and by consultants.

Problem-oriented research addresses a *class* of issues or problems, and typically it has at least limited generalizability across firms or situations. The topics examined are usually conceptual but oriented to applied problems—for example, an effort to classify the kinds of products and consumer purchase situations in which the hierarchy of advertising effects might operate in different ways.

The major criterion for assessing problem-solving research in marketing is whether it helps improve a specific business decision. For problem-oriented research, the criterion is whether it improves our understanding of particular kinds of phenomena in marketing and/or whether it contributes to advancements of theory and method in a basic discipline. The narrowness of the problem, the time frame for utility, and the context of the application all are factors differentiating problem-solving from problem-oriented research.

Problem-oriented research, particularly that done in academic institutions, may take on several forms depending on the research interests and training of the researcher. Thus, for example, behavioral science-trained academics have recently attacked the problem of television "clutter" by attempting to explain and test viewer perceptions about the number of, and time devoted to, commercials based on behavioral science theories of selective perception, information processing, cognitive structure, and so on. The extensive work by management science-trained academics in developing various types of "media models," or indeed any of the models developed for specific decision areas such as sales management, advertising, and so on, comprises problem-oriented research. The perspective is not company-situation specific. *Any* company might profitably use the findings or the model developed in that particular decision area. The immediate "client" is a scientific community of academic and professional peers, and the satisfaction of their professional standards, but as Churchman has noted,[75] the longer-range "client," particularly in the case of management science models in marketing, is the marketing manager. The success or failure of this kind of research is heavily dependent on whether or not managers adopt and use the model. The value of problem-oriented research is thus most directly measurable as its *utility* to the manager in assisting with decision making. As noted earlier, beyond this fundamental basis for evaluation, management scientists in marketing have developed numerous other criteria for evaluating problem-oriented research.

Problem-oriented research is done by both academics and professional researchers. It is the predominant research mission of the Marketing Science Institute, Cambridge, Massachusetts. MSI plays a unique role in marketing knowledge development by bringing marketing academics together with real-world marketing problems. Given its importance to knowledge development in the field, and the principal thrust of the Commission's efforts to assess the effectiveness of this kind of marketing research, much more will be said about MSI in Chapter 6.

What can be said in general about these views on knowledge development in marketing? The most important fact is that marketing knowledge is characterized by a diversity of "ends," "means," and "intervening states." The R & D on which the Commission focused is actually a widely differing set of goals, ways of doing research, and types of knowledge, none of which are necessarily more or less, important or relevant than others. All forms of knowledge development—basic research, problem-solving research, and problem-oriented research—are important to a profession such as marketing.

SUMMARY

We have offered some new perspectives on marketing research and on marketing itself. The idea that there exists a national research and development system for marketing, which in many respects parallels the research and development system for production, is the basic departure point. To describe, estimate, and assess this system requires a national accounting perspective. Currently, no studies at this level appear to be done by any organization in the public or private sector. Work is needed on this broadened view of marketing research and on the nature of the system involved.

The ideas presented here should lead to better and more rigorous specifications of concepts, estimates, and insights. We have sacrificed elaboration and detail in describing various aspects of marketing's R & D system in favor of presenting the major features of its many complicated parts. This system is, in many respects, what the Commission was charged with assessing, even though the major focus was on the industrial sector and its relations with the academic sector.

Many of the estimates in the chapter are best viewed as "guesstimates." We do have some faith in the generalization that at the end of the assessment period, 1977, the national investment in marketing R & D was much smaller than in production R & D. Resources devoted to marketing R & D have increased appreciably since the beginning of the assessment period but have not approached the equity level implicit in Ferber's 1949 forecast. Between 1973 and 1978, marketing research budgets in private-sector companies increased 65%, and more than half of all marketing research departments were formed in the 1968–1978 decade.

Our attempts to provide insight into marketing's R & D system from a national-level accounting viewpoint have probably raised more questions than they have answered. Hopefully, discussion will become more informed, and others will take up the challenge implicit in the three propositions given in the introduction. The elaborations and estimates of the national investment in marketing R & D are our own, and other commissioners should not be held responsible for any errors that we have made. The essential premise is that national R & D investments are divisible into the two broad categories of production R & D and marketing R & D. There is obviously much more to the world than production and marketing, but there are also advantages to thinking about R & D in this way and a need for leaders in government, business, education, and all sectors to begin doing so. The procedure of working from what we know about R & D, particularly in the rigorous definitional sense of the national accounting done by the National Science Foundation, to mapping out a parallel system serving marketing interests has many advantages. The least-developed concept in marketing seems to be that of marketing "development," and we have not attempted to estimate this as an investment. It is not the same thing as "knowledge development" as we use this term. In terms of what NSF calls R & D, it is the category that absorbs by far the largest share of the overall national R & D investment. If development in marketing from the academic perspective means the work of marketing professors, there is little question that exactly the reverse situation exists in marketing R & D. A much smaller share of the nation's investment is devoted to these kinds of activities than to research activities in the basic social science and social engineering disciplines.

Chapter 5 presents an elaboration of the knowledge-creation and utilization aspects of marketing's R & D system. What is involved is a process in which certain individuals and groups appear to play particular roles. The chapter spells out various viewpoints on the nature of these roles and the process involved.

NOTES

[1]See for example, David Allison, ed., *The R & D Game: Technical Men, Technical Managers, and Research Productivity* (Cambridge, Mass.: M.I.T. Press, 1969); Keith Norris and John Vaizey, *The Economics of Research and Technology* (London: Allen and Unwin, 1973); Fritz Machlup, *The Production and Distribution of Knowledge in the United States* (Princeton, N.J.: Princeton University Press, 1962).

[2]The federal government primarily through the Bureau of the Census compiles vast quantitites of statistical information useful for doing marketing research. But it does not appear to monitor, or even to recognize the existence of, a marketing research and development system.

[3]National Science Foundation. *Research and Development in Industry, 1975* (NSF 77-324) (Washington, D.C.: Supt. of Documents, U.S. Government Printing Office), p. 18.

[4]This definition was reported in "R & D Spending Patterns for 600 Companies," *BusinessWeek*, July 3, 1978, p. 58. Reprinted from the July 3, 1978 issue of BusinessWeek by special permission, © 1978 by McGraw-Hill, Inc., New York, N.Y. 10020.

[5]Robert Ferber, *Market Research* (New York: McGraw-Hill, 1949).

[6]Ferber, *Market Research,* pp. 3–4.

[7]Ferber, *Market Research,* p. 5.

[8]Ferber, *Market Research,* p. 4.

[9]Ferber, *Market Research,* p. 5.

[10]Ferber, *Market Research,* p. 5.

[11]Nor did Ferber in his 1949 book go on to elaborate the institutional components of marketing's R & D system or the scientific disciplinary base for marketing research. The book did argue effectively that statistics should be the base. Other views expressed later in the chapter that social science and social engineering, in addition to statistics, are the foundation disciplines of marketing research seem to have gained their greatest support from the Ford and Carnegie Commission Reports published three years later in 1951.

[12]*Research and Development in Industry,* p. 19.

[13]*Research and Development in Industry,* p. 18.

[14]*Research and Development in Industry,* pp. 9–11.

[15]One could even add a parallel exclusion of development activities related to production R & D in this definition.

[16]A review of forty-two case histories of product development focusing on development time from inception to large-scale or national marketing is given in Lee Adler, "Time Lag in New Product Development," *Journal of Marketing,* 30 (January

1966), 17–21. The review includes the discovery and introduction of products such as penicillin, transistors, and television, and indicates the scope of what are considered "products" from a marketing point of view.

[17]Kinnear and Taylor, in *Marketing Research: An Applied Approach* (New York: McGraw-Hill, 1979), devote an entire chapter to "the marketing research system." The meaning and their use of the term, however, is confined largely to elaborations of the research process for managing marketing research in an industrial organization ["The concept of a marketing research system implies a deeply involved role for research in the marketing management process" (p. 19)]. The authors do discuss basic and applied research in marketing, and they classify all marketing research as either "exploratory," "conclusive," or "performance-monitoring." As in most other texts, the assumption is that marketing research is applied research that takes on characteristic forms in the industrial sector, where the goal is to inform marketing management policy or decision making directly. The authors also provide a brief history of marketing research, identify seven areas of probable top management-marketing research conflict, and imply that marketing is a part of the social sciences ["methodological advances made by psychologists, economists, sociologists, political scientists, statisticians, and so on had a pronounced influence on marketing research methodology" (pp. 32–33)].

[18]Buzzell and others, in *Marketing Research and Information Systems: Text and Cases* (New York: McGraw-Hill, 1969), make the important point that marketing research and marketing information are not the same thing. They argue that "the term 'research,' properly speaking, denotes formalized procedures, based on the principles of scientific method and especially on statistical techniques, for collecting and analyzing information" (p. 15).

[19]We hasten to add that given the teaching and training purposes of marketing research textbooks, which focus student attention on learning data-collection and data-analysis procedures, such texts should be focused as they are. There is a need, however, for a national-level, macro perspective on the subject.

[20]Zaltman and Burger, *Marketing Research: Fundamentals and Dynamics* (Hinsdale, Ill.: Dryden Press, 1975), p. 13, identify five major institutions that do marketing research: (1) publishing companies and government agencies, (2) large companies with marketing research departments, (3) advertising agencies, (4) market research consulting agencies, and (5) academic researchers. With the exception of nonprofit organizations that are neither government nor education, this list basically encompasses our four-sector view of the system. They also report: "In terms of dollars, the largest amount of marketing research is performed by publishing companies and governmental agencies," but they provide no estimates of what these amounts might be.

[21]One of the first articulations of this idea was in Philip Kotler and Sidney J. Levy, "Broadening the Concept of Marketing," *Journal of Marketing,* 33 (January 1969), 10–15.

[22]FFRDC'S or Federally Funded Research and Development Centers are organizations administered by industrial firms, universities and colleges, or other institutions for the purpose of performing research and development almost exclusively for federal agencies. Examples of those administered by industry are Bettis Atomic Power Laboratory (Westinghouse), Knolls Atomic Power Laboratory (General Electric), Oak Ridge National Laboratory (Union Carbide), and Savannah River Laboratory (E. I. DuPont de Nemours).

[23]All data presented below are from National Science Foundation. *Research and Development in Industry, 1975* (NSF 77-324) (Washington, D.C.: Supt. of Documents, U.S. Government Printing Office).

[24]The latest report in this series is Dik Warren Twedt, ed., *1978 Survey of Marketing Research* (Chicago: American Marketing Association, 1978).

[25]The terms "primary" and "secondary" are usually used in reference to types of data rather than types of sources. Churchill in *Marketing Research: Methodological Foundations* (Hinsdale, Ill.: Dryden Press, 1976), for example, defined primary data as data originated by the researcher for the purpose of the investigation at hand, and secondary data as "statistics not gathered for the immediate study at hand but for some other purpose" (p. 127). As used in Figure 4-3, the terms identify the main external *sources* of primary and secondary marketing research data from the perspectives of the user corporation.

[26]For a chart identifying the various problems and decision areas facing top management and the types of marketing research data applicable to each, see Ferber, *Market Research*, p. 7.

[27]R. R. Coutant, "Where Are We Bound in Marketing Research?" *Journal of Marketing*, 1 (1937), 28–34, published by the American Marketing Association; F. LaClave, "Fundamentals of Market Research," *Printers' Ink*, February 16, 1945, 26 ff.

[28]Quoted by John G. Keane in "Some Observations on Marketing Research in Top Management Decision Making," *Journal of Marketing*, 33 (October 1969), 10–15.

[29]"R & D Spending Patterns for 600 companies," *Business Week*, 58ff.

[30]Data on these companies are given in *Standard Directory of Advertisers* (Skokie, Ill.: National Register Publishing Company, 1978). This directory, one of the so-called Red Books, is published annually by National Register, a subsidiary of Standard Rate and Data Service. A companion volume is *Standard Directory of Advertising Agencies*.

[31]Data supporting these propositions can be found in "The Largest U.S. Industrial Corporations," *Fortune*, May 8, 1978, 238 ff, and in "Top 100 Near $9 Billion in Ads," *Advertising Age*, August 28, 1978, 1ff. The Fortune 500 list does not include all large corporations but only industrial manufacturing corporations. Sears, Roebuck, for example, is not included, even though its annual sales of $17.2 billion in 1977 would otherwise rank it in eleventh place. Of the twelve largest U.S. companies in that year, five were oil companies, three were automobile manufacturers, and the other four were AT&T, IBM, General Electric, and Sears, Roebuck. Eight of the twelve made the list of "top 100" advertisers. Representative advertising-to-sales (A/S) ratios for that year were General Motors (.5), Exxon (.06), AT&T (.3), General Electric (.6), and Sears, Roebuck (1.7).

[32]The top one hundred advertisers in 1977 represented fourteen industry groupings: (1) airlines, (2) appliances, TV, radio, (3) automobiles, (4) chemicals, (5) drugs, toiletries and cosmetics, (6) food, (7) gum and candy, (8) oil, (9) photographic equipment, (10) retail chains, (11) soaps and cleansers, (12) telephone services, equipment, (13) tobacco, (14) wine, beer, and liquor, and a miscellaneous category of other companies such as CBS, Goodyear Tire, Hanes, Kimberly-Clark, Mattel, Scott Paper, Time, Inc., and the U.S. Government. (See *Advertising Age*, August 28, 1978, p. 30.). With the exception of advertising agencies and independent marketing research or consulting firms, all the main categories of companies having marketing research departments from the pool of 798 sampled in the 1978 AMA survey of marketing research are included in the top 100 advertisers; that is, (1) manufacturers of industrial products, (2) manufacturers of consumer products, (3) publishing and broadcasting, (4) retailers, and (5) financial service companies (e.g., banks, insurance companies). Financial service companies, the fastest-growing group with respect to new marketing research departments initiated, is least well represented in the top 100 advertisers list. See D. W. Twedt, ed., *1978 Survey of Marketing Research* (Chicago: American Marketing Association, 1978).

[33]This estimate is for U.S. agencies. There were an additional 400 foreign, a total of 4400, listed in *Standard Directory of Advertising Agencies* (Skokie, Ill.: National Register, 1978).

[34]"583 Agencies Record $2.9 Billion Income," *Advertising Age*, March 13, 1978, 1 ff.

[35]*Advertising Age*, March 13, 1978, p. 1.

[36]*Advertising Age*, January 8, 1979, p. S-8.

[37]This calculation was made by first computing the total gross sales of ninety-nine companies in the top one hundred advertiser list (excluding federal government) given in *Advertising Age*, August 14, 1978, p. 30. This amounted to $551.3 billion. Advertising expenditures by these firms in 1977 were $8.7 billion, an overall average A/S ratio of about 1.5%. Assuming the ninety-nine companies spent about 5% of advertising on all forms of marketing research, the estimated marketing R & D investment was $440 million. On the base of $551.3 billion in sales, this amounts to .0008%. The *1978 Survey of Marketing Research* reports marketing research expenditures as a percent of sales for 169 consumer-products manufacturers, 168 industrial-products manufacturers, 45 advertising agencies, and 78 financial service companies. These ratios range from .0001 to .01 (1%). The weighted average ratio for the 460 companies represented amounts to .0025%, which is comparatively much higher than our estimate. The more conservative .0008% seems reasonable, however, when considered in light of "all large advertisers" or of the tie to "all national media expenditures." It is known, for example, that about 45% of all media advertising expenditures represent "local" rather than "national" advertising, and there is unlikely to be much marketing research associated with local advertising. For an estimate that national advertisers spend 3% to 5% of their media budgets on copy-testing research alone, see Irwin Gross, "The Creative Aspects of Advertising," *Sloan Management Review*, Fall 1972, pp. 83–109.

[38]Jack J. Honomichl, "Research Top 20: Companies Posted 19% Gain Last Year," *Advertising Age*, April 24, 1978, 3 ff. Reprinted with permission from the April 24, 1978 issue of Advertising Age. Copyright 1978 by Crain Communications, Inc.

[39]These studies have been done about every five years since 1959 (1959, 1963, 1968, 1973, and 1978). The 1978 study reports on estimates made by marketing research department directors concerning organization, size, and growth of marketing research departments, marketing research budgets, types of marketing research done, and compensation of marketing research personnel. Data are gathered by mail questionnaire. In the 1978 survey, questionnaires were sent to 2780 marketing research executives (typically Director of Marketing Research or Marketing Research Manager) of companies represented on the AMA Membership Roster. All reported estimates are for fiscal year 1977. See Twedt, *1978 Survey of Marketing Research.*

[40]Twedt argues effectively that expenditures by these types of companies are *included* in the expenditures of marketing research departments of industrial, consumer, media, and financial service firms. The same argument, we feel, should be applied to the bulk of the marketing R & D expenditures of advertising agencies. Most is research done as a "supplier" for a client firm.

[41]J. H. Myers and R. R. Mead, *The Management of Marketing Research* (Scranton, Pa.: International Textbook Company, 1969); L. Adler and C. S. Mayer, *Managing the Marketing Research Function* (Chicago: American Marketing Association, 1977).

[42]Twedt, *1978 Survey of Marketing Research.* This report presents many useful statistics that we do not reproduce here. As noted, it supplies probably the best currently available data on industrial marketing research. For an overview of the major findings, see

"Survey Shows Research Grows; But Position, Lower-Level Pay Slip," *Marketing News,* January 12, 1979, 1 ff. That these studies may not represent a complete census is suggested by the fact that the 1949 study cited earlier of marketing research functions and decision areas was based on reports of "563 companies with research departments." See Ferber, *Market Research,* p. 7.

[43]Reported in Adler and Mayer, *Managing the Marketing Research Function,* p. 84, from a talk by Aubrey Wilson presented at an Industrial Research Seminar, Toronto, Canada, May 1976.

[44]Adler and Mayer, *Managing the Marketing Research Function,* (Chicago, Ill.: American Marketing Association, 1977), p. 73. The authors review many other issues of departmentalization, such as how big the department should be, whether to have a centralized or decentralized department, alternative types of reporting relationships, organizational structures, and so on. Eight different types of organization are presented in this book, and three different ways departments can be related to other functions: (1) centralized—single division, (2) decentralized-divisional, and (3) hybrid (often used in large, diversified, multinational firms). For an insightful discussion of department organization at RCA, Westinghouse, and other companies, see Lee Adler, "Companies Experiment with Research at Varying Levels," *Advertising Age,* July 15, 1974, 62 ff.

[45]James R. Krum, "B For Marketing Research Departments," *Journal of Marketing,* 42 (October 1978), 8–12, published by the American Marketing Association.

[46]Reported in *The Corporate Investor's Research Library* (New York: The Wall Street Transcript), Vol. 303, 1978, NK-445326. This volume contains the 10-K reports to the Securities and Exchange Commission submitted by all major publicly held companies in the United States.

[47]Donald R. Lehmann, *Market Research and Analysis* (Homewood, Ill.: Richard D. Irwin, 1979), p. 7.

[48]Adler and Mayer, *Managing the Marketing Research Function.*

[49]*Standard Directory of Advertising Agencies,* 1978.

[50]*Advertising Age,* March 13, 1978, p. 1.

[51]Some useful information is now available on the scope of this industry and the nature of the services offered by marketing research supplier firms. For listings, see Bradford's *Directory of Marketing Research Agencies* and *Management Consultants in the U.S. and the World* (Fairfax, Va. [biennial]), and *International Directory of Marketing Research Houses and Services,* published by the New York Chapter of the American Marketing Association. Lists with various breakdowns are also provided in the *Roster of the American Marketing Association* under headings such as communications, consultants, data processing, information systems and analysis, industry and service specialization, media and rating, personnel, product and packaging, research services (e.g., twenty-four firms who conduct consumer panels, thirty-eight who do field interviewing), sales management and promotion, and service. For reviews of the nature of the services offered by major suppliers, see Lehmann, *Market Research and Analysis,* pp. 208–52, and Elizabeth J. Heighton and Don R. Cunningham, *Advertising in the Broadcast Media* (Belmont, Calif.: Wadsworth, 1976), pp. 153–67 (copy-testing services) and 171–202 (audience research services). See also the two appendices in Kinnear and Taylor, *Marketing Research,* the first devoted to "Syndicated Sources of Marketing Data" and the second to "Library Sources of Marketing Data."

[52]Honomichl, "Research Top 20."

[53]*Advertising Age,* August 28, 1978, p. 30.

[54]The term "market research" can be found in the American Statistics Index. In

1977 twenty-one agency publications were listed under this heading, mostly having to do with imports and exports—for example, an article on China coal mine equipment imports. The term "marketing" is also present. Here again the six publications listed under this heading were virtually all foreign market analysis reports. "Advertising" is a more meaningful word. About forty publications were listed, many having to do with military advertising. SIC codes have major categories for "wholesale trade," "retail trade," and, under the "service" category, four-digit codes for advertising agencies (7311), R & D laboratories (7391), management consulting and public relations services (7392), and commercial testing laboratories (7397), but none called marketing research. There is also no occupational SOC code for marketing research, even though there are codes for "buyers: wholesale and retail" (432), "driver-sales workers" (433), and so on.

[55]Philip Kotler, *Marketing for Nonprofit Organizations* (Englewood Cliffs, N.J.: Prentice-Hall, 1975), p. 330. Kotler's case that government agencies should adopt a marketing approach to the management of their affairs is very persuasive. See Chapter 17 of his book for the arguments and implications. He argues that there are basically four types of government agencies: (1) business-type, e.g., the Postal Service, (2) service-type, e.g., public schools and public libraries, (3) transfer-type, e.g., the Social Security Administration, and (4) intervention type, e.g., the Federal Trade Commission.

[56]John M. Rathmell, "Marketing by the Federal Government," pp. 21–28, *MSU Business Topics*, Summer 1973. Reprinted by permission of the publisher, Division of Research, Graduate School of Business Administration, Michigan State University.

[57]National Science Foundation. *An Analysis of Federal R & D Funding by Function, Fiscal Years 1969–1978* (NSF 77-326) (Washington, D.C.: Supt. of Documents, U.S. Government Printing Office), p. iii.

[58]Honomichl, "Research Top 20." The Marketing and Development Group of BA&H comprises National Analysts, AD-TEL, and Market Audits, Inc.

[59]A representative publication of The Brookings Institution is Charles L. Schultze et al., *Setting National Priorities: The 1972 Budget* (Washington, D.C.: The Brookings Institution, 1971).

[60]Philip Kotler, *Marketing Management* (Englewood Cliffs, N.J.: Prentice-Hall, Inc. 1976), p. 5.

[61]For a list of these cases, see Ralph M. Gaedeke, ed., *Marketing in Private and Public NonProfit Organizations* (Santa Monica, Calif.: Goodyear Publishing Company, 1977), pp. 371–77.

[62]The question of what is a "nonprofit" organization is itself an interesting subject. We have adopted the National Science Foundation view of a "four-sector" economy in which nonprofit organizations are all those that are not business concerns, governments, or educational institutions. Etzioni calls them "third-sector" organizations (he includes educational institutions)—those serving needs not profitable enough to attract the private sector and problems that are not effectively dealt with by local, state, or federal government. See A. Etzioni, "The Untapped Potential of the Third Sector," *Business and Society Review*, Spring 1972, pp. 39–44. Oleck classifies all nonprofit organizations into five types: (1) charitable, (2) social, (3) political, (4) trade, and (5) government. H. L. Oleck, *Non-Profit Corporations, Organizations and Associations,* 2d ed. (Englewood Cliffs, N.J.: Prentice-Hall, 1965). Some appreciation for the number of nonprofit organizations in the United States can be gained by examining Margaret Fisk and Mary W. Pair, eds., *Encyclopedia of Associations,* 11th ed. (Detroit: Gale Research, 1977). Over 17,000 associations are listed, including 5000 or more foundations, 2000 "Mystic Fraternities, Secret Societies, and Unorthodox Groups," and so on. As of about 1974, there were over one hundred protest or consumer action groups identified by the Council on Economic Priorities. See also Max Ways, "Creative Federalism and the Great Society," *Fortune,*

January 1966, for an interesting discussion of the creative federalism that characterizes many organizations in the nonprofit sector—a borrowing of the efficiency and expertise of the business world while retaining the accountability, public interest, and planning of government.

[63]David A. Aaker and George S. Day, *Marketing Research: Private and Public Sector Decisions* (New York: John Wiley, 1980).

[64]For a discussion of these issues and examples of local and national public service advertising, see John G. Myers, "On the Search for Management Science and Marketing in a NonProfit Organization," TIMS College on Marketing Annual Meetings, Portland, Oregon, August, 1974. See also articles on "In the Public Interest," and "Illustrations of Selected Public Cause Campaigns of the Advertising Council," in Gaedeke, *Marketing in Private and Public NonProfit Organizations,* pp. 237-62.

[65]See the chapter on "Educational Services Marketing" by Philip Kotler and Bernard Dubois in Kotler, *Marketing for NonProfit Organizations,* pp. 344-64.

[66]For a book on university management, see Frederick C. Balderston, *Managing Today's University* (San Francisco: Jossey-Bass Publishers, 1974).

[67]In Chapter 5 we provide some additional elaboration of the nature of this type of scholarship core in the overall system. As will be seen, it is larger because there is also a group of researchers working in industry on similar kinds of research. Together, they make up what are called the "innovator research group" in the field of marketing.

[68]The field of organizational behavior, for example, deals with this subject.

[69]Kinnear and Taylor, *Marketing Research,* p. 150.

[70]See, for example, Darral G. Clarke , "Econometric Measurement of the Duration of Advertising Effects on Sales," *Journal of Marketing Research,* 13 (November 1976), 345-57, and Russell I. Haley, "We Shot an Arrowhead (#9) Into the Air," *Proceedings,* 16th Annual Conference, Advertising Research Foundation, New York, pp. 25-30.

[71]For a useful discussion of theories and models, see Joseph Berger and others, *Types of Formalization in Small-Group Research* (Boston: Houghton Mifflin, 1962).

[72]There is a vast literature on the topic of knowledge development and the philosophy of science generally. Names such as Whitehead, Northrop, Kemeny, Langer, Campbell, Snow, Popper, and Brononski come to mind. See, for example, Alfred N. Whitehead, *Science and the Modern World* (New York: Mentor, 1951), for a classic work on the subject. See also C. West Churchman, "Reliability of Models in the Social Sciences," in Peter Langhoff, ed., *Models, Measurement and Marketing* (Englewood Cliffs, N.J.: Prentice-Hall, 1965), for treatment of topics such as reliability, models, the model of geometry, facts, measurement, prediction vs. prescription, and realism vs. idealism.

[73]Donald S. Tull and Del I. Hawkins, *Marketing Research: Meaning, Measurement, and Method* (New York: Macmillan, 1976), p. 56.

[74]Adapted from Tull and Hawkins, *Marketing Research,* pp. 52 and 56.

[75]C. West Churchman, "Reliability of Models in the Social Science," in Peter Langhoff, ed., *Models, Measurement and Marketing* (Englewood Cliffs, N.J.: Prentice-Hall, Inc. 1965), p. 33. The relevant passage is: We must recognize a very significant difference between physics and geometry on the one hand and marketing on the other. . . . [O]ne ultimate test of a marketing theory is not the acceptability of the theory on the part of marketing researchers. Instead it is its acceptance by marketing managers."

5

The
Knowledge-Creation
and Utilization Process

The essential output of marketing's R & D system presented in the last chapter is information or "knowledge." From the perspective of the broadest possible views of marketing and marketing research, such knowledge should be useful to managers of *any* type of organization in the public or private sector. Marketing knowledge is that which is relevant to the management of "exchange processes," whether the thing being exchanged is a physical good, a service, an idea, or any other conception of this fundamental concept. Marketing R & D is research and development applicable to the management of exchange among and between human groups, organizations, and individuals. In other terms, all four sectors of the economy are involved in marketing's R & D system, and marketing knowledge is both produced by and used by individuals and organizations in all four of them.

This chapter deals with elaborations of the process by which such knowledge is created and used. Rather than attempting to explain the nature of this process for all components of the total system, much of the material focuses on the industry sector–academic sector interface. The interaction between these two sectors has been the most controversial and, at the same time, has received comparatively little formal analytical attention. Thus, for example, the concept

of "utilization" of marketing knowledge throughout the chapter is largely restricted to manager-users in industrial, private-sector corporations.

Another point of focus is the identification of sources of *new* knowledge, and particularly new knowledge that is useful or relevant to private-sector
corporation managers. How is new marketing knowledge created? Who plays
what roles in the process? Where do new ideas come from? Much of the face-to-
face meeting time of ERDMM commissioners was devoted to attempts to answer
these questions and to explain the processes by which new knowledge is created,
diffused, and used or not used by managers of companies in this sector. After
many hours of discussion over a long period, all members of the Commission
remain less than satisfied with the results. Although many studies have been done
of the analogous subject of "diffusion of innovation" in marketing, none to our
knowledge have focused on the diffusion of "new knowledge" in quite the way
it is being treated here. Like the idea of marketing's R & D system, the ideas
presented in this chapter have not been subjected to rigorous empirical study or
testing. The reader should nevertheless appreciate that they evolved from intensive discussion and debate among the eighteen members of the Commission, all
of whom are well-informed leaders in the field and who might thus be considered
"expert" on the subject.

The first section addresses the question of the interactions, if any,
among various types of new knowledge and different kinds of marketing
research. Next, the essential stages of knowledge creation and utilization are
identified and discussed in the context of innovation, diffusion, and adoption
constructs well known in marketing literature. The third section provides an illustrative example of the knowledge-creation and utilization process by tracing the
major stages and people involved in the creation and use of conjoint analysis.
Finally, various elaborated models of the process are presented, including discussions on characteristics of the "innovator research group" in marketing. Also
presented are the results of an iterative delphilike procedure (the "Mini-Guide"),
in which commissioners were asked to develop alternative views of the process
on each round.

RESEARCH ROLES AND KNOWLEDGE DEVELOPMENT

Chapter 4 presented numerous criteria for distinguishing types of
knowledge and types of research in marketing. The question addressed here is
how, if at all, do they interact? Are they "dependent" or "independent?" Does
basic research necessarily precede problem-oriented or problem-solving research
and always feed into them? Is context-free knowledge always associated with
basic research and context-specific knowledge always associated with problem-
solving research? These are fundamental questions about how knowledge is

created and used in marketing. If, for example, the output from basic research does not flow into and influence, to some degree, the output of problem-oriented and problem-solving research, its "effectiveness" from the viewpoint of the "ends" of marketing knowledge development—to improve marketing management decision making and practice—can be seriously questioned.

It is very unlikely that the direction of these flows is always the same in every important new piece of marketing knowledge developed. In some instances, problem-solving research may feed into basic research, or situation-specific knowledge may be the source of an idea developed by a basic researcher. In the words of one commissioner:

It is important from the beginning to understand that the identification of a new concept or technology in marketing is a relatively rare event. As such, it is somewhat presumptive to assume any formalized structure regarding the process. I have been involved in marketing for some time and possibly I can identify a handful—each of which followed a totally different path.

Given these qualifications, the Commission nevertheless developed a view of the nature of these interactions (see Figure 5-1), even though others could undoubtedly be developed. Basic research is shown at the core of the process of knowledge creation. Inquiries embarked on for their own sake produce new generalizable facts and laws, and they also facilitate problem-oriented re-

FIGURE 5-1

RELATIONS AMONG TYPES OF MARKETING RESEARCH AND TYPES OF KNOWLEDGE

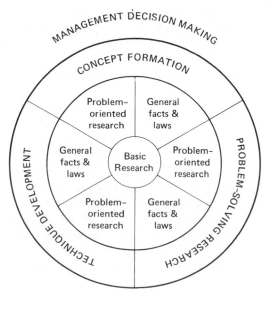

search. The process feeds on itself, so the flow of influence and communication is both inward- and outward-directed. Efforts at problem-oriented research and the accumulation of a body of facts produce "interesting questions" that may (or may not) appeal to basic researchers.

The growing stock of facts and the results of problem-oriented research contribute to all three entities in the next ring: concept formation, technique development, and problem-solving research. These, in turn, contribute to each other and to management decision making.

The process also works in the opposite direction. Management decision problems may trigger problem-solving research, or concept formation, or perhaps the development of a new technique. A call upon a company's marketing research or management science staff is a good example of the former. The invention of the experience-curve and product-portfolio concepts, and of the marketing concept itself, appear to have followed this "outside-in" path. The technique of zero-base budgeting arose out of a manifest management need rather than research findings.

STAGES OF KNOWLEDGE CREATION AND UTILIZATION

What steps or stages are involved in taking an idea from an initial conception to the point where it is useful to an operating line manager? The process has many parallels with the "diffusion" of any "innovation," and it is useful to begin with some background ideas from the diffusion literature in marketing. The subject of the diffusion of innovations has received a great deal of attention by marketing researchers over the assessment period because it is of inherent interest in new-product development.[1] Formal mathematical models have been developed,[2] as well as many sociologically oriented theories of the process,[3] and there have been numerous empirical studies of hypotheses derived from those theories.[4]

Much of the work in marketing on the topic has been done in the latter half of the assessment period, beginning in the mid-sixties. Insights from this literature can inform the discussion of knowledge creation and utilization, but readers should be aware of two fundamental differences of perspective. First, the Commission's interests were in understanding the *creation* of an "innovation" as well as its dissemination and diffusion. This was a crucial point of departure for the various views presented in this chapter. Second, the analysis unit here differs from the usual one in the marketing diffusion literature. It is not the behavior of the "consumer" or even of the "firm" that is of primary interest. Rather, the unit is primarily "researchers" or "managers," and the innovation is some type of "marketing knowledge." Many of the ideas from theories of diffusion and adoption are nevertheless applicable to understanding the knowledge creation and utilization process in marketing.

What do we know (or think we know) about the diffusion of an innovation? Katz and Lazarsfeld[5] offer the major insight that a "horizontal" as well as "vertical" flow takes place. Innovations do not simply "trickle down" (or up) from one social stratum to another as in fashion-adoption patterns. Rather, opinion leaders and followers exist within the *same* social stratum or group, and the process of adoption is much affected by what opinion leaders believe, feel, and do with respect to the social groups with which they are connected. From a mass-communications perspective, the adoption process is inherently two-step rather than one-step. It is argued that mass communication is first processed by opinion leaders before it works any significant effects on, or is passed along to, the public at large.[6]

A great deal of marketing research has been done on the characteristics of opinion leaders.[7] Opinion leaders, for example, in product categories in which they are interested, well tend to read, view, and listen more (expose themselves to more information sources). Traits such as "venturesomeness" have been shown to be meaningful. It is very likely that adopters of new marketing knowledge also have distinguishing characteristics analogous to "opinion leadership," whether considered from the viewpoint of an individual or an organization.

Rogers[8] was among the first to extend the Katz and Lazarsfeld view and develop a richer and conceptually more complex theory of adoption and diffusion. He postulated five rather than two stages:

Impersonal information (e.g., mass communication) plays its greatest role at the earlier stages, whereas personal information (e.g., opinions of friends and word-of-mouth) becomes most important at the later stages of evaluation, trial, and adoption. Rogers also argued that not just two "segments" were involved in the diffusion/adoption process (i.e., opinion leaders and followers), but five: innovators, early adopters, early majority, late majority, and laggards, and that the distribution of these types for a typical innovation was bell-shaped. The majority of individuals associated with any innovation tend to be in the early-majority and late-majority categories. In marketing knowledge creation the "innovators" are the important source of new knowledge; they differ from "opinion leaders," who in the Rogers theory are the early adopters of an innovation.

Important insights on the *rate* of diffusion and adoption can also be gleaned from this literature. Diffusion and adoption rates are largely determined by how the innovation is perceived by potential adopters. *Relative advantage* refers to the degree to which the benefits of the new thing are perceived as superior to those of the current product or idea. *Compatibility* concerns the degree of consistency of the innovation with the alternatives now being used to satisfy the potential adopter's needs. *Complexity* refers to the difficulty the recipient encounters in understanding the innovation. *Divisibility* has to do with whether the innovation is capable of being tried out with a minimum of financial or other risk (e.g., in a consumer context, does the consumer have to invest heavily to try the product—is "reversibility" difficult or easy?) *Communicability* refers to the ease with which information about the innovation can be transferred. In all cases, what is important is what the recipient perceives rather than what might be judged as "objective fact." Predicting the adoption rate of a piece of new marketing knowledge (e.g., a new decision model) might well be more informed by an analysis of its characteristics on these five dimensions.[9]

Theories of innovation, diffusion, and adoption can thus be very helpful as a reference point for explaining the knowledge-creation and utilization process in marketing. They must be extended, however, to take into account the creative activities involved in bringing these kinds of "innovation" into being. Much diffusion research assumes the existence of an innovation. The Commission was equally interested in the creative as well as in the diffusion aspects of the process. In what follows, we adopt the essential stage-theory notion from theories of innovation diffusion, but add an initial "idea-generation" stage and use terminology more appropriate to marketing R & D to identify the basic stages involved.

Three stages, referred to as idea generation, development, and application, can first be recognized. Figure 5-2 is a schematic representation of these basic features of the overall process, offering some insights into what goes on at each stage. The Commission concluded that two characteristics seemed to capture much of the basic task of creating new knowledge in marketing. First is the *idea*. This might come from a manager's insight into a new way to solve a marketing problem, a researcher's recognition of a better approach to data collection or analysis, or an academic's reflections on some basic social science theory with potential application to a marketing problem. The second is the *context*. New ideas are always associated with some context or reference point. Examples are a particular marketing problem, a theory, or a specific methodological development. Thus, as suggested in Figure 5-2, managers, professional researchers, and academics are the principal sources of new ideas and knowledge development in marketing, and new knowledge is invariably associated with some context such as a problem, theory, or method.

At the second stage, *development,* the idea goes through a process of definition and refinement. This may involve explicit empirical testing, "simulated" testing via discussions with other managers, researchers, and academics, or computer simulation testing, in which the effects on objective setting, strategy, or other aspects of marketing management are studied.

The third stage, *application,* refers to a more fully developed program

FIGURE 5-2

BASIC STAGES OF KNOWLEDGE CREATION AND UTILIZATION IN MARKETING

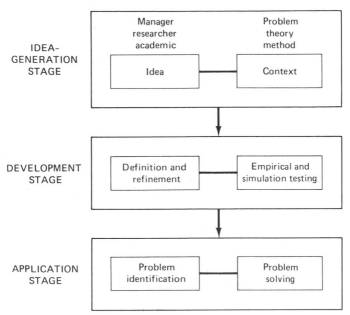

of testing and use by the firm in a specific area such as problem identification or problem solving. In the former case, the "problem" may have to do with strategic planning issues such as estimating market potential, market share, or short- and long-range forecasting; in the latter, with some aspects of product management, pricing management, advertising and sales management, or distribution management. The familiar tasks of management—planning and strategy, organization, implementation, and control—provide another way to think of the range of possible applications for the idea.

This representation of the stages of knowledge creation and utilization does not include what is really a "fourth" stage—the wide-scale dissemination of the idea to other firms and the industry as a whole. Also, it omits an important component of idea generation, as well as other aspects of the process that became evident as more discussion and thought were devoted to the subject. Figure 5-3 adds a fourth stage and presents an elaborated view of the first and fourth stages.

The important point at the first stage is what commissioners came to call idea-problem "matching." Ideas that end up being useful usually derive from a matching process at the early creative stages in which the idea is matched with a problem, or a problem is brought together with an idea that has potential for helping the problem solver solve it or at least understand it better. Also, it should be emphasized that the application stage can be quite complex, consume long

FIGURE 5-3

FOUR STAGES OF KNOWLEDGE CREATION AND UTILIZATION IN MARKETING

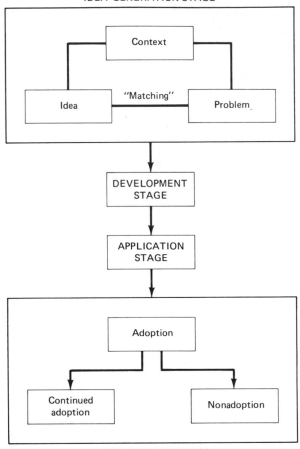

IDEA-GENERATION STAGE

DISSEMINATION STAGE

periods of time, and include several iterations of testing and retesting. The dissemination stage is characterized by the adoption of the idea by a larger group of firms or managers. The idea may continue to find useful applications (called *continued adoption*) or may be shown not to be applicable in another firm or industry context (called *nonadoption*).

There was considerable debate within the Commission whether the need for problem solving should be considered the *end result* of the process rather than the *initiating element*. The "matching" concept introduced in Figure 5-3 emphasizes the case in which the problem is the essential triggering element of idea generation. This process posits that, in essence, an idea is "invented" when someone takes his idea and finds a problem to which it is applicable. It is impossible to tell which comes first—the idea or the problem. Sometimes the same person can be both idea-developer and problem-definer. Once a matching has occurred, "development" takes place. Development generally includes "validation," when the inventor tests the idea in a problem setting. This is usually budgeted more in the manner of R & D than the later stages. The person is testing the technique against his own standards of credibility. There follows application to specific problems within the company, and finally dissemination to other companies and users ("General Foods is using it, so we should use it").

The degree of validity that has come to be associated with the concept or technique is the key factor determining movement from the development to the application and dissemination stages. A concept or technique under development is shepherded by an expert, usually one who has a personal stake in the success of the idea. More widespread dissemination requires that things be refined to the point where they can be used by the nonexpert. "Expertise" is a relative thing, and most marketing research techniques will, for example, always require more technical expertise than do general management concepts. Applications engineering for techniques is expensive and requires a commitment of resources. Even the use of a concept or technique by a nonexpert requires personal investment and risk taking. A certain minimum level of credibility for the idea or its author is required in order for these investments to be forthcoming.

The following two observations seem as appropriate for innovations in marketing knowledge generation as for new-product innovation in general:

1. *It is likely that any given concept or technique in the idea-generation stage will end in failure, if widespread adoption is the criterion. This does not mean that the idea and experience with it will not prove valuable in the generation of new knowledge.*
2. *Most ideas, concepts, or techniques that have not yet passed from development to application will not be judged as credible, useful, or relevant by very many people.*

While those having experience with the idea-diffusion process will recognize the potential importance of ideas, their track record for a priori identification of successful candidates will not necessarily be very good.

Another way to understand the idea-generation and subsequent stages is to consider that new knowledge is created by one of two fundamental processes. First, some new knowledge is essentially idea-, concept-, or methods-driven. It can arise in the academic *or* professional sphere because someone has an important insight and the energy and persistence to pursue the research, testing, and publication required to disseminate it.[10] Examples in marketing are the idea of a "hierarchy of effects" and the extensions to expectancy-value and other models to explain consumer decision making and information processing. Consumer information processing, in particular, is now a very popular academic subject that, some might say, is being driven mostly by the inherent interest of researchers in attempting to understand it.

Second, new knowledge can be developed by a process that is essentially problem-driven. A manager needs to predict his brand share for a new product, and this need leads logically into such things as sales forecasting techniques and new developments in this area,[11] consumer panels and stochastic models of brand choice,[12] basic concepts such as market segmentation,[13] and a variety of other new models and methods developments.[14] Much segmentation research during the early part of the period appeared to be basically "idea-driven" (researchers were more interested in testing new types of multivariate methods such as factor analysis, cluster analysis, and latent structure analysis),[15] whereas during the latter part, particularly with the publication of *Market Segmentation* in 1972,[16] research appeared more problem-driven, and efforts were concentrated on situation-specific variables.

It is useful to summarize the overall nature of the creation and dissemination process in terms of the degree of use of a successful new piece of marketing knowledge. Figure 5-4 shows the relationship between degree of use and each of the four stages. The idea-generation and development stages are characterized by relatively narrow use, in most cases confined to the organizational entity in which the creative and development activities are taking place. This could be, for example, within the marketing research department of a corporation, or in a university setting. The application and dissemination stages are characterized by wider use, represented in Figure 5-4 as a gradually accelerating curve. As many readers will recognize, this curve is not unlike the first stages of the familiar "product life cycle," and successful new knowledge developments in marketing may follow similar cycles of "birth" and "death." In other words,

FIGURE 5-4

RELATIONSHIP BETWEEN STAGE OF KNOWLEDGE CREATION AND DEGREE OF UTILIZATION

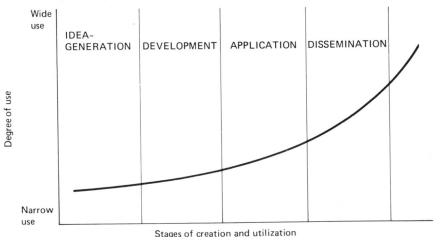

for some "innovations" in knowledge development the curve shown in Figure 5-4 will peak and turn down. A good example is motivation research. It is unlikely that TAT tests and numerous other techniques associated with motivation research that flourished in popularity during the mid-1950s and early 1960s are in such widespread use today. Focused group interviewing, surveys involving structured instruments, and physiological measures (eye-camera, pupilometrics, and so on) seem to have grown and surpassed the classical "clinical" methods, even though the latter still have some role to play.

The next section presents a case that illustrates the overall process. It highlights the roles played by various individuals, the diffusion vehicles used, and the time aspects of the process with respect to one widely adopted technique in marketing.

AN ILLUSTRATIVE EXAMPLE: CONJOINT ANALYSIS

Conjoint analysis, variants of which are known as "trade-off analysis" and "conjoint measurement," provides an excellent example of the matching of an idea with an important marketing problem. The success of this form of "new knowledge" in marketing is traceable both to managerial need and to basic research breakthroughs in the fields of mathematical psychology and marketing. The managerial need was for identifying in a rigorous and systematic way the relative importance that consumers place on various product attributes. Such information is obviously crucial in the development of new products as well as in decisions regarding advertising and communications programs. The need factor is well described in the following quotation from an article by Green and Wind:

When developing new products or services—or even when repositioning an existing one—a company must consider two basic problems. First, it must know its market, second, it must understand the nature of the product. It may find both problems hard to solve, especially when the nature of the product under consideration has several disparate qualities, each appealing to a diverse number of consumers with diverse interests. Beyond the fundamental need that the product is to fill often lie several others that the marketing manager would do well to consider. But how does he evaluate those needs? How does he evaluate which of the product's attributes the consumer perceives to be the most important? In order to market the product most effectively, marketing managers must have the means to answer these kinds of questions. In this article the authors demonstrate one research technique that has been used in evaluating consumers' judgments and show how to apply it to a number of complex marketing situations.[17]

Concerning the idea itself and the basic research breakthrough, it is generally held that an article published by two nonmarketing academics, Luce and Tukey, in 1964[18] was most significant. A long tradition of psychological and attitude measurement perspectives stemming from the work of Fechner,

Thurstone, and others preceded this article, but Luce and Tukey solved some of the fundamental problems needed to make the approach viable in marketing applications.

The first major publication on the topic in marketing appears to be an article by Green and Rao in the *Journal of Marketing Research* in 1971.[19] As with Luce and Tukey's article, much development work preceded publication.[20] Green and his colleagues at Wharton focused on developing what became known as the "full-profile" approach to conjoint analysis. It is particularly interesting that a professional researcher, Richard Johnson of Market Facts, Inc., Chicago, working independently from the Wharton group, developed a parallel procedure based on a "two-factor-at-a-time" approach. This became known as "trade-off" analysis. The first article from this point of view was published by Johnson in the *Journal of Marketing Research* in 1974.[21] In each case, a fundamental task is the generation of part-worth utilities on levels of attributes as well as overall importance weights on the attributes themselves.

Figure 5-5 shows the major individuals and institutions involved in the creation and diffusion of conjoint analysis. Each can be seen as a part of the overall system of marketing research and development given earlier in Chapter 4 (see Figure 4-3). In Figure 5-5 we use the term "nonmarketing academic" to distinguish these scholars from marketing scholars, and we further distinguish

FIGURE 5-5

PERSONS AND INSTITUTIONS INVOLVED IN THE CREATION AND DIFFUSION OF CONJOINT ANALYSIS

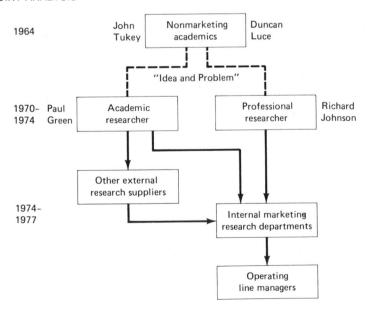

the "academic" roles within marketing from the "professional researcher" roles. In this case the professional researcher resided, from the corporation's R & D system viewpoint, in an "external" research supplier company (Market Facts). Important dates associated with the creation and diffusion process are also shown in the diagram.

Notice that in terms of a "development" stage the academic in this case was using real-world problems as the reference point for testing and refining the basic ideas.[22] A similar pattern from the professional researcher's viewpoint was going on through the normal dealings of a marketing research firm with numerous clients, many of whom were being introduced to the technique. Both persons also were appearing at conferences and presenting papers on the subject, further enhancing the diffusion process. Robinson and Associates (Philadelphia), another "external" marketing research firm, was also an early adopter of conjoint analysis and introduced the technique to many of its clients. Wharton students, particularly graduating Ph.D.'s who accepted positions at other universities across the country, were significant forces in the refinement and diffusion of conjoint analysis generally. One estimate is that there were over 300 commercial applications (separate and distinct studies) of conjoint analysis as of 1977. Interest remains high and is spreading to applications in the nonprofit and governmental sectors.

The development process required additional research, some of it probably rather technical and "basic," but there seems little doubt that this was guided by practical considerations. At the applications stage, computer software packages necessary for conducting conjoint analysis found their way to other universities, research supplier firms, and research departments, and the uses of the technique spread accordingly. Dissemination was enhanced as data-collection and data-analysis procedures were improved, and the credibility of the results began to become established.

The process of managerial concept formation also has taken a big step forward as a result of conjoint analysis. Consider the following scenario:

Taking a jet plane for a business appointment in Paris? Which of the two flights described below would you choose?

A B-707 flown by British Airways that will depart within two hours of the time you would like to leave and that is often late in arriving in Paris. The plane will make two intermediate stops, and it is anticipated that it will be 50 per cent full. Flight attendants are "warm and friendly" and you would have a choice of two movies for entertainment.

A B-747 flown by TWA that will depart within four hours of the time you would like to leave and that is almost never late in arriving in Paris. The flight is nonstop, and it is anticipated that the plane will be 90 per cent full. Flight attendants are "cold and curt" and only magazines are provided for entertainment.[23]

Obviously, the managerial problems to which conjoint analysis has been applied have existed for a long time. However, a necessary condition for a breakthrough was basic research work on the measurement of consumer utilities. The subject has been of interest to psychologists, economists, and management scientists for at least thirty years. The work of Luce and Tukey and other non-marketing academics surely was basic research, but the efforts of Green, Rao, and Johnson were also strongly basic in character, even though much of the development work was being done with "real" marketing problems. In conjoint analysis something interesting was initially pursued for its own sake, and something useful came out of it.

Two other managerially useful concepts were also offshoots of the basic idea: (1) The concept of couching questions of this kind in terms of trade-offs among specific scenarios or options. This concept has relevance for marketing planning regardless of any marketing research question. Management must trade off options, too, and it is helpful to express them in a trade-off format. (2) The concept that it is possible to measure consumer preferences in trade-off terms. This concept surely affected proposals for performing marketing research. Moreover, even the knowledge that something can be measured may change a manager's thinking in significant ways.

Over time the continued use of conjoint analysis should build up a store of knowledge from which useful generalizations about consumer behavior can be derived. There must be some commonality in the findings of the 300-plus studies based on conjoint analysis. If the data from many studies could be made available for analysis, new generalizations would be derived, leading to a new cycle of basic research—this time focusing on the substance of consumer behavior rather than solely on a technique for measuring it. This could lead to generalizable facts or "laws" with significant operational leverage.

In the next section many of these ideas are brought together and presented as a "model" of the knowledge-creation and utilization process. The section following focuses on the "innovator research group" and its characteristics in the field of marketing.

A MODEL OF MARKETING KNOWLEDGE CREATION AND UTILIZATION

In this section we present a more general model of the overall process of knowledge creation and utilization in marketing. There is significant parallelism with the view of marketing's R & D system given in the last chapter. Here, we focus on the process by which the system generates and disseminates new knowledge in the context of industrial sector–academic sector interactions. The conjoint analysis illustration identifies several major features, such as the role of nonmarketing academics and the patterns of interactions between industry and academic sector institutions. For many useful marketing knowledge innovations, creative efforts often appear, as in the conjoint analysis case, to span *both* academic and professional researchers. Another example drives home this point. In 1961, Lavidge (a professional researcher) and Steiner (an academic researcher) published a paper in the *Journal of Marketing* on a "hierarchy of effects" perspective to advertising research and management.[24] The patterns of borrowing from basic research (in this case in social psychology) and of the subsequent wide use of the ideas for planning and research in marketing have many parallels to the conjoint analysis case.[25] In both cases nonmarketing academics and marketing researchers in academic and professional contexts were involved.

One could also cite numerous examples of the impact of basic research outside of marketing on knowledge development within the field. The pioneering work of Dantzig in linear programming, for example, did much to set the stage for many applications of linear programming and model building generally in marketing applications.[26] Also, virtually every methodological variant of social science has its commercial equivalent in the context of some marketing research supplier company or marketing research application. Examples range from Skinnerian ideas of operant conditioning in commercial research applications such as CONPAAD, through Coombsian views on the "theory of data" applied to multidimensional scaling, to Bush and Mosteller's stochastic learning theory applied to stochastic models of brand choice, Johnson's econometrics ideas applied to sales forecasting, and dozens of others.[27] Both marketing's R & D system, and the process of knowledge creation in the field, are intimately tied up with basic social science and social engineering disciplines. This is not to say that *all* good ideas, particularly those that have been shown to be useful in marketing *management,* originate in these types of basic disciplines, but rather that many of them do and that, in developing a model of knowledge creation and utilization, this link should be made explicit.

Within marketing, the major sources of useful new ideas can be found in manager and researcher groups. Concerning the process of *developing* the ideas, researchers are the ones who have the time and technical expertise to see them through a development process, even though major supervisory efforts are often involved by operating line managers and marketing research managers. Researchers play the major role in knowledge creation and development because, in one way or another, this is the business they are in. Among researchers, it is important to recognize that (1) innovation flows from *both* academics *and* professionals and (2) not *all* academic or *all* professional marketing researchers are actively engaged in *creating* new knowledge. The majority in each case are best described as being involved in *disseminating* it. The group of active academic and professional researchers involved in knowledge creation we call the "innovator research group" *in* marketing. More will be said about the nature of this group in a later section.

What "vehicles" are used in disseminating marketing knowledge? This idea has not been formally presented in any of the views expressed thus far. It appears that four kinds of vehicles are most important in the diffusion and dissemination process. *Consulting* is a major avenue through which both academic researchers and some professional researchers keep in touch with practical marketing problems. *Teaching,* where this refers to formal classroom and executive training program work, is a second major vehicle. *Publication* refers to journal articles, working papers, books, and the variety of written materials in newsletters, trade papers, and so on that the innovator group produces. A very broad view is taken of this term to include, for example, computer programs, software packages, and other types of model development. Finally, *meetings and conferences* can be singled out. Innovators appear consistently at annual association conferences, workshops, special events such as the AMA's Doctoral Consortium, and numerous specialized marketing conferences such as the Attitude Research Conference of the AMA.[28]

Figure 5-6 presents a model of marketing knowledge creation and utilization that identifies these and other aspects of the overall process. The work of nonmarketing academics is shown as a major input into the work of the *innovator*

FIGURE 5-6

A MODEL OF THE KNOWLEDGE-CREATION AND UTILIZATION PROCESS IN MARKETING

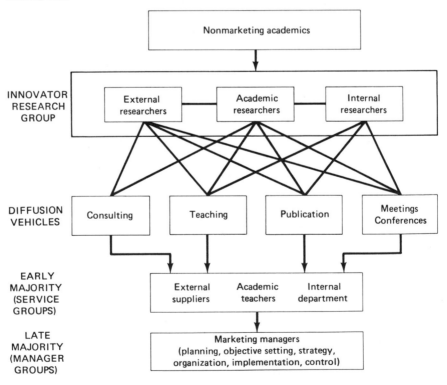

research group in marketing. The innovator research group is made up of academic researchers and professional researchers who are either *external* to the corporation (researchers in marketing research supplier firms and advertising agencies) or *internal* and encompassing marketing research managers and their staffs. Many of the "professional researchers" as a group hold the Ph.D. degree. In terms of scientists with Ph.D. degrees working in industrial-sector organizations, there are many parallels to production's R & D system, even though, in marketing, the pool of higher degree holders is undoubtedly much smaller. All three types are shown in the model as part of the innovator research group to identify their primary commitment to research and knowledge *creation* rather than to applications, teaching, management, or knowledge dissemination and *use*. They do, of course, engage in knowledge-dissemination activities via *diffusion vehicles* such as those shown (consulting, teaching, publication, and meetings-conferences), but the basic characteristic of this group is their primary commitment to the creation of new knowledge in the field, rather than to its dissemination.

The model in Figure 5-6 suggests that all three types of innovators use the four diffusion vehicles shown, with one exception: internal researchers do not do consulting. Although external researchers and academic researchers engage in various consulting activities, this avenue is not really open to those working in the marketing research or operations research department of a corporation. All, however, engage in "teaching" in one form or the other. For the academic researcher it is a primary activity; for professional researchers it is most likely to be secondary.[29] All are also prone to publish their work in some form or another and to be active attendees at meetings and conferences, usually as "speakers," "session chairmen," "discussants," and so on. More will be said on the characteristics of this group in the next section.

The four diffusion vehicles provide the avenue whereby new knowledge is disseminated first to what Figure 5-6 calls *early majority* or *service groups*. These are people who make up the staffs of external suppliers (marketing research firms and advertising agencies); academics whose primary focus is teaching; and internal marketing research department staffs of corporations. They provide the key interface between the creators of new knowledge and its users, the latter being referred to as the *late majority* or *manager groups*. Marketing managers (users of the knowledge) apply new knowledge to problem-identification or problem-solving questions ranging over activities such as planning, objective setting, strategy, organization, implementation, and control.

It should be reemphasized that this is but one conception or "model" of the process. Managers, for example, supply the key ideas for truly important breakthroughs in knowledge development in many instances. They are unlikely, however, to have the time or inclination to pursue their ideas through all phases of development and testing; they are much more likely to delegate them to be worked on by someone in the innovator research group. As the friend of the

Commission said: "The line manager does not have a tool kit; he has a staff!" Thus, although other models might be used to characterize other patterns through which the process works, this one appears to capture the predominant pattern in the field of marketing.

THE INNOVATOR RESEARCH GROUP

This section examines some characteristics of the innovator research group identified in Figure 5-6. The focus is on "researchers," both academic and professional—who they are and what they do. A leader-follower pattern *within* operating line managers with respect to new knowledge development also probably exists but is not examined here.[30]

Conventional wisdom often suggests that the academic community, or part of it, is the only source of new knowledge in marketing, knowledge which is then "diffused" via publications, teaching, consulting, and the like. This is not true. Important innovations are made, and new knowledge created, by people working in the industrial and other sectors as well as the academic. Indeed, there are much greater differences *within* sectors than there are between them. One of the commissioners drove home the point:

Rather than viewing the marketing academic community, external marketing research, internal marketing research, and marketing management community as playing separate roles, one needs to divide each of them into two segments. In each of these communities I think there is a group I might call the leadership cadre or club. It seems to me that these four clubs have almost a circular relationship in passing on early information of some new concept. At times a concept has been promulgated by the academic community and at times the business community. I think the first person to actually use the word market segmentation in print was Wendell Smith—a hybrid born of both. I don't know to whom to give the credit with regard to the concept of product positioning. The marketing concept was born where? Was it Ted Levitt? Or was it G. E.'s management in the early days? Or was it Neil Borden?—I'm not sure. What's important is that there is a leadership group (in both the academic and business sectors of marketing) that interchanges thoughts and ideas fairly intensely and that from that interchange all of the corresponding follower groups are influenced.

Leaders interact among themselves partly through journals and other formal channels and partly via word-of-mouth and working papers or reprints. The idea of a "club" is not too far off, except in principle this "club" is open to anyone of sufficient talent and training who is willing to play by the necessary rules of intellectual rigor.

The diffusion of ideas takes place through the formal channels, but it is likely that the mix is somewhat different because the majority group is much larger than the leader group. Word-of-mouth is important in the diffusion process, too.[31] It occurs as a result of the "sales activities" of external marketing research companies and by way of the comparison of notes among internal marketing researchers and managers in different companies—for example, at AMA chapter or national meetings. Data on sources of information used in the adoption of new concepts and techniques obtained from a broad sample of AMA members (see Chapter 6) doubtless are more representative of the majority group rather than of the leader group.

Much attention has been given in recent years to the ranking of leading universities and scholars in business and marketing. The sections that follow give results from some of these studies as well as some impressions of leaders and their characteristics in the industrial sector.

Academic Researchers

MBA Magazine regularly publishes its ranking of "leading business schools" from the perspective of alumni and deans. This has been supplemented by numerous other types of ranking studies. For example, the *Journal of Business* provided a study of the number of articles published in leading journals broken down by functional area (accounting, finance, marketing, and so on). Special studies have been commissioned to include academics (appropriately segmented by junior-senior faculty) as the rater pool. The business of business school and faculty rankings and ratings has flourished in the past few years!

The most recent types of studies involve what is called *citation analysis*.[32] Citation analysis concerns counting the number of times a researcher's article is cited in footnotes and bibliographies. This number is used as one measure of the impact of his or her work on the field and, in this context, is a useful way to identify key individuals in the academic side of the innovator research group in marketing.

A citation analysis study in marketing covering the period 1972-1975 was done by Robinson and Adler.[33] It is useful in at least two respects. First, it provides an indicator of the size of the academic innovator research pool in marketing that was alluded to in Chapter 4 in the discussion of the education segment of marketing's R & D system. Second, it identifies those scholars in the field during the 1972-1975 period whose work had the greatest impact based on the number of times it was cited. Concerning the first of these points, the pool of scholars whose work was to be analyzed in the study was 1656. This is larger than the 500 to 800 estimated in the preceding chapter. But many of the 1656 had publications that were not "cited" in footnotes and bibliographies. As the authors noted, over 50% of all citations over the four-year period was accounted for by only 3.1% (51) of the total number of scholars (there were 7179 citations recorded). Eleven percent accounted for some 80% of all citations, and *all* citations were accounted for by only 36.2% (599) of the pool of scholars involved. Thus, although there were 1656 scholars who published something in marketing during this period, only about 600 had that work formally acknowledged in footnotes and bibliographies.

Who were the leaders among the 600-odd people involved? The three most frequently cited were, in order: Paul Green (Wharton School, Pennsylvania), Philip Kotler (Northwestern University), and Frank Bass (Purdue University). The three universities whose marketing faculty members received the most citations per faculty member were University of Pennsylvania, Purdue University, and Stanford University. Those whose *graduate faculty alumni* received the most citations per graduate were, in order: MIT, University of Chicago, and Stanford University; and those whose doctoral graduates in *business* received the most per graduate, respectively, were: University of Chicago, Stanford University, and Carnegie-Mellon.[34]

Table 5-1 lists the thirty most-cited marketing scholars over this period, showing the institutional affiliation of each, the university granting the degree, and the number of citations broken down into articles and books. With a little stretch of the imagination, it is possible to classify the research of these individuals as either quantitatively or conceptually oriented. For example, the work of Frank Bass tends to involve mathematical equations and econometric analysis, whereas behaviorally oriented researchers such as Robertson, Ward, and Ray deal more with verbal concepts and sociological or psychological analysis methods. The list is interesting from this point of view because about half of those shown are quantitatively oriented and about half conceptually oriented. Of the top fifteen, however, eleven are best characterized as "quantitative," and this perspective dominates a significant proportion of the core of marketing knowledge, particularly at the basic research and problem-oriented research levels.

Numerous problems are associated with citation analysis, and much criticism has been leveled against it. The Science Citation Index, for example, lists only first authors.[35] Small coding mistakes can have major impacts on interpretation. One irate researcher complained to *Science* as follows:

For best results it would be wise to cite yourself as often as possible; insist that your work be cited in all articles that you review; and automatically pass articles that already contain a sufficient number of citations to you. Unfortunately, you will not get any credit if an author leaves out one of your initials, or, even worse, misspells your name. Nevertheless, if the above steps are taken, you should be able to push your "lifetime citation rate" over those of any immediate rivals. If all else fails, publish a paper containing a subtle misuse of the second law of thermodynamics.[36]

Citation analysis is nevertheless here to stay, and it will probably see increasing use for evaluating institutions and faculties. The Robinson-Adler study reveals much about the academic innovator research group during 1972–1975. It is a small group. Out of 1656 marketing academics studied, less than 600 accounted for all of the citations in this four-year period, and only 30 of them accounted for nearly 40% of the over-7000 citations recorded.

TABLE 5-1

THE MOST-CITED MARKETING SCHOLARS (1972–1975)

				Citations		
Rank	Name	Institutional Affiliation, 1976–1977	University Granting Doctoral Degree	Total	Articles	Books
1	Green, Paul E. [a]	Pennsylvania	Pennsylvania [b]	289	147	142
2	Kotler, Philip [a]	Northwestern	MIT [b]	264	159	105
3	Bass, Frank M. [a]	Purdue	Illinois	188	184	4
4	Frank, Ronald E.	Pennsylvania	Chicago	170	140	30
5	Howard, John A. [a]	Columbia	Harvard [b]	146	42	104
6	Little, John D. C.	MIT	MIT [b]	126	126	0
7	Sheth, Jagdish N. [a]	Illinois	Pittsburgh [b]	111	93	18
8	Engle, James [a]	Wheaton	Illinois	111	21	90
9	Farley, John U.	Columbia	Chicago	102	100	2
10	Robertson, Thomas S.	Pennsylvania	Northwestern	98	55	43
11	Pessemier, Edgar A.	Purdue	Harvard	88	65	23
12	Levitt, Theodore [a]	Harvard	Ohio State [b]	87	64	23
13	Ferber, Robert [a]	Illinois	Chicago [b]	86	60	26
14	Montgomery, David [a]	Stanford	Stanford	82	65	17
15	Massy, William F. [a]	Stanford	MIT [b]	74	36	38
16	Webster, Frederick E.	Dartmouth	Stanford	73	48	25
17	Morrison, Donald G.	Columbia	Stanford	65	65	0
18	Wilkie, William L.	Florida	Stanford	63	61	2
19	Ward, Scott	Harvard	Wisconsin	61	45	16
20	Aaker, David [a]	California	Stanford	56	45	11
21	Ray, Michael L.	Stanford	Northwestern [b]	55	48	7
22	Brozen, Yale	Chicago	Chicago [b]	54	50	4
23	Bucklin, Louis P.	California	Northwestern	53	28	25
24	Day, George [a]	Toronto	Columbia	53	33	20
25	Zaltman, Gerald [a]	Pittsburgh	Johns Hopkins [b]	51	16	35
26	Sturdivant, Frederick D. [a]	Ohio State	Northwestern	47	30	17
27	Huff, D. L.	Texas	Washington	47	43	4
28	Kassarjian, H. H. [a]	UCLA	UCLA [b]	47	43	4
29	Buzzell, Robert D.	Harvard	Ohio State	46	24	22
30	Stern, Louis W. [a]	Northwestern	Northwestern	46	26	20

Other scholars with 40 or more citations were (in alphabetical order): Harper Boyd (Tulane), John Fayerweather (NYU), Charles King (Purdue), Francesco Nicosia (California), and Glen Urban (MIT).

There are two other well-established scholars who publish in fields closely related to marketing, who might be included in the above list. They are Jacob Jacoby (Psychology, Purdue, 78 citations) and John Meyer (Transportation, Harvard, 59 citations).

[a]These scholars were also included on a list of perceived leaders in marketing thought published by the American Marketing Association in 1975. *Marketing News*, Nov. 21, 1975.
[b]These authors did not receive doctoral degrees in business administration.

Source: Larry M. Robinson and Roy D. Adler, "Citations Provide Objective Ratings of Schools, Scholars," *Marketing News*, 12 (July 28, 1979), p. 8, published by the American Marketing Association.

Professional Researchers

To our knowledge, no published study has attempted to identify innovator-leaders among professional researchers in the innovator research group. In this section we make that attempt. The primary criterion for identification is *publication* activity, and this eliminates many who, based on other criteria, would be classified as innovators in the creation of marketing knowledge.[37]

We remark first, as noted earlier, that many people in this group hold the Ph.D. degree—often *not* in business administration or marketing but in some applied social science field such as economics, psychology, or sociology. Second, we find leaders associated with *external* supplier firms as well as with *internal* marketing research departments—those who not only publish but also teach and are active in making presentations at meetings, conferences, and so on. It is interesting to note that some of the innovators associated with media (particularly newspapers) are located in an association rather than with an operating firm. Third, members of this group share a characteristic of the academic researcher group: there are not very many of them! Fourth, many are ex-academics—people who have moved into industry after spending some time doing teaching and research at a university. Finally, as with academics, each is identifiable with a particular contribution, stream-of-research, theory, model, managerial framework, technique, or methods development in the field of marketing.

Table 5-2 presents a listing in alphabetical order. It is not comprehensive but represents some of the more visible contributors to marketing knowledge at the "idea-generation stage." Note that three types of institutional locations are involved: marketing research departments, research supplier firms, and advertising agencies or associations. Also, specific contributions of each person are easily recognized. Banks, for example, produced one of the classic books on marketing experimentation; Wells is known for his work on psychographics; Gross for contributions to advertising budgeting and copy decisions; Warwick for his role as section editor of Computer Abstracts for *JMR;* and so on. Much of the published work of these people is read by academic researchers through the medium of the *Journal of Advertising Research.*[38]

We gain some idea of the nature of the "club" or "cadre" alluded to by the commissioner quoted earlier when we observe that many of the professionals shown on these lists were at one time professors of marketing in academic institutions (for example, Irvin Gross, Henry Claycamp, and Bill Wells). Furthermore, there is to some degree a reverse flow. Many academics now teaching marketing were at one point in their careers "professional researchers" (for example, Paul Green and Russell Haley).

Basically, members of the innovator research group, whether academic or professional, look to and interact with each other on an ongoing and continuing basis. They "speak the same language," read one another's work, and have

TABLE 5-2

A SELECTED LIST OF PROFESSIONAL INNOVATOR RESEARCHERS IN MARKETING

Advertising Agencies or Associations

Alvin Achenbaum, J. Walter Thompson
Seymour Banks, Leo Burnett
Leo Bogart, American Newspaper Publishers Assoc.
Ted Dunn, Benton & Bowles
Russell Haley, Grey Advertising
Lawrence Light, BBD&O
Ben Lipstein, SSC&B
Kenneth Longman, Young & Rubicam
Joseph Plummer, Leo Burnett
Stuart Tolley, American Newspaper Publishers Assoc.
William Wells, Needham, Harper & Steers
Shirley Young, Grey Advertising
Ruth Ziff, Doyle, Dane & Bernbach

Marketing Research Supplier Firms

Jack Abrams, Market Facts
Valentine Appel, W. R. Simmons
Douglas Carroll, Bell Laboratories
Irving Crespi, Gallup
Ernest Dichter, Dichter and Associates
Andrew Ehrenberg, Aske Research
Frank Goode, Market Facts
Marshall Greenberg, National Analysts
David Hardin, Market Facts
Richard Johnson, Market Facts
Jack Keane, Managing Change
Donald Kunstler, Elrick and Lavidge
Robert Lavidge, Elrick and Lavidge
William Moran, Ad Mar Research
Charles Ramond, Marketing Control
Patrick Robinson, Robinson & Associates
Irving Roshwalb, Audits & Surveys
Peter Sherrill, Field Research
Kenneth Warwick, Avrett, Free & Fischer

Marketing Research Departments

Henry Claycamp, International Harvester
George Fabian, Johnson & Johnson
Nelson Foote, General Electric
Lawrence Gibson, General Mills
Irwin Gross, DuPont
Neil Holbert, Philip Morris
Herbert Krugman, General Electric
Elmer Lotshaw, Owens-Illinois
J. Tony Lunn, Unilever (London)
John McMenniman, Norton Simon
Malcolm McNiven, DuPont
Bart Panettiere, General Foods
Robert Pratt, General Electric
W. R. Reiss, AT&T
Dudley Ruch, Quaker Oats
Leonard Simon, Community Savings Bank
Edwin Sonnecken, Goodyear
Roy Stout, Coca-Cola
Edward Tauber, Carnation
Lewis Winters, Standard Oil of California

similar interpretations of terms such as "quality work," "contribution," and "progress in the field." This mutuality extends to published material. Whereas the two books most widely used for teaching marketing management were written by academics (McCarthy and Kotler), three of those most widely used for teaching advertising were written by "professional researchers" (Longman, JWT; Kleppner, The Kleppner Company, Inc.; and Bogart, American Newspaper Publishers Association). A related phenomenon is the tendency for professional researchers to move freely from one type of organization *within* the industry sector to another; from a supplier to a marketing research department, and so on. Another is the tendency for people in this group to start new marketing research firms. Dozens of such firms are started in any one year by people previously working on the staffs of larger MR suppliers or corporate MR departments. A final observation is that "marketing research department" may not adequately represent all corporate departments in which new-knowledge innovators in marketing can be found. In recent years, the "management science" department in many larger firms has been the source of much that is new in marketing.

THE COMMISSION'S MINI-GUIDE STUDY

As noted earlier, the Commission conducted a study to elicit various conceptions of the knowledge-creation and utilization process from its members and friends. This study, which became known as the "Mini-Guide" study, involved a series of iterations in which a basic conception of the process was sent to each individual and then systematically elaborated upon in subsequent rounds. Many of the ideas presented in the early sections of this chapter evolved from this study. The first round began with a hypothetical representation or "model" based on conventional wisdom. Figure 5-7 shows the model sent out on the initial round. Note that it ignores the stage of idea development and the "innovator-majority" distinction. Also, respondents were asked to react to the model in terms of knowledge that was more general and concept-oriented than, say, the development of specific marketing models or research techniques.

For the first round, respondents were given the following instructions:

1. The enclosed diagram represents the *hypothetical process* of an idea conceived in the outside (of marketing) academic community and finding its way into the "tool kit" of an operating line manager. An alternative view would start with the line manager and his problem and then work backwards.

   – Is the process as hypothesized a fair representation of reality in your experience?

   – Where are the barriers to diffusion—at the academic/business interface, or intracompany between the market research department and line manager?

   – Is the diffusion being slowed by a lack of feedback from the line manager to the academic community?—i.e., are line managers aware of many concepts and tech-

FIGURE 5-7

THE BASIC MINI-GUIDE MODEL

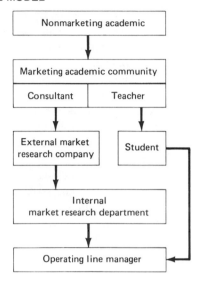

niques which have been developed by the academic community which cannot be used?

- Is the diffusion process, alternatively, being slowed by a lack of awareness by the line managers of the techniques and concepts?
- As a third alternative, is the organizational system and its "acceptance" of the techniques and concepts the source of any loss of effectiveness?

2. How do firms maintain an awareness of new concepts and techniques?

- What is the best method—an internal specialist, outside courses for line managers, encouragement to external market research companies to use new approaches?

3. What is the primary source of new marketing concepts and ideas to companies?

- Professional training
- New staff members in companies
- External market research firms
- A new technique specialist
- Consulting relationships with academics

This material was sent to all Commission members plus approximately ten "friends" nominated by the Commission for the first round. Many of the reactions concerning barriers to diffusion, awareness of new concepts and techniques, and sources of concepts and ideas are presented in Chapter 6. Here, we focus on commissioner judgments about an overall model of the process. The results described below are the synthesis of ten responses received from Commission members plus five friends. Two of the latter responses represent the views of more than one person taken from in-company meetings held especially for that purpose.

The major reaction to the first-round model was that, although it represented one possible view of the process, it was by no means the only possible view. A number of respondents suggested the addition of colloquia or seminars and publications as vehicles and channels through which academics communicated with the rest of the system. Another suggested that the marketing academic was not the sole channel of communication between the nonmarketing academic and the rest of the system: there is direct contact, but there is also contact via the "internal management science" departments in companies.

Based on these kinds of replies, the basic model was extended as shown in Figure 5-8. Advertising agencies were added to the system, as were other components such as corporate staff and field managers in addition to operating line managers. Reactions to this version emphasized the absence of, or lack of acknowledgement of, a central meeting ground for researchers and managers. This led to yet another iteration of the basic model, as shown in Figure 5-9, which served as the stimulus material for the second iteration.

These graphical displays do not capture all the flows and institutions and agencies that could conceivably be involved in the process. Probably there is no "one" way in which new managerially useful concepts and frameworks come into being and are diffused through the system. We present below, however, the

FIGURE 5-8

FIRST ITERATION OF THE MINI-GUIDE MODEL

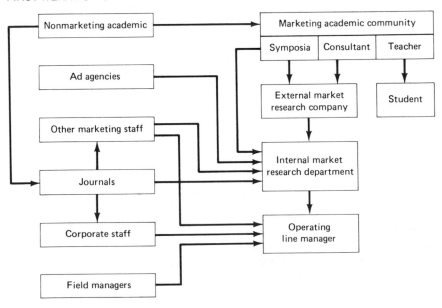

FIGURE 5-9

SECOND ITERATION OF THE MINI-GUIDE MODEL

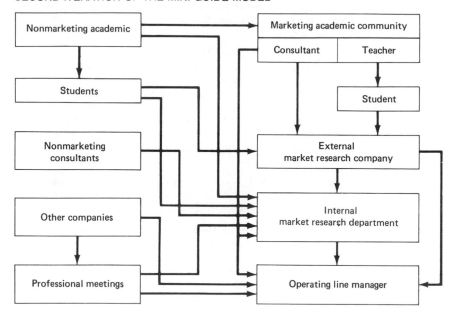

detailed response of a friend of the Commission, who explains the process in his company, a large and innovative packaged-goods manufacturer. The response is significant because it represents the joint efforts of several people in the company, even though this is probably not the only way the processes implicit in the three versions of the model might take place.

Most of the work on new concepts and techniques in marketing reaches our operating line management through the Market Research Department or through the Management Sciences Department. In any case, techniques which involve data collected from consumers or through syndicated services like Nielsen, SAMI, etc. must be approved by the Market Research Department before they can be used for decision-making purposes.

I have attached a slightly revised diagram which I feel better represents the process of new technique diffusion in (our company). For the most part, it just shows more lines of communication. Much of the information reaching our Market Research and Management Science Groups comes directly from the academic community via technical symposia, meetings and conferences and technical journals, working papers, etc. The Marketing Academic Community is obviously the most important source, but we also receive valuable ideas from academic sources in statistics, psychometrics, econometrics, and psychology as well as some input from other behavioral science areas. In a few cases, we have been experimenting with new techniques like multidimensional scaling, etc. at about the same time that the Marketing Academic Community first began its work [with the technique].

External market research companies are another important source of new techniques. Often these techniques come from the Marketing or Nonmarketing Academic Communities and are developed into commercially salable services by these research companies. In many cases, the same people originate a technique while working in the Academic Community and later develop it for commercial application as part-time or full-time employees of an external research firm.

(Our company) makes relatively little use of outside marketing consultants, mainly because of the availability of technical consultants within the company. The Market Research Department has access to consultants in the areas of marketing models, econometrics, statistics, and mathematics who are members of the (company's) Management Sciences Department. Outside consultants tend to be used only for occasional problems in which we have not yet acquired the necessary expertise, when our own consultants are overloaded with work, or when there are legal requirements for an outside expert judgment.

Some new concepts and techniques have come to us from the academic area via newly hired students at the Ph.D. level, or via Ph.D. level training of company employees. However, most techniques taught at the MBA level are already familiar to us.

Most new techniques introduced to our Market Research Department are evaluated by our internal Experimental Research Section before they are exposed to operating line managers. If the evaluation is favorable, a new technique may be used on a limited number of studies for line management with the understanding that the results are not fully validated and cannot be used, in isolation, for important management decisions. As favorable experience accumulates, the technique may be removed from experimental status and turned over to our Consumer Research Section as a standard procedure.

Other commissioners further emphasized, as we have done in describing marketing's R & D system in Chapter 4, the important role of nonmarketing academics. These two statements were made by nonacademic members of the Commission:

Many of the techniques I am familiar with, particularly those in quantitative and statistical areas, have originated in academic fields other than marketing. Marketing educators and researchers tend to be very eclectic in picking up ideas and then developing them through research and consulting activities.

I think when it comes to specific methods and techniques and their first original development it has dominantly been in academic communities other than marketing. Marketing people have typically transplanted methods that others have created.

Elaboration on this idea as well as the need for a "development" function was provided by a friend of the Commission. After noting that the really important new developments in the practice of marketing have been due to "technological innovations in fields other than marketing" (that is, factors such as mass production and mass advertising, discussed in Chapter 2), he discussed a number of "minor" concepts and techniques that have had some impact on marketing research procedures.

Most of these techniques originated in the behavioral sciences, or were originated by behavioral scientists working in some applied setting. The common element in all (or at least most) of them is that they have been drastically altered and adapted for use in marketing research.

In some cases the prescriptions of the originators of these concepts have been ignored or reversed. For example, the sample survey based on the probability sample (still described at great length in marketing research textbooks) has virtually disappeared from the marketing research scene. It is still employed on some government projects where unusually large budgets are available, and it is still sometimes forced on studies conducted by media; but the great cost and great difficulty of personal, in-home interviews has precluded their use in most marketing studies. Today, marketing research surveys are much more often conducted by telephone, by mail, or by shopping mall intercepts. As far as I know, the Consumer Mail Panel was developed in the marketing research context. It violates many of the principles of "scientific" survey work still extolled in marketing research textbooks and courses, and receives little attention there. However, because it is so much less expensive than personal interviewing, and because the samples it produces are good enough for most marketing research purposes, its use has increased greatly. If anything, the academic social science and marketing establishment has retarded the spread of this major innovation.

The semantic differential developed by a behavioral scientist (Charles Osgood) has contributed the seven-step bipolar scale to marketing research. However, the scales most commonly used in marketing research today are tailored to the product or service in question rather than designed to measure the more abstract semantic differential dimensions of evaluation, potency, and activity. (I still remember the bewildered look on a homemaker's face when I tried to get her to rate [one of our brands] as fast or slow.) Further, some marketing researchers have found that greater precision can be obtained by breaking the seven-step scale into two halves and asking the respondents to react to each pole separately. Again, a technique adapted from the behavioral sciences was radically transformed by marketing researchers as a result of their efforts to apply it to their specialized problems.

The formal attitude scaling techniques described by Thurstone and Likert received extensive trial in marketing research. They have now virtually disappeared, having been replaced by the rating scales described in the paragraph above. A lot of time, effort, and money was wasted in trying to use these "scientific" methods. The diffusion took place, but the method didn't work very well.

Projective techniques were imported from clinical psychology on the premise that they would reveal the "real" motives behind consumer behavior. Now, the only remnant of clinical techniques is the "depth" interview, usually conducted in group form. The group interview is very widely used today because it is such a rich source of information about consumers' reactions to goods and services, but it is seldom used in the original clinical spirit of attempting to uncover unconscious processes. Something useful emerged from all this, but only after a nearly complete revision of the technique to meet the unique needs of the marketing research setting. Incidentally, it is worth noting that this very useful and much used method receives almost no attention in most marketing research textbooks, and has never been a topic for academic research; while probability sampling, which is very nearly gone from the day-to-day marketing research scene, still gets lots of attention and space.

The techniques of multivariate statistical analysis (including nonmetric multidimensional scaling) did come directly from the behavioral sciences and have been used in marketing research in much the same way as they are used in psychology and sociology. This is the one case, among all the developments cited, that seems to have followed the flow chart developed by the Commission.

Like projective techniques, personality tests have received extensive trial—and then have generally been found wanting, although attempts to employ them persist. An offshoot—"psychographics"—which specifically rejects many of the concepts and principles of personality testing, is alive and well, however.

Dogged attempts to use laboratory-based physiological measures—GSR, eye movement, pupil dilation, and now voice analysis—keep reappearing. None has so far gained general acceptance, even with extensive modification. The exception is the tachistoscope, which appears to be useful when employed judiciously in package testing.

Experimental designs and their associated classical statistical models have proved useful in product testing and in some large scale in-the-market experiments. However, the notion of "significance," which came along with the classical models, continues to cause great confusion in marketing research studies. Formal Bayesian models have rarely been applied in practice because the information they require is usually unavailable. For some unknown reason, MBA's are [still] taught that these models are both valuable and in common use.

The common element in all these examples seems to be that someone in a marketing research setting saw something in the social or behavior sciences that might be useful and attempted to apply it. Sometimes the attempted application was a complete or nearly complete failure because the concept or idea was simply inappropriate to marketers' problems. Even when the idea or technique was appropriate, it usually needed extensive testing and revision before it could be adopted. The process was seldom if ever that of an information-bearer transporting a concept or method from a "nonmarketing academic" to a marketing practitioner.

Although the experiences of this professional seem not to acknowledge the role of marketing academics as part of the innovator research group, the eight examples given are excellent illustrations of the process described in the general model given in Figure 5-6. Each example highlights the role of the nonmarketing academic, and the necessary development activities. There is little question that parallel work was being done on each by marketing academics, even though one comes away with the impression that the latter did not significantly affect the developments (and in some cases, rejections) in each case. More will be said of this point in Chapters 6 and 7.

A final version of the Mini-Guide model was developed from a synthesis of the many comments received from commissioners. It is presented in Figure 5-10. Both within-field and outside-the-field factors are represented. Since there are no one-way flows among different groups within marketing, all the arrows in this sector are double-ended. Interactions with the nonmarketing world external to a given company are shown as one-way, even though certain members of the marketing academic community have been contributing to work in the underlying academic disciplines in recent years. Of course within-company flows tend to be—and definitely should be—two-way.

FIGURE 5-10
FINAL ITERATION OF THE MINI-GUIDE MODEL

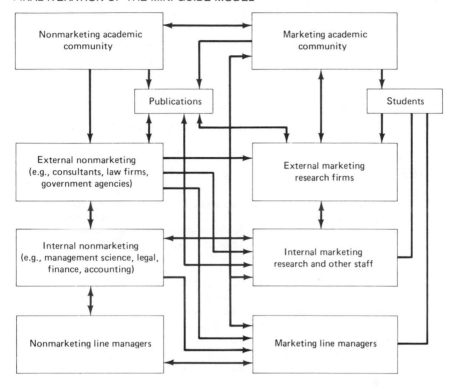

SUMMARY

The process of knowledge creation and utilization in marketing is very complex. This chapter has provided some insights into that complexity. Types of knowledge do interact with types of knowledge development (research), albeit in highly complex ways. It is impossible to generalize for the field of marketing that basic research *always* precedes problem-oriented research, which *always* precedes problem-solving research, even though this may be a dominant pattern. Other generalizations such as "academics always initiate the knowledge-creation process" are also tenuous at best. There do appear to be definable *stages* to the process and a generalizable model that recognizes the important role played by the *innovator research group* in marketing, but there are no easy ways to describe all the flows, interactions, and diffusion/influence processes taking place in all situations.

To this point in the book, we have focused on descriptive materials drawn from the work of the Commission and from marketing literature. As stated in Chapter 1, an important objective of the Commission was evaluative. Numerous types of assessments and evaluations were made, particularly concerning the scope or *degree of utilization* of various kinds of new knowledge developed over the period. These assessments are described in Chapter 6. Commissioner viewpoints are presented on the success or failure of particular theories, models, and techniques. Results of a rate-of-adoption survey are given, and an analysis is made of various types of barriers or blocks to the knowledge-utilization process. Chapter 6 focuses on assessments of the "effectiveness" of the knowledge-creation and utilization process and, by implication, the effectiveness of a major part of marketing's overall research and development system.

NOTES

[1]Diffusion of innovations and ideas and objects in general is a subject of continuing interest in many basic disciplines. The perspective in economics often sees the firm as the basic unit of analysis. Sociology and medical epidemiology often focus on the individual and the group processes that operate to affect adoption and diffusion rates. For classic works on the subject, see Edwin Mansfield, *Industrial Research and Technological Innovation* (New York: W. W. Norton, 1968); Elihu Katz and Paul F. Lazarsfeld, *Personal Influence* (New York: The Free Press, 1955. Copyright © 1955 by Macmillian Publishing Co., Inc.); Everett M. Rogers, *Diffusion of Innovations* (New York: The Free Press, 1962. Copyright © 1962 by Macmillian Publishing Co., Inc.).

[2]See Frank M. Bass, "A New Product Growth Model for Consumer Durables," *Management Science,* 15 (January 1969), 215-27.

[3]An excellent book on the topic, which pulls together much of the work done in marketing up to 1971, is Thomas S. Robertson, *Innovative Behavior and Communication* (New York: Holt, Rinehart and Winston, 1971).

[4]For early studies, see John G. Myers, "Patterns of Interpersonal Influence in the Adoption of New Products," *Proceedings,* American Marketing Association, 1966, pp. 750-57; Alvin J. Silk, "Overlap Among Self-Designated Opinion Leaders: A Study of Selected Dental Products and Services," *Journal of Marketing Research,* 3 (August 1966), 255-59; Harold H. Kassarjian, "Social Character and Differential Preference for Mass Communication," *Journal of Marketing Research,* 2 (May 1965), 146-53; James F. Engel and others, "How Information Is Used to Adopt an Innovation," *Journal of Advertising Research,* 9 (December 1969), 3-8.

[5]Katz and Lazarsfeld, *Personal Influence.*

[6]This conception of the way marketing communication such as advertising works has been seriously challenged and is not generalizable over all industry and product situations.

[7]A good review of what is known about opinion leadership is given in Robertson, *Innovative Behavior and Communication.* Dozens of additional studies on innovation and personal influence in marketing have been done since its publication in 1971.

[8]Rogers, *Diffusion of Innovations.*

[9]Although there have been studies of the criteria on which marketing models might be considered "useful" [see Larreche and Montgomery, "A Framework for the

Comparison of Marketing Models: A Delphi Study," *Journal of Marketing Research,* 14 (November 1977), 487–98], none to date appears to approach the question of model utilization from the perspectives of theories of innovation diffusion. Also, it needs emphasizing that diffusion and adoption rates are affected by many other factors than simply the "nature of the product" alluded to above. In marketing, pricing, advertising, and distribution factors all affect "diffusion rates." For further discussion, see David A. Aaker and John G. Myers, *Advertising Management* (Englewood Cliffs, N.J.: Prentice-Hall, 1975), pp. 358–91.

[10]An academic administrator once observed that even the most brilliant ideas have no social value if they remain lodged in the heads of their proponents.

[11]Frank M. Bass and Dick R. Wittink, "Pooling Issues and Methods in Regression Analysis with Examples in Marketing Research," *Journal of Marketing Research,* 12 (November 1975), 414–25.

[12]For one of the earliest papers, see Donald G. Morrison, "Stochastic Models for Time Series with Applications in Marketing," Program in Operations Research, Stanford University, Technical Report No. 8, 1965.

[13]See John G. Myers and Francesco M. Nicosia, "On the Study of Consumer Typologies," *Journal of Marketing Research,* 5 (May 1968), 182–93; Frank and others, *Market Segmentation;* and the recent review article, Yoram Wind, "Issues and Advances in Segmentation Research," *Journal of Marketing Research,* 15 (August 1978), 317–37.

[14]The evolution is represented in recent works such as Alvin J. Silk and Glen L. Urban, "Pre-Test Market Evaluation of New Packaged Goods: A Model and Measurement Methodology," *Journal of Marketing Research,* 15 (May 1978), 171–91, and V. Srinivasan and Allan D. Shocker, "Linear Programming Techniques for Multidimensional Analysis of Preferences," *Psychometrika,* 38 (September 1973), 337–69.

[15]A good overview of these perspectives and efforts is given in Jagdish N. Sheth, ed., *Multivariate Methods for Market and Survey Research* (Chicago: American Marketing Association, 1977), and Harry L. Davis and Alvin J. Silk, eds., *Behavioral and Management Science in Marketing* (New York: Ronald Press, 1978).

[16]Frank and others, *Market Segmentation.*

[17]Paul E. Green and Yoram Wind, "New Way to Measure Consumers' Judgments," *Harvard Business Review,* 53 (1975), 107–17. Copyright © 1975 by the President and fellows of Harvard College. All rights reserved.

[18]Duncan R. Luce and John W. Tukey, "Simultaneous Conjoint Measurement: A New Type of Fundamental Measurement," *Journal of Mathematical Psychology,* 1 (February 1964), 1–27.

[19]Paul E. Green and Vithala R. Rao, "Conjoint Measurement for Quantifying Judgmental Data," *Journal of Marketing Research,* 8 (August 1971), 355–63.

[20]For example, several working papers relating to the subject were developed as early as 1968 by Green and others at Wharton.

[21]Richard M. Johnson, "Trade-Off Analysis of Consumer Values," *Journal of Marketing Research,* 11 (May 1974), 121–27.

[22]This process of refinement has continued to the present and involves different types of data-collection procedures, different types of scale assumptions (nominal, ordinal, interval, ratio), and basic extensions such as categorical conjoint measurement and second-generation models such as componential segmentation. For a paper tracing these developments, see Yoram Wind, "Marketing Research and Management: A Retrospective View of the contributions of Paul E. Green," in *Proceedings of the Tenth Paul D.*

Converse Awards Symposium, Alan Andreasen, ed. (Urbana, Ill.: University of Illinois Press, 1978).

[23]Green and Wind, "New Way to Measure Consumers' Judgments," p. 107.

[24]Robert J. Lavidge and Gary A. Steiner, "A Model for Predictive Measurements of Advertising Effectiveness," *Journal of Marketing,* 25 (October 1961), 59–62. Lavidge, at the time, was president of Elrick and Lavidge, a Chicago-based marketing research firm, and Steiner was an Associate Professor of Psychology in the Graduate School of Business, University of Chicago.

[25]The tripartite structure of attitude (cognitive-affective-conative) on which the Lavidge-Steiner model was based is the foundation for most of the field of social psychology and research in attitude formation and change and can be traced to the original thinkers. The true roots go back to the Greek philosopher Plato, who conceived of the mind as constituting Affection (feeling), Conation (striving), and Cognition (thought). The first book to use the title Social Psychology was published by a sociologist, E. A. Ross, in 1908. For a review of the historical roots of the field (and the Lavidge-Steiner model), see Gordon W. Allport, "The Historical Background of Modern Social Psychology," in Gardner Lindzey, ed., *Handbook of Social Psychology* (Reading, Mass.: Addison-Wesley, 1954), pp. 3–56. The idea has had a profound impact on marketing research and knowledge development and has been expanded into formal theories of consumer behavior, models for marketing planning and control, and hundreds if not thousands of empirical studies of consumer behavior, attitudes, information processing, and so on, that relate to it.

[26]For a brief sketch of the history of linear programming, see G. Hadley, *Linear Programming* (Reading, Mass.: Addison-Wesley, 1962), p. 20. George H. Dantiz is generally credited with making the prewar theoretical developments in economics by Von Neumann and others operational. He formulated the general linear programming problem and devised the simplex solution in 1947. It was later published as a Cowles Commission monograph in 1951.

[27]For these examples, see Ogden R. Lindsley, "A Behavioral Measure of Television Viewing," *Journal of Advertising Research,* 2 (September 1962), 2–12; Clyde H. Coombs, *A Theory of Data* (New York: Wiley, 1964); R. R. Bush and F. Mosteller, *Stochastic Models for Learning* (New York: Wiley, 1955); J. Johnston, *Econometric Methods* (New York: McGraw-Hill, 1963).

[28]Students of mass communications may find it interesting that "print media" and more specifically "journals," rather than any form of "broadcast media," are the only ones used by knowledge innovators in marketing.

[29]Most business schools, for example, have at least one or two "practicing professionals" teaching at any given period, and they can make up a significant percentage of the faculty. Of approximately seventy faculty teaching marketing at a large eastern school, for example, about thirty-five (50%) are professional researchers or managers in the sense used here. This phenomenon is an interesting characteristic of marketing's R & D system.

[30]Part of the rationale for this focus relates to definitional problems in using terms such as "manager," "knowledge," and "innovation." For example, an important marketing "innovation" over the period was the discount store. Beginning about 1950, the growth in these types of retail units over the ensuing twenty-five years was spectacular (there were over 4000 of them as of 1971). E. J. Korvette was surely an important "innovator" in this development. From this perspective, innovators are really business entrepreneurs (when the company is small), and often become the presidents and CEOs when the company is large. Similar kinds of reasoning could be used to trace important innovations by operating line managers of major corporations (brand, product, sales,

advertising managers), and useful kinds of studies might be done in this regard. The emphasis in this section is on *research* leaders, and identification is heavily based on *publication* activity. It should be recognized that many persons who have not published their work but have made significant contributions to marketing in other respects are thus not included. This "invisible college" of innovators has obviously been of great importance to the development of marketing and marketing management over the assessment period.

[31]For an interesting article on the increasingly important role of word-of-mouth communication in science generally, see L. Thomas, "Hubris in Science?" *Science,* 200 (June 1978), 1459–62.

[32]For a good review article, see "Librarian Turned Entrepreneur Makes Millions Off Mere Footnotes," *Science,* 202 (November 1978), 853–57. Copyright 1978 by the American Association for the Advancement of Science. The entrepreneur in question is Eugene Garfield, president and chairman of the board of Institute for Scientific Information (ISI), the world's first multimillion-dollar corporation based on providing access to scientific literature. The Philadelphia-based company employs over 450 people, has offices in nine countries, has two Nobel Laureates on its board, publishes three different citation indexes, and in 1978 had annual sales of about $15 million.

[33]Larry M. Robinson and Roy D. Adler, "Citation Provides Objective Ratings of Schools, Scholars," *Marketing News,* 12 (July 1978), 1ff, published by the American Marketing Association. Citation analysis, although a useful way to document the impact of scholars and schools on knowledge development, may not be the best way to document the impact of that knowledge on marketing management and professional practice. This point is discussed in Chapters 6 and 7.

[34]The impact of the training an individual scholar receives and the university's orientation to research and knowledge development is rather dramatically pointed up by these data. One university, for example, which produced only five Ph.D. graduates who ended up teaching marketing during the four-year period, led the list of "citations per graduate," a total of ninety-three per graduate. Another, which produced 117 graduate Ph.D.'s teaching marketing during the period, averaged only three citations per graduate. The first university produced about three times more citations in total than the second, with about 4% of the number of people. Obviously, some institutions are much more research and knowledge-creation oriented than others.

[35]In response to this criticism, Garfield published a list of the 300 most-cited authors, including secondary authors. As *Science* noted, however, even this list did not contain the names of any of the most recent Nobel Prize Winners!

[36]"Librarian Turned Entrepreneur," p. 856.

[37]For a review of the "founding fathers" of advertising research and the founders of many of the marketing research supplier firms identified in various parts of the book, see the June and October 1977 issues of the *Journal of Advertising Research.* The careers and contributions of nine people are reviewed: Ernest Dichter, George Gallup, Alfred Politz, Henry Brenner, A. C. Nielsen, Sr., Hans Ziesel, Frank Stanton, Archibald Crossley, and Daniel Starch. Much about the historical development of this aspect of the marketing research industry can be gleaned from reading these accounts.

[38]A content analysis of the *Journal of Advertising Research* since its inception in September 1960 would expand our list. Much of the work of innovator research professionals has appeared in this journal, and a good study could be done of individuals and contributions based on *JAR* alone. The first issue, for example, contained articles by Lester Frankel (Audits & Surveys), Arthur Koponen (J. Walter Thompson), Brian Copeland (Hobson, Bates & Parteners, Ltd.), and an academic, Arthur Done (University of Illinois).

6

Assessments of the Knowledge-Creation and Utilization Process

This chapter presents assessments of various components of the models of knowledge creation and utilization presented in Chapter 5. Chapter 7 presents some general commentary on marketing's overall system of research and development. As the preface pointed out, much of the interest in marketing research and knowledge development derives from the ongoing debate about the efficiency and effectiveness of various parts of the system. As noted in Chapter 3, much controversy surrounds the questions of the effectiveness of applied research and of the internal role of the marketing research department as it interfaces with marketing management. The built-in frictions between marketing researchers and manager-users are discussed in several recent marketing research textbooks, and are reflected in the numerous studies we have reviewed in earlier chapters. The controversies become particularly heated about the relative effectiveness of basic research in marketing, particularly where this means the work being done by marketing academics in our leading business schools. Consider, for example, the following reflections of a distinguished professor of marketing who deplores the directions taken during the latter half of the assessment period:

So far as the present is concerned we marketing professors seem to be losing our mooring to economics. . . . It is very doubtful that today, after more than a decade of behavioral studies and theorizing, we know significantly more about consumer behavior than we did at the start. . . . Turning to refined statistical analysis and model building . . . it would appear that the "mountain has labored and brought forth a mouse ". . . . Marketing professors can continue on their present course by trying to create an academic discipline of marketing. If they do, they will become pariahs in the community, because there is no basic body of thought, and marketing professors will be quite properly viewed as poachers and panderers.[1]

   Westing is not alone in labeling much of what marketing academics do as "obscure," "arcane," "irrelevant," or focused on problems of "miniscule importance" relative to real-world concerns of management practice. If marketing academics make no significant contributions to advancements of basic social science or social engineering disciplines or to improvements in the practice and profession of marketing, as can be implied from such evaluations, then they and the field of marketing itself are in bad shape. As stated in the ERDMM Commission's Prospectus: "The fundamental question is whether all or most of these segments do really create useful knowledge. . . . The creation of knowledge that is inadequate . . . will not be viewed as an important investment. Those whose work is inadequate do not have a valid claim on resources." (See Appendix 1-1.) To this point in the book, we have attempted to describe what marketing's R & D system is. This and the concluding chapter focus on evaluation and assessment. Are Westing's charges warranted? To what degree is the system in its industry sector–academic sector aspects "effective"?
   Evaluative material presented in this chapter has two sources: (1) commissioner judgments taken from replies to polls and recorded in face-to-face meetings, (2) reactions of researchers and managers taken from an empirical study of members of the American Marketing Association. Materials are drawn from each of these sources with respect to each topic addressed. This method produces overlap and some duplication of thoughts and ideas—a disadvantage, we believe, that is far outweighed by the advantages of reading commentary in its original and largely unedited form.
   Materials are organized around the major components of the knowledge-creation and utilization models presented in Chapter 5. That is, we present assessments of the knowledge-innovator and knowledge-user groups and some reactions to the various diffusion vehicles and information sources involved. The first section offers background materials on the methods used in generating the assessment data. It is followed by a section on knowledge utilization in terms of commissioner judgments and the AMA membership survey. The third section reviews diffusion vehicles and information sources; the fourth, the innovator research group; and the final sections present material on manager-user groups and the relative contributions of innovator and diffusion agents. Some concluding comments are given at the chapter's end.

METHODS

Materials throughout the chapter are generally organized as commissioner judgments and as respondent reactions, the latter based on a survey of American Marketing Association membership. This section gives an overview of each kind of study and the questions and methods involved. Most of the commissioner evaluations derive from the first poll referred to in Chapter 2 and the Mini-Guide poll referred to in Chapter 5. Concerning the first poll, replies to the question: "What promising research approaches and techniques have, in your opinion, failed to fulfill their promise in terms of applications?" are presented in the section on knowledge utilization. Most of the other commissioner assessments derive from the Mini-Guide poll and replies to questions such as: "Where are the barriers to diffusion?" "Is the diffusion being slowed by a lack of feedback from the line manager to the academic community? By a lack of awareness by the line managers? By the organizational system and its 'acceptance' of the techniques and concepts?" "How do firms maintain an awareness of new concepts and techniques?" "What is the primary source of new marketing concepts and ideas to companies?"

It was decided to base the study on a much larger sample than the eighteen commissioners in order to objectively assess the current state of marketing-knowledge utilization and to check on commissioner judgments. Commissioners had been chosen for their interest and knowledge in the area, and, even though academics, professional researchers, and operating managers were included, the possibilities of serious biases in perceptions and opinions were obviously present. A survey of AMA membership was thus undertaken, and we describe the major features of the study in what follows. Some additional materials on sampling procedures and response rates are given in Appendix B at the end of the book.

The AMA membership study was developed in parallel with other Commission activities, and many of the ideas generated from the polls of commissioners were incorporated in the final design. It became evident, for example, that professionals and managers probably have a "tool kit" of concepts and techniques which they recognize or use in day-to-day operations. Ideas for the content of this took kit were derived from the commissioners' answers to the question on "major new useful approaches and techniques." Four broad questions evolved as the major departure points for data collection and analysis efforts: (1) To what degree had respondents tried and were they currently using various tools and techniques? (2) How confident were they with respect to each? (3) How relevant did they consider the techniques for either data analysis or decision making? (4) What sources of information did they draw on concerning new concepts and techniques?

For the first question it was decided to focus respondent attention on thirteen types of knowledge, all of which could conceivably be either used or not used and could be explained in a mail questionnaire format. The final pool chosen is shown below alongside the actual description given in the questionnaire.

Technique	Description Used
Time-series analysis	a. Time-series analysis—the statistical analysis of trends over time
Bayesian analysis	b. Bayesian decision theory—decision trees, personalized decision analysis
Focus groups	c. Focus groups
	d. Market segmentation
Demographic segmentation	1. Demographic (including socioeconomic) characteristics of present and/or potential consumers
Usage segmentation	2. Usage of products/brands by present and/or potential consumers
Psychographics	e. Psychographics—life-style analysis, attitude/interest/opinion studies
Multidimensional scaling	f. Multidimensional scaling–perceptual mapping
Cluster analysis	g. Cluster analysis
Factor analysis	h. Factor analysis
Conjoint analysis	i. Conjoint measurement—trade-off analysis
Formal experiments	j. Formal experiments using test and control areas and/or groups to test new products or elements of the marketing mix
	k. Marketing models—computer simulations of the response of a brand or consumer to answer "what if" questions in the formulation of strategy
Response models	1. Models to relate marketing expenditure inputs to market share and/or sales response
Computer simulation	2. Computer simulations of alternative marketing mixes

The items ranged over concepts such as various kinds of segmentation, through data-collection methods such as focus groups and experimentation, to complicated decision models and multivariate statistical techniques. Each exemplifies a type of marketing "knowledge" that might play some part in a professional researcher's or manager's "tool kit." In presenting results of the study, we refer to them all simply as "techniques."

Data collection involved a mail questionnaire sent to a sample of American Marketing Association membership. The AMA's membership roster was used as the sampling frame, and members were classified into four groups: marketing managers, research managers, commercial researchers, and academics. A random sampling procedure was followed in selecting respondents from each group. A total of 4292 questionnaires were sent out, and 1271 useable replies received. Of the latter, the usable replies by respondent type were marketing managers (218), research managers (433), commercial researchers (253), and academics (367). Appendix B discusses the representativeness of the sample and the classification procedure used, and gives data on response rates.

Most of the results reported are given as simple proportions and are designed to highlight the study's major findings. To briefly explain the analysis involved we will focus on the first research question concerning trial and use. Similar types of analysis were done concerning the other three questions. Trial and use were measured on a four-point scale: "used frequently," "used occasionally," "used once," and "never used." Respondents checked one of these categories for each of the thirteen techniques, and use, trial, and adoption measures were derived accordingly. Some simple notation will help clarify the nature of the measure of the constructs in each case. Each was developed for the four segments given above, and this is assumed in what follows.

Let:

u_i = a response to the category "used frequently" for technique i

where $u_i = \begin{cases} 1 & \text{if category "used frequently" is checked for technique } i \\ 0 & \text{if some other category is checked for technique } i \end{cases}$

b_i = a response to the category "never used" for technique i

where $b_i = \begin{cases} 1 & \text{if category "never used" is checked for technique } i \\ 0 & \text{if some other category is checked for technique } i. \end{cases}$

Then,

$$(1) \quad U_i = \frac{\sum_{n=1}^{N_i} u_i}{N_i}$$

where U_i = the proportion of respondents who use technique i frequently
N_i = the number of respondents in the subsample who rate technique i.

$$(2) \quad T_i = 1 - \frac{\sum_{n=1}^{N_i} b_i}{N_i}$$

where T_i = the proportion of respondents who have "tried" technique i.

U_i, or *use*, is thus a measure of the degree of use at one point in time of a particular technique by a particular subsample or segment. Like the familiar "penetration" construct in new-product research, it reflects the degree to which a technique is currently being used. T_i, or *trial*, is derived by assuming that those who checked any category other than "never used" had, at some point, used the technique. Here again, results are reported for each of the four subsamples involved.

An additional measure can be derived from these data. The degree of "adoption" of a technique is simply the ratio of the two proportions:

$$(3) \quad A_i = \frac{U_i}{T_i}$$

where A_i = the proportion of respondents who have tried technique i and continue to use it.

A_i, or *adoption,* is something like a "repeat purchase rate" in new-product research except that it is a measure at one point in time only and is based on stated trial and use rather than on actual trial and use. A low value of A_i could signify that the technique was heavily "rejected" by respondents; that is, having tried it, they no longer used it.

A value for each construct was derived for the four respondent groups—three professional and one academic. Professionals (operating managers, research managers, and research suppliers) were asked to report on their own use, whereas academics were asked to estimate how they thought professionals "would" respond.

Concerning the second question, proportions are reported for two types of confidence referred to as "applicability confidence," and "decision confidence." Applicability confidence was measured by the question: "How confident would you be in determining the *applicability* of the following technique to a specific problem?" and decision confidence by: "How confident would you be in *basing a decision* on your interpretation of analyses performed using the following technique?"

Question three was concerned with the *relevance* of the techniques. Respondents were asked: "How relevant do you feel the following techniques would be for data analysis and decision making by managers in positions similar to your own and with your own kind of background?" This was a projective question asking the manager to assess the relevance of the technique for a manager in his or her own position.

Finally, question four dealt with the respondents' evaluations of the *importance* of various types of information sources and agents. They were asked: "By assigning points totaling 100 percent, please rate the relative importance of the groups below in terms of their contribution to (a) the initial development of new concepts and techniques as applied to marketing, and (b) the diffusion of knowledge about new concepts and techniques and their application." Perceived shares and importance rankings of various agents were derived from answers to this question.

In the sections to follow, data from both these sources are presented with respect to particular topics and assessment perspectives. Commissioner poll results are presented largely by way of quotations of individual commissioners or our interpretations of them. The bulk of the AMA membership survey results are presented as tables of proportions with respect to each of the research questions and constructs discussed above. Analysis of association, statistical significance, or other forms of multivariate data analysis were not attempted, owing to time and cost constraints. Further analytical work, however, is being done in connection with the doctoral dissertation of John Bateson at the Harvard Business School, who served on the staff of the Commission.

KNOWLEDGE UTILIZATION

This section focuses on the degree to which new knowledge developed over the assessment period appears to be in current use by professional managers and researchers. In the AMA membership survey, the relevant reference point is the thirteen techniques chosen to represent a cross section of typical new knowledge in the field. Before reporting the results, we summarize the commissioner views on this question. We focus here on replies to the question in the first poll about research approaches and techniques that had failed to fulfill their promise in terms of widespread use and application.

In general the consensus seemed to be that almost any approach or technique could be accused of not having lived up to the expectations created at its "invention" and that many, if not most, were not being widely used. In most cases, this was thought to be due to "overclaiming" when the technique was first described. However, there were a number of things that the Commission regarded as "failures" no matter what standards were used:

The failure to cope with uncertainty in business decision making; notably, Bayesian decision theory had failed to be flexible enough.

The application of management science methods in marketing—notably media allocation models, brand planning algorithms, and call-plan models.

The stochastic approach to buyer behavior, which some believed had not justified the amount of time and money expended on it.

Marketing models, notably decision models and computer simulation.

Other knowledge and techniques cited as candidates for a "glorious failure" list were (1) personality variables and attitude research, especially with respect to predicting sales; (2) marginal analyses and microeconomic theory; (3) certain sophisticated multivariate statistical techniques; (4) formal experimentation; (5) total marketing information systems; and (6) some aspects of advertising research, such as the eye camera. The degree of intensity of feelings about these varied a good deal, and some failures were seen as being "at the margin" relative to expectations.

Somewhat different factors are probably operating with respect to each example listed above. For Bayesian decision theory, there is a big gap between the "theory" and the widespread ability to build models and generate data adequate to exploit it. Thus the problem may be partly technological. Assmus[2] provides a useful review of the problems of applying Bayesian analysis. Many commissioners noted, however, that a great deal of "Bayesian lore" has in fact crept into marketing management and research thinking, even though the formal procedures are not widely used. The basic idea of thinking of decision alternatives in terms of subjective probabilities has contributed something to the field.

The difficulties with models of other kinds are more subtle. Some problems must be due to the limitation of the current state of the art, especially since many of the models included in the assessments should be regarded as early-generation efforts. (A number of first-generation models did fail "gloriously"—e.g., linear programming for advertising media selection and complex marketing simulations).

Many commissioners felt, however, that the problems of the successful development and implementation of decision models were due to more than limitations of technology. In a nutshell, the use of models for close-in managerial support alters some fundamental properties of the decision-making process. Not the least of these changes is the need for new management styles and reward structures, for shifts of power relationships and the sharing of risks among corporate executives. There is a "sociology of model usage" that is to some extent independent of the technical characteristics of the model.[3] To some extent the same issues were beginning to be confronted a generation ago with respect to marketing research. Modeling is newer, and the problems are more difficult. Hence we should not be surprised that at present there are more "glorious failures" than unambiguous successes.

The overall pessimism reflected in many commissioner reactions and their recognition that many techniques and models in 1977 were in a relatively early stage of development is generally upheld in the following AMA Membership Survey results. The first section concentrates on trial and use of the thirteen techniques.

Survey Results: Trial and Use

Several of the thirteen techniques selected for the study are multivariate methods of data analysis. It is useful to set the stage by considering comments made by one of the commissioners, Robert Ferber, during a symposium on multivariate methods held in 1969:

It would appear that multivariate methods are widely known but not many people are familiar with their use, even fewer people have accepted their use, and these methods are certainly not used on a widespread basis. The problem is essentially one of communication, at several levels.

Possibly the first and most important level is to communicate to the public that we are living in a multivariate world. . . . Second, people working in particular areas of multivariate methods have to be induced to learn and to make use of methods from other areas. . . . Third, those who are trying to further develop the field of multivariate methods have to exchange their experiences with other people working in the same area. . . . The most important thing is that those who use and understand multivariate methods of any type communicate the value of these methods to the large body of marketing people.[4]

From the perspective of a sample of AMA members eight years later as reported below, such techniques are still not widely used by any of the professionals surveyed. Models, according to these data, are even less widely used.

Table 6-1 presents data on the U_i ("use") and T_i ("trial") constructs for three categories of user: operating managers, research managers, and research suppliers. Also, the perceptions of academics of "likely" use and trial by managers are given in the fourth and eight columns of the table. First note the major differences between trial and use for all thirteen techniques. In terms of Ferber's reference to "awareness," for example, trial (a stronger measure) by operating managers is comparatively high (above 50%) for ten of the thirteen techniques. Only segmentation, however, appears to have attained a level of penetration or "frequent use" above 50%. The last seven techniques shown in the table all are either "models" or complex "multivariate methods" of data analysis and have achieved penetrations of less than 11% in all cases. Only 4.2% and 3.8% of the 218 operating managers, for example, report regular use of Bayesian analysis and factor analysis.

Patterns of trial and use by research managers and research suppliers are consistently higher than for operating line managers, with the exception of models and computer or economic analysis techniques (time-series analysis, response models, computer simulation). This is not surprising. Models and simulation should be useful to line managers, and data-analysis techniques should be useful to researchers. But the penetration in the case of all of these more complex modeling or analysis techniques is dramatically small. Only four out of 433 research managers reported using Bayesian analysis on a regular basis.[5]

Equally interesting is the significant perceptual distortion in academic estimates of trial and use by operating managers. Academics consistently *underestimate* both trial and use of the less complex techniques (segmentation, focus groups, experiments) and *overestimate* trial and use of the more complex techniques (conjoint analysis, multidimensional scaling, Bayesian analysis, factor analysis).

Research managers represent "internal" managers of research in marketing research departments of corporations. Research suppliers represent "external" firms supplying research to those corporations. Suppliers, interestingly, report somewhat *greater* use of MDS, and cluster, factor, and conjoint analysis, and *lesser* use of time-series analysis. This is not too surprising, as economic forecasts tend to be done by economists in the planning departments of major

TABLE 6-1

TRIAL AND USE OF THIRTEEN TECHNIQUES BY USER TYPES [a]

Technique	Used Frequently ("Use")				Used at Some Time ("Trial")			
	Operating Managers	Research Managers	Research Suppliers	Academic [b] Perception	Operating Managers	Research Managers	Research Suppliers	Academic Perception
Demographic segmentation	54.9	64.1	72.0	30.0	91.2	95.7	98.3	60.3
Usage segmentation	52.0	59.9	68.6	27.5	91.6	91.3	94.6	61.4
Time-series analysis	43.4	45.2	27.8	18.3	81.6	87.2	69.9	65.6
Focus groups	35.4	51.1	62.3	8.6	76.6	85.9	95.6	77.5
Formal experiments	24.6	36.6	45.9	8.3	71.9	73.2	87.7	67.2
Psychographics	12.7	22.3	37.9	3.6	71.1	78.1	88.1	73.3
Response models	10.6	10.6	7.0	2.2	50.0	52.5	35.6	67.8
Computer simulation	10.1	8.7	6.5	5.3	45.5	47.6	35.6	61.7
Cluster analysis	5.2	7.7	16.5	6.1	53.6	62.2	76.3	65.8
Conjoint analysis	4.8	3.8	11.7	5.8	32.6	43.8	55.5	63.6
Multidimensional scaling	4.3	7.0	15.7	6.7	38.2	53.9	65.7	63.9
Bayesian analysis	4.2	1.5	2.2	6.1	59.8	50.4	45.3	67.5
Factor analysis	3.8	12.4	23.6	6.7	56.5	70.4	85.2	64.2
Means	20.5	25.5	30.6	10.4	63.1	68.6	71.8	66.1
Standard deviations	19.4	22.8	24.5	9.0	19.3	18.1	22.6	4.8

[a]All numbers in Table 6-1 are proportions. Columns 1, 2, 3, 5, 6, and 7 are derived from replies of 218 operating managers, 433 research managers, and 253 research suppliers to the question: "Which of the following techniques and concepts have you ever used? (used frequently, used occasionally, used once, never used)." The "used frequently" proportions are derived from responses to the first category. For example, 54.9% of operating managers checked "used frequently" for demographic segmentation. The "used at some time" proportions are derived from 1.00 − (never used) responses.
[b]Columns 4 and 8 are based on replies from 367 academics to the question: "A random sample of AMA members who are practicing marketing managers and who do not work for research companies and advertising agencies have been asked the following question. Please indicate the category which you think the majority of respondents will have checked for each of the items below. (If you are unfamiliar with a technique, please indicate in the box provided and do not answer further for that item.) Which of the following techniques and concepts have you ever used?" (used frequently, used occasionally, used once, never used)."

corporations using secondary data, whereas suppliers tend to be more oriented to primary field or laboratory data and to psychological data collection and analysis techniques.

Although this sample of 218 "operating managers" may be atypical of the field in general, it is clear, for them at least, that none of the more complex techniques is widely used. The discrepancy between what has been "tried" and what is being "used" is very great.

Table 6-2 presents additional data on this latter point. The ratio of use to trial gives an estimate of A_i, the "adoption rate," across the thirteen techniques. As noted, it is like but not the same as a "repeat purchase rate." What the table shows, particularly for operating managers, is that the more complex techniques have not been "adopted" in this sense, or at least in very low proportions of .07, .10, .11, and so on. Concerning Bayesian analysis, for example, although nearly 60% of the reporting operating managers had tried it, only about 7% continued to use it (4.2/59.8 = .07).[6] Even less complex techniques show a significant drop-off in adoption, particularly for operating managers. Academic perception is more accurate in estimating manager adoption rates, but there are still significant underestimates (segmentation, time series, focus groups, experiments) and overestimates (Bayesian and factor analysis).

Tables 6-3 and 6-4 provide a closer look at the distribution of operating-manager trial across industries and by the type of research supply alternative

TABLE 6-2

ADOPTION RATES OF THE THIRTEEN TECHNIQUES [a]

Technique	Operating Managers	Research Managers	Research Suppliers	Academic [b] Perception
Demographic segmentation	.60	.67	.73	.50
Usage segmentation	.57	.66	.71	.45
Time-series analysis	.53	.52	.40	.28
Focus groups	.46	.59	.67	.11
Formal experiments	.34	.51	.52	.12
Computer simulation	.22	.18	.19	.09
Response models	.21	.20	.21	.03
Psychographics	.18	.29	.43	.05
Conjoint analysis	.15	.08	.22	.09
Multidimensional scaling	.11	.13	.24	.10
Cluster analysis	.10	.12	.22	.09
Bayesian analysis	.07	.03	.05	.09
Factor analysis	.07	.18	.28	.10
Means	.28	.32	.37	.16
Standard deviations	.20	.23	.22	.15

[a]See footnote *a*, Table 6-1, for sample sizes and question formats. Adoption rates were derived using the formula for A_i given in equation (3).
[b] See footnote *b*, Table 6-1.

TABLE 6-3

OPERATING LINE MANAGER TRIAL BY INDUSTRY TYPE [a]

Technique	Consumer Products (n = 53)	Industrial Products (n = 43)	Advertising, Public Relations, Consulting (n = 38)	Banking, Finance, Insurance (n = 29)	Retailing (n = 10)
Demographic segmentation	94.4	75.0	97.4	96.7	100.0
Usage segmentation	94.3	82.2	97.3	96.7	90.0
Focus groups	92.5	68.1	64.9	90.0	80.0
Time-series analysis	84.6	80.4	78.4	86.2	70.0
Formal experiments	83.4	59.6	76.9	66.7	80.0
Psychographics	77.4	73.0	74.4	75.0	72.7
Bayesian analysis	67.3	75.0	55.6	46.4	20.0
Factor analysis	62.3	47.7	66.7	42.3	30.0
Cluster analysis	55.8	54.5	61.1	53.3	33.3
Response models	51.9	43.2	52.6	58.6	40.0
Multidimensional scaling	50.0	34.1	41.7	38.5	11.1
Computer simulation	43.4	44.4	55.3	58.6	10.0
Conjoint analysis	43.1	30.2	25.0	29.6	20.0
Means	69.3	59.0	65.2	64.5	50.6
Standard deviations	19.5	17.9	20.4	22.8	32.3

[a]See footnote a, Table 6-1 for question formats. All numbers are proportions of operating managers in each category who had used the technique "at some time."

chosen. In Table 6-3 it is evident that trial is consistently higher among consumer-goods companies than industrial-goods companies, except for computer simulation and Bayesian analysis. Based on overall average trial of the five industry types, consumer-products companies rank first; advertising, PR, and consulting companies second; banking, finance, insurance, third; industrial products, fourth; and retailing, fifth. All samples, particularly retailing, are rather small, even though these patterns appear to make sense. There is much higher variance in the retailing scores than others, and it is very doubtful that these data are generalizable to the entire retail industry. The banking, finance, and insurance company managers report the highest rate of trial of response models and computer simulation of any industry. All five types of companies are very similar in their trial of psychographics, and trial generally varies from high to low as the techniques become more complex.

Table 6-4 shows similar data broken down by the nature of the research supply alternative used. If the company has a research department, trial on average is considerably higher (65.7 vs. 51.5). If an outside research supplier is used, it also tends to be higher on average (66.5 vs. 57.1). If the company has a specialist person or group responsible for investigating new techniques, overall trial also is higher (65.8 vs. 55.2). A consistent exception to this pattern is

TABLE 6-4

OPERATING LINE MANAGER TRIAL BY RESEARCH SUPPLY ALTERNATIVES [a]

Technique	Research Department		Outside Supplier		Specialist Group	
	Yes (n = 143)	No (n = 52)	Yes (n = 107)	No (n = 83)	Yes (n = 142)	No (n = 60)
Demographic segmentation	94.7	80.8	95.0	85.5	93.7	86.7
Usage segmentation	94.4	82.7	97.0	84.4	94.2	84.5
Time-series analysis	87.4	45.4	84.5	75.9	85.8	71.7
Focus groups	79.6	62.7	72.4	75.3	84.8	54.2
Formal experiments	76.7	57.7	77.5	63.0	72.1	72.1
Psychographics	74.5	61.5	74.0	67.5	75.0	63.3
Bayesian analysis	58.6	61.7	58.2	59.5	58.6	62.1
Cluster analysis	55.6	46.9	58.9	46.2	58.0	44.1
Response models	54.5	35.3	59.6	36.7	55.1	37.3
Factor analysis	54.3	44.9	55.3	48.7	54.7	46.7
Computer simulation	47.6	37.3	50.0	37.5	47.4	40.0
Multidimensional scaling	39.9	31.9	46.2	33.3	39.1	35.7
Conjoint analysis	35.7	20.0	36.3	28.2	37.4	18.9
Means	65.7	51.5	66.5	57.1	65.8	55.2
Standard deviations	20.1	18.6	18.7	20.0	19.8	20.4

[a] Proportions of Yes/No responses to: "Does your company have its own marketing research department?" "Does your company regularly use outside marketing research specialist firms/consultants?" "Is any person or group in your company specifically responsible for investigating new techniques and concepts for potential use in the company?" Cross-classified by use of the technique "at some time."

Bayesian analysis, which, in all cases, shows a higher trial for those replying "No" to the three questions. Focus groups are also apparently tried more by companies that do not use outside research suppliers. These patterns suggest that a more general factor, "size of company," may be operating. Larger companies tend to have their own marketing research departments, use outside suppliers, and have specialists focusing on new techniques, and these are reflected in the higher overall trial figures shown.

It is interesting to examine the use of conjoint analysis in these data, given its choice as a "successful technique" in the Chapter 5 example. Many more operating managers have tried techniques such as usage segmentation than conjoint analysis (Table 6-1). This pattern generally holds for all types of operating managers (Table 6-3), and even for the three categories of research supply alternatives (Table 6-4). Furthermore, conjoint analysis is lowest in trial and next to lowest in use by research managers (Table 6-1), even though more than 55% of the research suppliers have tried it and nearly 12% indicate continued use. In sum, the example of conjoint analysis as a "successful" technique given in the last chapter (recall that commissioners reported over 300 separate studies using conjoint analysis as of 1977) must be qualified if these data are to be believed. It may be becoming part of the "tool kit" of research suppliers, but very few corporation managers, either line managers or research managers, as represented by AMA membership, seem to consider it part of their "tool kit" of useful techniques.

In general the following points can be made:

1. Overall, market segmentation, time-series analysis, and focus groups seem to be most widely used. In contrast, the level of usage of more complex techniques such as cluster analysis, conjoint analysis, multidimensional scaling, Bayesian analysis, and factor analysis is very low.
2. Research managers use all techniques more than operating line managers with the exception of response models, computer simulation, and Bayesian analysis, and to some degree conjoint analysis.
3. Research suppliers, not unexpectedly, report having used most of the data-analysis techniques more, and the decision-modeling techniques less, than have their counterparts within companies. The high percentage of researchers who have never used time-series analysis suggests that it is not used by commercial researchers on their own problems and is performed "in house" by their clients.
4. Similar patterns of continued use of the more familiar and less complex techniques are reflected in adoption rates by all three types of users.
5. When answering for "a marketing line manager," academics tend to underestimate the usage of time-series analysis, market segmentation, and experimentation. They also tend to overestimate the use of multidimensional scaling, cluster analysis, conjoint analysis, Bayesian analysis, and factor analysis. These distortions are similarly reflected in patterns of trial as well as use.
6. Trial of all techniques tends to be highest among consumer-goods manufacturers and may be lowest among retailers. Furthermore, trial appears to increase if the company

has a research department, if a research supplier is used, and if the company has a new techniques specialist. As noted, company size is probably the major factor underlying these patterns.

Table 6-5 compares the Commission's survey results with those of a study performed by faculty at Georgia State University,[7] in which there was overlap in eight of the techniques tested. The table shows data from two studies broken out by consumer companies use and research supplier use. The use rankings, from relatively high use of simpler techniques to relatively low use of complex techniques, particularly for consumer-company data, are quite similar. The patterns hold up even though quite different question formats, sampling frames, and differences in respondent classification were involved. The penetration given in the Georgia State results is higher in practically all cases, and this result may be accounted for by the phrasing of the use question as "used last year" instead of the Commission's "used frequently."

Although the studies differed in significant respects, many of the following overall conclusions of the Georgia State researchers appear well supported by the Commission results:[8]

1. Consumer-goods manufacturers make greater use of all the techniques (thirty-seven in the Georgia State study) than industrial, financial, or retailing companies.
2. Most of the research techniques have penetrated the industrial-goods manufacturing firms less than is true of the average of the groups of firms.
3. Fewer research techniques have penetrated the research efforts of retailers and wholesalers.
4. A broad range of research techniques is used by utility firms.[9]
5. Communications firms use relatively few of the available research techniques.
6. Market research and consulting firms are essentially data-gathering organizations.
7. The finance and insurance firms report the highest rate of usage among the industrial groups for analysis of internal company records, trade journal data, measures of dispersion, and telephone surveys.
8. "Simpler" techniques are the most widely used.[10]
9. Innovative techniques and their applications are diffusing into business research primarily through the large firms. These firms are the change agents—the innovators.

Although the Georgia State study suggests higher use of the most complex techniques than the Commission study, the proportions are still comparatively small—in the 30%-and-less category. This lack of penetration might be attributed to (1) the irrelevance of the technique to a manager's problems, (2) the nonrepresentativeness of these samples, (3) a lack of confidence by a manager in using them, or (4) some combination of such "causes." The next section presents data on confidence and relevance.

TABLE 6-5

A COMPARISON OF USE BY CONSUMER COMPANIES AND RESEARCH SUPPLIERS IN COMMISSION AND GEORGIA STATE STUDIES [a]

	Consumer Companies				Research Suppliers [b]			
	Commission		Georgia State		Commission		Georgia State	
Technique	Percent	Rank	Percent	Rank	Percent	Rank	Percent	Rank
Focus groups	64	1	81	1	62	1	61	1
Formal experiments [c]	54	2	67	2	49	2	49	2
Time-series analysis	42	3	67	2	28	4	39	3
Psychographics [c]	22	4	36	3	38	3	49	2
Factor analysis	17	5	36	3	23	5	27	6
Multidimensional scaling	10	6	29	4	15	7	30	5
Cluster analysis	9	7	21	5	16	6	33	4
Bayesian analysis	1	8	14	6	2	8	15	7
n	53		42		253		33	

[a]Source of Georgia State data: B. A. Greenberg et al., "What Techniques Are Used by Marketing Researchers in Business?" *Journal of Marketing,* 41 (April 1977), pp. 62–68. Estimates are based on "used frequently" in the Commission study and on "company used last year" in the Georgia State study.

[b]Category used in the Georgia State study was "marketing research and consulting."

[c]Referred to in the Georgia State study as "informal experimental designs" and "life style analysis," respectively.

Confidence and Relevance

One commissioner remarked on the notion of a manager's "confidence" in understanding and using new techniques.

The major barrier to new-idea diffusion within this company stems from the unwillingness of most line marketing personnel to sponsor projects involving techniques which are still in the experimental stage. This is particularly true when the techniques involve mathematical procedures which the line personnel do not fully comprehend and feel uncomfortable trying to defend with their own supervisors. Far more rapid diffusion would probably be achieved if our line marketing personnel were better trained in quantitative techniques. We do find more acceptance for these techniques among product development personnel who are more mathematically oriented.

Another commissioner alluded to the question of relevance:

Many academic marketing researchers and behavioral scientists have no real knowledge of marketing problems. This occurs because academic researchers tend to pick problems that are academically respectable rather than managerially relevant and because academics often do not know what problems are relevant.

How confident are managers in using the techniques? To what degree do they see the techniques as relevant or irrelevant to the problems they face? For purposes of discussion, we refer to their confidence in the applicability of a technique to a particular problem as *applicability confidence* and their confidence in basing a decision on the results of an analysis involving the technique as *decision confidence*.

Table 6-6 shows the results of asking respondents about their applicability and decision confidence for each of the thirteen techniques. In every case respondents are more confident in determining the applicability of a technique to a specific problem than in basing a decision on their interpretation of analyses performed using the technique. (The overall mean for applicability confidence is 1.89 versus 2.12 for decision confidence.) Also, the degree of both types of confidence progressively declines as techniques get more complicated. Assuming a score of "2.5" as the center point of the confidence scale (halfway between "somewhat confident" and "somewhat uncertain"), we find that operating and research managers register "confidence" for all techniques—the worst score is 2.49 for using interpretations of Bayesian analysis to make a decision. But there is a considerable range in confidence scores. For the "simpler" techniques, managers register comparatively high confidence in their ability to determine technique-applicability, and they even show fairly high willingness to base decisions on the results of using the technique. There is a marked decline in confidence as techniques get more complicated. Maximum decision confidence, for example, is associated with usage segmentation, demographic segmentation, and experimentation, whereas those techniques associated with decision making (re-

TABLE 6-6

OVERALL CONFIDENCE IN USING TECHNIQUES FOR APPLICATIONS AND DECISION MAKING [a] (*n* = 904)

Technique	Applicability Confidence [b]	Decision Confidence [c]
Demographic segmentation	1.37	1.64
Usage segmentation	1.39	1.59
Focus groups	1.49	2.29
Time-series analysis	1.53	1.78
Formal experiments	1.57	1.64
Psychographics	1.87	2.20
Factor analysis	2.07	2.18
Response models	2.13	2.42
Cluster analysis	2.15	2.20
Computer simulation	2.17	2.46
Multidimensional scaling	2.20	2.39
Conjoint analysis	2.25	2.33
Bayesian analysis	2.33	2.49
Means	1.89	2.12
Standard deviations	.36	.34

[a] Mean ratings of each technique on confidence scale: 1 = very confident, 2 = somewhat confident, 3 = somewhat uncertain, 4 = very uncertain, for total user sample.
[b] Based on operating and research manager replies to: "How confident would you be in determining the applicability of the following techniques to a specific problem?" and, for research suppliers: "How confident would you be in determining the applicability of the following techniques to a specific problem, assuming that a client has suggested you use it?"
[c] Based on operating and research manager replies to: "How confident would you be in *basing a decision* on your interpretation of analyses performed using the following techniques?" and, for research suppliers: "How confident would you be in *basing a recommendation* to a client on your interpretation of analyses performed using the following techniques?"

sponse models, computer simulation, and Bayesian analysis) receive the lowest confidence scores.

The confidence expressed in specific techniques leads to some interesting reflections. Focus groups are rated very high for applicability confidence but comparatively low for decision confidence. This makes sense. Few managers are willing to base final decisions on focus-group results. A similar, but less dramatic, result occurs in the case of psychographics: a manager feels relatively confident in applying it to a specific problem but relatively less confident in using the results to make a decision. The standard deviation of confidence scores in each case is about the same, even though the range differs across each construct.

Table 6-7 presents a breakout of the overall confidence scores by manager and researcher type, as well as academic perceptions of what managers *should* feel with respect to each technique. Note, first, that research suppliers are more confident than research managers, and research managers are more confident than operating line managers, in either applying the techniques or using

TABLE 6-7

APPLICABILITY AND DECISION CONFIDENCE OF USERS AND ACADEMIC PERCEPTIONS OF MANAGER CONFIDENCE [a]

Technique	Applicability Confidence				Decision Confidence			
	Operating Managers	Research Managers	Research Suppliers	Academic Perception	Operating Managers	Research Managers	Research Suppliers	Academic Perception
Usage segmentation	1.54	1.37	1.27	1.48	1.72	1.65	1.39	1.46
Demographic segmentation	1.49	1.36	1.26	1.43	1.75	1.72	1.44	1.43
Time-series analysis	1.53	1.48	1.58	1.73	1.82	1.82	1.70	1.84
Formal experiments	1.66	1.56	1.49	2.04	1.82	1.66	1.44	2.09
Response models	2.10	2.10	2.18	2.66	2.37	2.47	2.42	2.73
Cluster analysis	2.43	2.09	1.94	3.15	2.40	2.18	2.03	3.15
Psychographics	2.04	1.88	1.69	2.28	2.41	2.27	1.92	2.35
Focus groups	1.76	1.44	1.26	2.06	2.42	2.43	2.03	2.22
Conjoint analysis	2.41	2.18	2.15	3.32	2.43	2.39	2.16	3.32
Computer simulation	2.15	2.14	2.23	2.79	2.44	2.49	2.46	2.86
Factor analysis	2.40	1.99	1.81	3.09	2.44	2.15	1.94	3.12
Bayesian analysis	2.18	2.40	2.41	2.90	2.44	2.50	2.53	3.00
Multidimensional scaling	2.46	2.21	1.94	3.21	2.64	2.42	2.11	3.26
Means	2.01	1.86	1.79	2.47	2.24	2.17	1.97	2.53
Standard deviations	.37	.37	.40	.67	.33	.33	.39	.67

[a]See footnotes a, b, and c in Table 6-6. Mean academic perceptions of applicability confidence are based on the question: "A random sample of AMA members who are practicing marketing managers and who do not work for research companies have been asked the following question. Please indicate the category which you think the majority of them will have checked for each of the items below. 'How confident would you be in determining the applicability of the following techniques to a specific problem?'" For decision confidence academics estimated replies to: "'How confident would you be in interpreting analyses resulting from these techniques?'"

them in decision making. Operating managers, however, register more confidence in using Bayesian analysis for a specific problem or as the basis for a decision than either research managers or research suppliers. Research suppliers are more confident than either type of manager in applying the techniques in every case except time-series analysis, response models, computer simulation, and Bayesian analysis. Once again, the impression is that suppliers are strongly oriented to sociological and psychological data-collection and data-analysis procedures.

Academic perceptions of manager confidence are again highly distorted. In general, academic respondents feel that managers would be much less confident on both applicability and decision confidence than managers themselves state themselves to be. But academics are comparatively accurate in the direction of the confidence they ascribe to managers. In general, they appear to believe that more confidence will be placed in the simpler techniques and less in the more complicated techniques. This is consistent with what managers actually report. A characteristic of academic ratings is that there is greater variance in their judgments than in any of the self-ratings of either managers or research suppliers. This pattern is consistent with the distortions registered by academics in estimating patterns of trial and use.

In sum, operating line managers appear to be less confident in using or basing a decision on *any* technique than either research managers or research suppliers. They are more confident in using the "simpler" techniques and more confident in determining their applicability to a problem than in basing a decision on their interpretation of results based on a technique. Academics again significantly distort what managers actually feel, tending on the one hand to over-ascribe confidence to the simpler techniques and underascribe confidence to the more complex techniques.

Table 6-8 pertains to the perceived relative importance of each of the thirteen techniques for data analysis and decision making by *managers*. Both suppliers and academics were asked to estimate how managers would view relevance, and managers were asked a similar kind of projective question—to estimate relevance by managers in "positions similar to their own." The most striking result is to compare the relevance rankings of operating managers and academics. There is a high *inverse* rank correlation in the replies of each of these groups. Generally, operating managers see the simpler techniques as more important for data analysis and decision making, whereas academics see the more complex techniques as more important. Academics, for example, rank conjoint analysis, computer simulation, response models, and MDS as first, second, third, and fourth in relevance, whereas managers rank them ninth, seventh, sixth, and thirteenth, respectively.

Assuming that the relevance scale can be treated at least at the interval level of measurement, research managers consider all techniques slightly more relevant than operating managers. Research suppliers estimate overall relevance

TABLE 6-8

PERCEPTIONS OF RELATIVE IMPORTANCE OF TECHNIQUES TO OPERATING LINE MANAGERS [a]

Technique	Operating Managers		Research Managers		Research Suppliers		Academic Perception	
	Mean	Rank	Mean	Rank	Mean	Rank	Mean	Rank
Demographic segmentation	1.44	1	1.32	1	1.31	2	2.47	13
Usage segmentation	1.46	2	1.35	2	1.27	1	2.38	12
Time-series analysis	1.54	3	1.46	3	2.01	8	2.30	10
Formal experiments	1.72	4	1.68	5	1.53	3	2.06	7
Focus groups	1.89	5	1.59	4	1.73	5	2.34	11
Response models	1.91	6	1.95	10	2.36	11	1.85	3
Computer simulation	1.95	7	2.00	11	2.40	12	1.84	2
Psychographics	2.05	8	1.79	6	1.70	4	2.11	9
Conjoint analysis	2.12	9	1.86	8	2.07	10	1.83	1
Cluster analysis	2.19	10	1.91	9	2.00	7	1.94	5
Factor analysis	2.23	11	1.82	7	1.90	6	2.07	8
Bayesian analysis	2.30	12	2.32	13	2.76	13	1.99	6
Multidimensional scaling	2.33	13	2.08	12	2.06	9	1.87	4
Means	1.93		1.78		1.93		2.08	
Standard deviations	.31		.29		.43		.22	

[a]Based on replies by operating managers, research managers, and research suppliers to: "How relevant do you feel the following techniques would be for data analysis and decision making by managers in positions similiar to your own and with your own kind of background?" 1 = very relevant, 2 = somewhat relevant, 3 = somewhat irrelevant, 4 = very irrelevant. Academic estimates are based on replies to "How relevant do you feel the following techniques would be for data analysis and decision making by a line marketing manager?"

of managers very accurately (although with different orderings and wider variance), and academics estimate that managers would consider them overall slightly less relevant than actually reported by managers.

The downgrading of management-science techniques (response models and computer simulation) by research managers and research suppliers (to tenth, eleventh, twelfth places) in contrast to operating manager rankings of these techniques (in sixth and seventh place) probably accurately reflects their perceived utility to each of these three professional groups. All three groups are consistent in downgrading Bayesian analysis (ranked in twelfth and thirteenth places), in contrast to the comparatively high (sixth-place) ranking by academics of how important *they* feel Bayesian analysis is for the manager. The value differences reflected in these importance rankings for professionals and academics are indeed striking and may be one of the most significant barriers to the utilization of new knowledge in the field.

Concerning confidence and relevance, the following conclusions can be drawn:

1. All professionals appear more confident in determining the applicability of a technique to a problem than in using a technique as the basis for making a final decision.
2. Both types of confidence decline as techniques become more complicated.
3. Overall, research suppliers register more confidence in the techniques than research managers, and research managers are generally more confident than operating line managers.
4. Academic perceptions are distorted in ascribing less confidence to managers than they actually report, but are generally accurate in ascribing more professional confidence regarding simpler techniques, and less regarding the more complex techniques.
5. The relative importance of each technique to operating line managers given by professionals shows a striking inverse rank correlation pattern when compared with rankings given by academics. Professionals, for example, rank demographic and usage segmentation in first place, whereas academics rank them in last place. Academics rank conjoint analysis as the most important of all thirteen techniques, whereas professionals rank it eighth, ninth, and tenth.
6. As suggested in the analysis of trial and use data, operating managers tend to rank decision models as relatively more important than data-analysis techniques, whereas research suppliers tend to rank each in the reverse order.

It is obviously dangerous to generalize further from the results of this study and, for example, point to a lack of manager confidence as the "cause" of low penetration and adoption rates. Numerous factors are undoubtedly involved, including the "irrelevance" of some of the techniques as well as the sampling and nonsampling errors inherent in any piece of survey research. Professionals, according to these data, do seem to register less confidence in their capacity to understand and use complex techniques. Whether this, in turn, leads to a downgrading of such techniques as irrelevant or of little importance is an open question. Academic perceptions that complex techniques are "most" important could be attributed to self-interest as much as to any "objective" superiority as inputs to scientific decision making. This, too, is an open question.

ASSESSMENTS OF DIFFUSION VEHICLES
AND INFORMATION SOURCES

Chapter 5 (Figure 5-6) identified four kinds of "diffusion vehicles" as the major channels through which new knowledge is introduced and diffused: consulting, teaching, publication, and meetings-conferences. Elaborations of this model recognized several different kinds of change agents in the overall process, such as the internal marketing research department, advertising agencies, and commercial research suppliers. Concerning the four diffusion vehicles, it was argued that most knowledge innovators, whether academics or professional researchers in a marketing research department, a research supplier company, or some other entity, engage in all of these activities. From the manager-user viewpoint, these vehicles and agents can be considered "sources" of information and evaluated as good-bad or effective-ineffective. Each is also a potential barrier or block to the knowledge-diffusion and utilization process. Both an inhibiting and a contributing role can be assessed in each case. This section provides commissioner evaluations and AMA membership survey results with respect to diffusion vehicles and information sources. Although much of the commentary is quite general, essentially the role or utility of each vehicle or source is assessed from the viewpoint of the practicing marketing manager.

Consulting

Commissioners had varied opinions about the impact of academic consulting on the knowledge-diffusion and utilization process. They agreed, however, that it did have a role to play. Comments by two nonacademic members of the Commission are given below. Note the second commissioner's concern with what can happen in follow-up work in the academic community.

I feel that the barriers to diffusion are built into the academic/business interface with consultancy the best channel of diffusion. The academicians' work *seems* obsessed with theory and with methodology; the line managers *are* obsessed with practice, i.e., meeting this campaign's objective—dollar or profit volume. The professional marketing journals speak to researchers.

Let me give you another point of view [as opposed to the Mini-Guide]. Industry-top operating/marketing executives request academic help for real problems: David Learner of BBDO got Cooper & Charnes to work on the application of linear programming to media selection; Budweiser with the approval of Gussie Busch brought in Ackoff, Arnoff, and Rao to apply OR and experimentation to the beer business; DuPont also started a great deal of OR work including market experimentation plus financing a laboratory designed to use operant conditioning principles to measure many aspects of response to advertising; Pillsbury and Coca-Cola served as guinea pigs for John Little's ADBUDG model, etc.

Then, having got a taste of such real-world problems, academicians are driven by the "publish or perish" syndrome to spin out these models and concepts using any data they can lay their hands on. Often, these concepts achieve a life of their own in the academic world long after they've been discarded in the real world. Thus almost all advertising students are still being taught how to use linear programming to select media when industry dropped the practice almost ten years ago.

Continued success of academic consultants is associated with the business community's perception of at least potential relevance. However, business people often perceive the work of the marketing academic community generally as profoundly lacking in relevance. For instance:

I think the biggest (problem) is implied by Ted Levitt's article in *The Harvard Business Review* many years ago about "Which Business Are You In?" I suspect that most marketing academics do not consider themselves as being in the business of R & D for *marketing management* with the objective of learning things that *can* and *will* be *used* to *improve* the practice of marketing.

If they were, how could they do the research they do, write the textbooks they do, or write the journal articles I have to try to read? My view is that too many are in the business of doing their own thing and advancing their academic careers by virtuosity in stringing bibliographic references end to end or demonstrating one-upmanship in rarified vocabulary or mathematics. You can see what my *JMR* experience has done to my sweet disposition about those to whom we have entrusted our future concepts and techniques and the training of our young people.

This reaction comes from a highly respected professional marketing researcher. It is not an isolated feeling or one that can be dismissed lightly. Another commissioner sees the consultant role as of relatively minor importance compared with publications and professional meetings:

Now how does the transfer happen when it does? People in marketing research organizations are perfectly capable of reading, and they do read books and journals, especially intermediary journals like the *Journal of Marketing* and the *Journal of Advertising Research*. They are also capable of going to professional meetings, and they do that too. Frequently they employ entry-level researchers who have had recent technical education; these researchers help with the process of diffusion. Sometimes, but relatively rarely, the idea comes from a consultant.

There was thus a diversity of opinion among commissioners about the role of consulting, particularly academic consulting. There are also differences of opinion among academic administrators. A dean or department chairman is likely to view an excessive amount of consulting as distracting a faculty member from the primary duties of teaching and research. Consulting nevertheless seems to have a role to play in a professional school. Deans and department chairmen should encourage rather than discourage a reasonable level of consulting activity by their faculty. The essential argument is that the impact of a professional school's output on the progress of any of the professions it serves is enhanced by having its faculty engage in consulting activities. The faculty gains perspective on real-world marketing problems and the professional gains insights into literature and the latest academic thinking in the field. Business-school academics who do not "consult" or otherwise maintain lines of communication with the professional community risk losing touch with the realities of their profession and lose important opportunities for gaining insights into the tasks of creating new knowledge and having it used. Consulting activities should, however, be kept in balance with normal teaching, research, and other administrative duties.

This balance is a delicate one and difficult to maintain. Every marketing academic who consults successfully or whose services become widely in demand faces a point where the volume of activity begins to erode seriously his or her normal academic functions. At this point, the decision must be made either to cut back and maintain consulting activities at some reasonable level or to leave academia and go into business for oneself. Numerous examples of this latter pattern exist in marketing. The formation of Management Science Associates, Inc. of Pittsburgh by Professor Alfred Kuehn while on the faculty of Carnegie-Mellon University is typical.

Teaching, Specialists, Students, and Training Programs

Although the Commission did not undertake an evaluation of marketing teaching per se, it received many comments about teaching-related activities. For example, the Mini-Guide study asked: "How do firms maintain an awareness of new concepts and techniques? What is best: internal specialist, outside courses for line managers, encouragement to external market research companies to use new approaches?"

The roles of specialist, training programs, and related "teaching activities" are acknowledged in the following five commissioner replies to this question.

Outside courses received a majority of the endorsements [within this company]; each of the other alternatives received some support. I believe that all methods are required at different times. Line managers need awareness of the power of new techniques through practical examples so they will be receptive to their use and, in fact, promote their application. Obviously most companies need internal specialists who can do or coordinate projects (internally or externally) using the best methods.

Among the alternatives suggested in question 3, professional training received the most votes [among the respondents in this company], although I do not believe everyone interpreted this identically. Does it mean their own college training or seminars and conferences held at universities, or the training received by new staff members? Personally, I find that seminars and discussions with managers in other companies and with academics to be the most fruitful in stimulating interest. However, to really bring a new method into application, I believe a consultant or specialist experienced in its use must demonstrate through practical examples to others in the firm how it works and what it can be. I think we have more examples of that course of events being successful than any other.

I suspect one of the greatest problems is getting line managers to take the time to attend seminars and conferences where they will be exposed to their peers in industry and the advanced thinking of academics. This problem might forever be with us.

My experience is that in large businesses the staff personnel have sufficient knowledge of the new developments and that there is plenty of expertise in corporations with respect to newer developments.

I do not believe that the organizational system influences the acceptance of new ideas. In the systems area, very few companies have been willing to experiment with formal decision systems which cut across product lines and brands. There is probably good reason for this but it is troubling to find very little evidence of experimentation in this area.

The internal specialist serves a major role as a transfer agent in communicating and demonstrating new ideas to management.

Given the rarity of really new concepts, it's very difficult to indicate a source precisely. For the most part, it's the responsibility of the internal specialist to be aware of "what's going on outside." This is accomplished by extensive and intensive reading on the subject and attendance at various seminars, conferences, etc.

Generally, a line manager consults with his professional marketing researcher, not so much to gain knowledge of techniques, but more so to develop an information base with which he can solve a problem.

The organizational system and its "acceptance" of techniques are not particularly relevant. It's true that the professional does act as a screen. It's his job to operate in this way.

The rise of short courses by organizations like the American Management Association, AMR, and many universities, and also marketing conferences by our own AMA and the Conference Board are primary means by which firms maintain an awareness of marketing practices along with various trade periodicals—*Advertising Age, Sales and Marketing Management, Super Market News, MART, Industrial Marketing,* etc.

University teaching also plays a role in the diffusion process, because many line managers have MBA degrees from universities in which the academic faculty reside. Twedt[11] reported on a study of marketing teaching nationwide and concluded that about 25,000 students are graduated each year in the United States who are specializing in marketing. A significant seven-year decline in "market share" of marketing majors relative to finance and accounting was also noted in this study.

There is obviously also disparity between what the students are taught in the classroom and what they later face in real-world marketing situations. Some of this is traceable to the great variability in styles of teaching in the field of marketing. At some schools what is essentially taught is applied economics; at others, applied psychology or sociology dominates, at still others, the case method or, increasingly, computer-assisted cases is the dominant style. Some schools are heavily "practical" in orientation, and students learn such things as package design, how to develop advertising copy, how to close a sale, and so on. This variability was viewed by many as a *strength* of the system rather than a weakness. Every school cannot, and should not, attempt to be "everything to everybody." Nevertheless, academic administration should give attention to the balance between the poles of scholarly and practical as one way in which teaching and academic productivity could be improved.

Apart from the role of *students* as potential marketing managers,[12] it should be noted that students, particularly Ph.D. students, are themselves a type of diffusion vehicle and a very important source of new knowledge. Much of the development of new knowledge in the field takes place as a result of the interactions between a doctoral candidate and his or her faculty supervisor. Although one might attribute solely to faculty the responsibility for shaping the direction of the field, in many cases it is the curiosity of a student searching for something new to work on that results in a real breakthrough in knowledge development.

The other dimension of teaching considered by the Commission falls into the area of executive training programs. Many schools now offer a "night program" for practicing professionals, and they offer a mix of senior-management or middle-management short courses to supplement the regular teaching program. This type of education has shown explosive growth in recent years and is probably one of the more important avenues through which managers can "update" themselves and get exposed to current developments. Numerous associations and specialized executive education firms are also involved.[13]

Conferences, Meetings, and Word-of-Mouth

Conferences, meetings, workshops, and face-to-face communications provide for early dissemination of new findings, techniques, and theoretical developments in marketing. Conferences may be sponsored either by a professional association or by an industry group or government agency interested in specific areas of application.

Some sense of the "invisible colleges" to which researchers in marketing belong can be gained from a listing of their memberships in professional associations. Leaving aside applications-oriented associations, the listing of some American-based organizations that do *not* have "marketing" in the title, but to which many marketing faculty and marketing researchers in business and government belong, includes:

Association for Consumer Research
American Economic Association
American Institute for Decision Sciences
The Institute for Management Sciences
International Communication Association
American Association for Public Opinion Research
The Psychometric Society
Operations Research Society
American Psychological Association
American Sociological Association

Conference papers that are to be published in the proceedings are often refereed, but workshop papers are not. As a broad generalization, the average conference paper is not up to the same standards as a journal paper. However, conferences perform a valuable service by providing faster turnaround for publication than do journals and by accepting more "risky" or "limited-interest" material. The conferences or workshops themselves also provide an opportunity for face-to-face discussions between authors/presenters and interested members of the audience, thus accelerating both the diffusion process and feedback to the researcher.

It is noteworthy that the AMA has separate conferences for educators and practitioners, although some members of the opposite group typically attend the others' conference. Specialist workshops allow for in-depth treatment of specific topics of current interest. The Commission did not undertake an in-depth review of conference proceedings over the years. A casual analysis of the contents of several AMA Marketing Educators *Proceedings* suggests that many of the trends highlighted in the journal and textbook analyses presented in Chapter 3 are reflected in the *Proceedings*. Not surprisingly, the time scale is somewhat advanced for proceedings, because of their function in expediting early exposure.

Conferences serve three basic purposes: (1) They bring people together for informal dialogues and the sharing of ideas. (2) They provide a mechanism for formal presentation of studies and research findings in an environment that allows for audience feedback, questioning, and clarification. (3) They usually result in publication of *Proceedings* that provide an archival record of what was presented for future reference.

Because of the nature of conferences and the shorter lead time involved in preparation and publication (a characteristic further emphasized by publication of the AMA *Proceedings* in advance of the actual sessions), conference papers are likely to be more topical than are journal articles.

A brief comparison of AMA conference topics in 1976 and 1977 with those of twenty-five years earlier yielded the following conclusions:

1. Far fewer papers were presented at AMA conferences in the early 1950s as compared with the late 1970s (about twenty vs. one hundred nowadays).
2. There were a similar number of "circles" or "round tables" in the 1951 mid-year and 1977 Educators' Conferences (seventeen vs. eighteen).
3. Academic and business representation at the twice-yearly conferences in the 1950s appeared rather less segregated than today.

Meetings and conferences play a vital role in the knowledge-creation and utilization process. Academic and professional researchers in marketing increasingly face the dilemma of "too many" conferences, meetings, and associations to which to relate. As the field of marketing has grown, national, regional, and local meetings and conferences have multiplied. One need only add to this the growth in each of the social science and social engineering disciplines, and the associated growth in the number of their meetings and conferences over the period, to appreciate the scope of the pool of potentially interesting such events in any given year. The individual researcher must make tough decisions in attempting to maintain a balance between "missing something important" and incessant "conference-hopping." Particularly for the marketing academic who tries to maintain lines of communication with scholars in basic disciplines on the one hand and professional and managerial people on the other, this is a serious problem. It is one more reason why "specialization" in some one or a few topics, decision areas, or theoretical and methodological perspectives takes place.

Publications and Journals

Chapter 3 provided much information on the scope and nature of publication activity in marketing. As noted there, over 53 journals are published *within* the field (not counting trade magazines and some omitted journals), and hundreds in the broader field of social sciences and engineering on which marketing scholarship and knowledge-creation activities depend. Recall that Chapter 3 presented over-time content analysis studies of *JM, HBR, JMR, JCR,* and selected textbooks. Much information was given on changes in journal content over the assessment period, ratios of academic to professional authorship of articles, and status/utility rankings from the viewpoint of academics. We now explore the viewpoint of the operating line manager, particularly with respect to the role of these types of journals and their content in initiating changes in marketing management practice. Readers should be cautioned that these judgments are not based on an actual survey of manager opinion but rather on the opinions of the eighteen commissioners and their perceptions of how marketing journals do or do not serve operating line managers. There is, however, a reference to "journal usage" in the survey results presented at the end of this section.

The basic conclusion reached by the Commission was that existing marketing journals, particularly *JM, JMR,* and *JCR,* play little or no *direct* role in the knowledge-utilization process as far as most managers are concerned. Most operating line managers have little time to read academic journals and would not do so regardless of their content, or feel the potential benefits of a journal article are not worth the investment in time necessary to understand it, or perceive journal content as largely irrelevant to the day-to-day problems and issues they face. In contrast to trade magazines, journals provide a relatively minor source of information perceived to be directly relevant to a manager's activities. These viewpoints are expressed in the following four excerpts from commissioner comments:

Managers do not adopt, and often may not even consider, an innovation because of its being reported in an article. This applies to professional publications in general, and the *Journal of Marketing* in particular. Reasons range from the lack of manager time for journal reading to the nature of the journals themselves.

Whether journals are "on the manager's list" of possible sources of worthwhile new ideas is, to some degree, a function of the type of education a manager receives. For example, a case-oriented MBA course does little to expose a student to academic journals.

Only articles which discussed practice in a conceptual generalizable way (beyond reminiscences) would have any chance of producing direct change in "line management practice." Articles which, in the vernacular, are "success stories" but which are at a sufficiently conceptual level to be generalizable are likely to be most successful. The type of article published in *HBR* in contrast to *JMR* and *JCR* is an example of what is needed.

A major problem in synthesizing experience in an article is "context." Unless the context in which a particular strategy or approach has been assembled can be defined in great detail, it is difficult to produce generalizable results. This is a problem for research itself as well as publication. There are few if any incentives or "gold stars" for practitioners to publish these kinds of articles, and yet they are often the only ones with a sufficient base of real-world marketing experience to produce such articles.

These ideas were further reinforced by the general opinion that marketing journals essentially represent material that is of interest to, and serves, academic rather than manager needs. Also, several commissioners pointed out that the important proprietary work done in corporations often does not even get into marketing journals. Consider the following comments:

The bulk of the articles in the three principal marketing journals are written by academics, and thus tend more to reflect interests and trends in academic research rather than management concerns. The three AMA-supported journals plus *HBR* do not represent all of the manuscript activity in marketing.

Marketing journals do not represent the "state of the art" in many areas. Companies typically regard marketing research and the development of new techniques and concepts as a competitive marketing tool. Thus, there will always be an absence of proprietary materials in marketing journals.

Marketing journals tend to represent the *supply* of ideas rather than the *demand* for them. What gets published is a trade-off between the supply and the demand from the readership, with the editor as mediator.

Journals were nevertheless viewed as "important" in the process of knowledge utilization, but largely in an *indirect* sense as "reference sources" to be looked at by staff people in connection with a particular marketing problem or research technique. *JMR* was singled out as most representative of this kind of journal function; essentially it was viewed as a "storehouse" of the forefront work published in the field. Thus, although *JMR* is not regularly read by practicing managers (indeed, it is not regularly read by many academics), it was widely recognized as symbolic of the "latest developments" going on in the academic sector.

From the manager's point of view, the process of adoption is an extremely agonizing one. A seasoned marketing executive develops his own conceptual model of the world. Equally successful executives may have opposite points of view. A passive description in a complicated article is unlikely to result in any basic change in one's framework. What seems needed to stimulate consideration of change is "experience." This experience need not be direct, and even "generalized war stories" may play a role in helping to change a framework.

Concerning the *Journal of Marketing,* commissioner reactions resembled those to *JMR*. In general, managers do not adopt, and often may not even consider, a new idea or technique because of its being reported in an article in the *Journal of Marketing*. There was not much consensus, however, on just what this meant in terms of repositioning the journal. Some believed *JM* should be made more "readable" by busy marketing executives, while others acknowledged the basic heterogeneity of its audience. Grether,[14] in his forty-year review of the journal, points out that the criticism appears to have lost some of its sharpness, but it still remains. His arguments for keeping the journal from becoming too "practical" provide interesting insights into the issues surrounding it:

It is evident that the majority of AMA members regularly read some of the feature articles . . . but the issue of the relative balance between "practical" and "theoretical" or "academic" articles and of the relevance of the materials to individuals in their own work in business or education still remains. . . . [A] sizable proportion of the readership feels that the *Journal* is too "academic". . . . [W]ith reasonable editorial interest and care, the issue of being too "academic" may be expected to resolve itself in the foreseeable future. . . . [E]ven though the dominant membership is now overwhelmingly composed of practitioners, so called, many of these are in research, planning, consulting, and advisory roles in which it is mandatory to have sophisticated knowledge of, or ability to use, advanced tools and techniques. At a minimum, they must be able to appraise the results of the applications of such techniques. . . . Top management has become thoroughly aware of the extraordinary complexity of its problems and of the great need for professional and expert, sophisticated analysis. . . . It could be an enormous mistake to try to replace the "scholarly," the "theoretical," and the "academic" by something more "practical" at the very time when the sharpness of this dichotomy is becoming increasingly blurred and meaningless. . . . [A]ll educators and scholarly and professional journals have a responsibility for leadership, not followership. It would be tragic, indeed, if the *Journal of Marketing* were, at the time of its Golden Jubilee, appraised as "overly practical."[15]

In an effort to understand the roles of various types of journals better, and to sharpen the nature of the problems faced by the AMA in sponsoring a journal such as *JM* whose central purpose is to represent the entire field of marketing, the Commission developed a simple model (see Figure 6-1).

Each cell represents a type of journal distinguished on the basis of the character of the articles and the nature of the target audience. Type 1, for example, would be aimed primarily at practicing professionals whose articles were mainly conceptual in content. Type 2 journals would also aim at professionals, but their content would be more context-specific and immediate—more "concrete." The conceptual-concrete distinction for academically targeted journals (Types 3 and 4) basically captures the theory-methods distinctions in social science. A Type 3 journal would be heavily conceptual in character, whereas a Type 4 journal would emphasize empirical studies and the reporting of empirical results.

The content of Type 2 "journals" is the more down-to-earth, and that of Type 3 more ephemeral. The specialized character of trade-oriented material (Type 2) makes it unsuitable for the AMA, if for no other reason than lack of comparative advantage. The AMA *does* have an obligation with respect to Types

FIGURE 6-1

FOUR HYPOTHETICAL TYPES OF MARKETING JOURNAL

CHARACTER OF ARTICLE CONTENT

		Conceptual	Concrete
TARGET AUDIENCE	Practitioner	**TYPE 1** Practice in a conceptual, generalizable way (beyond reminiscences)	**TYPE 2** Practice in a concrete, specific way (what is the "x" industry like today . . . trade press)
	Academic	**TYPE 3** Theory development based on social science (one developer talking to another)	**TYPE 4** Empirical tests of theory, data oriented—"another market segmentation study"

3 and 4, even though the "academic-oriented" target audience is much smaller than the "practice-oriented" one.

It is likely that only Types 1 and 2 journals are read by managers and have any chance of producing changes in "line management practice" *directly*. The role of the other types as change agents will, in general, always be *indirect* via their influence on staff people, professional researchers, consultants, and so on. Type 1 journal content could be characterized as predominantly oriented to reporting on "success stories" but at a sufficiently conceptual level to be generalizable. The *Harvard Business Review* was cited as a good example of this type of journal. Type 2 would generally capture the trade magazine category, such as *Business Week* or *Fortune*. Type 4, in contrast, is oriented to reporting the results of empirical research and new-methods developments in the field, as the *Journal of Marketing Research* does. Type 3, in marketing, is currently most closely represented by the *Journal of Marketing*.

The problem of a journal such as the *Journal of Marketing* is that it must simultaneously attempt to serve the needs of both practitioners and academics and, in some senses at least, strive to appeal to readers represented by each of the four types. Given that the dominant share of its readership is practitioners, it has attempted to generate Type 1 articles while at the same time trying to serve the Type 3 needs of the academic segment. It thus tends to be damned by the innovator research group for not publishing rigorous research and damned by professionals for not publishing anything useful for what they do.

Several commissioners took the position that *JM* should be trying to influence managerial decision making *directly* by attempting to increase readership among marketing managers. In sum, it should be more like a Type 1 journal. All were in agreement, however, that this would be a very difficult task. One of the major problems noted was that much of what could go into a Type 1 journal in marketing might still be viewed as of little managerial use. The *Harvard Business Review* was nevertheless cited as the ideal kind of journal for reaching marketing executives and a model of the kind needed in marketing. The authorship of *HBR* articles has a higher proportion of managers (42% compared with 30% for *JM*), and the articles tend to be topical. For example, *HBR* had articles on ghettos in 1968, health care in 1971, and inflation accounting in 1972. It is not limited to a single trade, industry, or function. Even when authorship is academic, articles are carefully reviewed for style as well as content to make them as readable as possible by busy executives.

The following suggestions were made for improving the flow of Type 1 manuscripts that would interest marketing executives:

1. Use of material illustrating actual successful cases of marketing programs or plans that were sufficiently conceptual to be generalizable over industry or context-free situations.
2. Use of the public/private track approach in which "sanitized" results that have been developed from consulting work are published.[16]

3. Use of the "critical-incidents" method to pool the experiences of many executives on a particular problem.

The gap not now being filled by *JM* or any other marketing journal that purports to serve as an interface between academia and management is probably associated with failing to reach *senior marketing executives* or CEOs of major corporations. That is, manager-users who are most important in influencing changes in practice are top management and not so much the "line operating manager." The AMA should take this gap seriously and seek to publish a journal or some type of publication that will reach these busy people. Publications of the Conference Board, the American Management Association, the Sales and Marketing Executive Association, the Association of National Advertisers, and the American Association of Advertising Agencies all probably do a better job of reaching top marketing executives. Article content that is "case-oriented" and follows the lines of the suggestions made above is what is needed.

In certain respects, journals are the most important type of publication and the most visible of the "diffusion vehicles." They are hard copy. They are widely available through individual, company, or library subscriptions. Typically they are sponsored by professional organizations, such as the AMA or ACR, or else published under the auspices of leading schools. Unlike books, they have a continuing identity that transcends the specific contents of any one issue; their "packaging" often remains little changed for many years. Whereas a successful book may reappear in new editions every three or four years, new issues of most journals appear every two to three months, thus creating a strong impression that their contents are up-to-date and state-of-the-art. Being hard copy, rather than ephemeral, and usually saved rather than discarded, journals come to represent archival material that is available for subsequent consultation.

Nevertheless, even though journals play a significant role in the diffusion process, it is easy to overstate their importance. Availability does not necessarily lead to their contents' being read. Skimming may not lead to retention. Even where the contents of an article are carefully read and digested, there is no guarantee that this will lead to changes in management practice. Moreover, the impression that a journal's contents represent the state of the art may be illusory. As noted, much proprietary research is not submitted to the journals at all. Further, the heavy preponderance of academic authors may result in academics' talking to one another principally about areas of mutual interest to themselves rather than paying much attention to issues of current concern to management and executives. The Commission recognized that different journals should be positioned to play different roles; target audiences may be either academically or practically oriented, and their needs will vary accordingly. The articles viewed as most likely to have an effect on line management practice or on senior executives were those that presented success stories in the vernacular, but at a sufficiently conceptual level to be generalizable.

The need for precise targeting of readership has grown more critical in recent years because of increasing *specialization* within the field of marketing and because of the proliferation of journals generally. One need only reflect on the academic's complaint that it is "impossible to keep up with what is going on"[17] to appreciate what the manager must face. Virtually his only avenue of keeping up to date is via staff assistance, consultants, and experts of all kinds. Any journal, in order to be read, must be highly tailored to the manager's own needs and to the minimal time available for journal reading. It is becoming increasingly difficult to have one journal be "all things to all people," even though, because of its role as the major journal representing the field, *JM* should continue to seek ways to do so.

Information Sources

In the Commission's survey of AMA membership, respondents were asked what would be the most useful sources of detailed information and guidance concerning a new technique they were attempting to use. They were also asked to give the *sequence* of their choices and to indicate any source they would definitely not use. Because of differences in the types of sources likely to be used by managers versus research suppliers, slightly different lists of alternatives were presented to each group.

Table 6-9 presents the results as "utility rankings" of each of the sources presented, and it gives the proportions of managers and suppliers who stated they would *not* use the source. As can be seen, the first source turned to by all three groups is "colleagues within the company." The data show a remarkable consistency in the sequence of information sources chosen, particularly across the two manager groups. Similarly, their views are very close regarding the percentage who would definitely *not* use a particular information source. More specifically, a logical flow pattern of searching emerges—from colleagues, to the literature, to research suppliers and friends outside the company, and then to authors/originators of ideas.

It is important not to confuse the *sequence* of information search with the *usefulness* of the source. Note that *none* of the first five sources is viewed by more than 11% of the managers and research managers as "not useful." Only advertising agencies, research firms with which one ordinarily does not deal, and (to a lesser degree) academic consultants are seen as relatively less useful sources, and even these are presumably "used" by over 65% of the operating managers responding.

Somewhat surprising is the relatively high rank accorded to literature searches of the journals. This may simply reflect the relative ease of performing such a check—as is also true for the highest-ranking initial source, one's colleagues. A pattern of sources similar to that used by line and research managers is

TABLE 6-9

SOURCES OF INFORMATION USED BY OPERATING LINE MANAGERS, RESEARCH MANAGERS, AND RESEARCH SUPPLIERS [a]

Source	Operating Managers		Research Managers		Source	Research Suppliers	
	Utility Rank	Percent Not Use	Utility Rank	Percent Not Use		Utility Rank	Percent Not Use
Colleagues within company	1	9.1	1	9.4	Colleagues within company	1	4.2
Literature search	2	5.3	2	3.1	New-techniques specialist	2	14.4
Own marketing research company	3	11.0	3	7.3	Literature review	3	2.5
Acquaintances in other company	4	7.2	4	7.7	Acquaintances in other research companies	4	12.7
Author/originator	5	11.0	5	10.8	Researchers in client companies	5	11.9
Advertising agency	6	34.4	6	39.7	Author/originator	6	9.7
Academic consultant	7	18.2	8	22.3	Academic consultant	7	12.7
Different marketing research company	8	28.2	7	32.7			

[a]Based on replies to: "Now please assume that you have heard about a technique of data collection or analysis that is new to you, which you think might be useful to you in approaching an important problem. You are looking for more detailed information and guidance in attempting to use it. Please indicate the sequence in which you might try the following sources in order to obtain the information and guidance that you need. ('1' would try first, '2' would try second . . . , etc. Please indicate any source you would definitely *not* try by an 'X')." Utility rank is based on mean sequence rank for each information source.

used by commercial researchers. Again a literature review figures relatively high on the list, and only 2.5% report *not* using this source. No information source is rated by over 15% of the commercial research respondents as one they "would definitely not use."

Commercial researchers and academics—who were viewed as having the best perspective in this area—were asked for their assessment of how important the sources would be to line marketing management. Table 6-10 presents a comparison of the self-rankings of managers for each source with the perceived rankings assigned by research suppliers and academics. As can be seen, there is considerable perceptual distortion by both suppliers and academics. Research suppliers downgrade the importance of a literature search and, in some sense, upgrade their own importance by assigning the company's "own marketing research company" the first-rank position. Academics, interestingly, agree with suppliers on this ranking, whereas both manager types rank it in third place. A similar phenomenon of "feathering one's own nest" can be seen in the elevation of "academic consultant" to fourth place (by the academics), compared to the seventh and eighth places given to this source by both managers and research suppliers. Furthermore, suppliers indirectly see their own role as more important by assigning "different marketing research company" to fifth place in contrast to

TABLE 6-10

COMPARISONS OF SELF-DESIGNATED AND PERCEIVED UTILITY RANKINGS OF MANAGER INFORMATION SOURCES

Source	Self Utility Ranking		Perceived Utility Ranking	
	Operating Manager	Research Manager	Operating Manager [a]	Operating Manager [b]
Colleagues within company	1	1	2	2
Literature search	2	2	6	3
Own marketing research company	3	3	1	1
Acquaintances in other companies	4	4	4	6
Author/originator	5	5	3	7
Advertising agency	6	6	8	5
Academic consultant	7	8	7	4
Different marketing research company	8	7	5	8

[a] Ranks assigned by *research suppliers*, based on mean sequence rank for each information source that an operating line manager would be likely to use.
[b] Ranks assigned by *academics*. The question to both research suppliers and academics was: "Please state your own view of how important you think the following would be to a line marketing manager who is looking for more detailed information and guidance on a marketing technique of data analysis or collection, new to him, which he has read or heard about."

the seventh- and eighth-rank positions assigned by both managers and academics. Academics also do not appear to realize that going to the author/ originator is a viable alternative for managers. They rank this source seventh, managers rank it fifth, and suppliers rank it third. There is relatively strong agreement across all four groups on the importance of "colleagues within the company" and "acquaintances in other companies."

The perceived importance of checking with the company's own research suppliers, a source both logical and accessible, is most significant. Although the high "self-ranking" by suppliers suggests ego involvement, the independent high ranking by academics supports the logic of this step. Research suppliers tend to downgrade the importance of the literature search to managers and tend to upgrade the importance of checking with the author/originator of the idea. This may reflect a closer professional relationship between suppliers and idea originators. Academics, whose ranks contain many author/originators, rank the importance of this source quite low. It is interesting to note that of the two "diffusion vehicles" included as potential information sources, a literature search (publication) appears consistently more important than consulting. Consulting is nevertheless considered by about 80% of all groups as something they would use.

The next two sections present commentary by commissioners together with some additional survey results that focus on assessments of the effectiveness of the knowledge-innovator and knowledge-user groups. Again there is some unavoidable overlap and duplication of perspective in the materials. Also, some gaps occur in the commentary. For example, the first section—assessments of the innovator research group—is heavily focused on the academic component and not on the professional component. In many respects, however, the ideas are probably applicable to both academic and professional innovator researchers, even though most comments single out the academic people only.

ASSESSMENTS OF THE INNOVATOR RESEARCH GROUP

Recall that the concept of an innovator research group, presented in the context of the knowledge-creation and utilization model in Chapter 5 (Figure 5-6), refers to a group of academic and professional researchers in the field of marketing who account for the bulk of new-knowledge development. This group exists *within* the field in the sense that its members are pursuing marketing careers either as researchers in commercial settings or as academics teaching and doing research in marketing in university settings. In terms of the Figure 5-6 model, the group does not encompass "nonmarketing academics" in the social and engineering sciences, even though many fundamental breakthroughs in knowledge development flow from this latter source. Also, it does not encompass manager groups, even though we argued that many important developments occur as a result of the initiation of a stream of research inquiry by operating line managers or senior marketing executives. From an adoption point of view, it is also evident that "opinion leader" managers or corporations play a vital role in their willingness to invest in, and experiment with, new-knowledge development.

This section focuses on assessments of the innovator research group *within* marketing, those who appear to be at the forefront of new-knowledge developments in the field. The next section presents assessment material pertaining to managers as "users" of new knowledge. In each case, commissioner commentary is generally "critical," and the lack of effectiveness can be traced to a number of factors, many of which are seen as barriers to the knowledge-utilization process. In other words, commissioner assessments focused on where and why communication and information flows between the knowledge generators (academics) and knowledge users (managers) tended to break down.

As noted earlier, virtually all comments in the first section pertaining to the innovator research group are focused on academic rather than professional researchers. Apart from some specific insights that are best understood when these two subgroups are distinguished, most commentary is probably equally applicable to both. The principal reason for the focus on academics is that assessment material is drawn mainly from the Mini-Guide study in which professional members of the Commission were asked for their judgments and their experiences, within their own organizations, of how the process works. Questions were generally cast (see Chapter 5) in terms of the academic/business interface, and the professional commissioners thus tended to identify sources and barriers in terms of "academics" and "managers."

The following commissioner comment might be interpreted to mean that the professional researchers are the only significant part of the innovator research group.

At the outset, forgive me for saying that I cannot associate any new concept or technique with the academic community as a primary source. Most often the genesis is with some marketing research professional—either within a manufacturing company or in a marketing research company. Quite often an individual leaves a "parent" company to set up his own marketing research company as a result of work and experience gained as a participant in the parent company. . . . It would indeed be unusual for the academic community to have direct access to line management.

Another commissioner argued that the flow of new significant concepts has been *from* innovative companies *to* the academic community, but that academics play a major role in diffusion.

In my opinion most of the major new concepts that have had a significant impact in marketing have actually originated in innovative companies and have found their way to the academic field . . . Academics have played a major role in the diffusion of these concepts by writing and speaking about them. In addition, *academics usually* play the dominant role in investigating all of the possible ramifications and variations of these ideas.

The following four comments seem to recognize additional roles and contributions of academic researchers in one way or another.

Since 1948, my experience has all been as a staff "problem solver." In that role, I have seen many concepts brought into operating use, including a number that clearly originated in academia.

The one thing that you may not have allowed for is the process by which marketing executives obtain ideas from academic people by attending workshops, conferences, and short courses.

In addition, there is the . . . approach . . . of a marketing executive bringing a problem to the attention of an academic person who then develops a technique for dealing with the problem.

It appears to me that the communication and interaction between academic and business marketing community has been increasing recently and that the flow of ideas in both directions has been increasing. This flow is especially apparent to me between large businesses and the academic community. It has been facilitated because of the increased sophistication and knowledge of staff personnel in large well-managed business firms. Smaller firms, including marketing research firms, are often reluctant to accept new ideas or to experiment. One reason for this is the more limited resources and risk-averse attitudes.

When we are prompted to looking to new concepts to solve a particular problem, we will turn to research firms, technique specialists, and academic consultants as appropriate. Also, much new knowledge is acquired when we hire either experienced people or those who have just graduated from school—indeed, knowledge of new concepts and ideas is an important criterion in hiring new personnel.

Although the role of marketing academic researchers is implicitly or explicitly recognized in five of the comments above, commissioners were generally critical about the "effectiveness" of the knowledge innovations such researchers produce. Much of this criticism is expressed in the context of identifying "barriers" to the knowledge-utilization process. Barriers were seen to emanate from a lack of researcher knowledge of real-world marketing problems, a failure to test concepts adequately, problems of obscure language, and many other shortcomings. Three lengthy comments—the first from a friend of the Commission and the latter two from professional members of the Commission— refer to these factors as types of "barriers" to the diffusion and utilization process. As a group these obstructions were generally referred to as *substantive and communication barriers*.

It seems to me that there are three principal barriers to the diffusion process. One, alluded to above, is that some "nonmarketing academic" techniques and concepts are simply inappropriate to marketers' problems; or, when they are appropriate, they need extensive testing and revision. This process is slow, inevitably.

A second barrier is that communication between academic marketing researchers and practicing applied marketing researchers is much poorer than it could be. Part of the problem lies with the journals, especially the *Journal of Marketing Research*. Even under its new editor, *JMR* continues to be esoteric, abstruse, and jargon-laden. The academic marketing researchers who fill its pages are obviously writing to each other (and to the appointments and promotions committee), and a great many marketing practitioners simply will not go to the effort to decipher their cryptic inscriptions. Another part of the communication problem lies in the setup of the annual AMA marketing meetings, which appear to be designed so as to keep academic marketing researchers and marketing research professionals separated. The "academic" meetings and "professional" meetings are held at different times of the year and usually in widely separated locations. I do not know how this practice originated, but it appears to me to be a major barrier between two groups.

The third barrier to diffusion is that very many academic marketing researchers (let alone behavioral scientists) have no real knowledge of marketing problems. They tend to focus on a very narrow range of techniques and concepts, and they ignore many of the problems that practicing marketing researchers find most pesky. In part this lack of relevance comes from the fact that academic researchers tend to pick problems that are grand enough to be academically respectable; in part it comes from the fact that academic researchers simply do not know what is important to practitioners and what is not. Again, the separation of the AMA's "academic" and "practitioner" meetings seems to be a major contributor to this lack of communication.

In my opinion, the major deterrent or barrier to more rapid diffusion and acceptance by practicing marketing people is the lack of empirical testing of these techniques by marketing academicians. In many cases, the academics are simply ignorant of the problems of practical implementation. Many intelligent practitioners recognize this situation and, as a result, frequently overgeneralize about the lack of usefulness of other academic research results.

A second important barrier is the failure of many academics to make sure that the problem they are addressing is, in fact, relevant when compared to the other problems faced by practitioners. When practitioners see equal treatment being given to a trivial problem and one of major importance, they tend to discount the output of all academics.

Once a technique has been exposed to practitioners and has passed the tests of practicality and relevance, I think the major barrier is simple inertia. In most organizations there is a body of experience with the old procedure. The tendency is to say, "At least we know how to get things done the old way," and we're concerned about whether the new approach will be accepted by management at higher levels.

In my opinion, the best way to promote awareness of new concepts and techniques within an organization is to make sure that managers and research professionals maintain broad contacts and information sources with other organizations as well as the academic community. Although there is some reluctance in a number of firms to divulge much of anything, there are a number of trade associations which have off-the-record meetings where techniques can be discussed with some degree of frankness. I also believe that seminars for operating management are an excellent source of new ideas and concepts in companies; however, if there is a lack of expertise permanently residing in the organization, the chances of any new concepts being adopted are very slight. Hence, it is very important to have new hires coming into the organization with good training and new ideas.

Part of the interface problem is that marketing management has no media vehicle edited to reach a marketing management audience. The MSI publications come close—but I believe they would be more effective if the editorial emphasis were balanced even more to the *Harvard Business Review* mode and less to the "standards" of academic publication.

Since there is no broad vehicle for reaching marketing *management,* we rely on academic and business consultants, research companies, and a few innovative industry or ad agency research people as the communication pipeline to operating management.

Meanwhile, the line managers get their ideas from sources who know what business they are in—influencing the decision and action of line managers—such as management consultants, advertising agency account executives from other companies, as well as trade conventions geared to communicate with managers—on their terms!

Research management in a company is one source of new marketing concepts, but not necessarily the only or most creditable source. How effective they are depends on the kind of role they have *earned* in the organization. Only a limited number of research managers have earned the role as a source of concepts or knowledge that can affect the *practice* of marketing management in a company. More have earned the role as a technically competent source of "facts" that can contribute to a specific marketing decision. Most have earned the role of contributor of a narrow range of kinds of facts that the marketing management has decided it wants from research.

Hence the knowledge generators would be well served to develop more client-effective channels of communication with the marketing managers—if they ever decide that they are in the business of developing knowledge and theory to be *used* in the practice of marketing *and* if they ever *straighten* out their own institutional arrangements so that the things necessary to be in the business are legitimate and rewarded.

The last comment about a researcher's credibility being a function of the kind of role *earned* in the organization seems to us particularly insightful and to apply to academics as well as professional researchers. The effectiveness of a knowledge innovator depends to a considerable degree on the reputation he or she has gained in terms of providing useful new concepts and ideas, and this applies internally within the organization as well as externally. It is one more manifestation of the requirements for being a member of the innovator research group.

Alluded to by several commissioners, the problems of communication that arise from the requirements of "language" alone appear formidable. Another barrier is the fact that unfamiliar ideas will tend to be seen as irrelevant and, in many cases, threatening. Both phenomena retard the flow of ideas from the development to the dissemination/utilization stage.

The mode of expression of an idea can be a very serious barrier, especially if the language is mathematical. Unfortunately, though, some ideas that are highly relevant to marketing (especially marketing research) cannot be expressed with the necessary precision without the use of mathematical notation, and they cannot be understood without knowledge of mathematical processes. This phenomenon is not unique to marketing. For instance, Smith and Karlesky[18] stated, "The economist of thirty years ago would probably have scoffed had someone told him that by 1977 every serious undergraduate student in his discipline would be expected to study calculus, linear algebra, and introductory mathematical analysis."

The problem of language also is related to the well-known time lag between the performance of basic research and its reduction to practice and widespread adoption. We think of physical engineering as both highly technical and highly pragmatic and problem-oriented. Yet this profession has had its time lags in achieving an appropriate level of mathematical literacy and the diffusion of basic research findings. Consider this comment about mathematician Norbert Weiner's wartime paper on the analysis of stationary time series:

It was written primarily for electrical engineers, even though most electrical engineers of the 1940's could not read it. This was perhaps not a bad thing; the results were sufficiently interesting to provide a stimulus to engineers to acquaint themselves with enough mathematics so that they could read it. In 1965 most theoretical communications and control engineers can read it, and in fact are fairly conversant with its contents. There is now probably not a graduate program in the country in which [this] material is not offered.[19]

Thus, a basic research finding that is at first inaccessible to the majority can, in time, revolutionize practical applications in a field.

A major problem in assessing the state of R & D in an applied field is that most professionals are likely to conclude that what is currently in the pipeline is of dubious value. This is not unreasonable, since most items may well be destined for failure. Also, it is perfectly reasonable for individuals and companies to wait until ideas reach the stage of credibility before paying attention to them. However, what may be good policy for individuals will be bad policy in the aggregate if the indifference of the majority leads to closing down or seriously constricting the pipeline of new ideas in the field.

The strong reaction of many people to the problems of language is well expressed by Westing:

Marketing research is and always will be a vital activity. Probably marketing professors have contributed more to this activity than to any other. However, our progress here seems to have been from the simple to the obscure to the arcane. The typical research study today relates to a subject of minimal importance, is analyzed by methods so refined that they are probably not fully comprehended by the researchers, and produces conclusions of dubious validity, which interest only the next would-be article writer.[20]

Although some of this criticism is undoubtedly justified, it is in our opinion a mistake to categorize all attempts at formal reasoning as "obscure" or "arcane." Such observations, among other things, ignore the important role of the computer in modern marketing management and research, and the fact that mathematical specification is often a necessary prerequisite to its use. Westing offers numerous other reflections that are very germane to the Commission's work. For example, he attributes much of the "misdirection" of current marketing scholarship to the Ford and Carnegie Commission reports, which were, in part, used to define the twenty-five-year span of the assessment period:

... marketing may have got onto the wrong track at the time we were all reacting to the Ford and Carnegie reports. ... Since the critics charged us with being superficially descriptive, we determined to become an academic discipline, with all its trappings. The fact of the matter is that we are not an academic discipline. ... There is nothing wrong with discovering something on our own, but that is not our primary purpose. Our goal should be to try to make business more proficient and efficient—and this is not an unworthy goal. It is similar to the goals of engineering, law, medicine, pharmacy, agriculture, and education. We are all professional disciplines, rather than academic disciplines. ... Beyond being descriptive, we should have become prescriptive. ... [W]e should content ourselves with borrowing from basic disciplines and concentrate on applications which will enable business to do its job better and cheaper.[21]

Westing's thesis that marketing is a "professional" rather than an "academic" discipline seems to us correct and is consistent with the thrust of the Commission's work. Marketing academics, whether teaching or researching, need to maintain this perspective. It does not follow, however, that all current scholarship is necessarily on the wrong track, or that the Ford and Carnegie Commissions were the only cause of this supposed misdirection. We need to take account of the invention and development of computers and television over the period and to apprehend the meaning of terms such as marketing information and useful marketing knowledge in this context. Westing's recommendations that marketing academics become more prescriptive and less descriptive and devote their energies to more important problems seems to ignore these developments as well as the facts that much modeling, for example, is now prescriptive (even though perhaps not "widely used") and that many of the issues cited are the focal points of much current academic research. In sum, although the content of academic research needs constant appraisal and attention, we are less than convinced that it is "irrelevant" to marketing management practice.[22]

The next section highlights some additional "causes" of barriers to the diffusion and utilization process as indicated in commissioner comments on the manager-users of marketing knowledge.

ASSESSMENTS OF MANAGER-USER GROUPS

The foregoing materials represent a generally critical reaction to the productivity and impact of the innovator research group in marketing, particularly the academic component. Criticisms of the group range from the irrelevance of the problems they choose to work on through a wide range of communications and language-related factors that serve as barriers to knowledge diffusion and utilization. Commissioners were equally critical, however, of the "receivers" of the information—the manager-user groups to whom new knowledge should be useful.

Much of the commentary was generated in the context of the Mini-Guide study and the request made to commissioners to identify "barriers" to the diffusion process. The commentary here focuses on what became known as *structural and organizational barriers* within the business community. Factors such as manager inertia, conservatism, and limited opportunity for, or motivation to, communicate with the knowledge innovators are identified in the four following comments from commissioners in operating companies:

More line managers [in our company] believed the barriers to be between academia and business. Staff people tended to believe they were between line managers and staff. My own thoughts are that both interfaces present barriers. Line managers do not have much contact with academics, they do not find time to go to seminars and meetings, and the published journals seem to be written more for other academics than for practitioners. Seminar presentations and consultants actually are more practical in their recommendations, but they do not have much opportunity to speak to line managers. The barrier within the company differs in the resistance it offers, depending upon the line manager. Does he make the effort to find out the capabilities of new methodologies and ask questions of his staff that require their use? Or does he resist techniques if he does not understand all the details of the mathematical analyses used? My belief is that the barrier within the company is the more serious one since its presence limits the demand.

The principal barriers to diffusion of new marketing concepts and techniques are the same that apply to other subject matters. I believe that most managers are conservative in adopting new techniques. Both sloth and an understandable reluctance to apply something new and untried are involved. Beyond this, the principal problem is lack of incentive on the part of management to adopt new techniques. Management has its hands full with current problems and has very little time for the study and reflection required to gain knowledge and confidence in new techniques.

I recall research I did a number of years ago on the types of infant feeding formulas prescribed by pediatricians; I found what they prescribed closely correlated with when they graduated from medical school. The same applies to management, and, as you know, one of the big challenges in management education is keeping those in practice up-to-date. The same problems exist intracompany, as many marketing researchers are not good teachers and line managers are often poor students.

Diffusion is slowed by limited communication between those developing techniques and those using them—i.e., the line manager. Short courses offered by business schools, AMA, MSI, and The Conference Board are all excellent for this purpose, and they do a reasonably good job reaching many of the large companies . . . but this is only scratching the surface. Feedback is also a problem. Many companies are very secretive about their experiences . . . but the academic community is not a very good listener either. Here again, I'm not talking about the leaders in both business and the academic community, but they are too few.

With regard to channels of communication between line and staff (including both inside and outside consultants), there are many impediments. Among the more critical, I would include:

1. The N.I.H. factor—"not invented here."
2. The feeling on the part of certain line managers that staff people are not very realistic in their approach to practical problems.
3. The natural inclination of administrators to concentrate on "short-term" problems.
4. The lack of opportunities for line managers to participate actively in professional groups (such as AMA) where they can get acquainted with professors actively interested in their areas of concern. This barrier has been made even greater by the increasing dispersion of companies from central cities into the suburbs.

Taken together, these comments comprise a position that commanded a strong consensus within the Commission.

INNOVATOR AND DIFFUSER ROLES

From the foregoing, one gains an impression that significant communication and structural/organizational barriers impede the flow and utilization of new marketing knowledge. Based on their own experiences, the commissioners commented on who appeared to play what roles. Some saw professional rather than academic researchers as most significant at the innovator stage. One commissioner asserted: "I cannot associate any new concept or technique with the academic community as a primary source." Another stated that academics "have played a major role in the diffusion of the concepts by writing and speaking about them, and in investigating all of the possible ramifications and variations." Another said, "I have seen many concepts brought into operating use, including a number that clearly originated in academia." Obviously, the experiences and opinions of these observers differ, reflecting some of the many possible conceptions of the nature of the knowledge-creation and utilization process.

That there is an "innovator research group" in marketing made up of professional and academic researchers appeared to be generally agreed on by the Commission. There was also general agreement that, for the barrier reasons alluded to in the last two sections, the impact of the knowledge they produced over the assessment period was generally less than it might have been. The latter proposition was, in effect, reported on in the first section of the chapter pertaining to knowledge use. Here, we focus on the former proposition. More specifically, within the innovator research group, do academics and professionals play the same roles with respect to creating and diffusing knowledge? How important is each as the source of new ideas or as the major "diffuser" of new ideas?

Some insight into this question can be gained from the results of the AMA Membership Survey. Academics and research suppliers were asked to rate the *relative* importance of eight different kinds of change agents in terms of the contributions of each to the initial development of new concepts and techniques and to the diffusion of those concepts and techniques. Table 6-11 presents the first results from this aspect of the study.

The most significant impression one gains is that professional researchers (in this case commercial research supplier respondents) and academic researchers rate *themselves* as most important in both the initial development and diffusion aspects of the process. Once again, a kind of self-fulfilling prophecy is evident. Academics rate "academic research and publication" as most important at both the initial-development and diffusion-of-knowledge stages, with "shares" of 32.8 and 24.3, respectively. Research suppliers, on the other hand, rate the contributions of "marketing research and specialist firms" number one in each case, with "shares" of 30.6 and 28.8, respectively. Academic consulting activities are ranked third by academics and fourth by research suppliers behind the activities of academic research and publication and of marketing research specialist firms. Consulting firms rank fourth and third, respectively. The rankings of the last four agents (company marketing research departments, advertising agencies, academic teaching programs, and line marketing management) are identical for both academics and suppliers at the initial-development stage.

Perceptions differ also about the role of various agents in the diffusion process. Academics rate academic teaching programs highly (second place), whereas suppliers relegate such programs to fourth place behind their own firms, academic research and publication, and consulting firms. Otherwise, academics and suppliers are comparatively similar in their ranking of the other agents in the diffusion process.

Both academics and suppliers are highly consistent in relegating the last (eighth) place to "line marketing management." Neither group perceives them to be important agents either in the development of new knowledge or in its diffusion.

In sum, with respect to both development and diffusion, the academics and research suppliers hold somewhat parallel views. However, each group contends that it is the major force in each area, although each gives the other relatively high grades as well. Research supplier firms and academic research/publications are viewed by both groups as central sources of both initial development and diffusion of new concepts and techniques for marketing. Academics tend to see their own teaching programs and consulting as relatively important sources of knowledge *diffusion*.

Table 6-12 summarizes these data in terms of academic and supplier perceptions of relative "shares" of initial development and diffusion activity of four groups: academics, research suppliers, marketing research departments, and operating managers. As can be seen, academics and suppliers perceive that their own two groups do about 87% of the initial-development activity and about 90% of the diffusion activity. They rate marketing research departments consistently as more important than operating managers in both kinds of activity. Academics

TABLE 6-11

IMPORTANCE OF KNOWLEDGE-DEVELOPMENT AND DIFFUSION AGENTS AS PERCEIVED BY ACADEMICS AND RESEARCH SUPPLIERS [a]

| | Initial Development | | | | Diffusion of Knowledge | | | |
| | Academics | | Research Suppliers | | Academics | | Research Suppliers | |
Agent	Share	Rank	Share	Rank	Share	Rank	Share	Rank
Academic research and publication	32.8	1	23.1	2	24.3	1	21.5	2
Marketing research specialist firms	16.3	2	30.6	1	14.1	3	28.8	1
Academic consulting activities	13.0	3	10.7	4	11.5	4	7.4	7
Consulting firms	10.0	4	10.8	3	10.5	5	11.1	3
Company marketing research departments	9.5	5	10.2	5	5.9	7	8.3	6
Advertising agencies	8.3	6	7.3	6	8.3	6	10.1	5
Academic teaching programs	6.3	7	4.5	7	22.2	2	10.5	4
Line marketing management	3.8	8	2.8	8	3.2	8	2.3	8
Totals	100.0		100.0		100.0		100.0	

[a] Based on academic and research supplier replies to: "By assigning points totaling 100%, please rate the *relative* importance of the groups below in terms of their contribution to (a) the *initial development* of new concepts and techniques as applied to marketing, (b) the *diffusion of knowledge* about new concepts and techniques and their application."

TABLE 6-12

PERCEIVED SHARES OF KNOWLEDGE-DEVELOPMENT AND DIFFUSION ACTIVITY OF ACADEMIC AND PROFESSIONAL RESEARCHERS AND OPERATING LINE MANAGERS [a]

| | Initial Development | | | | Diffusion of Knowledge | | | |
| | Academics | | Research Suppliers | | Academics | | Research Suppliers | |
Agent	Share	Rank	Share	Rank	Share	Rank	Share	Rank
Academics	52.1	1	38.3	2	58.0	1	39.4	2
Research suppliers	34.6	2	48.7	1	32.9	2	50.0	1
Marketing research departments	9.5	3	10.2	3	5.9	3	8.3	3
Operating managers	3.8	4	2.8	4	3.2	4	2.3	4
Totals	100.0		100.0		100.0		100.0	

[a]See footnote a, Table 6-11.

claim that the largest share of both initial-development and diffusion activities is done by academics, and suppliers claim that the largest share of each is done by suppliers.

Although there is probably no "objective" way to conclude which group is the more important in these activities, and there is certainly reason to argue for a certain amount of perceptual distortion on behalf of all groups in the AMA survey, academics and professional researchers appear to be identifiable as the essential components of the innovator research group, and thus they engage in both knowledge creation and diffusion activities. Even operating managers appear to recognize these roles. For example, although operating managers "use" literature searches and their own colleagues more, about 89% reported using their own research company (e.g., a supplier) and "author/originator" as a useful source for information and guidance with respect to a new technique. That is, operating managers appear to look to them as sources of relevant information. Even the concept of "academic consultant," although rated in seventh place as a source by operating managers, was still reported "not used" by only 18% of the operating manager sample.

SUMMARY

This chapter has examined the models of knowledge creation and utilization given in Chapter 5 from an assessment point of view, using commissioner commentary and the results of the AMA Membership Survey. We conclude first that the various models are reasonable representations of the process in the industrial and academic sectors. There does appear to be an "innovator research group," and concepts such as "diffusion vehicles," "information sources," and "manager-users" appear to be useful and generalizable representations of basic components of the knowledge-creation and utilization process in marketing. There are many places where the different kinds of evaluative commentary do not appear to "fit" well with the general models, and probably no one model could adequately describe all possible ways in which the process works.

The assessments presented are generally critical of the efficiency, effectiveness, and functioning of the knowledge-creation and utilization aspect of marketing's research and development system. In Chapter 7 we summarize the book in a way that highlights much of this assessment material, and we will not attempt to summarize it here. As will be seen, apparently much new knowledge in marketing is not being used. We consider this neither particularly alarming nor totally assignable to any one "cause" such as the irrelevance of what the knowledge innovators create. The situation stems rather from a number of complex factors, barriers, and differences in perspectives and values that characterize marketing's research and development system. Many of these were identified in the various sections of this chapter. In Chapter 7 we pull them together as we summarize the book's major ideas and our major conclusions about marketing's research and development system.

NOTES

[1]J. Howard Westing, "Marketing Educators Must Switch to Helping Real World Meet Real Problems," *Marketing News*, 11 (July 29, 1977), 16, published by the American Marketing Association.

[2]Gert Assmus, "Bayesian Analysis for the Evaluation of Marketing Research Expenditures: A Reassessment," *Journal of Marketing Research,* 14 (November 1977), 562–68.

[3]For an excellent discussion of these issues from the point of view of federal, state, and local government, see Martin Greenberger, Matthew A. Crewson, and Brian L. Crissey, *Models in the Policy Process* (New York: Russell Sage Foundation, 1976).

[4]Robert Ferber, "Antecedent Conditions for Diffusion of Multivariate Methods," in J. N. Sheth, ed., *Multivariate Methods for Market and Survey Research* (Chicago: American Marketing Association, 1977), p. 331.

[5]This result is particularly interesting and appears to confirm the impressions of many commissioners. From a textbook viewpoint, Bayesian analysis has been suggested not only as an approach to all kinds of marketing management problems and decision making, but also as the formal way to determine the value of marketing research information.

[6]It may be that the nine manager-users of Bayesian and factor analysis are "innovators" or "early adopters" in the sense of the model. They might, however, also be considered "laggards" in the sense of the high rejection of these techniques by other managers!

[7]B. A. Greenberg, and others, "What Techniques Are Used by Marketing Researchers in Business?" *Journal of Marketing*, 41 (April 1977), 62–68, published by the American Marketing Association.

[8]Greenberg and others, "What Techniques?" pp. 66–67.

[9]The authors make the point that techniques such as store audit and test marketing, which show little penetration in utilities, are by and large inappropriate for them.

[10]The authors argue that "simpler" does not imply lack of sophistication but rather "the more complex techniques are perhaps not necessary." They go on to argue that marketing research courses should include intensive study of these "simple, albeit less sophisticated, techniques." Greenberg and others, p. 67.

[11]Dik W. Twedt, "Business Degrees Show Steady Increase, But Marketing Education's Share Shrinks," *Marketing News,* 10 (July 30, 1976), 1 ff. Further analysis of these data revealed that only institutions granting a degree "in marketing" were included. A large proportion of leading business schools only grant a degree in "business administration" and thus are not included. Among the latter schools, at least, marketing generally ranks behind accounting and finance as a major area of concentration for the student. The addition of these types of students would probably raise the Twedt estimate above 25,000 nationally.

[12]Many critics of marketing education in the better business schools appear to forget that the dominant "product" of these schools in marketing is a potential marketing *manager* rather than a potential marketing *researcher*. Marketing management is the

subject that dominates the curriculum, and the demand for MBA's with marketing majors has been consistently strong over the period, particularly during up-phases of the business cycle. Also, we suspect that the recent generation of marketing managers from such schools are probably more comfortable with computers and quantitative techniques, given their likely exposure to them in such programs.

[13]The participation of academics in these kinds of activities needs additional emphasis. Although we do not have hard data on the number of marketing faculty who contribute to these types of training programs on an annual basis, our impression is that there is a high demand for them, and that a significant amount of faculty time is spent in executive and middle-management type training programs.

[14]E. T. Grether, "The First Forty Years," *Journal of Marketing,* 40 (July 1976), 63–69, published by the American Marketing Association.

[15]Grether, "The First Forty Years," pp. 68–69.

[16]Many forces oppose this, not the least of which is any explicit monetary reward for publication activity by professionals. Also, there is a problem of enforcing sanitized rules to protect confidential data. Despite these problems, the Commission endorsed this as an effective way of building the desired combination of experience and concepts.

[17]This was aptly stated by Green: "Today a single individual cannot encompass the breadth of material being ground out in the quantitative and behavior sciences." See Paul E. Green, "Where Is the Research Generalist?" p. 442. This comment was made in 1968; the explosion of such material since that time makes the job of today's scholar even more difficult.

[18]Bruce L. R. Smith and Joseph J. Karlesky, *The State of Academic Science* (New York: Change Magazine Press, 1977), p. 120.

[19]From William L. Root, "Contributions of Norbert Weiner to Communication Theory," *Bulletin of the American Mathematical Society* (1966), quoted in Smith and Karlesky, *The State of Academic Science,* (Change Magazine Press).

[20]Westing, "Marketing Educators Must Switch," p. 16.

[21]Westing, "Marketing Educators Must Switch," p. 16.

[22]For papers that address the question "What Is the Appropriate Orientation for the Marketing Academic?" see *Proceedings of Annual Conferences* (Chicago: American Marketing Association, 1979), papers by William H. Peters, J. Howard Westing, Jeffrey Maiken, George Swartz, and John G. Myers.

7

Summary
and
Conclusions

This chapter summarizes our views on marketing research and knowledge development and its contributions to marketing management practice over the past quarter-century. Many of the conclusions emanate from the work of the ERDMM Commission.

This book offers a new perspective on marketing research. The basic argument is for a much broader viewpoint than what is currently popular, one which looks at marketing research and development as an important national resource about which not much is known and that deserves more attention. The perspective is embodied in the concept of "marketing's research and development system." Evaluation of the effectiveness of this system for marketing management is a major focus of this chapter and of the book.

Significant controversies surround the subject of the effectiveness of R & D for marketing management. Some of these issues might be considered "traditional." The questions indicating the ways in which a marketing research department interfaces with a marketing management team, and what the role of industrial marketing research is in decision making, have been subjects of continuing interest since marketing research began. We have argued that the subject and the issues surrounding it are much broader and more fundamental than the problems associated solely with line-staff relations in a corporation. The fundamental issue is whether a "system" of marketing research and development, servicing the profession of marketing and resting on scholarly work in the basic social and engineering sciences, exists. To those who would reply "Obviously yes," we would point out that it does not appear to be described, researched, or monitored in any systematic way. Basically, it is not well understood. To those who would say "No," we would point to the need to repudiate many of the facts presented in this book.

A pervading theme has been the accountability and relevance of basic research and knowledge-development activities, particularly those engaged in by the marketing academic community. To evaluate their role and contributions, we must first reach agreement on whether they are part of marketing's research and system. Again, we would have those who say "Obviously" consider the fact that much of the research productivity of this group appears to have had little effect on marketing management practice. There is a widespread and firmly held belief that "science" and the people who adopt the perspectives of scientific inquiry in the field have little to contribute to improving management. This is not only the dominant belief of many marketing executives and managers but is shared by government officials and many scientists and scholars in the basic disciplines. As we have pointed out, it is also shared by some marketing professors.

The basic debate thus concerns the role, contributions, and place of "science" and established methods of scientific inquiry in the field of marketing. If one believes that the profession of marketing is (or should be) based on science, it is logical to assume that a scientifically based system of research and development exists to serve the profession. If, on the other hand, one believes that marketing is largely an art in which decisions are based on experience and on methods of "tenacity," "authority," or "intuition" rather than on the methods of science, then our notions of an R & D system for marketing management that extends into the marketing academic community and ultimately into the academic communities of the basic social sciences and social engineering will not be readily accepted.

We doubt that this book will change many minds. It will be successful, however, if it succeeds in focusing the debate on the scope, nature, and functioning of what we have called marketing's research and development system. Hopefully, more and better studies will emanate from such discussion, leading to better understanding of the system. Our position is that science does have a role to play in marketing, that a system of scientifically based research and development does exist, that it is an important national resource, and that much remains to be learned about it.

The first section of the chapter summarizes the nature and scope of the system and some important new concepts associated with it. The major forces that appear to have shaped it also are summarized. The second section considers the system's effectiveness—in terms of both knowledge creation and knowledge utilization—from the viewpoint of marketing management in the private sector.

The next section summarizes the major factors that appear to inhibit knowledge utilization—factors specifically associated with knowledge-generators and knowledge-users as well as more general factors. A fourth section presents our opinions and advice on the role of the marketing academic community, particularly with respect to the place of basic and problem-oriented research. The final section offers some conclusions on marketing research and knowledge development, the need for conscious efforts to support marketing R & D, and the national investment in these types of activities.

MARKETING'S RESEARCH AND DEVELOPMENT SYSTEM

This book appears to be the first publication that attempts to map out marketing's research and development system. Current marketing research textbooks do not present materials on the subject of marketing research in this way, nor does any organization or individual currently provide a national accounting perspective that allows estimates of the national investment in the system. National accounting is not done on the size, nature, scope, and investment in this system as it is for production research and development. This is a major finding, and we hope it will lead to continued study, concentrated attention, and better understanding.

In the review that follows, we highlight the major features and scope of marketing's R & D system. People within and outside the field of marketing will disagree upon many points. Some ideas might be labeled pure speculation. We nevertheless feel they are important and provide a useful new way to think about marketing research and the field of marketing as a whole.

Nature and Scope

The departure point for the argument that there exists a national system of research and development for marketing lies in the assumption that all R & D efforts are divisible into a production-related component and a marketing-related component. As we have noted, there are many shades of gray at the boundary, particularly with respect to the meaning of terms such as "product research." The distinction seems viable, however, in terms of formal definitions of R & D currently in use by agencies such as the National Science Foundation (definitions that specifically *exclude* marketing research activities) and in light of the fact that marketing research departments and R & D departments often are treated as separate entities in corporate structure. There are investments in marketing R & D that are distinct from investments in production R & D.

The other basic departure point is that there exist "users" and "suppliers" of marketing R & D. Again, this is a slippery concept, but it does serve to identify particular organizations and the roles played by them in the overall system. We further argue that users and suppliers of marketing research and development exist in all four sectors of the economy, and that the national scope of the system should, as with production R & D, be viewed from this perspective. The definitions of research and development, the methods used to monitor investment expenditures, and the nature of the reports generated by the National Science Foundation serve as a model to which marketing should aspire. The four-sector view is viable if one adopts the increasingly popular assumption that marketing principles are generalizable to the management of nonprofit organizations. If so, it is but a simple step to argue that the marketing concept and the consumer or "publics" focus implied lead logically to the need to conduct "marketing research" for the management of such organizations. This, in turn, leads to the insight that many organizations in the nonprofit sector are in the business of conducting "marketing research."

The most concrete conceptions of the system currently refer to an industrial corporation in the private sector. From a national accounting perspective, this is also where most of the investment in marketing R & D takes place, and it has been our focus in elaborating various parts of the system and its functioning. Figure 4-3 presented the basic perspective. Marketing R & D is juxtaposed with production R & D, recognizable internally as the marketing research department and externally as organizations that perform primary and secondary research activities on which the corporation draws. Like production R & D, the system rests on basic "sciences." It differs, however, both in that marketing R & D rests on the social and social engineering sciences and in that investments tend to be much smaller.

Our attempts to provide a specific number that reflects the size of the national investment in marketing R & D were restricted to this sector. As of 1977, it appears that something over $1 billion is a reasonable guesstimate of the expenditures involved. Compared with a *Business Week* report on industrial investments in production R & D for that year, the amount devoted to marketing works out to about 5.5%. Industry, and the nation as whole, continues to invest a much smaller share of resources in marketing-related research activities.

The "system" upon which marketing management rests and from which it draws new knowledge and decision-making insights is thus much broader than the marketing research department of a corporation, and it goes beyond current meanings of the term "marketing research" or even "marketing information system." It is intimately intertwined with other sectors of the economy, particularly the academic sector. Although many corporations and leaders in marketing appear to recognize this interdependency and successfully capitalize on it, many others do not. Much of the controversy surrounding the subject of marketing research and knowledge development ultimately reduces to conflicting beliefs about either the basic existence or the nature and scope of this system.

Universities, and business schools in particular, play a vital role, both in replenishing the pool of professional marketing manager and marketing researcher talent and in contributing to the development of new knowledge in the field. The MBA and Ph.D. students graduating from these institutions who opt for careers in marketing are the ones who ultimately give the field of marketing its semblance of professional stature.

Chapter 5 addressed the question of how knowledge is created and utilized in marketing largely from the perspective of the industry-academic sectors of the overall system. Although no one viewpoint seems capable of capturing all possible channels, all sources of influence, or the nature of the process for every single advance of meaningful new knowledge, the various models presented represent the basic nature of the process in many instances. As noted, there are many parallels in the creation, diffusion, and adoption process with respect to any innovation, and a "stage theory" appears most applicable. Certain concepts seem particularly important or new to the field, and we focus on them in what follows.

The first is the role played by the *nonmarketing academic*. Much new knowledge in marketing is an adaptation or refinement of basic knowledge developed in the social or social engineering sciences. This can be recognized in the comments of many commissioners as well as in the examples of new-knowledge developments in marketing presented in various parts of the book. The diversity of the surrounding sciences from which specific examples can be traced is represented in Figure 4-6. Marketing, in this sense, is a truly "interdisciplinary" subject, even though the scope of the major supporting disciplines is largely constrained to social engineering and the social sciences. One implication of explicitly recognizing these as supporting disciplines is that, in some senses at least, we can then consider them *part* of an overall national system of marketing research and development. Many such scientists will not adopt this proposition, but it is difficult to escape, given all the arguments that have been presented. The nature of the commercial research supplier industry, in which virtually every social science methodological perspective is represented, appears to us to further support these arguments.

The second important concept is that of an *innovator research group*. This "group," as explained at length in Chapter 5, is comparatively small and made up of leading scholars and thinkers in the field, not restricted to marketing academics. There is, in effect, a small "college" of such people that transcends university boundaries and includes a wide range of professional researchers in advertising agencies, research supplier firms, media, and marketing departments of major corporations. The stereotype that all important new ideas leading to improvements in marketing practice flow from academia is thus without foundation. Nor is the innovator research group in marketing the only *fundamental* source of important new ideas. "Nonmarketing academics," "managers," or even a "wife, husband, or child" can also be considered fundamental sources of new ideas. The point is that an idea is not worth much unless it is developed, refined, tested, and in some way or another put to practical use. Members of the innovator research group perform much of this function in the field of marketing. In an R & D sense, much of their work might best be described as "development." But it can also be described as "basic research" where, for example, the choice of the unit of analysis as "consumer" or "retail store" is relatively unimportant to the underlying theory or model being proposed or tested. Or it might be considered "problem-oriented research," where a specific managerial or organizational problem and not a general contribution to scientific knowledge is the basic motivation or departure point. We discuss further the nature of marketing academic research in a later section of the chapter.

The third important new concept is that of *problem-oriented research.* This term has found its way into the language of marketing, particularly among marketing academics. It has not, however, found its way into marketing research or marketing management textbooks. It is worthy of formal introduction into marketing literature. Not the same thing as "basic research" or "problem-solving research," in many ways it lies between them and combines many of the perspectives of each.

It has become popular among academics in marketing to declare that one has two fundamental options: (1) to do "poor-quality" research on a "relevant" problem, or (2) to do "high-quality" research on an "irrelevant" problem! This maxim expresses a fundamental dilemma of the academic researcher in marketing and, indeed, a dilemma that faces the field as a whole. One interpretation is that "high-quality" research extends the forefront of knowledge (either theory or method) in the social or engineering sciences. It is characterized by extensive literature review into previous research on that topic in the sciences, much footnoting and referencing, and should truly build on what can be a fifty- to hundred-year knowledge foundation! The result from a managerial perspective, however, can appear totally irrelevant to anything the manager deals with and totally uninterpretable within the manager's time and ability constraints. A relevant problem, on the other hand, often results in "poor-quality" research because (1) the nature or complexity of the problem can reduce the researcher to mere description of what appear to be the major factors involved, (2) the problem is phrased so broadly that it cannot be empirically addressed, or (3) the researcher is simply not well versed in the social sciences. We comment further on this point later in the chapter.

A fourth concept is that of *matching.* New knowledge that has the best chance of being widely diffused and adopted is that which, at the point of origination, results from the "matching" of an idea with a problem. In fact, many commissioners took the position that if it came down to a trade-off between the two ways of doing research alluded to above, the probabilities of "successful" research or knowledge generation as measured by managerial utility would be higher when a specific managerial problem was the main reference point for the inquiry. Relevant research from the viewpoint of directly influencing changes in marketing management practice appears to be that in which a new idea is tied directly to a specific managerial problem. It may, however, as argued later on, not be the most "relevant" for management over the long run.

Forces That Shaped Marketing's R & D System

Chapters 2 and 3 reviewed some of the major changes in marketing management and marketing knowledge development and the factors involved over the past twenty-five years. These are the influences that shaped the current nature of marketing's research and development system, particularly in the industrial sector. The first, as noted in Chapter 2, was simply the *marketing concept*. This change in managerial philosophy and in "the way of doing business" had far-reaching consequences for marketing research and development as well as marketing management practice. Among other things, it resulted in a demand for more and better "market research." The external and consumer focus it implies inevitably had much to do with the creation of marketing research departments and, in academia, the creation of significant academic interest in and concentration on consumer motivation and behavior as well as the emergence of the subject of marketing research. The marketing concept has broadened to encompass the management of nonprofit organizations. It has had much to do with improvements over the last quarter-century in marketing planning, organizing, implementing, and control.

Technological developments, particularly in the areas of *computers* and *television*, were very significant in shaping marketing's research and development system. Each created the need for research expertise and brought into the field of marketing a vast array of technicians, statisticians, computer and management scientists, creative experts in audiovisual communications, and so on. It has been said that the computer essentially "quantified" marketing, or at least made some minimum level of quantitative skill a prerequisite to its use. Many developments in mathematical model building and in complex multivariate methods of data analysis (and increasingly in methods of data collection) are directly attributable to the invention of the computer. The computer, in some sense, is both the means and the ends of these developments. Without it, most of the formal model developments could not have been "tested" in either a simulation or a data-gathering sense. And, without it, there would have been no rationale for developing the kinds of models that were developed in the first place.

A final force was the fundamental change in *educational philosophy* promulgated by the Gorden and Howell and Pierson reports in 1959. As noted in Chapter 6, much that is basic about the relevance or irrelevance of the knowledge-producing sector's activities is inherent in a debate initiated two decades ago by these two reports and continuing up to the present day. The principal message was that business education should be "liberalized" and given a scientific base. In marketing, this evolved into the position that research, knowledge development, and scholarly activity in general should rest and build upon the social sciences such as economics, psychology, and sociology and upon disciplines such as engineering and statistics. This position underlies our attempts to map out the full complexity of marketing's research and development system. These disciplines are seen as the academic knowledge base. The nature and characteristics of knowledge developments, the people involved in them, the criteria of "quality," "academic worth," and so on, have been governed accordingly. The "new-look" business schools such as M.I.T., Carnegie-Mellon, Chicago, and later Stanford, Harvard, Wharton, Northwestern, and Berkeley were among the first to adopt this perspective, and from these institutions much of the "new knowledge" in marketing has been generated.[1] The perspective has since been broadly adopted in many American universities and research-oriented marketing departments.

Not all informed academic and professional people in marketing support this position, however, nor should one expect them to. It seems to us that the profession of marketing is best served by the same principles of freedom of choice and heterogeneity that serve the economic system as a whole. There is no one "proper" way to teach and do research in marketing, just as there is no one proper way to manage a marketing operation. What exists is a heterogeneity of educational and professional philosophies that is well suited to the heterogeneity and diversity of the field of marketing itself. Modern marketing is a complex interdisciplinary and multivariate subject that, in its professional aspects, must relate to giant corporations and tiny ones, and increasingly to nonprofit organizations as well. On the academic side, the training and research needs are filled by schools that range from virtually pure-science orientations through more applied case-method orientations to totally applied and tradeschool-like orientations. It would be a grave mistake to constrain all marketing education and scholarship into one monolithic mold.

The next section offers concluding comments on the effectiveness of marketing's research and development system. Materials are organized into sections on knowledge creation and knowledge utilization.

EFFECTIVENESS OF THE SYSTEM

It is useful to think of effectiveness in knowledge creation as distinct from effectiveness in knowledge use. From the creation side, one could argue that the system is not very effective if it does not generate significant amounts of new knowledge. By analogy, a new-products group can be assessed for its generation of worthwhile new ideas that might eventually become vital products or services. From the utilization side, one might ask how many of those new ideas find their way to the marketplace and do indeed become profitable products or services. In general, there appears to be a wide disparity in the "performance" of marketing's R & D system between the two criteria.[2]

Knowledge Creation

New-knowledge creation activities and "products" flourished over the twenty-five year assessment period. Compared with overall marketing knowledge development since the turn of the century, the last quarter-century was characterized by a sharp increase in the volume and a major shift in the nature of marketing knowledge produced. During this period numerous new marketing journals came into being, such as the *Journal of Marketing Research,* the *Journal of Consumer Research,* the *Journal of Advertising Research,* and the *Journal of Advertising.* As noted in Chapter 3, at least fifty-three journals and trade papers now provide an outlet for marketing-related publication, and at least ten to twenty additional academic journals publish the works of marketing scholars and professional researchers.

Hundreds of new textbooks on marketing and marketing-related topics were published during the period. The subject of consumer behavior is particularly impressive. In the early fifties few if any universities were teaching consumer behavior as a regular part of a marketing curriculum. One reason was that there were no textbooks with this title from which to teach. By 1977 probably fifty books bore the title *Consumer Behavior* or something very close to it, and few universities were not teaching the subject as a regular part of their marketing curriculum.

Another indicator is the increase in marketing research books and in quantitative or management-science-in-marketing books, which paralleled in scope and volume the consumer-behavior trend. Whereas there were dozens of books on marketing and advertising in the 1950s, there were relatively few on marketing research and virtually none on model building or quantitative methods in marketing. In Chapter 4 we have reviewed some examples of marketing research books. It is useful to show here the pattern of parallel developments concerning management science, quantitative, or model-building books in marketing. Consider the following nineteen examples published in the period 1961–1972.

FRANK M. BASS AND OTHERS, eds., *Mathematical Models and Methods in Marketing* (Homewood, Ill.: Richard D. Irwin, 1961). There were eight other editors of this readings book.

RONALD E. FRANK, ALFRED A. KUEHN, AND WILLIAM F. MASSY, eds., *Quantitative Techniques in Marketing Analysis* (Homewood, Ill.: Richard D. Irwin, 1962).

WROE ALDERSON AND STANLEY J. SHAPIRO, eds., *Marketing and the Computer* (Englewood Cliffs, N.J.: Prentice-Hall, 1963).

MARTIN K. STARR, *Product Design and Decision Theory* (Englewood Cliffs, N.J.: Prentice-Hall, 1963).

RALPH L. DAY, ed., *Marketing Models: Quantitative and Behavioral* (Scranton, Pa.: International Textbook, 1964).

ROBERT D. BUZZELL, *Mathematical Models and Marketing Management* (Boston: Division of Research, Graduate School of Business Administration, Harvard University, 1964).

FRANK J. CHARVAT AND W. TATE WHITMAN, *Marketing Management: A Quantitative Approach* (Boston: D. C. Heath, 1964).

PETER LANGHOFF, ed., *Models, Measurement and Marketing* (Englewood Cliffs, N.J.: Prentice-Hall, 1965).

ARNOLD E. AMSTUTZ, *Computer Simulation of Competitive Market Response* (Cambridge, Mass.: The M.I.T. Press, 1967).

WILLIAM R. KING, *Quantitative Analysis for Marketing Management* (New York: McGraw-Hill, 1967).

FRANK M. BASS, CHARLES W. KING, AND EDGAR A. PESSEMIER, eds., *Applications of the Sciences in Marketing Management* (New York: John Wiley, 1968).

DAVID B. MONTGOMERY AND GLEN L. URBAN, *Management Science in Marketing* (Englewood Cliffs, N.J.: Prentice-Hall, 1969).

JAMES H. DONNELLY AND JOHN M. IVANCEVICH, *Analysis for Marketing Decisions* (Homewood, Ill.: Richard D. Irwin, 1970).

LEONARD S. SIMON AND MARSHALL FREIMER. *Analytical Marketing* (New York: Harcourt Brace Jovanovich, 1970).

WILLIAM A. CLARK AND DONALD E. SEXTON, *Marketing and Management Science: A Synergism* (Homewood, Ill.: Richard D. Irwin, 1970).

BEN M. ENIS AND CHARLES L. BROOME, *Marketing Decisions: A Bayesian Approach* (Scranton, Pa.: Intext Educational Publishers, 1971).

PHILIP KOTLER, *Marketing Decision Making: A Model Building Approach* (New York: Holt, Rinehart and Winston, 1971).

DAVID A. AAKER, ed., *Multivariate Analysis in Marketing: Theory and Application* (Belmont, Calif.: Wadsworth, 1971).

STANLEY F. STASCH, *Systems Analysis for Marketing Planning and Control* (Glenview, Ill.: Scott, Foresman, 1972).

These volumes represent the contribution of a considerable amount of creative effort and "new knowledge" to marketing during the time period. Much of their content reflects applications of decision theory to problems facing *marketing management*. They also indicate what we mean by a ''social engineering'' base to the field. The dominant perspective is managerial decision making and the application of many mathematical forms, tools, and techniques familiar to the field of engineering. In its preface the Frank and others volume prophesied in 1962:

> The material contained in this volume can be looked upon as reflecting a feeling of the authors as to one of the principal trends that is occurring in the field of marketing (and will continue to occur over the long run). In our opinion the analysis of complex marketing problems will gradually move in the direction of increased reliance upon a rather extensive array of quantitative techniques. Eventually these techniques may become as familiar to the marketing analyst as are break-even analysis and sampling theory now.[3]

The prophecy certainly has been supported by the volume of creative effort and publication that followed.[4] A ''models'' course is now a regular offering in most well-run marketing programs. In terms of widespread adoption and use, however, these books on ''marketing management'' have made comparatively few inroads as basic introductory foundation texts in the marketing management curriculum. None have approached the sales or adoption rates of the marketing management and marketing principles books reviewed in Chapter 3. Few to date have gone into multiple editions. And, according to commissioner judgments and the AMA Membership Survey results, although one might conclude that awareness (trial) of many of the techniques presented is high, as of 1977 it is also apparent that usage across three types of professionals in the field is very low. The Bayesian approach to decision making, for example, which is a recurring theme throughout many of these texts, appears to have had no significant effect on marketing management practice to date.

Thus, although the amount of knowledge created during the period was considerable, comparatively little appears to be widely used in day-to-day marketing practice. Any of the new theories, managerial frameworks and approaches, models, or research methods and statistical techniques given in Table 3-2 could probably be considered as failing to meet everyone's expectations. Commissioners also identified many problems and problems areas that appeared to be unsolved despite research efforts to address them. The following reaction is typical:

> In my opinion, in spite of the fact that this profession has matured considerably it is still a neophyte. That is, there isn't a single problem area with regard to the practice of marketing management that one can truthfully say marketing research or the world of technology and concepts has mastered. We may have well made more progress in some than in others. But I think it is pretentious to take a position that any problem area has been mastered by the net contributions to theory and methodology that have occurred in the last twenty-five years. In general, I think the field has progressed much farther in high-velocity grocery products than it has in consumer durables. In fact, you could make an argument that we

know the least about the most important products that consumers buy, as the purchase of insurance or a home. If we broaden our perspective it can be argued quite strongly that more progress has been made in consumer products than industrial products. In general, it is my opinion that industrial products are something like a decade or maybe two decades behind consumer products with regard to the concepts and the approaches that are used with respect to marketing problems.

A wide range of problems or problem areas were identified by commissioners as needing further research. Examples are listed below in four categories: organizational problems, the environment, specific problems, and problem areas.

1. *Organizational problems*

Executive decision making (what do brand managers really do or use?)

Research on the diffusion and adoption process of marketing management models and the high rate of "product failure" in this area

Educating and developing marketing personnel to use new information techniques

The tendency for marketing decisions to be made either without research or on the basis of extremely sloppy research

Overall emphasis on tactical, often at the expense of strategic, marketing decision making

The lack of integration between marketing research and marketing management

The effectiveness of alternative organizational structures for marketing effort

The development of formal learning systems of marketing experience

The need for multidisciplinary approaches to problem identification and solution

The need for detailed consequential links between marketing theory and practice to strengthen communications

Development of organizational behavior theories/concepts relevant to product management, salesforce management, etc.

2. *The environment*

Environmental/consumerism/ecology/legal issues—how to incorporate them formally into marketing management thinking

Impact of marketing decisions on the social environment and its converse

Ability to understand, influence, and predict major changes in the socioeconomic environment

What impact will the increasing cost of energy have upon marketers of goods and services?

3. *Specific problems*

Copy research that gets at the process of communication

The inability to provide direction to R & D in the development of new products except for the modification of existing products

How can one (a) generate, (b) evaluate new-product concepts?

Identification of new *needs* as distinct from new products

How advertising influences sales

The lack of understanding of how advertising precisely works

How does television advertising affect children? What does music do in TV commercials? Ditto humor?

Does sex and/or violence in magazines or television affect consumers' attitudes or behavior toward the product advertised? If attitudes are affected, do they in turn affect behavior?

Optimizing advertising budgets

The setting of advertising budgets

Do ads wear out? If so, do different ads wear out at different rates under different circumstances? If so, which, when and how?

Investment allocation

How do you measure the sales effectiveness of an advertisement? Of a package?

Optimizing sales promotion budgets

Market performance measurement

Predicting market response to controllable marketing variables

When is market segmentation a profitable strategy, and when is it not?

What is the best way to conduct group interviews? To train group interviewers? In what situations is the group-interview method liable to produce misleading results?

4. *Problem areas*

Sales management

Models of competition and competitive behavior

Distributive research

Personal selling problems

Not enough clinical research on buyer behavior with the objective of understanding it in its own right

Data drought for academic research

Knowledge Utilization

In general, it appears that a great deal of knowledge available in marketing was not being used in practical day-to-day management operations as of 1977. In particular, numerous types of decision aids and research techniques that could be potentially useful were not being used. A widely held view is that many marketing decisions are made based on very ad hoc research input or no research input at all, as expressed in the following comment:

In my opinion, the major problem area in the practice of marketing from a research point of view is something that may not have changed much over the past twenty-five years, namely, the tendency for many marketing decisions to be made either without any research or on the basis of extremely sloppy research. The fact that the vast majority of new products put on the market turn out to be failures may be a manifestation of this phenomenon. In many ways, marketing management may be about as gullible from a research point of view as it was twenty-five years ago, exhibiting a pronounced tendency to misunderstand how and when research should be used and caring little about such key aspects as data quality and reliability of analytical methods. The lack of integration in many companies between marketing research and marketing management is a symptom of this poor understanding.

The general impression of "low utilization" is confirmed by individual commissioner comments and by the empirical study of the extent of penetration of thirteen representative techniques into operating manager, research manager, and research supplier groups. (The results of this study were detailed in Chapter 6.)

Based on the AMA Membership Survey results, the picture in 1977 was doubly bleak when one considers that the amount of "trial" of the thirteen techniques was comparatively high (the average overall trial by the three types of professionals was about 68%), but "use" was comparatively low. Average overall use was only about 25%. A picture emerges of professionals "giving something a try," concluding that it is not useful, and subsequently discontinuing its use. As Tables 6-1 and 6-2 showed, the more complex models and multivariate analysis techniques are both least tried and least used. Bayesian analysis, for example, the lowest-used of the thirteen techniques, had an average use across the three types of professionals of only 2.6%. In contrast, the use for demographic segmentation, the most frequently used, was 63.7%. Even when we discount for the possible nonrepresentativeness of the samples involved and for problems associated with question interpretation and other forms of nonsampling error, the picture is rather bleak.

Given below are some of the major conclusions regarding knowledge utilization as of 1977, based upon the findings of the AMA Memberships Survey.

1. Marketing professionals, represented by operating managers, research managers, and research suppliers, have "tried" thirteen different techniques at a comparatively high "rate" (68%). The continued use of those techniques, however, is comparatively low (25%).

2. Trial and use both range widely according to the complexity of the technique. Simpler techniques are much more widely adopted and used (i.e., use rates above 50%) than complex techniques.

3. Among the complex techniques, trial and use vary by the type of user. Models, computer simulation, and Bayesian analysis tend to be used more by "managers" than by "researchers." Data-analysis techniques (cluster analysis, conjoint analysis, MDS, factor analysis) tend to be used more by "researchers" than by "managers." The proportions in all cases, however, are generally low (below 20%).

4. Trial and use vary by type of firm and by size of firm. Consumer-products companies tend to be the heaviest users, and large firms have higher use rates than small firms.

5. Academics have a distorted view of professionals' trial and use. They consistently underestimate the trial and use of the simpler methods and overestimate that of the more complex methods.

6. The overall applicability and decision confidence of all three types of users varies by the complexity of the techniques. Users are more confident of the simpler techniques and less confident of the more complex ones.

7. There is high agreement among all three types of professionals concerning the most important information source for managers in learning about a new technique. The most important source is the manager's "own colleagues within the company." Academic consultants are ranked comparatively low (seventh or eighth) as an information source. Some use of all sources, however, is reported by over 80% of the three manager and professional researcher groups.

8. A near-perfect inverse rank correlation exists between academic and manager perceptions of what *should be* the most important techniques for managers. Academics perceive the more complex techniques as the most important. Managers perceive the simpler techniques as the most important.

9. There is high agreement between academics and research suppliers as to the groups that are *least* important in knowledge generation and diffusion (both agree that marketing research department personnel and operating managers are least important in these two activities). There is high disagreement between academics and research suppliers as to the groups that are *most* important in knowledge generation and diffusion. Academics believe that academics are most important, and research suppliers believe that research suppliers are most important.

Even allowing for predictable distortions in perception (and these distortions are undoubtedly an important part of the lack-of-utilization problem), the general picture that emerges is that a great deal of "available" knowledge is not being used. Marketing's R & D system from this perspective is currently not very "efficient" or "effective."

The principal factors that appear to inhibit the rate of new-knowledge utilization in the field are reviewed in the next section.

FACTORS INHIBITING KNOWLEDGE UTILIZATION

Dozens of general and specific factors representing barriers to knowledge utilization can be identified and have been alluded to in one way or another throughout the book. Each is in some way tied to characteristics of either the knowledge "generators" or the knowledge "users" or is a "general" factor.

Knowledge-Generator Factors

Four factors involving knowledge-generator groups and individuals may inhibit the utilization process: (1) research philosophy, (2) lack of experience and time, (3) inadequate marketing, and (4) inadequacies of diffusion vehicles. Each is briefly discussed below.

1. Research philosophy.   The way in which a researcher approaches a project and picks a topic on which to work, his or her commitment to testing the replication of a new technique, and the basic research motivations and reference points used in guiding the research are potential inhibitors to the utilization of marketing knowledge. Much research is being done that is not practical or relevant. Furthermore, it is not adequately tested in a real situation before being offered as a "solution" to some problem. Criticism is particularly directed to those whose only research motivation or reference point is "advancing science" and those who remain insensitive to the applied and professional aspects of marketing.

2. Lack of experience and time.   Several commissioners alluded to the fact that researchers, particularly those in academia, often have had no real-world managerial experience or exposure. As one commissioner put it: "They have no real knowledge of marketing problems. They tend to focus on a very narrow range of techniques and concepts, and they ignore many of the problems that practicing marketing researchers find most pesky . . . they tend to pick problems that are grand enough to be academically respectable . . . they simply do not know what is important to practitioners and what is not."

A lack of time can also be a factor. It is often overlooked that researchers, too, are "busy people," and in some cases time does not permit extensive interaction with practitioners in the development and completion of a research project.

3. Inadequate marketing.   Much of the utilization of marketing knowledge appears typified by a series of "Edsels"! Among the many reasons for product "failure" is inadequate or poor marketing. This seems a particularly appropriate "inhibitor" when applied to many of the management science models that have been developed. Considering a typical marketing mix of consumer, product, price, promotion, and distribution, it might be said that the knowledge generators in many instances had an inadequate understanding of "consumer" needs and wants and failed to involve the manager-user in the development process. From the product level, there appears to be an inadequate understanding of the impact of the "product" on organizational relationships or a lack of understanding of "competitive alternatives." In many cases the price (or cost) of implementing models was overlooked. Promotionwise, many early models were vastly oversold, and what amounts to promotional communication was often in the language of the sender/generator rather than the receiver/user. Finally, many developers of new knowledge appear to overlook the nature of "distribution" of ideas in marketing and lack an understanding of marketing's R & D system and how it works.

4. Diffusion vehicles. Inadequacies in the diffusion vehicles of knowledge generators were alluded to in many comments. Existing marketing journals were generally seen as representing the supply of ideas rather than the demand for them, as representing "academics talking to one another," and as generally inappropriate for managers. There also appears to be an unfilled need for a good, managerially oriented marketing journal to provide communication between professional and academic researchers and senior marketing management.

The AMA's two-annual-conferences structure, one for professionals and one for academics, was singled out as potentially inhibiting to communication and knowledge utilization.

The language used by the innovators is a factor. In the words of one commissioner: "*JMR* continues to be esoteric, abstruse, and jargon-laden. The academic marketing researchers who fill its pages are obviously writing to each other (and to the appointments and promotions committee), and a great many marketing practitioners simply will not go to the effort to decipher their cryptic inscriptions."

Knowledge-User Factors

1. Management philosophy   Two aspects of management philosophy appear to inhibit knowledge utilization. First is management's attitude toward research and its use—at worst, an attitude that discourages the use of research or has no respect for it. The extreme is decision making without "research" of any kind, the absence of a research group or department, and decision making by intuition, fiat, or political pressure. Second is management's attitude toward research innovation. Even for corporations that have a research group or otherwise use research, commissioners concluded that great differences exist in management's willingness to experiment, try something new, or otherwise be the first in adopting new techniques. References were made to manager inertia, conservatism, the "not-invented-here" syndrome, and so on.

2. Lack of training and time.   A lack of manager training in quantitative methods or abstract thinking and reasoning was cited as an inhibiting factor. Also, as stated by one commissioner, "Management has its hands full with current problems and has very little time for the study and reflection required to gain knowledge and confidence in new techniques."

3. Secrecy and lack of feedback.   The competitive environment in which most firms operate leads to a natural inclination to suppress information and keep secret much that would be useful as input to the knowledge-generator group. Issues, problems, and ideas that would otherwise inform the knowledge innovators and guide research developments often do not reach external researchers for this reason.

4. Reluctance to invest; inadequate infrastructures.   A final user-related factor is simply a reluctance on the part of management to consider marketing "research and development" a worthwhile investment opportunity. Much of this reluctance stems from the difficulty of applying the usual cost-benefit type of analysis to marketing research and knowledge-development activities. In order to apply much of the new knowledge that has been developed, a considerable investment in computer hardware and software (specifically to service marketing research), the development of large and expensive data banks, and the retraining of personnel (particularly management personnel) in their use is often required. Much new knowledge is not being used simply because the infrastructure for applying it does not exist.[5]

The foregoing are some of the more important factors inhibiting knowledge utilization. Others appear more general and in some sense characteristic of the system as a whole. Three such factors are discussed below.

General Factors

1. Specialization and different values.   Marketing has progressed to the point where it involves numerous types of research (and managerial) "specialists." This situation, the usual one for any advancing discipline, creates its own set of built-in barriers to communication. The problem applies not only to manager-researcher interaction but to researcher-researcher interaction. As pointed out earlier, research specialists in marketing have trouble communicating with one another or in simply keeping up with developments in their own area of specialization. The general complexity of the field has increased dramatically.

Also, basic values differences between managers and researchers inhibit knowledge utilization. Researchers by inclination are often reflective, concerned with methods, and scholarly in their orientations. Managers are likely to be concerned primarily with results and generally to be more action-oriented. More than a "lack of time" interferes with communication between these groups.[6]

2. Incentives and reward structures.   A major factor is the lack of incentives or rewards for knowledge generator and knowledge user. On the generator side, particularly among academics, there are often few rewards for engaging in "relevant" research or interacting with practicing managers and great rewards for making "scientific" contributions. Promotion committees are much more inclined to judge performance on research quality and its contributions to the advancement of science. On the user side, there are few if any rewards for seeking out the knowledge generators or for engaging in publishing activities that would foster communication and feedback. Performance is much more likely to be judged over the short term and on the basis of "sales" or "profitability."

    3. The formative stage of scientific marketing.   Finally, underutilization of existing knowledge may be attributed to marketing's primitive or formative stage in terms of scientific information and procedures. We elaborate on this point below.

    There is great ambiguity in many of the concepts in marketing because so many of them are cycling through the development process. This fuzziness may lead to their being "written off" too soon. The problem is compounded when the people who do the "judging" are not analytically trained. The fact that many concepts and techniques do not get down to the development or dissemination stages also leaves a residue of skepticism. The major bottleneck at the development stage is *matching ideas with problems*. The "problems" typically reside with the people least trained to articulate them. The challenge is to find ways to communicate the problem to researchers so that they can work from a base of reality. Much of the criticism of the academic community was of their inability to recognize meaningful and relevant marketing problems. An analogous situation typically exists in advertising when a client accuses an agency of not providing advertisements that solve the client's problems. Too often, the real issue is not the agency's ads but the agency's or the client's lack of understanding of what the client's problems are.

    The division of labor and of organizational relationships in such terms as staff/line and insider/outsider is a built-in barrier. Also, there is currently no marketplace in which ideas and problems can "marry up," and innovative individuals in an organization are often not being given the support or resources to pursue development.

    A very important question addressed in some Commission meetings was what makes resource-rich organizations innovate—or, more pointedly, not innovate—with respect to creating or using new marketing knowledge? Two organizational attitudes appear necessary: (1) an attitude in favor of conceptualization and an acceptance of some degree of abstraction, and (2) an attitude that will deal with the *process* (and is prepared to give credit for the process) and not just the results. This has a lot to do with an individual's ability to share risk with his or her department or working group. Companies where innovation can flourish have an attitude of "Why not?"—that is, they are risk takers; noninnovative companies have an attitude of "Why?"—that is, they are risk minimizers.

    There seems to be little hard evidence about whether innovator companies are more successful than members of the majority. Based on anecdotal evidence, innovativeness, which includes sophistication in modern management and marketing research techniques and an openness to considering new ideas, may enhance the chances for success. On the other hand, it is possible that the costs of innovation and the extra risks it may entail are not worth the candle.

Many of these barriers reduce to attitudinal factors in the makeup of managers and researchers. Managers, often uncomfortable with complex quantitative and abstract materials, or having no time to learn about them, are prone to dismiss much that could be valuable as academic nonsense. Patterns such as the "not-invented-here" syndrome, antiintellectualism, and other defenses develop to rationalize the basic position. Researchers, particularly those who are scientifically inclined, are prone to write off practical marketing problems as irrelevant to what they do or as an interference with their scholarly progress. Patterns of "let them learn what I am doing" develop, and there is little or no commitment to translating ideas into the practical world of the marketing decision maker. These value differences are rather strikingly portrayed in the inverse rank correlation between professional and academic judgments concerning what techniques are most important (Table 6-8 of Chapter 6).

Although knowledge utilization, at least in terms of the examples used in this study in 1977, was considered by many commissioners to be "disappointingly low" and the effectiveness of this aspect of marketing's R & D system over the period was best described as "mixed," it does not follow that ways of doing research, or the ideas and problems on which researchers work, should be radically changed. This pertains particularly to academic work. In the next section we discuss the role of the marketing academic community in this regard.

ROLE OF THE MARKETING ACADEMIC COMMUNITY

Research along with teaching is a primary objective of the academic community in marketing as in other fields. While notable exceptions can be found, the performance of what we have called the marketing academic component of marketing's R & D system is perceived as somewhat disappointing by many members of the business community. Doubtless there is a reciprocal feeling on the part of many marketing academics—business people are not very quick to adopt the ideas that seem clear and logical to marketing professors.

Given the ambiguity and criticism of the marketing academic community's role in knowledge creation, we shall attempt to interpret what is happening in somewhat more detail. First, it is clear that there are distinct innovator-majority segments in the field. These segments cut across academic, professional research firm, and operating company lines. Also, most studies of the innovation process in other fields indicate that there is not a one-to-one correspondence among the creators and early adopters of different kinds of innovations. We suspect that this is true in marketing, too, including the academic sector.

No one doubts that some innovators in the marketing academic community have seen their ideas widely applied and utilized. What our findings show, however, is that these contributions are a rather small fraction of all the new knowledge developed by marketing academics during the last twenty-five years. We do not find this alarming, given the relatively small number of people involved, the far greater resources available to professional researchers compared to academics, and other factors to be discussed presently.

What is the role of the "majority" segment of the academic community? One answer is that it is to study the work of others (including business practices) and teach it to successive generations of students. Education is a noble calling because it deals directly with the human problems of students and their development—in terms of character and identity as well as intellect. An increasing number of voices both inside and outside marketing are calling for an unabashed return to these basic values in education based on the assumption that research is unimportant.

We believe that engaging in research is important for the "majority" academic segment. First, the process of staying abreast of developments and understanding them is enhanced if one goes through the discipline of writing and getting professional feedback from time to time. We would go so far as to say that effectiveness in education *requires* broad participation in research and thoughtful commentary about concepts and techniques being used in business. The very criticism one hears, for example, within the American Marketing Association is part of a process of feedback and correction. Listening to innovators (both academic and nonacademic) and talking to students (especially undergraduates) are not very good ways for "majority" academics to maintain their intellectual productivity. Writing and receiving criticism can be viewed as providing the feedback to academic researchers that in management and professional research circles is provided by the market.

Suppose a certain piece of research or commentary is judged to be of good quality but not pathbreaking and innovative in the sense that it is not likely, by itself, to make a discernible difference in the practice of marketing research or marketing management. Is it valueless? We think not. Any field, including marketing, has a strong need for "journeyman" research that replicates previous findings (sometimes they are found to be wrong), provides additional observations, and adds to the inventory of verified facts and examined concepts.

While such results are not breakthroughs, an accumulation of them over time is a necessary condition for continued progress. Also, there is a need for interpreting previous work, preparing teaching materials, and so forth.

Many questions posed to Commission members and friends and our survey respondents were inevitably put in such a way that the contributions of the innovator research group in academia and business were seen as the only ones that matter. We want here to dispel this notion. The research of the majority group is important, too. The criterion of effectiveness should not, however, be "a directly attributable change in business practice," any more than "an attributable change in earnings per share'' should be the criterion for the majority of journeyman managers and marketing researchers.

All researchers in the marketing academic community must address the question, ''What business are we (and should we) be in?'' We next discuss some answers to this question.

Basic Research

Most university researchers in fields other than marketing would argue that the ''business'' they are in is basic research. It is true that ''basic'' is defined relative to the field in question: for instance, ''basic'' work in finance is likely to be less basic than in, say, economics or mathematics. But the essential idea that the researcher should be driven more by what is truly interesting than by what is immediately relevant cuts across all basic research.

Basic research in marketing tends to deal with topics such as:

Consumer behavior and attitude formation and change
Communication and information processing
Brand switching models
Measurement and multivariate statistics
Distribution channels and systems
Allocation of marketing resources
Marketing information and decision systems
Market definition and measurement

These topics certainly are relevant to marketing, and it would seem that the results of the research should be useful. But the ''business'' of following one's own interests does not lead to relevance except as a byproduct or follow-on with problem-oriented research.

How should basic research be evaluated? This is a perennial problem in all fields, because the character of the work requires evaluation by peers, and this can lead to an actual or perceived lack of accountability to those who provide the resources. But there is no way to avoid this, so there is always a built-in tension at the boundary between basic research and the world of affairs.

People with responsibility for basic research in universities tend to use these two criteria in making judgments about programs, people, and projects.

1. Is the work of high quality? Does it contain deficiencies or omissions or is it internally consistent, rigorous, and highly linked to related findings? Is it shallow or deep? Is it new or is it a rehash of old results? In other words, does it truly contribute to the stock of knowledge?

2. Is the subject of the work intrinsically important? Does the work address important questions or is it trivial? Is such a contribution to knowledge likely to lead to other answers or even other questions? In other words, is the work relevant to the future evolution of basic research?

Note that relevance is at issue, but relevance in terms of the internal logic of the field rather than in terms of external standards. Payoff is defined in terms of knowledge for its own sake rather than the facilitation of some external goal. Even so, it is hard to make judgments about even the "internal" relevance of specific basic research results, because tomorrow the conception of the field may be changed by some new finding. Therefore the most hard-nosed evaluations of basic research are in terms of the first criterion—quality—as judged by peers.

What business *should* academic researchers in marketing be in? Is the mix too far toward basic as opposed to problem-oriented research? Should marketing, and the American Marketing Association in particular, encourage basic as well as problem-oriented research, or should basic research be left to the "underlying disciplines" such as psychology, economics, statistics, and management science?

We have two firm conclusions:

1. Basic research *is* very important *in* marketing and it should be continued. Also, it is in better health than ever before.
2. There ought to be more problem-oriented research in universities. Except for people who are *both* active researchers and active consultants, the problem-oriented "business" in universities is *not* in good health.

The first conclusion is rooted in deep personal convictions that the base of knowledge in marketing now is far more substantial than it was a decade or two ago. A great deal has come from outside, particularly in terms of new kinds of multivariate marketing research techniques. But much basic research has occurred within the field of marketing as well, as anyone will attest who has studied the best of today's textbooks or attended the AMA Doctoral Consortium programs. It is not totally presumptuous to state that many of today's scholars within marketing know as much or more about how to study human behavior and communications than those in basic disciplines.

Doubtless many readers remain skeptical about the value of basic research. Such skepticism is common in all branches of science: "What good is particle physics when our problems are energy and the environment?" In marketing the problem is compounded because basic research on management-type problems is young enough and the problems hard enough that breakthroughs have been few and far between. Marketing *is* a professional or applied field and not an "academic discipline." It is hard even to speculate on the precise kinds of contributions that will be made in the future, so the justification for basic research is largely a matter of faith—as it is to a considerable extent in all fields.

Basic research findings in the area of financial portfolio management provide an example of what *can* occur. Until recently the financial community (including the security analysis sector, which corresponds to our marketing research sector) was strongly focused on how to do a better job of "beating the market." But an intrepid group of basic researchers on finance faculties were saying, "That's the wrong question." Eventually the sheer accumulation of empirical and theoretical research findings began to convince people that for practical purposes it is impossible to beat the market and that the proper question is how to optimize the risk-return trade-off through diversification and leverage.

There is plenty of controversy in the financial community about whether the "perfect-market theory" is correct. But the professors are in the thick of it, and increasing numbers of business people are demonstrating agreement by placing their company's money on the line. There is no longer any question about relevance, and problems of language and unfamiliarity are being overcome because of the enormity of the stakes involved.

We do not presently have anything like this degree of theoretical development in marketing, and maybe we never will. Product-portfolio theory, for example, is heavily constrained by problems of market definition and measurement. But these difficulties should not lead to a conclusion that basic research on market definition and measurement is thus irrelevant.

A relatively small but active group of innovators in basic research in marketing will continue to work no matter what. We believe it is in the best long-run interest of the field to keep them "hooked into" marketing rather than nudging them back into the underlying disciplines, where the length of the road to eventual marketing applications will be far longer.

The environment of marketing also can pose a problem with respect to those who stay. They are bombarded regularly with calls for relevance to today's problems. But the *comparative advantage* of many of the most-talented and best-trained professors is in basic research, although compared to the majority of academics they may also have an absolute advantage at problem-oriented research. There are strong incentives for creative researchers to leave academia to obtain access to resources for problem-oriented research, to experience the satisfaction of managing, and sometimes to obtain monetary rewards. And some excellent academics have done so. Forays with problem-oriented research and consulting are very valuable, but the marketing profession as a whole loses something important whenever such a person leaves basic research.

Problem-Oriented Research

This is the biggest area of disappointment with respect to the academic sector. We offer four speculations about the reasons for the lack of progress.

1. Good problem-oriented research requires very close coupling with the business community. It is hard to do it well without access to the "guts" of

management issues, and this is hard to come by for many academic researchers. Extraordinary statements by managers and sales-oriented journal articles by consultants and research firms, are not sufficient "access" to the world of marketing management issues. Concept formation is particularly difficult for people who are not involved in, or regularly exposed to, real management problem solving. Few institutions (such as the Marketing Science Institute) exist whose mission is to bring together practically oriented academics with conceptually oriented practitioners.

2. Problem-oriented research dealing with technique development can be very expensive by the standards of university budgeting. Consulting aside, this has been a major barrier to performing such work in universities, even where there is good intellectual coupling with managers. In contrast, these costs are not so great a problem for firms whose business depends on successful innovation.

3. It has become fashionable to some extent to try to "clothe" basic research results in a mantle of relevance, even where the work is essentially basic in character. In large part this is due to demands by students and professionals (including publication boards and editors) for relevance, coupled with the difficulty of actually doing relevant work on a minimum budget and in isolation from business inputs. However, even the best-known researchers (who need not be concerned about "image") are prone to this malady from time to time.

4. Some work is published that qualifies neither as good problem-oriented research nor as good basic research. While some articles that contain faulty or obsolete methodology sometimes get past reviewers, we would hazard the guess that the main problems are due to (a) selection of subjects that are essentially trivial in terms of contributions to knowledge or a marketing problem, and (b) loss of potential relevance because of the difficulty of generalizing from the sample used. There often is a problem in achieving external validity out of a low budget!

In sum, we believe that some research is done in the marketing academic community that ought not to be done. Doubtless the causes are the publish-or-perish pressure and the difficulty of doing *either* good basic or good problem-oriented research in marketing. Perceptions about the output of the academic community also are hurt by mislabeling and by the difficulties with specialization and language discussed in Chapter 6. Finally, there is a tendency to confound the goals of basic and problem-oriented research, and to discount the former because of short-run needs.

What is to be done? We believe that some of the structural barriers to problem-oriented research in universities can be alleviated. If so, we would expect that (1) the potential portfolio of research opportunities will be broadened, thus reducing constraints and improving average quality; (2) there will be a better coupling of interests between the researchers in many universities and professionals, thereby increasing both the fact and the perception of relevance; and (3) education for marketing management will be improved because of the better coupling between business and academia.

CONCLUDING COMMENTS

Marketing management is an important function encompassing analysis, planning, implementation, and control activities in connection with product, pricing, distribution, communications, and other program and decision areas in an organization. Any organization needs marketing management; in many respects, organizational health and vitality depend on it.

This book represents a detailed examination of the research and knowledge-development base on which marketing management rests. We have argued, particularly in Chapter 4, that a "system" of research and development for marketing management is identifiable, even though it has not been well recognized, monitored, or researched. It is not well understood, and there is much disagreement about its nature and scope. The system, as we see it, rests on the basic social and social engineering sciences. Biology recognizes a relationship called symbiosis—a consorting together in mutually advantageous partnership of dissimilar organisms. There should be a "symbiotic" relationship between marketing management and these sciences. Each has much to contribute to the other. Like production's R & D system, the best conceptualization of such a system for marketing includes explicit links to academia and science, and it entails widespread respect for the roles and contributions of basic research, applied research, and development. Science can make contributions to marketing management and the advancement of the profession, and the profession can make contributions to the advancement of science.

Although many people in marketing agree with this viewpoint, many others do not. Marketing's R & D system is relatively small, ill-defined, and comparatively primitive. There is no widespread recognition of either its worth or its existence. Many professionals and even academics are fundamentally skeptical about the contributions of science to marketing management. This attitude is manifest in rejection of the use of marketing research information, a disrespect for scholarship and scientific method, and numerous kinds of antiintellectualism alluded to throughout the book. It is part of a more broadly based skepticism about science in general and the numerous problems that science appears unable to solve. The demand for relevance in marketing is part of a more general demand for relevance in science as a whole.

Much of the Commission's effort was devoted to evaluation and assessment of the contributions and functioning of the system over the past twenty-five years. The major and disturbing finding from these efforts is the discrepancy between the amount of new knowledge developed and available, and the amount being applied in day-to-day marketing management operations. A significant amount of marketing research effort, new-knowledge development, model building, and theorizing has had relatively little impact on improving marketing management practice over the period. It should be recognized, however, that this phenomenon also is not unique to marketing. Knowledge generation and use in any field will always be to some degree "inefficient." There will always be wasted efforts, false starts, and blind alleys. The underutilization of scientific and technical information in the physical sciences and the relative "inefficiency" of the process by which any new product is successfully marketed should give pause to those who would point to this as a fundamental failing of the system.

In retrospect, the functioning of marketing's research and development system as it has evolved over the past quarter-century is best characterized as mixed. The impacts of research and new-knowledge development activities on marketing management have been significant, but much less than "what might have been." As in other fields, some reasons for this inefficiency lie in the numerous kinds of barriers to the knowledge-diffusion and utilization process reviewed earlier. Progress also has been impeded by a failure of many managers, researchers, and academics to recognize the nature of the overall system in which they participate and the symbiotic relationships that should exist among them. Basically, there is a need for more and better communication and better recognition of, and respect for, the total system of marketing research and development. Appendix A offers twenty recommendations that flowed from the Commission's efforts, many of which suggest specific actions to increase communication and improve the effectiveness of the system.

What has been the investment in the system? Can the generation of new knowledge be taken for granted? Will the fuel renew and enhance itself solely by the process of its application, as in a breeder reactor, or does continued progress demand the explicit investment of talent and money in knowledge creation? If investment is required, how should the process be managed and the necessary resources made available in order to increase the yield of usable knowledge?

We are confident at this point that no one knows precisely the size of the national investment in marketing research and development. Obviously, much depends on what one includes in the "system." Agreement must be reached on what the system is before one can identify the size of the investment involved. No agency or organization has yet developed the requisite conception on which to base such estimates. Hopefully, this book provides a start in this direction. In the industrial sector, investments in marketing R & D appear to be of the order of $1 billion as of 1977. As for production R & D, the investment could be assigned to categories of "basic research," "applied research," or "development."[7] At present the major classification is into various kinds of problem-identification or problem-solving research.

The investment in the academic sector is more difficult to define and remains unmonitored or reported on by any agency or group. In human-resources terms, if the academic component is assumed to be solely marketing academics, then a relatively small investment is involved, represented by something like 500 active researchers in the nation's universities and business schools. If all social and engineering science is assumed part of the system, the investment is obviously much larger. Perhaps one hundred times as many scientists work in these disciplines as work directly in marketing, and the "investment" is considerable. A study could be done to document these aspects of the overall system along the lines of the NSF reports referred to in Chapter 4. At this point we are unable to say how much of the national investment in marketing R & D goes for basic research, applied research, or development in the academic sector. We have introduced and used the terms basic research, problem-oriented research, and problem-solving research to represent the main forms of research in marketing. Each form is recognizable and plays a role in the overall system.

All forms and types of marketing research increased in both quality and quantity over the twenty-five-year assessment period. Paralleling the developments in basic social science, research within marketing increased in quantitative and behavioral science sophistication. This sophistication has been manifested in the professional marketing and marketing research communities and particularly in the ways marketing is taught in business schools. The latter in turn feeds the world of practice at the entry level. There is, however, much room for improved research and concept development, and there is a basic need for better understanding and study of marketing's R & D system and the knowledge-creation and utilization process.

Although one might sensibly conclude that the evolution of marketing's R & D system was a natural "self-generating" process attributable to the overall growth of industry or other causes, we think it is not inherently self-generating and requires explicit investments and commitments of funds to sustain it. Basically, marketing research and new-knowledge development cannot be done without investments of funds. Funding, particularly in the areas of basic and problem-oriented research, has a major impact because it often dictates the kinds of research that gets done. A good example of the phenomenon in marketing over the review period is the relatively large amount of basic and problem-oriented university research on consumer behavior and advertising, funded by agencies such as the A.A.A.A. Educational Foundation, and the comparative dearth of such university research on problems related to sales management and personal selling. From a research point of view, advertising and sales management are very similar decision areas. In many corporations, similar amounts of investment are made in each. The amount of new knowledge, journal articles, textbooks, and so on generated over the period associated with advertising, however, far surpassed that associated with sales management. Although many factors were undoubtedly involved, a significant one was simply the availability of more research funds to study advertising.

In sum, we are left with the conclusion that there has been progress in marketing, though it is spread unevenly, and there is still much that is not known and debatable about its R & D aspects from a national investment accounting point of view. Marketing R & D is an important national resource that deserves continued study and broader recognition. Much of the progress has been due to conscious research and development efforts. We believe this has been worthwhile, and that efforts to improve the productivity of marketing R & D and the diffusion and use of its results are worthy objectives. The agreement for continued investment in such activities rests in a certain faith in the efficacy of "progress." In a sense we are all working as researchers in our day-to-day activities, as we continue to penetrate the unknown. While much progress has been made, the road ahead is still long and arduous, and some areas of our profession have traversed more of it than others. In short, marketing management, together with the R & D system on which it rests, is in transition.

The need for greater recognition and study of the system and conscious effort to improve its effectiveness is intensified by the significant challenges that currently face marketing management and that will continue into the decades ahead. Inflation, energy and raw-material shortages, consumerism, and dozens of new and old problems (and opportunities) must be faced. Research and new-knowledge development in marketing take on increased significance in the light of these challenges.

NOTES

[1]Many other schools not included in this list have been significant generators of new knowledge in marketing over the period. Columbia, Purdue, and Illinois are particularly noteworthy. For a list of the twenty top institutions in the 1972–1975 period, based on number of citations of their faculty, see Larry M. Robinson and Roy D. Adler, "Citations Provide Objective Ratings of Schools, Scholars," *Marketing News,* 12 (July 1978), 1 ff.

[2]As we have noted, it would be highly unlikely for every new idea or knowledge innovation to result in a successful application. The models of knowledge creation and utilization presented in Chapter 5 are not unlike the "stage" notions in new-product development: search, screening, business analysis, development, testing, commercialization, and evaluation. The percentage of new-product ideas that become commercially successful new products across six industries was reported in a Booz, Allen & Hamilton report as varying between 1% and 5%. See *Management of New Products* (Chicago: Booz, Allen & Hamilton, 1968), p. 12. In other words, it takes a large number of new ideas to create one successful new product, and the same phenomenon appears to occur in the new-knowledge area. This report gave the overall average as fifty-eight ideas to generate one successful new product. For new food items, another study revealed that in the period 1954–1964, preintroduction "research and development" expenses averaged $94,000 per item (based on 111 new foods analyzed); for those placed in test market, an additional $248,000 was spent on each; and for those actually placed on the market, $1.4 million of first-year promotional expense was incurred on average. The R & D expense was further broken down into $26,000 for market research and $68,000 for "research and development." See Robert D. Buzzell and Robert E. M. Nourse, *Product Innovation in*

Food Processing 1954–1964 (Boston: Harvard University, Graduate School of Business Administration, Division of Research, 1967), p. 113.

[3]Ronald E. Frank, Alfred A. Kuehn, and William F. Massy, eds., *Quantitative Techniques in Marketing Analysis* (Homewood, Ill.: Richard D. Irwin, 1962), p. vii.

[4]No marketing professor has yet won a Nobel Prize for his or her research contributions, but the first such prize to a member of a business school faculty was awarded to Herbert A. Simon of Carnegie-Mellon in 1978. Although the prize was "in economics," he was honored for his contributions to decision making and to social science in general. James March, a professor at Stanford's business school, describes him as "an economist, psychologist, political scientist, sociologist, philosopher, computer scientist, and not a bad tetherball player," and goes on to review his contributions to decision making in the period 1947 to 1958 and to human problem solving and artificial intelligence in the period of 1958 to 1978. Simon's award, among other things, is symbolic of the value placed on works such as the nineteen books listed above in economics and basic social science. It was exceptional also in the eclectic and multidisciplinary character of his contributions. Although neither Paul Green nor John D. C. Little appears as author in any of the works cited above, their contributions to model building and marketing research were also recently acknowledged in the form of the Paul D. Converse and Charles Coolidge Parlin Awards in marketing. See James G. March, "The 1978 Nobel Prize in Economics," *Science,* 202 (November 24, 1978), 858–61, "Little Sees Wiser Marketing Ways," *Marketing News,* 11 (June 30, 1978), 1 ff., and Yoram Wind, "Marketing Research and Management: A Retrospective View of the Contributions of Paul E. Green," in *Proceedings of the Tenth Paul D. Converse Awards Symposium,* Alan Andreasen, ed. (Urbana, Ill.: University of Illinois Press, 1978).

[5]The point is best understood in the context of a small firm. One might begin, for example, by arguing that "formal marketing plans" should be drawn up and that a "marketing information system" is needed. The costs, however, of proceeding in this way could easily reach 20% to 30% of projected sales, and other uses of the funds would undoubtedly take priority. Without such an infrastructure, much new knowledge is by definition "inaccessible" or "irrelevant" to the small firm. Even this situation is changing, however, as computer hardware costs come down.

[6]The notion of "two cultures" popularized by C. P. Snow seems to be as valid in marketing as in any other discipline. In our opinion, the two cultures are not so much "academic-business" as they are "researcher-manager." The idea has also been characterized in terms of communication difficulties between "those who think and never act" and "those who act and never think"!

[7]Although we have not attempted to put a dollar figure on "development" activities in marketing as the National Science Foundation reports do, the idea is explicitly recognized in the knowledge-creation and utilization models presented in Chapter 5 as the "development stage"!

Appendix A

RECOMMENDATIONS OF THE ERDMM COMMISSION

This appendix presents twenty recommendations of the ERDMM Commission. They represent the culmination of the Commission's work and its prescriptive charge. The recommendations are organized into sets directed to specific constituencies of the field of marketing as a whole. Many pertain to specific actions that should be taken to improve communications, reduce the barriers to use of knowledge, and improve the overall efficiency and effectiveness of marketing's research and development system. The hope is to stimulate specific actions as well as discussion and to improve the effectiveness of knowledge-generation and diffusion efforts.

The first sets are addressed to four constituencies: "the academic community," "the business community," "government," and "associations, institutes, and foundations." The final set is addressed to any and all of these interest groups. Each of the twenty recommendations is numbered according to block and sequence, R.1.1., R.1.2., and so on.

Academic Community

R.1.1. *Marketing educators and university administrators must be made aware of the crucial need to maintain open lines of communication with professional researchers and practicing managers. They should be persuaded to support teaching, consulting, and research activities that foster this communication and involve real-world marketing problems.*

The broad objectives of knowledge development in marketing should be improvements in management decision making and practice, whether over the short or the long run. Toward this end, academics need to open up and maintain lines of communication with professionals and management people. It is insufficient to maintain a stance of isolation from the real world or to adopt an attitude that the discrepancy between generation and use "doesn't matter." Some segments of the marketing academic community need to realign priorities and devote more time to "utilization" of what has been produced. This does not imply an abandonment of quality or scholarship, but rather a need for attention to the gap that exists and a redressing of the balance of priorities in this direction. Logical mechanisms are consulting, participation in executive development programs, conference attendance in which managers and professional researchers are involved, and publication that includes these latter groups as the intended audience. Academic consulting, when kept in balance with normal teaching, research, and administrative duties, should be considered a legitimate academic activity and be recognized as an important institutional means of fostering communication with the professional community.

This recommendation basically argues for a better balance of faculty interests and talents in an academic marketing department: we certainly need basic researchers, but we also need better translators and more people working on problems that are closer to immediate practical management concerns and interests. It relates to earlier comments on "two cultures": too many marketing academics think that "being practical" is not desirable (and may even be explicitly undesirable). This tendency can become exacerbated when academics from nonbusiness disciplines are involved, as in universitywide promotion reviews. Understanding practice, and contributing to it, can lead to major contributions to knowledge-development in and of itself.

R.1.2. *Nontechnical reviews of new concepts, findings, and techniques in marketing should be published far more frequently. At the same time, publications that permit researchers to communicate with other researchers need to be preserved and encouraged.*

This recommendation addresses both ends of the knowledge development/utilization spectrum. For scholarly journals, it underscores the importance of having an "archival resource" that not only provides a channel for publication of new research results but also permits ready access to such work by other researchers over time. "Relevance" is not the appropriate criterion on which to assess such journals. The *Journal of Marketing Research* is an obvious example of the type needed in marketing.

At the other end, nontechnical reviews represent one way of attempting to break the technical-jargon impediment to good communication. Complex ideas must often be expressed in formal, mathematical terms, but they should be communicable in terms that a broader audience can understand. "Annual reviews" and "state-of-the-art" articles are examples of what is needed.

In a complex field such as marketing, many types of journals and communication vehicles should be developed, as should many types of research (basic, problem-oriented, and problem-solving). But the "research innovator group" in marketing must find more and better ways to communicate to the larger majority of users and potential users. Nontechnical reviews should not automatically be relegated to a category of "lower-quality" or "insignificant" work by academic promotion committees. The recommendation applies also to professional researchers working with complex ideas and techniques. One suggestion is to publish "sanitized" results that have been developed from consulting work. We acknowledge the problems of lack of corporate incentives for this kind of work and of the difficulty in protecting confidential data. These kinds of publications nevertheless are of major importance in the dissemination and knowledge-utilization process. A great deal of "knowledge" that currently exists is not being used, not because it is irrelevant, but because it is not understood.

R.1.3.   *Teaching and research of the knowledge-creation and utilization process and the evaluation of the effectiveness of research and knowledge generation on marketing management practice should be introduced into university course curricula.*

Marketing students should be encouraged to examine the work of the Commission and challenged to build upon many of the thoughts and ideas put forth. The broadened perspective on marketing research presented in this book is a new and important one, and students should be made aware of it. We need to know more about how marketing's R & D system works and under what conditions it is most efficient and effective. Commissioners suggested that academics provide special encouragement for this activity at their institutions, that corporate members combine to offer a significant monetary prize for outstanding efforts, and that the American Marketing Association and the Management Science Institute consider a grant or competition toward this end. Also, it was suggested that Program Committees of AMA Educators' Conferences develop sessions on this topic.

Business Community

R.2.1.   *Senior executives of major corporations in the consumer, industrial, and services sectors should be encouraged to develop a climate within their organizations that is amenable to exploration and experimentation with new ideas and techniques. Conscious efforts should be made to improve communications between researchers and senior executives and to elicit the support of the latter in utilizing current marketing knowledge and investing in the development of new knowledge.*

The term "management" refers to several kinds of executive and managerial positions. The two broad classes of particular importance are senior executives and middle line managers. The most significant communications gaps may well be between senior executives and researchers rather than between middle management and researchers. Currently, marketing has no association or interest group that successfully serves as an interface between senior executives and knowledge generators or basic researchers, with the possible exception of the Marketing Science Institute. Other associations, particularly the American Marketing Association, should be encouraged to devote more attention to, and to open up active lines of communication with, senior marketing executives in large corporations. A basic premise is that it is senior executives who need to be convinced, if knowledge-utilization rates are to be raised and if support of all kinds from the industrial sector is to be maintained.

Concerning knowledge utilization, certain corporations and executives stand out as innovators or leaders in the adoption of new techniques. The basic attitude of senior executives permeates the corporation and can do much either to encourage or discourage innovation and knowledge utilization. It is senior management that is most crucial in establishing the right climate of line-staff relations within the organization. These basic attitudes need to be encouraged across a broader spectrum of executives, particularly in the industrial and service sectors of the economy.

Concerning investments in marketing's R & D, senior executives need to understand the nature, workings, and scope of the "system" involved, the forces and factors that brought it about, and what is required to maintain and sustain it. Marketing executives should be persuaded to support the advancement of marketing as a "profession" generally. Although opinions differ on the degree to which marketing is now a "profession," there is little question that the goals of professionalism for this field are highly desirable. University education should be acknowledged as an essential ingredient of training for the professional aspects of the field, even though many successful "entrepreneurs" undoubtedly will continue to come forward without a university degree. For reasons largely associated with the technical complexity of marketing, however, particularly in larger corporations, this latter pattern is becoming more the exception than the rule.

R.2.2.   *The criteria for evaluating marketing managers and their past or potential performance should be expanded to include assessments of their capacities to conceptualize, to develop relevant "theories" or models of their operations, and to initiate and supervise the gathering, analyzing, and interpreting of information relevant to marketing decision making.*

As discussed in Chapter 4, criteria for evaluating manager performance in marketing should be expanded beyond such things as "sales," "profits," "good judgment," and "good interpersonal skills" to include factors such as those given in this recommendation. As noted earlier, in many respects these are the characteristics of the "scientist" in terms of objectivity, respect for systematic data gathering, and use of research information in decision making.

R.2.3.   *Marketing managers should be encouraged to maintain open lines of communication with academic and professional researchers, to develop habits of continuing self-education, to participate in conferences and meetings where new marketing knowledge is presented, and to "listen effectively" to support staffs in marketing research, management science, and academic groups involved in the process of knowledge generation.*

Practicing marketing managers are very busy and must deal with day-to-day problems of coordination, implementation, and control of marketing operations. But this attention to detail should not lead to a fixation with "keeping things as they are" or to automatic rejection of new forms of decision aids, new theories, new data-analysis techniques—or of the people who develop them.

Managers should not propagate a spirit of antiintellectualism in marketing on the premise that there is nothing further to learn or that academics as a class are irrelevant to what they do. What is needed is greater recognition of mutual interests by all researcher and manager groups.

The next recommendation arises from the needs of marketing researchers for data by which to test new ideas, theories, and propositions. It pertains to the shortage of funding for academic research, the general need to increase the external validity of much of that research, and—what became very evident in Commission discussion—the fact that corporate marketing research is ahead of academia in many aspects of research development.

R.2.4.   *A "clearinghouse mechanism" should be established in which data files and historical corporate records are made available to academic and professional researchers. This mechanism should assure the confidentiality of the data where this is appropriate. The activity should be well supervised, systematic, and carefully controlled and monitored.*

A clearinghouse mechanism for such data would do much to advance the state of shared marketing knowledge and reduce the incidence of wasteful and ill-conceived research in the field. It would have potential value in theory building, development of generalizations and propositions about markets and marketing, and in testing both hypotheses and the applicability of new statistical techniques to various types of marketing problems. Many companies now have what amounts to a "gatekeeper"—a person who has been explicitly given the role of monitoring new developments, or who adopts the role as career-advancement strategy. More firms could benefit from introducing or formalizing such a role. It could be made doubly significant if it were also associated with a formal clearinghouse mechanism to which the corporation was contributing.

The following comments of two commissioners elaborate on the nature of such a "clearinghouse" and some of the problems involved:

An attempt should be made to facilitate the "pooling" of multicompany data and results, to be shared with the academic community. The result would not only add more realism for the academic research, but also through synergy provide some additional "currently useful generalizations" for the companies themselves. This would involve extensive planning in order to protect the companies, as well as to enhance the likelihood that the academics' research will be addressed to meaningful issues. The value for companies would lie in the larger data base on which analysis could be made.

MSI/AMA should develop a data archive of data sets from industry and academics to facilitate interest in secondary analysis. Guidelines for such an archive would be tricky to develop, but if one or two companies could agree to contribute old data it might get started. Judgments would have to be made about whether or not any particular data set if reworked might contain information of general interest and usefulness as one tries to move toward a richer set of generalizations in our field.

This is not a new idea, but one that should receive continued attention and efforts toward making it happen. It would do much to meet the needs of academics and professionals doing basic research for empirical data and would increase the usefulness (real and perceived) of their work.

The difficulties of implementing such an activity are widely recognized. Two major ones are the concerns of companies regarding proprietary information and the lack of congruence of categories and questions from study to study (even studies done by the same company). Although much time and careful effort is called for, these problems can be mitigated. Companies contributing data should suggest particular perspective and approaches of interest to them without imposing undue restrictions on possible research uses of the data.

Government

R.3.1. *Federal, state, and local governments should be encouraged to take an active and supportive interest in the development and use of marketing knowledge and to include marketing representation in numerous types of government and non-profit organization affairs.*

Marketing and marketing management has heretofore been considered largely a "business" affair, and the predominant government stance toward it has been one of regulation. This stance, reflected in a general lack of government support for marketing research and knowledge development over the twenty-five-year assessment period, contrasts sharply with heavy government investments in research associated with basic social science disciplines such as economics, psychology, and sociology. Governmental policy-setting boards and regulatory proceedings tend to be dominated by the inputs of economists and lawyers.

This recommendation proposes that energies and efforts be devoted to changing these basic attitudes. Marketing ideas are becoming increasingly relevant to the management of government and nonprofit organizations. At a minimum, governments should take a more active interest in the development and use of marketing knowledge and should divert some resources to fund and support it. Concerning regulatory policy, marketing management and marketing research representation should be explicitly included in the analysis and formulation of pertinent regulation and in decisions to deregulate certain practices and activities.

Associations, Institutes, and Foundations

JOURNALS

R.4.1. *The* Journal of Marketing Research *should remain largely unchanged in its current thrust, content, and direction.*

The *Journal of Marketing Research* is the principal research journal in the field of marketing. In recent years much criticism has been aimed at the "esoteric" and "academic" nature of its content. While recognizing the sincerity of these judgments, we must also recognize that the journal serves a very important function as an outlet for forefront work in marketing research and knowledge development. It should continue to perform this function. *JMR* is oriented to, and primarily serves, the "innovator research group" in marketing, and its important role in this regard should not be changed. Criteria for assessing *JMR* and related journals such as *JCR* should not be solely readership or profitability. In addition to the "outlet" function for academic and professional researchers, they perform important functions as scholarly references and documentation of the latest developments in the field.

R.4.2.   *The* Journal of Marketing *should strive to represent the total field of marketing to the academic and professional world, and it should recognize and attempt to respond to the wide diversity of interests and needs within and between these two groups.*

There are now more than sixty journals and trade magazines that publish marketing-related materials. The *Journal of Marketing* should be the one that most fully represents the field of marketing in all its diversity and scope. Students, for example, being introduced to the subject for the first time, should find this the most useful journal, representative of what the field of marketing is all about. As such, *JM* should strive to publish high-quality articles while recognizing the diversity in its readership—students, practicing line managers, professional researchers, marketing teachers, senior executives, academic researchers, government officials, and so on.

The journal does not currently bridge the communications gap between senior marketing executives and the "knowledge generators" of the field. This problem, alluded to in connection with recommendation 2.1, is a serious one, needing concentrated interest and attention. Currently, the *Harvard Business Review* appears to service this market segment, and marketing scholars should consider managerially oriented journals such as this as a potential outlet for some of their work. A few commissioners proposed that a new journal, the *Journal of Marketing Management,* be considered as a possible way to bridge this gap, and that some articles in *JM* should be written in action-oriented and practical terms to make it a more worthwhile and interesting publication for busy marketing managers and executives.

R.4.3.   *As the quantity of basic and problem-oriented research increases in quality and scope, and as new specializations of theory, method, and technique are developed, new journals should be introduced to take up the expanding supply. This pattern is consistent with what happens in any profession or branch of applied science.*

The proliferation of journals is a widespread phenomenon in higher education and the professions, and the beginnings of this pattern in marketing should not be considered unusual or threatening. There is a danger of losing basic researchers and leading scholars in marketing to other fields, particularly management science, consumer behavior, economics, and psychology, if journal outlets for their work are not provided within marketing. It is also important that the American Marketing Association, in its role as the major association representing the field, provide supports and incentives to keep the expanding flow of scholarly specialization focused on marketing problems and basic research.

CONFERENCES

R.4.4. *Conferences, workshops, seminars, and other opportunities for researcher-manager interaction should be encouraged. Efforts should be made to broaden the base of researcher-manager representation at national conferences.*

Several commissioners pointed out that the two annual conferences of the AMA, one a "professionals" conference and the other an "educators" conference, represented a built-in barrier to communication between these two constituencies. Steps should be taken to assure broad representation at each of these conferences and perhaps to juxtapose them in time and place. Also, workshops, seminars, and other forms of educational exchange should seek to accomplish the breaking down of professional-academic and researcher-manager communication barriers.

RESEARCH SUPPORT AND FUNDING

R.4.5. *The paradox of funding for basic research in marketing needs to be recognized and new ways to coordinate and support funding found.*

No government agency, industry group, foundation, or association now has a vested interest in funding basic research in marketing. Such funding is best described as "ad hoc," and what gets done is determined largely by the idiosyncratic interests of the individual researcher (often in a university setting). There is no Markle Foundation, Russell Sage Foundation, Carnegie or Ford Foundation dedicated to the advancement of basic research in marketing. Federal funding agencies such as the National Science Foundation are generally inaccessible to the marketing scholar because the research is not considered "basic" enough—it is not "pure" psychology, sociology, or economics. From the industry viewpoint it is generally considered "too basic" and "irrelevant" to marketing management and practitioner interests.

What gets done, then, is largely achieved by marketing academics scrambling for any source they can find. Funds may come directly from the academician's school or department. Another method is to "hook into" an ongoing project in one of the social sciences that has been funded by a government agency as a kind of outside consultant with some freedom to pursue the "marketing aspects" of the project. Finally, far-sighted corporations, research suppliers, or advertising agencies have, from time to time, provided funds to individual scholars on a "no-strings-attached" basis. The situation with respect to federal government funding is particularly paradoxical. For example, marketing academics who hold Ph.D.'s in a basic discipline and move into marketing are generally at an advantage in securing government funds relative to those who hold Ph.D.'s in marketing (at least for the first few years), because they can be clearly identified with that basic discipline. With time, however, they will face the same wall of rejection from this source. Even the College on Marketing of the Institute of Management Sciences has not succeeded in opening an avenue of federal government support for basic research in management science and marketing. The Association for Consumer Research has been somewhat more successful, but largely through the work of a few persons who have succeeded in bridging the barriers between behavioral science and marketing.

Energies should be devoted to establishing a reference point or funding agency that will coordinate basic research in marketing and provide a systematic source of funding for it. Unlike accounting, medicine, and law, where mechanisms of accreditation and funding are well ingrained into the supporting fabric of the professional and government communities, marketing is much more diverse, multifaceted, and difficult to identify in terms of its boundaries. It is, nevertheless, no less important, and conscious and continuing efforts are needed to coordinate and support basic research in the field.

R.4.6.   *Problem-oriented research in marketing should be acknowledged for its contributions and value to the field, and fund-raising efforts for its support should be accelerated.*

One of the Commission's important conclusions was a recognition of the importance of problem-oriented research for the field of marketing as a whole. Business and academia have given it too little recognition. As noted earlier, problem-oriented research has not even found its way into marketing research textbooks as an explicit kind of scientific inquiry.

Funding for problem-oriented research suffers problems like those of basic research in marketing. It is largely a stepchild, not considered "basic" enough to gain support from institutions geared principally to the "harder" sciences, and not immediately practical enough to warrant support from company operating budgets. A few institutions, notably the Marketing Science Institute, the (now phased-down) National Science Foundation's Research Applied to National Needs program, and the American Association of Advertising Agencies' Educational Foundation, do have problem-oriented research as their major focus. The support for this type of research has been rooted in institutional systems, such as MSI's, that catalytically bring together conceptually oriented professionals with practically oriented academics. But the scope of such support is limited.

Both the professional and the academic marketing communities need to give "problem-oriented" research much more attention. The role of firms here goes beyond providing financial support to contributing data and information on their own experiences. In this way, more progress can be made to develop experience-based "conditional generalizations"—that is, knowledge and concepts that apply under specified kinds of product, market, or consumer conditions. On the academic side, more appreciation is needed of the "respectability" of such research for academic knowledge building.

R.4.7. *The Research Priorities Program of the Marketing Science Institute involving inputs from business leaders, professional researchers, and academics in developing research priorities for problem-oriented research should be considered a model for the field.*

This recommendation calls for broad representation in the priority-setting process without constraining research to the immediate needs of a particular funding source. Problem-oriented research is particularly susceptible to "fashion," such as the appearance of topics related to energy conservation to the MSI Research Priorities list very soon after the oil crisis. Fashion extends not only to topics but also to the research approach. Quantitative research currently dominates in most academic departments, and little qualitative research is done. These tendencies should be guarded against, and a broader perspective of "searching for gaps in knowledge" adopted in most instances. One of the reasons for the current smaller flow of problem-oriented research is the difficulty of setting research priorities. Whereas basic research tends to be defined by the researcher, and problem-solving research by the company, problem-oriented research is best defined through a *dialogue*. This type of process is being stressed in the recommendation. Some commissioners believed that government representation should be considered as an input to the process.

CONTINUING AND PUBLICITY EFFORTS

R.4.8. *An ongoing researcher-manager committee similar in makeup and representation to the Commission should be established.*

This proposal envisages a type of "watchdog" committee as a follow-on effort to the work of the Commission. The new committee (or perhaps "council") could serve a number of useful functions. It could, for example, monitor or conduct new studies of the knowledge creation and utilization process in marketing. It could seek new ways to encourage research utilization and communications between researcher and manager groups. It might seek to stimulate investment in marketing's R & D and might lobby on behalf of marketing educational or professional interests generally. All the problems alluded to throughout the book would be grist for its mill. Representation on this new body might be further expanded to include government interests.

R.4.9. *The American Marketing Association and the Marketing Science Institute should publicize broadly the work and findings of the Commission on the Effectiveness of Research and Development for Marketing Management and seek ways to stimulate interest, reactions, and further study.*

Specific Project Recommendations

R.5.1. *A study of current funding sources for problem-oriented and basic research in marketing management should be undertaken.*

Although the general nature of the types of research being done in the field is quite well known, no readily available document identifies the nature and scope of its funding. Such a study will provide important insights into "gaps" in our current knowledge and into current sources of funding and new ones that might be tapped. It would also do much to illuminate and clarify the present boundaries of the field and would point to new areas of real and potential expansion of benefit to all constituencies involved.

R.5.2. *Studies of the diffusion and use of marketing knowledge, the characteristics of innovative and noninnovative managers and corporations and tracking studies of knowledge utilization are to be encouraged.*

Leaders in marketing and all those who have some sort of vested interest in the profession need to know how effective its R & D efforts are, how the process of knowledge creation and diffusion works, what the barriers are, and much about the "state of the profession" at any point in time. The Commission's work represents a beginning in this direction, but more needs to be done. The types of needs are identified in the following commissioner comments:

More detailed studies are needed of the diffusion of different methodological advances. This is best carried out by case studies, which might include companion case studies of methodological innovations that were not adopted. They might also include study of the individuals doing the adopting (or nonadopting), as well as of the individuals bringing about the methodological developments.

Detailed studies are needed of the extent to which innovator companies actually benefit from the innovation. These studies should include investigation of what sort of companies do accept innovations, under what circumstances, the intercorrelation between acceptance of one type of innovation and acceptance of other types of innovations.

R.5.3. *Creation and funding of a special project to determine the effectiveness and impact of recently introduced computer-assisted teaching materials for teaching marketing management in several of the nation's leading business schools is recommended. The focus of this project would be on an evaluation of the degree to which this new form of teaching pedagogy is serving, or will serve, to reduce barriers to the knowledge-creation, diffusion, and adoption process in marketing management.*

A significant number of marketing managers holding the MBA degree have been taught marketing management via the so-called "case method." Traditionally, rather than emphasizing the existence of a body of marketing knowledge in terms of published journal materials or forefront methods and techniques in the field, case-method teaching has emphasized the desirability of developing skills of "good judgment" and "managerial insight" in the handling of people and money. The idea that "wisdom can't be told" and that management is basically a set of attitudes, behaviors, and competitive styles to be inculcated into the student body is the basic premise of this philosophy. Recently, these ideas have been expanded to incorporate the computer explicitly as a major assist in the decision-making processes of marketing managers, and "cases" have been developed accordingly. To participate in case discussion, students are in effect forced to learn much about modeling, quantitative techniques, and computers, and to develop skills in these directions. This phenomenon is of major importance to the field as a whole and the work of the Commission generally and may signal a type of revolutionary change that will greatly affect marketing practice and the nature of problem-oriented and basic research. A study is needed of the current scope of this teaching pedagogy, what problems and opportunities are associated with it, and the degree to which it reduces, or perhaps increases, barriers to the diffusion and acceptance of new knowledge.

Appendix B

THE AMA MEMBERSHIP SURVEY

This appendix provides additional information on the survey of American Marketing Association membership reported on in Chapter 6. The survey was to provide a check on commissioner impressions about the degree of use of techniques and the nature of the diffusion process. To what degree were representative techniques a part of the "tool kit" of professional managers and researchers? Four questions generally guided the development of the instruments and the survey that evolved: (1) To what degree had respondents tried the various tools and techniques, and were they currently using them? (2) How confident were they with respect to each? (3) How relevant did they consider the techniques for either data analysis or decision making? (4) What sources of information did they draw on concerning new concepts and techniques? Chapter 6 lists the thirteen techniques that became the focal point of the study and the major results.

The study was funded jointly by the American Marketing Association and the Marketing Science Institute. Commission staff at MSI, particularly Professor Christopher Lovelock and John Bateson, assisted greatly with all phases of the project.

Design and Sampling

The study involved a cross-sectional survey by mail questionnaire sent to 4292 members of the American Marketing Association. A stratified random sampling procedure was adopted, using the AMA's membership roster as the sampling frame. Each member was first assigned to one of four groups: marketing managers, marketing research managers, commercial researchers, and academics, and a random sample was selected within each group. The commercial researchers sample was in fact a "census" of this category of AMA membership, given their relatively small numbers compared with other groups.

The four-group classification was done as follows. When joining the Association, AMA members classify themselves according to "primary interest" as marketing management, market research, or teacher/academic. Some 75% of the membership report themselves to be in one of these categories. From these data, the Commission staff further split the market research category into marketing research managers and commercial researchers, using the member's company affiliation as the criterion.

From the initial mailing to 4292 potential respondents, 1271 usable replies were received, an overall response rate of 29.6%. Table B-1 shows a

TABLE B-1
SAMPLE SIZES AND RESPONSE RATES

	AMA Membership [a]	Samples		Responses Received	Response Rate
Marketing managers	4,147	1,125	(29.5%)	218	17.8%
Research managers	3,256	1,114	(34.2%)	433	38.9%
Commercial researchers	828	828	(100%)	253	30.6%
Academics	2,157	1,125	(52%)	367	32.6%
Total	10,388	4,292	(41.3%)	1,271	29.6%

[a]Includes only those members for whom an area of special interest is known as of 1976–1977.

breakdown of the population of AMA membership into the four groups, the size of the samples, the number of replies received, and the response rate for each group. Marketing managers had the lowest response rate (17.8%) and research managers the highest (38.9%).

As we noted in Chapter 6, despite its size (about 18,000 members overall in 1976–1977), the AMA membership profile is not a true representation of the total American marketing community. Academics and university professors doing teaching and research in marketing are probably the best represented of the four groups. Concerning the two categories of professional researcher, we suspect that AMA members tend to be among the more sophisticated and experienced people in that sector. Marketing managers are probably least well represented by AMA membership. There are undoubtedly many more marketing managers in the United States and abroad than the 4147 AMA members who report themselves in this category. We suspect that operating line managers and senior marketing executives from large marketing-oriented companies are particularly underrepresented among AMA members. Their response rate also was the lowest. In sum, the survey may tend to inflate usage of the thirteen techniques by "representative" marketing researchers, and deflate usage by "representative" marketing managers. The reported differences between trial and use rates of managers and researchers, however, are *not* extreme, and in many cases they appear reasonable.

Obviously, in any questionnaire, particularly one that relates to technical expertise, respondents are highly self-selecting in terms of their own familiarity and comfort with the topics involved. In the present survey this holds especially among the managers, for whom the response was the lowest. However, the initial premise behind the survey is only reinforced by any self-selecting bias. The results are likely to reflect the "best possible" characterization of the state of trial or use of these concepts and techniques. From a purely statistical point of view, the samples are large enough in each case and the standard errors small enough that proportions in the population would not be expected to vary widely from those reported in each sample.

Index

299

Fairleigh Dickinson University Library
Teaneck, New Jersey

T001-15M
3-15-71